THE BERNARDS OF ABINGTON AND NETHER WINCHENDON (VOLUME 3); A FAMILY HISTORY

THE BERNARDS OF ABINGTON AND NETHER WINCHENDON (VOLUME 3); A FAMILY HISTORY

Sophia Elizabeth Higgins

www.General-Books.net

Publication Data:

Title: The Bernards of Abington and Nether Winchendon
Subtitle: A Family History
Volume: 3
Author: Sophia Elizabeth Higgins
General Books publication date: 2009
Original publication date: 1904
Original Publisher: Longmans, Green, and co.
Subjects: History / General

How We Made This Book for You
We made this book exclusively for you using patented Print on Demand technology.
First we scanned the original rare book using a robot which automatically flipped and photographed each page.
We automated the typing, proof reading and design of this book using Optical Character Recognition (OCR) software on the scanned copy. That let us keep your cost as low as possible.
If a book is very old, worn and the type is faded, this can result in typos or missing text. This is also why our books don't have illustrations; the OCR software can't distinguish between an illustration and a smudge.
We understand how annoying typos, missing text or illustrations can be. That's why we provide a free digital copy of most books exactly as they were originally published. Simply go to our website (www.general-books.net) to check availability. And we provide a free trial membership in our book club so you can get free copies of other editions or related books.
OCR is not a perfect solution but we feel it's more important to make books available for a low price than not at all. So we warn readers on our website and in the descriptions we provide to book sellers that our books don't have illustrations and may have typos or missing text. We also provide excerpts from each book to book sellers and on our website so you can preview the quality of the book before buying it.
If you would prefer that we manually type, proof read and design your book so that it's perfect, we are happy to do that. Simply contact us for the cost.

CONTENTS

1

SECTION 1

Mills – Thomas Bernard's Strictures upon the System in Force – Regulations suggested by him – Strength of the Mill-owning Interest – Sir Robert Peel introduces a Bill for the Amelioration of the Children's Condition – The Opposition to the Bill – The Second Bill 846

THEBEENAEDS

ABINGTON AND NETHER WINCHENDON

CHAPTER I

ScropeBernard'sOxfordDays

Scrope Bernard wins the Christ Church Prizes – William Wyndham Grenville's admiration for Scrope Bernard – Scrope Bernard takes his Degree – Rev- Timothy Shaw, Vicar of Bierton – George Shaw – An Election Song- Letters from William Grenville to Scrope Bernard – Scrope Bernard's English Prize Essay – Verses by William Grenville – Scrope Bernard's visit to the North – The Aylesbury Races – George Shaw's Career.

Thegrave had scarcely closed over the earthly remains of Sir Francis Bernard, in June, 1779, when his children became aware that, through the confiscation of his American estates by the Revolutionary Government, their lot was cast in comparative poverty. This news had probably reached England, and appeared in the public journals, before Sir John Bernard arrived to confirm it.1In consequence of his father's death he visited Aylesbury during the ensuing autumn. As the war with America still continued, there remained a chance that the Acts of Confiscation might be revoked or annulled; but it was a slender chance, since the Americans had been reinforced by French troops, andfortune was turning against the mother country, to the amazement and consternation of her people.

1It appears, from a message in a letter, that Sir John Bernard was in England at this time, and made some stay. I have not ascertained the precise date of the New York Confiscation Act, but it may not have affected the family so severely as the Massachusetts Act, since Sir F. Bernard had not apparently begun to' settle' his 30,000 acres in New York Province.

VOL. Ill, B

It must have been almost immediately after the decease of his father that Scrope Bernard discovered himself to be the winner of the Christ Church prizes, as they are designated in a private letter. Of the composition, whether in prose or verse, which obtained this reward, I have no account beyond the statements of William Wyndham Grenville, already mentioned as the third son of the Prime Minister. His mother was Elizabeth, daughter of another statesman, Sir William Wyndham, and of Catherine, sister of the seventh Duke of Somerset.1Possibly some feeling of compunction, for the trouble which his father's Stamp Act had brought upon the Bernard family, first induced young Grenville to cultivate Scrope's acquaintance during their residence at Christ Church; but, whatever may have been the originating cause of his regard, it is evident from Grenville's gushing epistles, that he soon became enthusiastic in his admiration of the Governor's son.

Mr. Grenville writes2concerning the prizes: ' Dear Bernard, you may judge by your own feelings of the real and excessive satisfaction which I have in sending you the enclosed list; it was given out last night.' Scrope headed a list of four candidates.

' Jackson ' – afterwards Dean – ' says that yours was incomparably the best; there being no doubt at all of the decision. Randolph desires me to tell you that, if it may be done with propriety, he wishes you to be here on Monday, as Wednesday next is fixed for the recital.' The expression ' with propriety,' contains, I imagine, an allusion to Sir Francis Bernard's recent death, and thus serves as a clue to the date, which is not given in the hastily penned note. This epistle is endorsed, by Scrope, ' sent express.'

On September 7, in the same year 1779, about threeTIMOTHY SHAW 3

1See Debrett'sPeerage,17th Edition,' Duke of Somerset,' and ' Earl of Egremont.' Also preface toThe Grenville Papers,vol. i.

2This and other extracts in this chapter are from MS. Letters at Nether Winohendon, written by W. W. Grenville to Scrope Bernard.

months subsequent to the family bereavement, Julia Bernard married the Bev. Joseph Smith, and went to reside at Wendover. The home at Aylesbury appears to have been then broken up. Fanny Bernard had been promised a welcome by Julia, and joined her some little while after the marriage. Emily, or Amelia, had evidently arranged to live with her sister Jane White at Lincoln. Sir John Bernard probably spent his time in visiting friends and relations and in urging his claims on the British Government, until he returned to America in the following spring or summer; there he will be found once more battling against adverse fate. Thomas continued his legal studies in London, and Scrope remained at Oxford studying medicine.

The first Earl Temple died on September 11, 1779, from the effects of a carriage accident;1and his nephew George, the eldest brother of William Wyndham Grenville, succeeded to the title.

Scrope Bernard took his B. A. degree in 1780, * and apparently spent the long vacation in his old neighbourhood, at the vicarage of Bierton, a parish adjoining Aylesbury. The vicar was a man of some note, whose biography has been condensed by the county historian3as follows:

Timothy Shaw, A. B. inst. 1752. He was of St. John's College, Camb., A. B. 1740, A. M. 1763; kept a very reputable school in the village during many years, and was highly esteemed by his pupils. He was inst., August 30, 1763, to the Vicarage of St. Michael, St. Albans, but resigned in 1777. He was indefatigable in the discharge of his clerical functions, and of so friendly and accommodating a temper, that, though he constantly officiated in his parish church and its members Stoke Mandeville and Buck- land, he very frequently extended his assistance to the neighbouring clergy of less activity, and among his familiar acquaintances obtained the title of 'The Angel of the Seven Churches' from having at one time no less than that number to provide forsimultaneously. He died in 1786, having been long infirm, and for some time was assisted in the performance of his clerical duties by his younger son.

1Debrett and BurkePeerages, 'Buckingham, Duke of,' until 1889. See also ' Baroness Kinloss,' and ' Earl Temple,' in more recent editions.*Oxford University Calendar. 'Lipscomb,History of Buckinghamshire,vol. ii.,' Bierton.'

This younger son, George, eventually attained a more widely spread reputation than his father, by whom he had been early initiated into various branches of natural history; he first studied medicine, but was afterwards admitted to deacon's orders, and acted as his father's curate in Bierton and the adjacent parishes for about ten years, during which period Scrope, who had probably been well acquainted with this cultivated family in the lifetime of Sir Francis Bernard, became an inmate of the parsonage. Soon after his return to Oxford, in November, 1780, George Shaw wrote *1*:

It is with great pleasure that I hear of your being so agreeably and usefully engaged in the attendance of Dr. P.'s Clinical Lectures, which I am certain must be of the greatest possible advantage to you, especially if you continue regular and constant in your attendance on the Hospital, and take proper notes from the Lectures; at the same time I cannot help observing that unless the celerity of your pen be equal to that of Dr. P.'s tongue your extracts will not be very considerable; at all events, however, I shall be happy to read them, and shall therefore depend upon your promise of bringing them with you when you mean to return to Bierton, and above all I beg you will remember to take the history and progress of any uncommon or curious case.

I shall be glad to hear in your next letter who the pupils are that constitute the clinical; I think if I was at Oxford for any length of time I should be strongly tempted to make one of the party; I suppose you do not take the range of a great part of the Hospital, but only select a certain number of cases for the clinical pupils; at least that used to be the custom at Edinburgh, and I think it greatly preferable to the confused practice of a large London Hospital, where the multiplicity of business and variety of cases rather tend to puzzle than inform the student. I remember when I was at St. Bartholomew's Hospital I used to neglect the generality of cases, and confine myself to a very few, which I used to observe and attend in my own way, exclusive of seeing them in company with the physicians.

For some time past my time has been engaged in writing over several old lectures of a miscellaneous nature, on a variety of 1 MS. Letter at Nether Winchendon.

AN ELECTION SONG 5

subjects, and which had lain by so long, quite neglected, that some appeared in such a state of inextricable confusion as to oblige me to burn them to prevent further trouble. When we have the pleasure of seeing you again at Bierton you shall see them, and copy any that may happen to please you. Amongst them are several clinical cases from Edinburgh, &c.

This letter contains some further information, which may relate to an old acquaintance of Sir Francis Bernard.

The Queen's Regiment under Colonel Dalrymple is quartered at Aylesbury, and Sir William Lee has made the officers an offer of Sir F. B.'s house, which is accordingly inhabited by the gentlemen of the military.

Sundry letters were exchanged between Scrope Bernard and William Grenville in the course of this year. I possess only the Grenville side of the correspondence, except in one instance, when Scrope left a rough draft among his papers which shows his growing interest in politics; it contains some crude but spirited verses entitled, ' Smith's the Man,' to the tune of the ' Dusky Night,' and was written during his stay at Mr. Shaw's house, with this explanation:

As I was leaving Aylesbury about one o'clock to return to Bierton, I happened to hear an election song, in favour of the other party, when it struck me that I might have been useful in that province myself. In my walk I composed the underwritten, which on reaching home I put to paper, and returned with it to Aylesbury, but found matters too far gone, and the poll almost concluded, which I had been told would not have been done till the next day. Perhaps this was a lucky circumstance, for I doubt whether it would have done most injury or service to the cause.

Of this effusion three stanzas may suffice:

The rest your favour wish to buy,
But this is all their plan –
To sell themselves full twice as high;
But Smith must be your Man.
They bow and cringe for place and gains,
Get pensions if they can;
But Smith such sordid arts disdains
Then Smith must be your Man.
'Gainst courtiers he your trade defends,
Protects each artisan,
Your lace and lacemakers befriends,
Then Smith must be your Man.

You will observe [continues Scrope in his letter to William Grenville] that Smith proposed himself as a Minority Man, in opposition to the noted principles of the others – hence all the abuse of courtiers, &e. You will at least allow that it was calculated for the meanest capacities, among such it was to be disseminated.

After some further allusion to the election, followed by a paragraph in Greek, the writer ends by requiring his friend to burn his letter.1But he kept the original draft. I find no clue in the local histories to the candidature of Mr. Smith, although two gentlemen of that name were returned for Wendover; the members elected to represent Aylesbury were Anthony Bacon and Thomas Orde; those for the shire, Ralph, Earl Verney, and Thomas Grenville. It was the polling for the borough that Scrope had witnessed.2He writes in the same letter: ' At the late election for Aylesbury, with the warmest wishes for Smith, I could go no farther than talk with my late Taylor and such persons as had been our Servants, upon the subject.' And: ' The County Election I hear is fixed for this day se'night.'

Scrope Bernard seems to have been capable of more elaborate efforts, if any reliance is to be placed on the following utterances of William Grenville, of which the meaning from the first was so slightly veiled as to be quite evident. He dates from Tunbridge Wells, October 12, 1780:

My dear Bernard, – I write these few lines in haste to beg that you will tell me seriously whether you know anything of a copy of verses which came to me by the post to-night. They are addressed to me on the occasion of my coming of age, and areA COPY OF VEESES 7

1Possibly the letter may have been much altered, if it was sent at all, after the enthusiasm of the moment went off.

' Lipscomb,*History of Bucks,*vol. i.; ' General History,' vol. ii.; ' Aylesbury with Walton,' Gibbs (Robert);*History of Aylesbury,*chapter xxv.; ' Parliamentary History' (resumed).

such as I did not imagine any person now living, much more in the confined circle of my acquaintance, was equal to. I should be inclined to speak more largely still in my admiration of them if they were not so flattering to myself as to prevent me from commending them without the imputation of vanity.

I apply to you, because I remember, in one of the letters I received from you the other day, your enquiring about the day on which I shall be of age. I have no time now for a longer letter, but am so impatient that I would not delay a moment writing to you. I beg that you will answer me as soon as possible, and let me know whether you can satisfy my curiosity on a subject respecting which I am very desirous to be informed.

Believe me

Ever most afftely yours

Gbenville.

There is a postscript – ' Direct to me at my brother's in Pall Mall, but do not enclose your letter to him.' Grenville wrote again, a little later, on other topics; and that letter will be presently quoted at length. It contains one allusion to the birthday greeting: ' You have probably by this time received the note I wrote the other day about the verses. Pray tell me if you know anything about them, for I am on the rack of curiosity.' Scrope's answer I do not possess, but the following letter from William Grenville refers to its contents, and is dated November 7.

My dear Bernard, – You will doubtless think it very strange that after the confession, if I may call it such in a matter of such infinite honour to yourself, contained in yr last letter, you should have heard nothing from me for so long. All I can say in excuse is that I have been following most exactly the dictates of a certain inspired Bard, who has counselled me to persevere in my undertaking.

' Tho' Dissipation's frantic sons deride,' &c.

' Tho' gaudy fashion,' &c., &c., which stanza, you will observe, I think one of the best, if not the best, in the whole. If it were not that the matter contained in the last is such as I cannot praise with any face at all, I should be inclined to give that the preference.

I do not know whether you will think it any compliment to you when I tell you how much the verses alluded to exceed theopinion I had of your poetical abilities; but to myself it is one, and of the most flattering nature; since you must allow me to be vain enough to imagine that the enthusiasm of the Muse was a little assisted by that of very warm and sincere friendship, such as I have always experienced from you, and such as it shall always be the pride of my life to cultivate.

After this complimentary exordium, Grenville continues:

You must permit me now to play the critic a little, at the same time assuring you that, except what I am going to mention, there is not a word that I could wish otherwise than it is.

Then follows a good page of severe analysis, after which the writer adds:

But something I will say, as hoping that it will be more agreeable to you than the greatest encomiums I could bestow on the verses. What I mean is this, that they came to me at one of the most discouraging moments that I have yet encountered, or hope to encounter, and were, as well as continue to be, of very great use and real service in raising my spirits, and pointing them to their true end. This is a very uncommon effect of modern poetry, which consists chiefly in the*nugcR canorce;*while your poem would, if it were divested of all its fine imagery and strong expression, make as good a serious discourse to a man in my situation as could be addressed to him. The difficulties you state are the very difficulties I feel, at least many of them, and the answers you make to them are the real and true answers, and those which suggest themselves in my most confident moments.

It is unfortunate, considering the encomiums lavished by Mr. Grenville on this poem, that no copy should have been preserved in the composer's family; but I have not found any copy or even memorandum amongst the papers at Nether Winchendon.

Two other letters, belonging to this correspondence, and dated October1 of 1780, are here noticed together, because they refer to a special subject, distinct from the birthday poem. From these two epistles it is evident that William Grenville was prepared to see his friend a physician, in fullTHE CHOICE OF A PROFESSION 9

1The figures in the dates of these letters are not very clear. I believe them, however, to be October 3 and 15, as stated below.

confidence that he would prove a distinguished member of the profession; but that he had a decided objection to his becoming more closely attached to the University.

As for your sub-librarianship, I must still say that if it prevents your attending either Parsons, or whatever else might be of use to you in your studies, you can never answer it to yourself hereafter – considering especially that from the circumstance of Parson's being of so much longer standing than yourself, it is your business to push yourself in point of time as much as possible. I am dreadfully afraid of your involving in some speech or other which will be only a fresh interruption without any one advantage. Everything that can be done in point of character at Ch. Ch. I consider as already done. Would not some medical prize (for I believe there are such things) at Edinburgh be a much more rational object of pursuit? As for the point of income, I will not hear of it. Without being impertinent, or going into particulars which do not belong to me, that cannot be an object to any man whatever who has a profession to pursue. You should consider that you are not obliged to any expence which is in any degree inconvenient to you.

I have said perhaps too much on this subject, but you will, I know, attribute it to its true cause. There is still another objection behind, which is the continuance of a college life to a man bound to go out into the world bye-and-bye, and who already wants something of the manners of the world, a deficiency which will grow upon you more and more every day. I wish you to think these things over and over.

' Nocturne versare animo, versare diurno.'

See how others have succeeded in your line. The practice of such men is the best lesson for you. Without being able to speak from any previous knowledge, I am confident you will find it militate against your present ideas. Unless you are as fixed as fate, pray let me hear from you soon, with your answer to all these objections. Nevertheless wherever you are, and whatever you are, either Censor at Ch. Ch. or King's Physician, believe me ever

Most afftely yours
Tunbridge Wells,
Oct. 3rd 1780.

P. S. – See how even Randolph was able to reconcile a college life with your pursuits, and then ask yourself whether you expectto succeed better. As for the command of books, I am sure that except in critical pursuits, which you have no business with, they rather distract than assist you – too great a number of them I mean – such as you will find the Library will afford you.

Direct to me still at my Brother's, Pall Mall, but do not enclose your letters to him.

Then came the already discussed verses, and the enthusiastic epistle which has been quoted. Scrope, however, still maintained his own views against his confident juvenile mentor. And so it was that William Grenville wrote, on October 15:

My dear Bernard, – I sit down to confess the weight of your arguments. If it be really true that the advantages of Oxford are equal or nearly so to those of other places, it certainly is an object to you to keep up your connections and your name there. Your arrangement with Pell is in one point of view very satisfactory, but not in all equally so; for if it is to keep you, as it did Sawkins at Oxford, in vacation time, it will hardly do you less harm than if it was to stop you from attending Lectures. Indeed it would fall under that objection precisely – it would debar you from the most useful of all lectures – lectures in worldly manners – lectures which, to the shame of Oxford, are not to be got there, but just their reverse – lectures which, say what you will, we both stand in need of, and you from character perhaps less, but certainly now from situation more than myself – lectures in short which I am studying to very little purpose. What a happy man you are to love dancing 1 Remember that I by no means admit all that you say, hardly indeed any part of it, about your own disposition for bustling and putting yourself forward. Fortunately you have a noble ambition – the most so of any – the ambition of distinguishing yourself by honest means. That will I hope supply the place of a more active turn, but be not too confident. Pray tell me whether you look so far forward as to next summer, and what is to become of you then? I have a reason for asking.

With regard to the profession itself, I think you undervalue its consequence – the consequence which it gives, I mean – for, as to the study, I perfectly agree with you that Hippocrates, Ghrysostom, and Lord Coke are indifferent (do not let Sawkins see that I) I know but of one which gives more of the*Hie ille Wardus, &o.,*than Physick, and by that you may guess I mean Law. As to your E – s, your L – s, &c., &c., peace be to all suchCORRESPONDENCE WITH W. W. GRENVILLE 11

– such peace I mean as can be enjoyed by people who have neither opinions nor characters of their own, but are obliged to borrow them from the reflection of some red-heeled luminary or other. God forbid that any one whom I value but half as much as I do you, should engage in the most toilsome of all drudgery, and I think the most unprofitable, since its means and its end are both that greatest curse in Nature – Dependence.

I laugh at your Eudiometer, it is true, but at the same time
I rejoice in it. What the had you to do with Gas? I do not
see how, when the particular view which had to do with that was at an end, it was at all better than mosses and toadstools.

And now I think I have pretty well answered your letter. The print was left there for your approbation, and if it met with that, for your acceptance.

There is no description to indicate the subject of the print; but the passage about the verses, already quoted, follows. There is also an allusion at the close of this letter to the possibility of Scrope entering the Militia. William Grenville was averse from the idea of his friend joining that corps, apparently because he thought it would tend to divide his energies. The step, however, had probably been suggested by Lord Temple, or those around him, for it was the Bucks Militia which Scrope eventually joined, perhaps some time later. At this period the correspondence between the two young men was briskly carried on; Scrope wrote speedily, perhaps more than once, in response to Grenville's desponding remarks, warning him against indulgence in the feelings which had prompted them. The next letter in my collection is dated, ' Pall Mall, November 30, 1780.'

My dear Bernard, – You seem to have taken in too strong a sense what I said about the difficulties I find in attaining what I am so very sensible that I want; or perhaps (for I really forget) my letter might have been written as you suppose in an unlucky moment. But you certainly misunderstood the cause, or rather the object, of my despair, be that more or less according as the wind is in the East or the West; you wonder that I should suppose myself incapable of acquiring what is already attained by so many men for whom, as you justly suppose, I must have so perfect a contempt; and you state that by using the proper means nothing is more easy – why then should I despair? You give me here, I see, credit for a modesty and diffidence of myself which I have. I have treasured up in my mind a saying of Lord Cobham's which was repeated to me frequently by my Uncle, 1 after having been confirmed to him, as he said, by all his experience. This was that there is nothing within the compass of a reasonable man's wish which he may not be sure of attaining, if he will use the proper means. If, then, I hold nothing to be impossible to me which I in my sober senses desire, how much less must I imagine those things to be which the most contemptible of mankind possess? But it is the road to them of which I despair. I have no doubt if I could bring myself to attend Mr. Hart's school, where grown gentlemen are taught to dance, that I should acquit myself as well as any Alderman of them all. But you are too good a logician not to know that the premises being taken away, the conclusion follows it [sic]. And certainly if I set out on the Oxford road, that will not carry me to Scotland; that is to say, that the being a student at Ch. Ch. for four years and then moving to Lincoln's Inn, or at least living in Pall Mall as if I was at L. Inn, is not the ready way to carry off a rich heiress. And so much for that, observing only – that I think myself already improved, notwithstanding that I can reproach myself with no neglect of my Blackstone, but on the contrary can affirm with truth, that at no time, hardly even when in the *furor* of prize-writing did I employ myself better, I mean in point of application, or even so well, in the quiet shades of Oxford, than now during my first month's residence in London.

The next paragraph apparently refers to some assistance which Scrope gave to Lord Wellesley, eldest son of the Earl of Mornington, in translating the ' Odyssey,' he being senior by nearly two years to the young lord.

You may perhaps expect that I should attack you on what Wellesley had told me about Homer's ' Odyssey'; but on the contrary I approve very much – in great measure on your account, and infinitely more on his. It was the greatest act of friendship you could show him, and I think you will find your account in it.

Perhaps you will not think the following lines equally exTHE ENGLISH PRIZE ESSAY 13

1The uncle mast have been the Earl Temple recently deceased; and the 'Lord Cobham,' Bicbard Temple, Viscount and Baron Cobham (died 1749), whose sister Hester, created Countess Temple, was wife of Eichard Grenville of Wotton, mother of the first Earl Temple and grandmother of the second, and of William Wyndham Grenville. See Debrett's and Burke's*Peeraget.*

disable, since I could derive no benefit from making them, and I am afraid they only show how soon disuse swallows up whatever little one has had that way, &c., &c.

Then follow some Latin verses about Medea. Further on Mr. Grenville adds: ' I am glad to hear from yourself and from Wellesley, to what good account your time is turned in Oxford.'

There is a postscript to this letter, which refers to Thomas Bernard:

I saw your Brother in the Court of King's Bench the other day, taking the oaths (without his wig) on being called to the Bar.

Then Mr. Grenville returns to the old topics:

Do you come to town at all at Xmas? and when, for I would contrive to be here. ' 'Gainst the soft magic' has a peculiar beauty from being connected with ' Victor unto bondage charmed' in the next line.

In the following year, 1781, Scrope Bernard was the fortunate writer of the English Prize Essay. A rush of congratulatory epistles from friends and relatives proclaimed their satisfaction, in some cases approaching to delight, at his triumph. There is scarcely one of these letters more jubilant than the following effusion from William Grenville dated ' Lincoln's Inn, June 18.'

My dear Bernard, – I am sure you do not expect a formal congratulation from me, but judge from your own feelings what mine are on the occasion. I heartily wish it was in my power to come down on Saturday, but it is absolutely necessary in order to keep the term that I should be one day in Hall next week. That day shall be Sunday, and unless anything should intervene (which is just possible) you may expect me on Monday time enough for the ceremony. At all events nothing but an immediate offer of the Seals should make me miss Wednesday. Can you get me any rooms for that week? I am afraid not. If so, you must engage lodgings for me at Brown's or anywhere that you can get them.

I am overjoyed, but not surprised, so Adieu.

Ever most afftely yours

Thomas Bernard wrote kindly and calmly as ever, though his letter was evidently penned in haste.

My dear brother, – Accept my congratulations. I did not venture to say how much I set my heart on your success, as in possibility it might add to a disappointment. It is exactly what your friends would wish for you. Mr. Jackson wished me joy on your success just before I came to my chambers and found your letter.

I have every reason to expect that I shall be able to be with you on Wednesday. I certainly will come if I can. May I recommend you to try (and to be sure of) the tone of voice which you can command, which will best suit the Theatre; it is the fault of all young speakers; a jury of your friends*who Jiave ears*would enable you to decide upon it with precision.

The other subject I reserve till I see Oxford.

Yours ever with the warmest wishes,

Tho. Beenakd.19 June, 1781.

Mr. Harwood, who has just come in, desires to add his congratulations.

How this Commemoration passed off and especially how Scrope acquitted himself in the Theatre, I have not been able to discover. A printed notice of his life in the ' Annual Biography and Obituary of 1831 " gives the name of his essay ' The Origin and Use of Fable.' This is probably correct, although the notice contains some mistakes on other points. But it is curious that Scrape's sister Julia, writing to one of his sons after his death, on the subject of the proposed obituary notice, entitled his essay ' Antiquity,' and states that Dr. Hall, afterwards Dean of Christ Church, recited the Latin Prize Poem on the same occasion. No copy of Scrope's Essay is now to be found amongst the family papers.

When the excitement was well over, Scrope Bernard evidently sent a copy of his treatise to Dr. Drury, who must have been his tutor or master at Harrow; perhaps at the doctor's request. The reply is extant.

1'*Annual Biography and Obituary,*1831: A General Biographical List of Persons who have died in 1829-30.'

VEESES BY W. W. GRENVILLE 15

My dear Friend, – I thank you for your excellent Essay, which I have already perused twice with infinite Pleasure. It is a close, compact, and elegant Peace*[sic]*of Reasoning, and without protruding any*ambitiosa ornamenta*on the reader, it engages his attention, satisfies his enquiries, and commands his approbation. That you may continue to enrich your mind with various knowledge, and ever meet with Honors suitable to your Deserts is the sincere wish of your

Affectionate Friend

J. Deury. Harrow, Sept. 25th, 1781.

Scrope Bernard's success inspired William Grenville with some grandiloquent Long Vacation verses, written while he was staying with other friends in Cornwall, near the Land's End. They are headed:

Bernarde salve, maxime Physice!

Bernardo salve! Te Boerhavius

Hippocratesque Galenusque

Suspicient Dominumque dicent.

Then follows a Greek introduction, after which the poet bursts into English verse which he terms Pindaric.

Bernard, whom rebel Jersey bore

There, where the hostile shore

O'er the vast Atlantic frowns,

Where Indians howl away the night

And Yankees tremble while they fight

To shake Imperial George's crowns;

Nursed in the lap of Power
And in a luckless hour
Doomed to cross the foaming main,
Thee Medycina gave
To be the ever-scowling Jackson's slave
O'er Logic's gulf to yawn in vain.

And so on. Scrope's appearance on the occasion of taking his B. A. degree is noted with:

Bare was thy hallowed head
Which Phoebus circles with his laurel wreath,
A lambskin o'er thy shoulders spread
Emblem of innocence and honours new.

The young graduate is then depicted as spurning ' un- hooded undergraduates,' and beholding them ' with exulting joy,' placed beneath his feet in church.

Nor this thy soaring mind could satisfy,
Ever to ambition true;
Such as when William passed th' ensanguined Boyne,
You viewed with ardent eyes,
You seized the envied prize, &c. &c.

Grenville and his friends, for it was probably a joint composition, continue:

Bernard all hail!
From that remotest bay
Lashed by the salt sea's whitening spray,
Where scowls the fabled Michael's Mount,
The seat of warrior and of chieftain bold,
O'er Marazion and Pensanza's hold.
The youths, who spread the daring sail
From Foy to Mevagissey's rocky pier,
And braved perfidious Gallia's threat'ning privateer,
With votive verse thy footsteps greet.

This might mean that Scrope had joined the party, or was about to join it; but I have no note of any journey that year except in a northerly direction. The Latin and Grecian Muses are next described as showering ' lyric chaplets ' and scattering ' epigrammatic lays ' before Scrope. And then:

Though not the briefest, next the British maid,
Daughter of Freedom, on Pindaric wing
Soaring aloft, spurns metre's iron chains
And times to thee her native strains,
Rejoiced one loyal Yankee's worth to sing.

Sundry learned Latin annotations illustrate and explain this interesting effusion.

From a letter, of September 15, written by George Shaw to Scrope Bernard,1 it appears that the latter must haveSCARBOROUGH 17

1MS. Letters at Nether Winchendon.

visited Scarborough before that date. From that gay resort he wrote an ' extremely picturesque' description, from which his friend gathered that it was 'an excellent place for killing time,' but that its medical merits were doubtful. Probably Scrope either met his cousin Mrs. Edmunds there, or visited her at Worsborough, and through her made the acquaintance of a young lady who will be mentioned again more than once, but whose name has not transpired.

Mr. Shaw's letter is addressed to Oxford; it is therefore probable that the query which follows may be answered in the negative, and that Scrope, having once returned from the north, did not travel in that direction again; indeed, although the idea of studying in Edinburgh had at one time apparently crossed his mind, I cannot find any evidence of his having visited that city at all.

Do you still continue your intention of taking a much longer Northern journey this season, or do you mean to pursue your medical studies at Oxford or in London? The London Lecturers, I observe, are already filling the newspapers with their advertisements, and promising great advantages to a rising race of homicides. If you continue in Oxford during the winter I make no doubt of your attending Dr. Wall's Lectures, which I venture to predict will be excellent and well attended.

After some reference to a controversy on respiration, Mr. Shaw adds:

If I remember right, a great part of your own studies during your residence at Bierton was directed to this sublime subject; in particular, I remember, a treat of air which you was ambitious of having reputed greatly superior to common atmospheric air, but which, from some perverse circumstances attending your experiment, proved, so far as could be guessed from the trial of common sense and perception, to be not quite so good as the air we are obliged to make shift with in general.

After all, however, I do by no means ridicule the investigation of this important fluid, but am inclined to express a doubt whether Dr. Priestly's experiments are so conclusive as he persuades himself to believe.

To descend at once from these lofty speculations. Aylesbury
VOL. III. 0
races you know are almost at hand, but the expectations of people do not seem to be raised very high on this subject; and I believe it is generally thought that these will be the last Aylesbury races. If they should prove any temptation to you to leave more important pursuits for a few days, we shall rejoice very much in the hope of seeing you at Bierton.

Scrope must have accepted this invitation, since he writes to Mr. Edmunds:*l*

The Aylesbury races, or rather the races of Buckinghamshire, have been particularly good this year, and have made a great noise in this part of the world. I will not flatter the county by comparing them with Doncaster; nor shall I flatter Yorks if I say that in consideration of Doncaster they were very insignificant; we had no Pilots, or Fortunes, no Mansion-house for our balls; no playhouse or company of players. However, we exhibited some decent gallops upon the race-grounds, had one or two hops at night, and made altogether a snug party, and what the Bucking- hamshires called a magnificent meeting.

To return to Mr. Shaw's letter, the following postscript bears witness to his love of horticulture, and to his friends attentive care:

When you write to Mr. Wickham, be so good as to give my compliments to him, and tell him I am extremely obliged to him for the trouble he has taken in preserving a specimen of the cactus.   That any other plant he may think curious, if not too troublesome to him, would be extremely acceptable.

There is another postscript relating to a Mr. Hare, who had been admitted to Holy Orders somewhat late, and who seems to have regretted this step. George Shaw had apparently entered his sacred profession too early to have ascertained his vocation. When, soon after this period, his home was broken up by the successive deaths of his mother, sister, and father, he reverted to his medical studies. This indeed would not have been conclusive, since many clergymen of the time combined the practice of the healing art with their clerical duties; but Mr. Shaw,2after takingGEOEGE SHAW 19

1MS. Letters at Nether Winchendon.

2Lipscomb,*Hist, of Bucks,*vol. ii.,' Bierton.'

his M. A. degree, devoted himself entirely to natural history, lectured in London on botany and zoology, became a Vice- President of the Linnsean Society, a Fellow of the Royal Society, and Principal Keeper of the Natural History Collections at the British Museum. His brother the Rev. John Shaw, D. D., of Magdalen College, Oxford, wrote a Latin epitaph, describing his career, for his grave in St. George's churchyard, Bloomsbury.

2

SECTION 2

CHAPTER II

THE DISPERSED FAMILY

The Competitors for the Christ Church Prizes – Letters from William Wyndham Grenville – Life at Wendover – Julia Smith*ne*Bernard – Fanny Bernard and Julia's Wedded Happiness – A Remarkable Garment – The 'Courting Bower' – Rev. Richard King – Mrs. Edmunds – Fanny Bernard's Engagement to Mr. King – Thomas Bernard – His Matrimonial Engagement with Margaret Adair – Their Marriage – Scrope Bernard's First Love – Fanny Bernard's Determination – Her Marriage.

Itwill of course be concluded that Scrope Bernard had many college friends besides William Wyndham Grenville, but he was probably first on the list; I certainly have not the same amount of correspondence from any other youth. Mr. Godschall, who continued to express himself chiefly in careless verse, comes next; and I ought not to omit Mr. Sawkins, whose name occurs immediately after Scrope Bernard's in the list of competitors for the Christ Church prizes. The others were Buckle, and Harwood whose congratulations to Scrope on his University Prize Essay have been mentioned. Mr. Sawkius wrote several letters during the continuance of a college quarrel; he seems to have been a sensitive young man, and believed for a time that Grenville and Bernard, who may have been somewhat exuberant in their mirth, were turning him into ridicule. The bundle of letters, labelled by Scrope Bernard, ' Letters, Negotiations, &c.,' shows that every effort was made to soothe him, and that William Grenville gave himself much trouble in the matter; the result being a complete restoration of harmony.

It would be interesting to follow the career of this gentleman, and of others con- nected with those Oxford days, butLETTERS FROM W. W. GRENVILLE 21

this I am unable to do in all cases. In the case of William Grenville, there are ample materials, owing to his originally distinguished surroundings, and his eminent public career, which is only touched upon in these volumes when it has any bearing on the Bernard history. And it must be added that, by reason of his early advantages, and of the use which he made of them, being, even in youth, not only a scholar, but a thinker, his early letters are the most interesting of the collection.

Soon after the Long Vacation of 1781, William Grenville wrote to Scrope Bernard from Lincoln's Inn,1one of those epistles no longer to be met with – lengthy, erudite, and well-thought out – which have vanished before the penny post and the general scramble for existence:

My dear Bernard, – I rejoice exceedingly in your account of your industry, espe- cially as I know you have not exaggerated it from my having often observed how little you are disposed (less than any man I know) even to do justice to your own merit. And I say merit, because I think it would be preposterous if men were allowed to arrogate merit to themselves for their abilities, which are such as God has given them; or their rank or fortune, which they owe too often to the guilt of their ancestors, or to their own, and that none should be allowed to the sacrifice of time, pleasure, or health to laborious and useful pursuits. When therefore you tell me of your adding to your other advantages that alone which is wanted from you, I already see you at the head of a lucrative and honourable profession, doing credit to it, both by that extensive circle of knowledge for which it is so distinguished, and by your own gentleness of manners and a natural humanity which is too often wanting in the profession.

If this should sound a little too grave you will excuse me, and attribute it to my pleasure in hearing that you was leaving step by step. The medical society, especially*under such auspices,*is not a hobby horse; it is the steady and trained horse, assigned you in that troop of life in which you have a commission, and you cannot exercise yourself upon it too often, since it is upon that that you are to exert yourself*in certamine,*and by that, that you acquire, not wealth only (which, by the by, is not in itself to bedespised, but the vicious desire for it and the bad use of it).

1MS. Letter of William Orenville, at Nether Winchendon, dated Lincoln's Inn, November 23,1781.

But: –
Honour, Love, Obedience, troops of Friends,
Praises both loud and full – heart-honour – 1

Immediately after this quotation the writer makes a digression from his theme by entering into questions of style, as a vehicle for thought more especially; but it appears in the course of a page of the large letter-paper then in use that he kept the original subject in view, and that the digression was subsidiary. It begins:

At the same time you must give me leave to tell you my opinion upon your St. Johnian or Bolingbrokian*furor,*which appears to me more likely to vitiate and corrupt your title than if you had a taste for all the bad writing that was*never*read. This perhaps you'll vote a paradox. My idea is grounded upon the clear distinction which appears to me to exist between the didactic and the epic stile of prose, between the simple, clear, elegant and philosophical stile of Addison and Swift, and the oratorical and declamatory effusions, I might almost say rhapsodies, of Boling- broke; which are nevertheless as well suited to his subjects as the stile of the others is to theirs.

Mr. Grenville then instances Steele as an author who made the mistake of writing in the same style in his essays as in his political pamphlets.

Now if Bolingbroke wishes, either by a speech, a pamphlet, or a craftsman, to raise or to foment a faction against a minister, it is for his purpose to inflame the passions of his countrymen. He is to raise in them a certain degree even of phrensy, before he can hope to accomplish that end to which his labour is directed. Is this the case with a moralist or a philosopher? And is it not still less so with a man who is explaining the theory of a science, or deducing practical consequences from its nature and principles?

A 'MUTUAL IMPBOVEMENT' CORRESPONDENCE 23

1I do not know whether Mr. Grenville altered Shakespeare in this instance himself. The passage in Johnson and Stevens, and in Theobald runs:

' And that which should accompany old age,
As honour, love, obedience, troops of friends,
I must not look to have; but, in their stead,
Curses, not loud, but deep, mouth-honour, breath,
Which the poor heart would fain deny, and dare not.'
*Macbeth,*Act V., Scene III.

Certainly you say very truly that the Thoracic Duct is a bad subject for a declamatory composition. But it does not follow that it is so for a clear and elegant composition. Observe what is the practice of a great man, and great master of both stiles.

This means Cicero, and after illustrating his meaning from his works, Mr. Grenville proceeds to instance Virgil for a like purpose, ending with: 'It is an endless and inexhaustible subject, but I will release you at last'; and then alludes to the project of a sort of ' mutual improvement' correspondence:

I shall be most sincerely obliged to you for such letters as you mention, which will afford me a most agreeable relaxation from my own studies, and will in some degree supply what I always considered a deficiency in my Oxford education. My own hobby at present is the following (tho' I must do myself the justice to say that I give little time to anything but law) – I want to collect what I call historical parallels. Such is, tho' it is a very trite example, that of the deaths of Epaminondas and Wolfe, or that of the resignations of Charles Vth and Diocletian or that more extraordinary one of Sylla. By throwing these together one sees how different men have acted in the same events, and one derives a certain degree of advantage with some little amusement in the composition. If you should happen to meet with or recollect any at all remarkable, I wish you would, whenever you have leisure, send me either a simple note of the names, or – what I should like much better – a little parallel drawn up by yourself. You will observe I mean them to be short, as the plan merely goes to one incident and not, like Plutarch's, to whole lives. Whenever I see you I shall have one or two to show you. It is at least a harmless, and perhaps not quite useless, lounge.

But do not let it interrupt better, much better things, such as Anatomical Discourses and Harangues on the Diseases of Children. It would be a curious speculation on that subject, to know whether more have not perished since it has become the fashion for all mothers to suckle their children. I own I should think that a cow, or a farmer's wife, would be a much fitter nurse than the Duchess of Devonshire. But I am going very far *ultra crepidam,* so I shall return to my reports, and wish you good night.

But the writer had not quite finished yet. A postscript or short appendix, originally, no doubt, jotted down on astray bit of paper, is stuck by sealing-wax to the end of the letter.

I never knew what good, or rather fine criticism was, till I dipped the other day into Longinus, and read his observations on the passage in Demosth. ' De Corona': Ou /iaTovsev "M. apaOS1vi TrpoKivSuvtva'avTas,&c., &c. You may easily find it out, and pray read it if you have leisure. I have even found time to translate both text and commentary, but not satisfactorily to myself.

That Scrope was now commencing in earnest the battle of life is evident from this and other letters, and that he was, as part of the necessary effort, vigorously striving to concentrate his energies on the profession he had chosen, an effort always painful to persons conscious of varied abilities, and obliged, as it were, to suppress a portion of themselves in order to achieve success. He was so far his own master, being left without father or mother, as to make the effort doubly hard, since he lacked the external support and pressure of parental authority, the only substitute being the wise and kindly counsel of his brother Thomas, and of other members of the family in their degrees.

At this period the current of life flowed onward with a peacefulness, probably unexpected, for all the family of Sir Francis Bernard, notwithstanding their previous bereavements and disappointments – for all, that is, except the unfortunate eldest son in America. Scrope, while at Oxford, was not precluded by distance from an occasional visit to Wendover, where an unmarried sister lived with Julia, ordinarily Fanny, but in her absence, Emily. The Rev. Joseph Smith's parish, nestling under the shelter of the Chiltern Hills, was divided into the ' borough and forrens,' land the said borough returned two members to Parliament, having done so since the 28th of Edward I., except for an interval in the following reign. It was disWENDOVEE 25

1Lipsoomb,*Hist, of Bucks,*vol. ii.,' Wendover.'*England's Gazetteer,*1751, vol. ii.,' Wendover.' It sent members to Parliament the 28th of Edward I., and intermitted the two first years of Edward II., but was restored to that privilege with Amersham.

franchised by the Reform Bill of 1832, at which time it contained 264 houses and 1,387 inhabitants.

The situation [says Lipscomb] is pleasant and even picturesque, the town being partly enclosed by lofty irregular eminences whose surfaces, clothed with beechwood and firs, or dotted with sheep, are in full view from the streets, whilst, in an opposite direction, the eye ranges over the contiguous Vale of Aylesbury, rich with corn and pasturage, to the bold hills which are its northern boundaries. The town, properly so-called, is situated about the middle of the parish; the forrens, consisting of detached farmhouses and cottages, interspersed among some dwellings of superior description, being chiefly southward of the town.

The population was almost entirely agricultural, and the women made lace, then an important industry in Bucks. The site of the old vicarage is still shown, though it has been pulled down some years, and another built in a different part of the parish; and Wendover is a pretty village, notwithstanding the nearness of a railway which has cut up that line of country. The value of the living must have been small indeed when Julia Bernard married its vicar, if, as I have heard my father say, their income, from all sources, did not exceed*300l.*per annum; by no means a large sum, even in those days. Julia wrote, in her ' Reminiscences': ' His good prudence and my willing acquiescence enabled us to get on pretty well. Certainly it was a small style I had not been accustomed to, but a willing and contented mind made us very happy.' I have been told that the young wife, conscious of her inability to give her friends luxurious dinners, yet anxious for her reputation as a housekeeper and hostess, used to ask them to name some favourite dish, that she might provide it when they visited her, and which was brought, of course, as nearly to perfection as previous study and practice could achieve.

And the vicarage, as appears from glimpses given of the life in her letters, was not entirely left to solitude, quiet as its social intercourse must have been. Julia has noted in an especial manner the continued kindness of the Hartwellfamily under the new circumstances: ' Good Sir William and Lady Elizabeth's first visit to us was a family dinner; only themselves.'

From her rural home the vicar's wife corresponded in French with Scrope at Oxford; and, in spite of mistakes, such as were to be expected, her letters show a considerable aptitude for entering into the spirit of the language. They are not dated; but one of those in my possession was probably written very soon after her marriage.

In this epistle Julia tells her brother that want of time prevented her from writing the day before, that he will no doubt smile at this, she being a ' jeune dame' living in the country, but that she would gladly borrow from those who have too much time; and does he not sometimes wish for more leisure than he can obtain? She continues: ' I wish to do all that can be done; I wish to read very many books, I wish to play well, to do all that a good woman ought to do in her own house, not only to work much, but also to look after everything; yet when we have company I am obliged to devote myself to conversation, to excursions, to cards, to badinage, and very often to etiquette only.' After sundry philosophical reflections, she informs her brother that she has been reading Eobertson's ' Charles V.,' Voltaire's ' Peter the Great,' and' Charles XII.' and has greatly enjoyed the visit of a Mr. Crowe, who had spent three weeks in Eome and had much to relate about his foreign experiences.

Fanny Bernard joined her sister soon after this time, and Julia's wedded happiness became the subject of a grandiloquent poetical effusion from her ready pen. In this quaint production Jove is brought upon the scene. After commenting on certain scandals in high life with an amount of indignation scarcely reasonable, if his own conduct be taken into account, he sends two sylphs to ascertain if the*menage*at Wendover vicarage is really as harmonious as it appears to be. These airy visitants are taken for benighted travellers, made welcome, and hospitably entertained, the evening winding up somewhat incongruously'THE EVERLASTING HABIT' 27

with family prayers; and the next day they are able to carry a most favourable report to Jove.

Fanny's spirits seem to have risen in this congenial atmosphere; it must have been in the early part of 1780 that she wrote ' The Lamentations of the Everlasting Habit.' This habit was, or rather had been, the gorgeous pearl-coloured garment, trimmed with gold lace, and lined with costly fur, which many years before had caused a memorable sensation in Lincoln Minster, when Mrs. Terry – not her daughter, Mrs. Hastings, as Fanny erroneously supposed – in the bloom of youth and beauty had disturbed the devotions of the worshippers.1It must apparently have descended to Mrs. Hastings, who left it by will to Jane Bernard – according to Fanny – and this is probably correct. Jane, after wearing it for some time in its original state, took off the gold and fur, and had the cloth dyed a dark blue. In course of years she seems to have tired of this too durable vestment, and passed it on to Fanny, when the latter was about twelve; and now Fanny, having worn it ten years, had caused it to be dyed a dark brown, and proceeded to make it up once more with her own hands, as a hack habit. She writes: ' It was cloth of such fabric, that it seemed neither threadbare nor thin after sixty years' wear.'

As the young seamstress plied her needle, she pondered over the possible feelings of the old garment, until her thoughts found utterance in a poem from which I give some extracts.

O'er a half-finished button-hole she hung
While in harmonious numbers thus she sung.
Having informed the habit that it is in future to be only a hack:
The offended garb, convulsed in every thread,
Thrice sighed, thrice gaped its seams, while thus it said,
After enumerating its former glories:
When pious Inet filled the chanter's chair;
1See vol. i. of this Family History, chapter viii., p. 188.
the habit continues:
When I engaged his powerful prying eyes
He sent the verger to express surprize,
That thus famed Hastings should attract each eye
From Heavenly things to such frail vanity.
Then, contrasting with this proud remembrance its present state:
Is this the conduct to old servants used?
A button grudged, a skein of silk refused,
In all your wardrobe to bring up the rear,
And only in bad roads and rain appear!
Shame on such conduct, my complaints attend,
Nor in the years of age neglect a friend;
Let me enjoy my long-sought, wished repose
Snug in a trunk among thy cast-off clothes,
Or grant me all my former rank and power,

And let me deck thee in thy gayest hour!
The angry maid, spurning the rebel prayer,
Stuck in her needle, and refused to hear.

In one of the French letters to Scrope, Julia mentions a projected excursion to Winchendon, which was about eleven or twelve miles distant from Wendover, and hopes that he will arrange to meet them there; if he wishes to bring ' Monsieur Le Roi,' he is welcome to do so. Fanny adds a postscript desiring that Scrope will on no account bring this gentleman, whose name in plain English was Mr. King; if he does, she cannot go. Apparently, however, Scrope did bring his friend, and Fanny was induced to join the party; for it must have been on this occasion that – according to tradition – an offer was made at Winchendon to one of my grand-aunts, and accepted, in a bower which long bore the name of the ' Courting Bower' in honour of the event.

About this time, but whether before or after the declaration I know not, Fanny wrote a poem: ' On a young gentleman taken out of a cottage and patronised by Mr. K,' which poem was of course a panegyric onTHE KING FAMILY 29

Mr. King, who had rescued this youth from the mortifications and deprivations incident to unrecognised talent. His name was George Anderson; he became an accountant to the East India Board, and maintained through life a reputation for superior intellect and irreproachable conduct; but his career must have been somewhat prematurely brought to a close, since he died several years before Mr. King, whose life was not remarkable for duration. In the words of an obituary notice:l' An interesting account of his (Mr. King's)' fostering kindness to that eminent young man, and of the distinguished talents of his*protegi,*may be found in a work published a few years ago under the title of ' Necrology.'

The Rev. Kichard King, Fanny's accepted suitor, was a Fellow of New College, Oxford;2he belonged to a family which claimed descent from the ancient monarchs of Devon. To this lineage Robert King, first Bishop of Oxford; John King, Bishop of London; and Henry King, the poet Bishop of Chichester, belonged. At one time the family possessed land in the parishes of Wonninghall and Shabbington, Bucks, in both of which it had built almshouses; but I doubt whether it had retained any of this property down to the days of the Bernard courtship. As to the place in which Fanny made her suitor's acquaintance, it was probably either Oxford or Wendover; and Mr. Smith is more likely to have been responsible than Scrope, because he was evidently a more intimate friend of Richard King.

Mr. King was vicar of Steeple Morden in Cambridgeshire, but his benefice did not afford sufficient emolument to justify marriage, and, as neither he nor Fanny Bernard were endowed with large private means, the young lady's brothers considered her engagement imprudent. Thomas, who still had the burden of his father's unsettled affairs to sustain, strongly deprecated any alliance tending to increase the family difficulties, and apparently Scrope soon saw matters in the same light. It would seem also that Mr. King's offhand manner caused a further amount of friction, while his views on questions of the day did not always harmonise with the Bernard ideas.

1*The Gentleman's Magazine,*vol. Ixxx. part ii., Dec. 1810,' Obituary Notice of the Rev. Richard King.'

2This account of the King family was communicated by the late Miss Collinson. It may also be found in Lipscomb, *Hist. Bucks.* I was informed through Miss Collinson that a notice of a Miss Alice King, an author, had appeared in a newspaper, stating her descent from the first Bishop of Oxford and also from John of Gaunt.

The engaged couple, however, adhered to their determination. At one time Mr. King was looking forward to the possibility of becoming vicar of Whitchurch, near Aylesbury; but he had apparently hampered himself by some promise, which, being strictly construed by the recipient, so diminished the income, that when offered the living by his college he felt compelled to decline it. Nether "Winchendon was then thought of for a moment, and Fanny would have rejoiced in the return to her old haunts, and must almost inevitably have made the deserted Manor House her home during a portion of the year; but it is doubtful whether Mr. King's views of life would have rendered him equally contented there, and the stipend was so insignificant as to be scarcely worth taking into consideration, even if the parish could be held together with Steeple Morden, according to the fashion of the time. So the idea was dropped. Then a chaplaincy was suggested as a means of tiding over the difficulty; but this plan also fell through.

Meanwhile Fanny paid a visit to Lincoln, or was perhaps driven there by her anxious relatives, who thus hoped to keep her away from dangerous company; a letter/from Mrs. Edmunds to Scrope, who had left Worsborough shortly before, evidently belongs to this period; it is dated ' November 18.'

V/e have been perpetually on the ramble since you left us, and are but just sat down composedly at home; our visit to Lincoln at last took place, and I had the pleasure to see your sister well. But poor Mr. White was confined to his room all the time we stayed, except two days, and I find he continues still in the same place.

1MS. Letter at Nether Winchendon.

FANNY BERNARD 31

Mr. White, as other letters show, suffered at times from gout, which is no doubt the ailment noted in this letter.

We stayed one Assembly, your sister being Queen; but there were but a very thin room, tho' esteemed a good Assembly. Mr. Edmunds danced with a Miss Taylor, who really is a fine young woman. Don't be too much amazed! when I tell you that Fanny returned with us to Worsbrough for the winter, where she now is to the Surprize of every Body that we left, and those we came too [to]; nay they can hardly think it is herself. Mrs. White thought that it was Better for her to be with her in the Summer, and she was not very reluctant to comply. We stayed a few days at Ferbeck and a few at Norton, saw Lord Scarbrough's sweet place and passed our time very agreably with our friends. Fanny came from Norton last night after paying a week's visit; they set off for town to-morrow morning for the winter.

Then follows a budget of local news – marriages, births, misfortunes, &c.; after which Mrs. Edmunds adds: ' We are going to lead a very quiet domestick life this winter; I want only a little concert to enliven our evening hours.' But after this declaration she reverts to the subject of a visit just made to a lovely spot, ' everything in the highest perfection,' including a new church on the top of a hill built by the last owner – neither he nor the actual owner are named – and also an orangery, which must have been something uncommon. She adds indeed: ' My little girls are at work by me,' and there are various allusions to her children in other letters, showing that pleasure did not exclude them from her thoughts.

Apparently Fanny Bernard did not leave the north until the autumn of 1781. Scrope says, in a letter to Mr. Edmunds: ' We have got Fanny home again at last, and think that on the whole she does credit to your Yorkshire air; she played off all her Doncaster airs at our race with very great success' – that is, in Aylesbury. But in one respect the sojourn in the north was a failure; Fanny was resolute in maintaining her engagement to Mr. King.

I have few particulars of Thomas Bernard's existenceduring the years immediately following his father's death. He dined once, but apparently once only, with Governor Hutchinson, on January 14, 1780.1' Strahan, Maseres, Mauduit, Galloway, Livius, and T. Bernard' formed the party. Strahan was the King's printer, Maseres was Attorney-General of Canada and afterwards cursitor-baron of the Exchequer; the other guests may be called old acquaintances – they are mentioned in the second volume of this history. Billy Hutchinson, the Governor's son, was then in a rapid consumption. He died in the following month, and the Governor survived only till April. Thomas Bernard must also have gone through the terrible experience of the Gordon riots this year, but he achieved his call to the Bar, and was soon in good practice as a conveyancer. It would be interesting to know what further intercourse he kept up with the loyalists of America, but, except in the case of Sir William Pepperell, I have no materials to quote from; the ranks of the exiles were indeed every year thinned by death and dispersion.

Early in 1782, Thomas-formed a matrimonial engagement with Margaret, daughter of Patrick Adair, a London merchant, and niece of Serjeant James Adair, whose professional relations with Thomas were probably the means of introducing the young couple to each other. The father of Patrick and James Adair had been an army agent, and one at least of his sons appears to have continued the business3; but they came of an old lineage, according to the Serjeant's biographer, who says:

This family, being of the Geraldines, emigrated from Ireland,circa1300; acquired Portpatrick, which they subsequently sold to the Montgomeries, but remained seized of large possessions in Galloway till near the close of the seventeenth century. They had previously acquired considerable property in Antrim, to which they eventually betook themselves. Sir Robert Shafto Adair, PEOSPECT OF THOMAS BEENARD'S MAEEIAGE 33

1Diary and Letters of Governor Hutchinson,vol. ii., chap. vii. *Life of Sir Thomas Bernard, Bart.,by Bev. James Baker. Lipscomb,Hist, of Bucks,vol. i., ' Nether Winchendon.'

'This I gather from a list in an Almanack of the time.

of Ballymena, Antrim, and Huxton Hall, Suffolk, is the head of the family.1

A letter from Jane White to her brother Scrope depicts the excitement caused by the prospect of Thomas's marriage:

Lincoln, 29 April 1782.

Dear Scrope, – Amongst the numerous congratulations bandied about on this joyful occasion, I must not forget my dear brother at Oxford, who I know takes a large share in the felicity of the Templar, but I am not without apprehension that this letter will not find you at Gh. Ch., which may for some little time delay the enclosed proceeding by the newsman to Wendover. I conclude the wedding will be next week, and am much pleased that Brother Smith is chosen to perform the ceremony. I imagine you will not be there at that time, as I suppose it will be a point of delicasy with my brother not to have more than two of his own family present, in order to show the greater respect to hers. Indeed I think she must be already half-frighted at hearing of brothers and sisters without end. I wish in the midst of our American Brother [sic], for I think his situation at present must be disagreeable, and the new ministry have given a turn in his disfavour, but if a peace should be accomplished in the course of this summer it would fully compensate.

Your favourite printroom was in high glory last Thursday, being as full as it could possibly hold. A commerce-table in the middle of sixteen; a llly quadrille-table in one corner, and the harpsichord very well engaged in the other. In order to expunge all engagements we had a great route; 70 invited and towards 60 came; we had 3 whist tables and 3 quadrille.

After some news about two charming young ladies who had recently been in Lincoln, and whom Scrope might meet in London, followed by the expression of a wish that the writer could entice Julia into the bracing air of Lincoln – Jane continues:

If you was but in Orders, perhaps Brother Smith could come too, but I doubt as it is there would be some difficulty in gettinga proper person to attend his living. You will hear how my cause is likely to go. The children are very well, but if you don't come to see them soon, they will almost forget Uncle Scrope, of whom they seem to have but a faint remembrance. Dr. Sibthorpe has been a good deal here, and talks much of your botanical abilities, as does the Subdean, with whom you are a great favourite.

1Woolrych,*Lives of Eminent Setjeants-at-Law,*vol. ii., ' James Adair.' The biographer erroneously calls Margaret Adair the Serjeant's daughter. Her father's name was certainly Patrick, and he was a merchant. Serjeant Adair had one daughter only, married to Admiral Sir John Colpoys.

VOL. III. D

If this letter was written soon after Mrs. White became aware of her second brother's engagement, the marriage must have been somewhat hurried; and no doubt by reason of Mr. Adair's state of health he probably wished to see his daughter married before he died. This was the more easily arranged, that a numerous attendance was not in those days usual, and far less preparation was therefore required, notwithstanding that some formalities were observed which have since been dropped. Thomas Bernard and Margaret Adair were married on May 11, 1782, and in a letter written on June 10, the bridegroom says to Scrope: ' We are all well at present, except in respect of the anxiety and melancholy we have suffered from Mr. Adair's death, who was released from his sufferings last Friday.' Mr. Adair left apparently two daughters only, Mrs. Bernard, and another who never married – they were motherless.

It appears that Scrope Bernard's poetical talents had been called into exercise on this important occasion of his brother's marriage. In a letter of May 20, when Mr. Adair must have been still alive, Thomas wrote:

My dear Brother, – You will think me very ungrateful in not having taken a more early notice of your charming Poem. I have shown it to Margaret, and she is extremely pleased with it. We think the most beautiful passages are the 3rd stanza, the simile of the vestal in the 6th, and the whole passage (and that is our great favourite) which refers to music.

I have shown it to nobody but her and Emily, partly because there are passages in it which mark haste, and some repetitions, which I think you would alter. The passage on music is so pleasing to me, and comes so home to my dear Margaret's ' Harmony of Disposition,' that I wish it to conclude there, and a few of the thoughts, though not the ruling idea of the 2 lastFANNY BBRNARD 35

stanzas, thrown into other parts in order to give variety. Suoh is ' the severity of my criticism.' Mrs. B. finds no fault at all, so that you must say with the Critic: – ' Well! the women are the best judges after all.' However, a proof of its merit is that it is commended and admired (spite of poetical envy) by a brother author, and he all the while continuing

Your affect. Brother

The Emily mentioned in this letter was no doubt Thomas's sister, who had probably come up for the wedding and remained with her brother and sister-in-law. Fanny also had come to town, probably with Julia and her husband; she addressed a letter from Soho Square, in May, to her youngest brother. The independent style of this epistle, the defensive, or even antagonistic, attitude she had felt bound to assume with regard to her own family, were consequences of her attachment to Mr. King. She was of course staying with friends – in all likelihood still with the Smiths; but speaks of going about on her own account in a manner scarcely usual at that epoch; and the letter further reveals the secret that Scrope Bernard was then passing through the ordeal of ' first love,' or what his sister supposed to be such, and that Fanny was most anxious to be of use to him, not only from sympathy, but probably also because she hoped thus to enlist his feelings in favour of her own views. She writes:

Your letter met me here last night on my arrival, too late to answer it by that post, and indeed I delayed answering it from a hope that I should have been able to have said something positive from the regions of St. James's, for though I am come to town with a resolution to see no one, I meant to have paid a visit there this morning, if I possibly could, to have learnt the time of their stay in town, their peregrinations for the summer, &c.; but it is a very rainy day, and the horses cannot go out after their two days' journey, so I must delay it till to-morrow, when I mean if possible to go, and if I see any reason for your coming to town immediately I will write again, but on the whole, if your not coming now is a great object to you, it certainly is at this moment – before I have been – too uncertain a cause to sacrifice much in. I am, however, much interested in it, and if friendship for theSister could inspire love for the Brother, I will leave no stone unturned to recommend myself to her.

The young lady to whom allusion is here made was evidently Scrope's Yorkshire acquaintance; I do not know whether he came to London, nor indeed whether the energetic Fanny was able to give him any ground for hope. The rest of her letter relates to her own affairs, and is most resolute in tone. She writes:

With respect to the last subject of your letter, it is become a very painful one to me, and as I think I am most competent to judging [sic] on the subject, it being now a matter of mere inclination, I wish as little as possible to talk about it to others, but yet it would be painful and a hard thing upon me to conclude the whole of this, till lately unpleasant affair, by having myself and my future Husband slighted by Brothers, and by no one else, but in that case I shall consider myself as between two evils and chuse the least.

The remainder of the letter is in the same strain, and Fanny Bernard was so far a champion of the rights of women as to declare: ' It must rest solely within myself to guide my own conduct.' She complains of Thomas's cold, legal way of looking at the subject, and vindicates Mr. King. Admitting that he might be somewhat regardless of etiquette, and too easily duped by ' unsuspected artifice' – which is, of course, an allusion to his promise concerning Whitchurch – she winds up with ' in heart and disposition I know not his equal.' As to her future residence:

With respect to Whitchurch, if the income is repaired that is no fair release to me, for he knows, you and most people know, that Whitchurch itself was no object – for I hated the house, the situation, and the neighbourhood, and never meant to live there; you know it, for I understand you was the first who suggested the idea of living at Winchendon – a scheme infinitely more agreeable to me.

The conclusion is calmer, but quite as determined:

I don't thoroughly understand you in your hope against positiveness on my side. I am now of an age to have a consequence and a conduct of my own; so if my own mature reasonMARRIAGE OF FANNY BERNAED 37

and judgement directs me to any object I shall be steady in my pursuit of it – steadiness and consistency of conduct is what I have hitherto wanted, but what, at my age, and in such a cause, I ought to want no longer.

Whatever happens on yours or my Brother's side, I shall not forget that you have both been warmly actuated by your interest for my welfare, tho' possibly mistaken in the pursuit – and if I can, consistent with my own ideas, make you both happy, I shall be very happy myself – at all events I shall ever feel myself

Your very affectionate Sister

As to farther details I am but very imperfectly informed. It is certain that when Thomas Bernard wrote to Scrope on June 10 he believed that he had induced Fanny to give up Mr. King, indeed she had desired him to write to that effect and to express her wish that no further communication should take place except through her brother. But this was evidently an arrangement prompted by some necessity of the moment, and something must ere long have happened to release Fanny from its restrictions – in her own estimation – since she was certainly married to Richard King in August. The event took place, I believe, in London, and an uncle – not then born – subsequently asserted that she went from Thomas Bernard's house but without his knowledge. Thomas and Scrope appear indeed to have been both out of town in that month; whether Thomas left her free to take the decisive step, which he could not legally prevent, merely refusing the sanction of his presence, I do not know; nor who acted as chaperon or gave her away – possibly Mr. and Mrs. Smith came up for the purpose.

Fanny was then five-and-twenty, and had therefore some reason for announcing that she was competent to judge for herself; and it will be seen in these volumes that she was justified by the result. None of the evils anticipated by her friends befell her – her relatives became thoroughly reconciled to her husband, and the marriage proved one of more than average happiness.

3

SECTION 3

CHAPTER IIIScropeBernard'
sIntroductionToPoliticalLife

Scrope Bernard's Interest in Politics – His Project of taking up a Tutorship – William Grenville's offer of Assistance – Scrope Bernard accepts a Tutorship – A Sudden Change in his Prospects – He gives up his Medical Studies and becomes Private Secretary to Earl Temple in Ireland – His First Visit to Ireland – The State of Parties in Ireland – The Coalition Ministry – Earl Temple Resigns the Vioe-Royalty of Ireland – Letter from Lady Roche – The Irish Volunteers – The Earl of Hillsborough – Earl Temple's Vice-Royalty.

Itmust be assumed, from the tone of the following letter from William Grenville, that Scrope Bernard early took a strong interest in politics, perhaps, indeed, to some extent for the sake of his friend. The letter is dated ' March 25, 1782.'1

My dear Bernard, – As I know the impatience you must feel at the present moment, I send you the following list, on which you may depend. It was settled only a few hours ago, so that you will have possibly the first news of it at least as early as anyone.

Cabinet.

The Chancellor to stay if he thinks fit; if not, to be succeeded by Dunning.

1st Lord of the Treasury. Ld. Rockingham
1 Ld. of ye Admiralty. Adml. Keppel
Commander-in-Chief. General Conway
Secretary of State. Ld. Shelburne
Do. Ch. Fox
President of the Council. Lord Camden
Privy Seal Duke of Grafton
Chanc. of the Exchequer. Lord John Cavendish
Master of the Ordnance. Duke of Richmond

1The letters in this chapter are in the Collection at Nether Winchendon, when nothing is said to the contrary.

A TUTORSHIP 39

This last is not a Cabinet office, but the Duke takes it to make the other arrangements easy, and is to be called to the Cabinet.

Lord Howe has the Channel Fleet – Barrington is talked of for the W. Indies – Barre is Secretary at War – Burke and Townshend Paymaster of ye Army and Treasurer of ye Navy, on a reduced scale of profits.

I am vastly sorry to hear that you do not think of coming to town this Easter as I shall not stir from hence. Could you contrive to spend a day or two here?

Ever most sincerely and afftely yours

It is just come into my head that I don't know where to direct to you. I believe the safest place is Oxford, but there my news loses its freshness which is all its merit. I send it, however, to show that I wished to have satisfied your curiosity tho' I fear I have not done it.

The nearness of Easter may have suggested this doubt; otherwise Scrope's address was certainly Oxford in the early part of this year. He was continuing his medical studies; but was apparently becoming uneasy at the length of time which must elapse before he could earn any money, while his unavoidable expenses during this preparatory interval were, and would continue to be, considerable. It was probably in this year that his brother Thomas wrote him a scrap of a note in Latin, interspersed for greater security with many blanks – which were of course quite intelligible to the recipient – in which he delicately offered pecuniary assistance, on the ground that Scrope's idea of earning a little money by a short tutorship – although less objectionable than another project, which is not explained, might lead to failure – in his intended profession no doubt. An invitation from Lord Bristol, in April, to undertake the tuition of Lord Sandys's nephew, was evidently the occasion of Thomas Bernard's letter. This scheme was not carried out; but Scrope declined his brother's offer, promising, it may be supposed, to apply to him whenever he felt a real need of help, since he did avail himself of Thomas's kindness at a later period.

It appears that Mr. Grenville had, in a letter I do notpossess, made Scrope an offer of assistance couched in the most generous terms, and that Scrope had partially accepted. The date of a second epistle, with the address, except the words ' Lincoln's Inn,' has disappeared with the seal, but it is approximately fixed by the contents of the letter, and the presumption that Scrope received it before his brother's proposal. William Grenville writes:

As the main object and intention of my proposal was no other than the enabling you with ease and satisfaction of mind to pursue the road into which you have entered, and which will I hope in your instance lead you so much beyond Parson's situation, to which you refer as the ultimate end of your labours, and as I had originally some difficulty with myself how to make it in a manner most agreeable to your feelings, I certainly can have no objection whatever to acquiesce in any modification of it which may unite those two objects. You must allow me, however, to entreat that you will not be over hasty nor over scrupulous in putting an end to it. That however is a future consideration. On the present arrangement I beg you to believe that you put me to no kind of inconvenience, and that even if you did, I could by no other means employ the matter in question more agreeably to my feelings than by being of service to you, nor more agreeably to my conscience than by going to my country instead of a parson buried in obscurity, and a tutor whose abilities would be choked up and overgrown by a college life, a man useful to himself, his friends, and to mankind.

I am very glad that you yourself have mentioned the scheme which you propose for your two next winters. It was the very place which I should have wished to have suggested to you. I can by no means allow that the failure of your views at Ch. Church is of such consequence as to put an end to your other hopes. Without that advantage you set out on a level with other people, with it you have much the start of them. As to Bagot's offer, tho' you do not mention what it is, I should hope you could no longer have any difficulty on the subject. The only one which remains with me, is how you can manage to observe the secrecy which I absolutely require of you, and to reconcile the world and your friends to the abandoning your present advantages. As to the first you may very well say that you have found your present avocations incompatible with your professional studies, and consequently with all your views hl life. To the latter you must make such apologies as you can best invent, but remember thatA TUTOESHIP 41

you are by no means at liberty to communicate the true reason to any person nor in any degree. One thing more I would mention is that whatever your feelings might induce you to do hereafter in case of our both living, if I should die before you are in a situation to comply with those feelings, you must consider what has passed between us as done away, and keep it as a tacit bequest of which no trace whatever will be found among my papers. I am not quite fixed either about my going abroad or my degree. There are difficulties attending both.

It is clear that Scrope was unwilling to accept help from his friend, unless arrangements were made guaranteeing its repayment. The allusions to Oxford matters in this letter I am unable to explain; but before Mr. Grenville had dispatched it he received from Scrope intelligence of the offer of a tutorship to Lord Sandys's nephew, and he opened his letter again to inform his friend that he had been consulted by Lord Temple on this very subject. The tutor was to be ' a Ch. Church man and an Etonian.' Somewhat reluctantly he had been persuaded to incur the responsibility of mentioning some of his own friends.

The names were – 1st Harwood, supposing that an Eton man was absolutely necessary; if not, Sawkins, and Bernard, supposing that he would accept the charge. But I made no difficulty of saying that I wished the choice to fall upon the*former*of the two.

This of course will have no influence when compared with Bagot's recommendation. But I mention it because it is more proper that you should know it from me than from anyone else. I am sure you will give me credit for the true reason, which is my utter abhorrence and aversion to your undertaking such a charge. It would be very useless for me to repeat the reasons I have so often urged, or to appeal to your own experience. I would only ask you what possible advantage – supposing the lad good for anything, which you cannot know – supposing your temper suited to his, which you can still less know – supposing the uncle grateful to you, which you can least of all know – what possible advantage can you derive from the utmost success of such a project, equal to the blessings of an honest, independent affluence? As for your argument about study &c., if any attention is required to any object, you cannot as an honest man give it; if any attainment is necessary, beyondwhat you have, you cannot as an honest man acquire it; and if neither is the case why do not you practise now?

Scrope declined this tutorship, but almost immediately after this decision he must have undertaken the tuition of a son of Dr. Buller, of Alresford, Hants; and I find no intimation that either Thomas Bernard or William Grenville objected to this engagement; apparently it was only for the Long Vacation. When the time drew near, Scrope was invited by the father of his pupil, in a highly eulogistic epistle, to spend the whole period of tuition at his house; and at this house he appears to have been when a sudden change occurred in his prospects which changed the whole current of his life.

The reader of the foregoing letters can hardly doubt that William Grenville had set his heart upon seeing his friend a distinguished man; and, while urging him to persevere in his chosen profession, the idea was perhaps often present to his mind that, if it were possible to start Scrope Bernard in the political line, it might better suit his varied talents, and eventually place him in a more exalted position than medicine ever could. It is indeed not unlikely that Scrope's constant intercourse with Grenville had led, perhaps unconsciously, to his imbibing ambitious dreams. Although I have no record of the fact, he may very possibly have been already an occasional guest at Stowe, the mansion of Earl Temple; and here he would be introduced to society, English and foreign, likely to indispose him for the drudgery of professional work.

Of the foreign guests I know nothing save in one case – the Comte du Roure wrote to Scrope in this year regretting that the invitation, sent him through Scrope, to visit Oxford for the purpose of receiving an honorary degree, had reached him too late in consequence of being wrongly directed. I conclude that this nobleman was a friend of Lord Temple, and a person of some importance also, since he was thus complimented by the university.

William Pitt, second son of the great Earl of Chatham, and of the first Lord Temple's sister, Hester Grenville, THE COALITION MINISTEY 43

was then very young, but was already on the high road to power and fame. The Lord Wellesley of Oxford days, who had become Earl of Mornington by the death of his father, was another youth destined to achieve celebrity, and there were probably others starting in life with numerous advantages, whose companionship must have been gratifying but also disturbing.

The Marquess of Rockingham died on July 1. On the 12th, Lord Mornington wrote to William Grenville, from Dangan Castle:'

We are all thrown into the utmost consternation by the apparent confusion in the British Cabinet; at this time instability of counsels will be absolute destruction. W. Pitt, Secretary of State! and Lord Shelburne Premier! Surely the first cannot be qualified for such an office, and the last is, in my opinion, little to be depended upon. He certainly has not the confidence of the people.

Among the many changes consequent on the formation of this coalition ministry, Earl Temple was appointed Lord Lieutenant of Ireland. William Wyndham Grenville became his brother's public secretary; and, in answer to Scrope Bernard's congratulations, wrote – without any date beyond the day of the week:

My dear Bernard, – Your intelligence is true, though rather premature, as it was not till yesterday evening after much serious deliberation that I accepted the situation in which I now stand. How it will turn out for me God knows. I have at least the satisfaction of thinking that it cannot but prove advantageous to you, as I have a commission to desire that you will come up to town immediately so as to be with me at Lincoln's Inn on Friday morning as early as you can – before ten, if it can be done by travelling all night, if necessary. Believe me ever, most afftely yrs.,

Pray don't be later Scrope Bernard, Esqre

if you can help it, Rev. Dr. Buller's

Wednesday night. Alresford Hants.

1*The Manuscripts of J. B. Fortescue, Esq., preserved at Dropmore*(Historical Manuscripts Commission), vol. i., p. 162.

Lord Temple proposed to take Scrope Bernard with him to Ireland as private secretary. Against this tempting offer Scrope was not proof. He gave up the tutorship of young Buller, and, what was more serious, he gave up his medical studies.

The following letter from a friend, afterwards Dr. Austin, who succeeded him in the tutorship, explains itself:

Oxford, August 7, 1782.

Dear Bernard, – I am much obliged to you for your instructions respecting Mr. B., from which I perfectly understand the path I have to follow. It is lucky for Mr. B. that you have undertaken the correction of his poetical exercises, as I had never paid the least attention to the very arduous task of making myself a poet, and did not even know that poetical exercises were regularly called for by any college in the University.

Though I have some fear from your late appointment that you will be drawn from a profession to which I am obliged for introducing me to your acquaintance, yet I cannot but congratulate you upon your preferment, which I daresay you would not have accepted of unless it afforded you some compensation for the sacrifice you have made. I am happy to find, however, that you have not yet absolutely forsaken us, and that you have still a wish to preserve a name in the Medical Society, which I am sure would be very sorry to part with you. Whether you persevere in this line or find it more eligible to adopt some other – for I take it for granted you will pursue some profession – as you justly observe that politics are precarious matters to depend upon, you will always have my best wishes.

Should you continue with Lord Temple for a year or two, you will enter upon physic as early as I did; and will I doubt not return to it with some valuable connections. I shall be happy to see you on your way to Ireland, and am

Yours very sincerely,

Wm. Austin.

Flattering as was Lord Temple's selection of Scrope Bernard, I am by no means certain that this new career was not the ' objectionable' plan of life against which his brother Thomas had written. Thomas had himself been thoroughly sickened of politics, and he had gained sufficient experience to perceive that Scrope ran some risk of beingA SEEIES OF CONGKATULATIONS 45

stranded in life altogether. If, however, this was the case,

he showed no resentment at the failure of his advice. Other,

friends were ready with congratulations. Dr. Drury wrote: ',

My dear Friend, – I sincerely rejoice at your late appointment and flatter myself it will prove as beneficial to you as it is honorable. Your ability and known Industry leave me no Eoom to doubt but that the attachment you have now formed will be lasting, and attended with the best of consequences; pray let me hear from you. I promise you my pen shall never fail to thank you for your attention, or to assure you with how much sincerity and affection, I am at all times your Friend and Servt

J. Druby. Aug. 2nd 1782 Harrow.

Shute Barrington, Bishop of Llandaff, wrote from ' Mongewell, Oxon,' most kindly, though with episcopal solemnity:

When the die is cast, to calculate chances is but lost time and thought misspent.

Nothing can be more flattering and honorable to you than the friendship of Mr. Wm. Grenville, or the appointment of Lord Temple's to so confidential a situation. You carry with you into the new scene, active talents, much industry, and I am persuaded, much attachment to your Patron. That they may be rewarded as they deserve is my earnest wish. My goodwill and good opinion will always accompany you, as I cannot entertain a doubt that they will always be merited.

Accept my thanks for your kind congratulations.

This last sentence evidently refers to the Bishop's impending translation to the see of Salisbury.1

There is one more letter of this time in my collection which deserves notice. It is from Cyril Jackson, who in the following year became Dean of Christ Church.2This letter ' does not contain congratulations on Scrope's appointment, for these had probably been expressed at an earlier moment; but refers to a present made by Lord Temple to Christ Church, without any further description. The writer thanksScrope for forwarding Lord Temple's letter, and states that he has written to him and to Mr. Grenville in return. He continues:

1Beatson,*Political Index,*vol. i.,' Archbishops and Bishops ' (Edition of 1788).

*A History of the University of Oxford, <tc.,*printed for H. Ackerman.

I can very truly assure you as indeed I have said to himself, that I consider it as the highest compliment that has been paid to Xtch on the present occasion – I have a very real pleasure in it. There is a liberality and a rightness of mind in his thinking of it at all,&it is done in the most handsome way. I am very sure that both the Chapter and the Society at large will view it in the same light.

I am really sorry to miss you. It is not, however, quite impossible that I may catch you for one day. You may assure yrself that I will take care yr rooms shall always be ready for you. Believe me with great truth Dear Sir Yr very faithful & affectionate servt

CtbJackson. Stamford, Sept. 12, 1782.

Scrope Bernard must have started for Ireland very soon after the receipt of this letter. And he was not the only member of the family connection who accompanied Lord Temple to Ireland. The Rev. Joseph Smith was a member of the suite, apparently as one of the Lord-Lieutenant's chaplains. He had been sufficiently long curate of Wad- desdon – a parish in which the Grenvilles had property, and which adjoined where their ancestral home was situated – to have won the Earl's goodwill, and spoke of him in after years as having been a kind friend. The journey to Ireland must have taken place before the end of September; in the course of October, Richard and Fanny, soon after their marriage, took charge of Wendover, then temporarily bereft of its pastor. Julia took the opportunity of paying a visit to her sister, Jane White, at Lincoln, accompanied by Emily, who had been her companion of late.

There are very few memorials of Scrope's first visit to Ireland in my possession. The only allusions to its commencement are contained in a letter from his lively cousin Mrs. Edmunds, dated ' 7th Oct., 1782,' and are as follows:

THEGOVERNMENTOFIRELAND47

I have the pleasure of your letter this day, and you see I take the first moment to reply, and send you my congratulations on your safe arrival and [the] pleasure you enjoy at the Castle; you would almost fancy yourself in Fairyland, that you was become a Sovereign of the first magnitude when you made so magnificent an entry.

Of this entry I have no further account. The writer adds, with an allusion to the convivial habits of the day: ' But you see every situation has its inconveniences; we at our little villa can sit down to our sober meal without danger of excess, whilst you must retreat to avoid it.'

In Lecky's ' History of Ireland in the Eighteenth Century,' 1 the recent changes in the mode of governing Ireland, which had culminated in what the historian terms ' the Constitution of 1782,' may be read at some length. The compiler of the Buckingham Memoirs2more briefly states that:

Lord Temple entered upon the government of Ireland at a crisis of serious agitation. A short time before, under the Duke of Portland's administration [Lord Temple's predecessor as Lord Lieutenant], a Bill had passed the Imperial Parliament, recognizing in full and in the most explicit manner, the sole and exclusive right of the Parliament of Ireland to make laws for Ireland. The Bill had given complete satisfaction to the popular leaders. But the factious and jealous spirit of the Irish was subsequently disturbed by indications on the part of the English Legislature, of a disposition to depart in some particulars from this settlement.

' Things were never more unsettled than they are at present,' Mr. Perry writes to Mr. Grattan, in October, 1782; ' some of the Ministry here are at open enmity with each other, and everybody seems to distrust the head ' – that is, Lord Shelburne.

From the 'Buckingham Memoirs' it appears that Mr. William Grenville was sent back to London to communicate with the Government confidentially on the part of his brother the Lord Lieutenant. About the same time, in November, apparently, Mr. Grenville encountered anxiety of a different sort as to the fate of his possessions at

Lincoln's Inn. Mr. Wickham, who must have written to Scrope Bernard on the subject of a fire, says, in a second letter dated ' Cottingley, December 1782':1

1Lecky,*History of Ireland in the Eighteenth Century*(Edition 1902), vol. chap, v., p. 334.

J*Memoirs of the Court and Cabinets of George III.,*vol. i., 1782.

I was made very happy this morning, after no small apprehension, by a letter from Bierton, informing me that all Grenville's books, which were removed on account of the late fire at Lincoln's Inn, were lodged in his chambers, and had received no injury whatever – they will all be replaced immediately. I thought it necessary to give you the information immediately, to relieve Grenville from any apprehension he might have been under on hearing the account of the fire, in case no other person had written to him on the subject. I should hope, however, that some [one] of his friends has been beforehand with me in the communication of his narrow escape.

Your brother, I fear, must have been under much greater apprehensions. I hope he has not suffered in the hurry and confusion of removing. Probably you will hear particulars from him, at present I am as ignorant of everything as you can be – excepting only that we may both congratulate each other on a very imminent escape.

The writer goes on to say that Grenville had arrived in town a few days before he left, but that he did not venture to trespass on his time. By the tenor of the letter it is clear he cannot have been aware that Mr. Grenville was still there, and must therefore have been well informed already of the calamity at Lincoln's Inn. There are some allusions towards the close to friends:

I heard last week from Oxford that Milner's voice, I am sorry to say, was just as I left it. G. Markham going to town in great spirits – his brother Jack is arrived from the W. Indies, after being in no small danger from the terrible storm which proved so fatal to our fleet.

Mention is made in the ' Memoirs ' of a ' network of small difficulties' in which Mr. William Grenville was involved during his mission to London ' by the want of unity in the1MS. Letter at Nether Winchendon.

THE STATE OF PARTIES IN IRELAND 49

Cabinet, especially between Mr. Townshend and Lord Shelburne on the Irish question.' Lord Temple, according to those ' Memoirs,' had always been in favour of keeping strictly to the compact with Ireland; and, in consequence of these complications, his brother was detained the whole winter in England.

In the collection of letters preserved at Dropmore, the home of William Grenville's later years, Scrope Bernard's presence in Ireland is first made known through a long letter from Lord Temple to Mr. Grenville, dated ' December 1st,' /and descriptive of the state of parties in Ireland, which is noted as being 'in Mr. Bernard's handwriting, except the last paragraph.' In January, 1783, there are various allusions to him in the Lord Lieutenant's correspondence with his brother, as, for instance: ' The slip of information you enclosed under cover to Bernard, dated the 24th (which is the last date from you), makes no alteration in my ideas '; and ' The death of the Chancellor's fat Hewitt and another arrangement enables me to give Bernard 400Z. per annum; this therefore is off my mind; and if I could provide for you, the brother of my affection, my task is done to my content.'

At length, after a few more weeks of uneasiness and constraint, a decided ministerial crisis in England determined Lord Temple to resign the Viceroyalty. He writes to Mr. Grenville, on ' March 20th ':"

I have thought it fair to apprize some few individuals of this event, and therefore it cannot remain a secret; and if it is known to Mr. Fox, it will not long be a secret here, as Sheridan has spoken to Bernard about my letter to the Duke of Portland, and has offered him ten to one that I stay. So much for delicacy, and therefore it need no longer be a mystery.

Fox was one of the ministry which had gone out in the previous year, and he appeared very soon after the date of this letter in the list of a new ministry, under the Duke ofPortland, which obtained the name of ' the " Coalition" Ministry, from the remarkable union of Lord North with Mr. Fox.'

'*The Manuscripts of J. B. Fortescue, Esq., preserved at Dropmare,*vol. L, pp. 165-8.

* *Ibid.,*vol. i., p. 202.

VOL. III. B

On March 23, Scrope Bernard writes, at Lord Temple's desire but in his own name, to William Grenville from ' Phoenix Lodge ':*l*

*I*do not pretend to describe my feelings upon the receipt of your most kind letter of the 12th instant. But I must break off from this subject to obey your brother's commands by writing you a detail of what occurs to me as most striking in the situation of things here. The addresses go on with tolerable spirit; nine already presented, and others voted but not yet arrived at the capital. A very warm and affectionate one from the county of Galway, presented this day, seems to curse the consequences of the coalition, when it concludes with this sentence:*We cannot without anxiety hear that some change is meditated in his Majesty's ministry in England, only because we fear it may lead to the departure of your Excellency, which, whenever it may happen, we must feel with regret, and meet with reluctance.*This regret upon the apprehension of the event is, I assure you, so general that, exclusive of the addresses, it resounds from every quarter, and notwithstanding there are necessarily a few Ponsonbyites and others, who do not feel it, yet on account of the general disposition of the people, there is not one of them who dares avow their unfriendly sentiments.

Then follow sundry details respecting the machinations of Lord Temple's opponents, and the dismay of another political set who had reason to dread the Duke of Portland as Prime Minister, and the appointment of one of his friends as Viceroy; these persons, however they might previously have demeaned themselves towards the Lord Lieutenant, were now earnest in desiring him to remain. Mr. Bernard continues:

As for the general mass of the people, abstracted from party, their addresses will fully show their sentiments, from which, notwithstanding the almost extravagant warmth of some of them, not a single man, however from passions unfriendly disposed, dare express his dissent or disapprobation. The numbers that flockedRESIGNATION OF LORD TEMPLE 61

1*The Manuscripts of J. B. Fortescue, Esq., preserved at Dropmare,*vol. i., p. 203.

to vote the address from Galway were so great that they could not assemble at their usual place, but were obliged to meet in the church, as at the famous Belfast meeting.

I feel an anxious suspense to see what effects will first show themselves upon your brother's resolution first getting abroad. At present all is mere surmise, and the very household continue to amuse themselves with speculating whether they are to lose their warm berths in the Castle. We shall have quitted this place at the very pinnacle of our glory, and shall leave a great many friends jealous of our honour and regardful of our memory; and who will not patiently suffer any slur to be thrown on the splendour of these six months of your brother's government, which I am confident, are not to be paralleled.

The letter is continued, apparently, on the same paper, by Lord Temple, who says: ' Bernard has been writing this while I have copied mine to the King. I send it open, and you have the former envelope in which you may put it, as I write at the park, where I have not my wafer seal/ He then goes on to discuss politics.

In this letter to the King, the Earl tendered his resignation of the Viceroyalty, and from that time forward he occupied himself more or less with the arrangements consequent on this step. In a letter of April 6/he adverts to the condition of his friends and dependents:

The total and absolute failure of Mr. Tunnadine, Master in Chancery and Commissioner of Appeals, makes it necessary to dismiss him. These offices provide for Doyle and Coppenger, and give me a satisfaction which I cannot express. All other considerations are indeed trifling, but I own I feel them strongly for some of my unfortunate household, out of which number, however, Sir Scrope Bernard and Dame Eleanor his wife are happily excepted.

Scrope Bernard was not then a baronet, nor a knight, nor was he married. But it is curious that both the title and the wife are mentioned in a document – little more indeed than a scrap of paper – signed ' Mornington, K. P.,' and addressed ' SrScrope Bernard, Bart., Castle, Dublin. To the care of Dame Eleanor Bernard." It begins ' Lord Apsley desires to acquaint SrScrope Bernard, Bart., that his Majesty has been pleased to sign a patent of the dignity of a Baronet of Nova Scotia,' for him with remainder to his children by ' Eleanor his now wife – the consequence of his faithful services as Examinator of the Hearth money in Ireland.' The missive is dated ' Secretary's Office, Whitehall, Ap. 1, 1783,' a significant day. There was no doubt some joke involved, but it cannot be fathomed so long after the event as the present time; ' Dame Eleanor' remains a mystery, and was probably a mythical personage. She is not mentioned again. Scrope had written to Mrs. Edmunds in unflattering terms about the ladies of Dublin, perhaps because his mind was engrossed by memories of the Yorkshire lady which his cousin seems to have carefully kept alive as long as possible. Lord Mornington, the ostensible perpetrator of the joke, was then in Dublin.

1*Manuscripts of J. B. Fortescue, Esq.,*vol. i., p. 209.

Scrope Bernard had known very early in March that the retiring Viceroy intended to retain him as his private secretary after his arrival in England. This disposed of all idea that he might, as suggested by Mr. Austin, return to his medical studies, for which indeed he was probably becoming every day more unfit, and William Grenville had already written to express his complete satisfaction in the following letter:2

Pall Mall, March 12th, 1783.

My dear Bernard, – I am very sure that you know too well the interest which I take in what concerns you, and the sincere satisfaction of my mind from your letter of the 5th (which I have this instant received) to make it necessary for me to expatiate further upon that subject. I can truly say that I am by it relieved from what has been a burden upon my mind ever since I have foreseen an event which is now almost certain (you will understand to what I allude). It was a most sensible mortification to me to think that I had contributed to take you from a line of life in which you must have succeeded, and to have thrown you into one so different, without your receiving any adequate compensation for what you have sacrificed.

As it is I own I am satisfied for the present. You may dependLADY ROCHE 53 1MS. at Nether Winchendon. =Hid.

upon it that the present situation of things will not last. Probably their change may again place you in a situation in which my brother or myself may derive advantage from that industry, those abilities, and above all that integrity and character which I was sure (and experience has proved it in the instance of my brother) wanted only to be known to be as much the subject of admiration and affection in others as in

Your most sincere and affte friend

There was some difficulty in filling the office of Lord Lieutenant, several persons refused; but eventually Lord Northington was appointed. Lord Temple remained until after the King's birthday, June 4, sorely against his wish, because his successor was not ready to undertake the duties of his post, and it was considered inexpedient to leave the country without a representative of royalty.1

I possess a manuscript letter addressed to Scrope Bernard by the lively Lady Roche, wife of Sir Boyle Eoche, described by Lecky as ' a member of Parliament who was well known for his buffoonery, but who was also a prominent and a shrewd debater, closely connected with the Government and chamberlain at the Castle.' This letter is too characteristically Irish to be omitted. It is dated ' Limerick, April ye 18, 1783.'

I had yesterday an opportunity of seeing all the volunteers of Limerick, who made a most martial appearance, when they attended the funeral of a brother volunteer, a dyer in the town; the procession was closed by a corps of cavalry commanded by the Speaker's son, and it was with difficulty I could recognize amongst them some honest traders of my acquaintance, and some good hack horses which I know, through the splendour of their dress and arms, and the richness of their furniture. I could not help fancying that the volunteers were not sorry for the death of their brother, which had enabled them to display such military parade.

On Monday our Assizes are to begin; I know not who is to behanged, but the ladies are making great preparations for dressing and dancing, and the gentlemen ought to be sharpening their pistols, as balls in these parts are commonly followed by duels.

1Lecky,*History of Ireland in the Eighteenth Century*(Edition 1892), vol. ii., chap. 5, p. 350;*Memoirs of the Court and Cabinets of George III.*,voL i. 1783.

2MS. Letter at Nether Winchendon.

The objectionable practice of organising assize balls at which the gentry of the neighbourhood danced, flirted, and feasted, while the wretched prisoners, many of them condemned for slight offences, were awaiting the hour of execution, was probably as common in England as in Ireland; but duels were much less frequent.

With regard to the Irish Volunteers, their position had just at this time become one of great importance, and some persons looked on it with alarm. Originally organised as a temporary expedient through dread of foreign invasion, they held their ground after the necessity had ceased.' ' Peace had been signed, but there was no prospect of a dissolution of the volunteer body. The last reviews had been the most splendid hitherto celebrated, and the institution had become a recognised national militia, discharging many important police functions, and bringing the Protestant gentry and yeomanry into constant connection with each other'; indeed, the force threw itself into the reform agitation, and ' the relations between the Castle and Charlemont'2 – a leader in the volunteer movement – ' became very cold.'

The mention of another and more important letter, from a family point of view, as well as from the fact of its writer being a prominent statesman only a few years before, has been reserved to conclude this Chapter. This was the Earl of Hillsborough, so often mentioned in Vol. II. of this History. On September 8, 1782, Lord Barrington had written to his young cousin Scrope Bernard from Hills- borough congratulations on his appointment as secretary to Lord Temple, accompanied by best wishes for his success in his new career, by favourable prognostics and encomiums; he continued: ' I have passed a very agreeable month withTHE EARL OF HILLSBOROUGH 55

1Leoky,*History of Ireland in the Eighteenth Century*(Edition 1892), vol. ii. chap. 5, p. 851-2.

* Lord Charlemont commanded the Ulster, and at one time also the Leinster, Volunteers.

my old friend Lord Hillsborough, who, as you know, was a most sincere and useful friend to your Father. I wish my time would have allowed me to have paid my respects to the Lord Lieutenant and embraced you.' Scrope Bernard can hardly have left England when this letter reached Dublin, and probably, by the wording of it, he did not meet Lord Barrington, who may have crossed the channel, while Lord Hillsborough perhaps sent some intimation that it would give him pleasure to hear from a son of Sir Francis Bernard. A letter from Scrope seems to have led to the following reply from his father's old ally dated,' Hillsborough, 21st of December':

Sir, – Upon my return to this place after a tour of visits which I have been making in this county, I found upon my table a most obliging letter from you dated the 6th inst., for which I take leave to return you my best thanks. I am much obliged to my friend Lord Barrington for making me acquainted with you, and lament that my leaving Dublin so soon prevented that acquaintance from becoming personal, but I shall hope for some other opportunity either of meeting you in London, or when I return to Dublin, or if curiosity or business should lead you into this part of the country I should be happy to see you at this place. You do me the honour to take notice of the connection I had with your excellent and worthy Father; I assure you, Sir, I entertained the highest esteem for him as a gentleman very meritorious in the service of his King and country, and shall be very glad to show every mark of respect and regard in my person to any of his Family. These sentiments make it particularly agreeable to me to have this opportunity of assuring you that I am

Sir, your most obedient Humble
Servant

Hillsborough.

Scrope Bernard, Esqr.

Castle, Dublin.

The tone of this letter is so cordial that it seems not unlikely the young secretary may have found it possible to make the acquaintance of a minister of whom he must have heard much in his boyhood. But I have no record of the fact.

Lord Temple quitted Ireland on June 5, 1783; and itmay be assumed that Scrope Bernard accompanied him, and also his brother-in-law the Vicar of Wendover. The viceroyalty of their chief had been so short that it afforded little opportunity for memorable deeds. The creation of the Order of St. Patrick must have been its most showy act, and Scrope had doubtless been a witness of the ceremonial attending it, but of this there is no record in his letters. Lecky states also that Lord Temple ' succeeded in detecting and punishing several instances of great peculation in administration,' and that' he announced to Lord Charlemont his firm intention of reducing " that impolitic and unconstitutional influence which has been the bane and ruin of both countries." ' This determination he had of course no time to put into execution.

SCROPE BERNARD'S EOMANCE 57

CHAPTER IV

EXCURSIONS AND RETUBN TO NETHEE WINCHENDON

Scrope Bernard's Romance – Crazes of the Time – Mrs. Siddons – Scrope Bernard's Plans – The Hon. George Pulke Lyttelton – Scrope Bernard's Visits to France – His Interest in Poor Law – Marriage of Amelia Bernard – Rumours of Scrope Bernard's approaching Marriage – His Anxiety to become Possessor of Nether Winchendon – Mr. and Mrs. King – Life in a Country Parish – Scrope Bernard becomes Lord of Nether Winchendon Manor – He is Offered and Accepts the Secretaryship to a Commission of Inquiry into Public Offices.

ScropeBernard'sfriends were not backward in supplying him with news on topics likely to interest him while he was under the disadvantage of being separated by the sea from his old haunts.

Mrs. Edmunds, always a sympathetic relative, did not forget her cousin's attraction towards the lady mentioned by his sister Fanny some months previously, whose home was apparently in the neighbourhood of Worsborough. She writes, in the letter already quoted, soon after Scrope's arrival in Dublin*l:*

*I*know that any intelligence from this quarter will be acceptable; first then the St. James Street Party. I spent a very agreeable day at her own house in this neighbourhood lately; she looks very well and enquired how long you continued in Ireland of my daughter who sat next her at table. They have been at Wakefield and Doncaster races, and are to be at the Mayor's feast this next week. I hear of no overtures at present.

Alas! in a later letter Mrs. Edmunds says:

Only returned on Saturday from Heath and Nowland Park Lady Georgina enquired after you; we spent a day and eveningthere very agreeably, for our visit was to the old lady. We left that part on the day of the ball, in honour of the Queen's birth; it had no charms to detain us; you would have felt yourself differently affected; a certain lady was to make her appearance; report speaks of an alliance I don't wish to take place, how true, time will discover, to a young man of very moderate parts, but ample fortune.

1This and the two following extracts are from MS. Letters at Nether Winchendon.

Two rich mountains of Peru,

Eush to wealthy Marriage too,

And make a world of love.

I have learnt long since not to wonder at what I see and hear, we have so many unaccountable events that all astonishment ceases 1 You will, I hope, find some worthy kindred mind that will make disappointment sit easy.

But there is a further allusion to this subject in a third letter:

I am informed the news I sent you in my last is not True, the young Lady begged it might be contradicted from herself, so you see while there is Life there is Hope. She is at present in a poor state of health from Ague and Fever.

This is the last mention of the affair I can find, and whatever may have been the reason, it is evident that it came to nothing about this time. So ended Scrope Bernard's romance, if it was one.

Two other letters from Oxford friends are interesting, as touching on crazes of the time. The first is especially notable as a craze. Mr. Godschall, Scrope's eccentric friend, had been captivated by the feats of an alchemist, apparently at Oxford, and so, it would seem, had many other persons. Scrope, indeed, took an interest in the reports which reached him, by reason of his love for chemistry. Mr. Godschall writes from ' Weston House ':

You enquire concerning Dr. Price and his experiments. I was present at one of them; and will relate what I saw there, and then leave you to judge for yourself. Tho doctor mixed borax, charcoal, and quicksilver in a crucible; he then put in some of his gold-making powder, and after the crucible had remained in the fire for a certain time, he broke it, and produced several bits1MS. Letter at Nether Winchendon.

MES. SIDDONS 59

of yellow metal, which being carried to the refiner, were proved to be pure gold; if it is objected that gold is an ingredient in the powder (I suppose that granted), by one grain of the powder are produced five or six grains of gold. The process for making silver is less complicate. A quantity of quicksilver is mixed with a white powder, by which it is converted into a paste; the gross particles are then blown off by fire, and there remains a round ball of silver, which was also proved to be such.

Dr. Price evidently had a run; but it appears from a subsequent letter that his reputation had not been well maintained. The following account relates to the early days of a career of more enduring renown. The writer 'was Mr. Frankland, formerly of Christ Church, who was then a Fellow of All Souls:

Old Bond Street,

January 2nd 1783.

My dear Bernard, – . All the world is wild here after Mrs. Siddons, the new actress. She is I understand all in all; she has the sweetest voice, most accurate pronunciation, and the most dignified action that ever graced the stage. In short you may say of her without flattery what Horace(*whom we both I know particularly admire*)said of Augustus with a great deal of truth,'*Nihil oriturum alias, nihil ortum tale fatentw.*'This is all very fine, vague, and poetical, and can give you no possible determinate idea. I assure you if I had seen her myself I would not have given you so undiscrimmating, unphilosophical a description.

I endeavoured last night to mob it into the pit as the boxes were all taken. I was at Drury Lane half an hour before the doors open, but it was too late as I found by experience, for the passages leading to the pit contained people enough to fill it, so that after being squeezed and sweated for an hour I was forced to return. A night or two ago the fine Mr. Hampden was in the same situation, though he did not make so disgraceful a retreat. He and his friend, who was going to the East Indies, tried the boxes, were repulsed, descended to the pit door, could not get in, went up to the two shilling gallery, ditto. The one shilling gallery was now their only resource, to which they at length forced their way, and thrusting their heads in at the door hollowed out*[sic]* – ' Is there any honest fellow in the front row, who will take five shillings for his place?' 'I will, Sir, I will, Sir,' resounded on all sides, and two men presently came out from the centre division, andhaving received half a guinea between them, probably went to the next ale-house and got drunk, while our two heroes entered their seats in triumph, having found that money has the same effect in Britain as Philip of Macedon found it had in Greece.1

After this account it may be assumed that Scrope, on his return to London, took an early opportunity of attending a performance at Drury Lane, but he has not left his impressions on record; they must have been favourable, however, as he was a frequenter of those theatres at which the Kembles acted for many years.

Soon after his arrival in England, he formed plans for utilising the interval of leisure afforded him by circumstances. The following letter2to Thomas Bernard partly explains itself:

Cross Inn, Oxford, Aug. 17, 1783.

My dear Brother, – Your letter, though calculated as well as mine, met with little better success. After searching for me in vain at Christchurch, it reached me at Stowe, which place I did not leave till this very day, near a fortnight after the time I had fixed in my letter to you. I have a train of plans for the rest of the Vacation, with the precise dates fixed to each, and a firm intention on my part to adhere to them, though Heaven only knows whether I shall; and yet my ideas of the usefulness of punctuality are as strong as any person's. On Monday the 25th I return to Stowe, where I am to meet my friend Mr. Lyttelton, who takes me with him on the 27th to Hagley, where I am to spend a few days which I limit to three. This brings me to the 30th of August. I then set out to prosecute my plan, which Lord Temple not only consents to, but has spontaneously revived and recommended, of my going abroad. His advice coincided very much with my inclination not to go immediately to Paris, but to take up my residence in some provincial town, of which he thinks Lille is as good as any. I will therefore trouble you to recollect your knowledge of that place, and to think of some house for lodging and dieting myself, or to put me in the way of finding one. The time for my stay is limited to six weeks at the utmost. You best know what sum of money will be sufficient to carry me through that, allowing for a few days' excursion before my return, and if you still think you can for the present spare me such a sum, will be kind enough to assist me at least as far as the state of my1MS. Letter at Nether Winohendon.2*Ibid.*

THEHON. GEORGEFULKELYTTELTON61

purse requires it. You will wonder perhaps, as I am to go, why I do not set off immediately, but I have engaged myself strongly to Mr. Lyttelton, and at the same time am so much bent on seeing Hagley and the family in so advantageous a manner, that I cannot break into this part of my plans, and after all – the remainder of the Vacation will allow me ample time for the purpose of launching me into the French language.

Part of my plan is not to take a servant, but to trust to Lisle for suiting myself, which I think you will approve of. I am happy in hearing of our Brother; if there are any particulars respecting him, you will inform me when I pass through town.

This is Cross pen, ink, and paper, and therefore no wonder if it does not please you, or makes me write ill.

Yrs affectly S. B.

Addressed:

Thomas Bernard Esqre,

Lincolns Inn,

London.

What the news was about Sir John Bernard, and whether it had arrived from him or some one else, does not transpire; but there was nothing cheerful to tell about this sojourn in America, as will appear when Sir John's experiences are related.

Scrope's friend, the Hon. George Fulke Lyttelton, was the eldest son of Lord Westcote, afterwards Lord Lyttelton.1Although he writes in one of his letters of their having read together, Scrope probably took the lead on these occasions, since he was five years older than Mr. Lyttelton. This youth was related to Lord Temple and William Grenville, but only as second cousin, and I know not whether the Bernard intimacy commenced in Oxford or at Stowe. Lord Westcote was married to a second wife, by whom he had a young family; the second of the two sons by his first marriage had been killed in battle in 1781, leaving George somewhat lonely, and inclined to melancholy; a studious youth, he appears to have shrunk from pleasure, so called, and to have been indifferent to general society. For many years he corresponded with Scrope, but hismost interesting letters belong to a later period. That Scrope should desire to visit Hagley was natural, not only for the sake of its own attractions and those of the family then residing there, but also because the reputation of the first Lord Lyttelton, elder brother of Lord Westcote, had made it classic ground. It was believed to have been the scene of wedded happiness, as intense as it was shortlived, which Lord Lyttelton had commemorated in his then famous monody on the death of his wife.1The reckless career of his son, the second lord, and the legend attaching to his end, had given the family a celebrity of another sort.

1See Debrett, Burke, and other*Peerages,* 'Lyttelton, Baron, now Cobham, Viscount.'

I have no record of Scrope's impressions of Hagley, nor of the results of his Lille visit. Why Lille should have been chosen for the study of French is a puzzle. Thomas Bernard, it appears, had already been there, with what object is not stated; but I am disposed to think that the choice of that town in both cases may be attributed to Lord Temple's influence. It is noted in a subsequent letter that Lady Temple had a relative, the Hon. Mrs. Storer, daughter of Lord Carysfort, at Lille, and that Scrope Bernard made the acquaintance of a family named Descouelle, well-known to that lady; it seems probable that by the recommendation of Mrs. Storer, transmitted originally through Lord Temple, he boarded with that family.

In the August of the following year a correspondent who signs ' C. Macartney,' and who was evidently George Lyttelton's maternal aunt, thanked Scrope for his kindness to the young man during a recent illness at Richmond. The lady says: ' Accept my best thanks for the favourMONTEEUIL-SUEMEE 63

1Lucy Fortescue; Lord Lyttelton's*Dialogues of the Dead,*were also much read, and he wrote other books. ' By the death of his father [in 1751] he inherited a baronet's title with a large estate, which, though perhaps he did not augment, he was caretnl to adorn by a house of great elegance and expence, and by much attention to the decoration of his park.' Johnson (Dr. Samuel),*Lives of tlie Moat Eminent English Poets,*vol. ii.,' Lyttelton.' The pedigree may be found in Debrett and Burke's*Peerages,*since 1889, under the heading of ' Cobham, Viscount.'

you did me in coming to the relief of your poor sick friend, for the comfort you gave him, and for having relieved many a sad and gloomy hour of distress for me by your attentions and your cheerful and agreeable conversation,' and continues her letter in the same tone of praise.

In the autumn of the same year, 1784, Scrope made another attempt to master the French language; he went for his holiday to Montreuil-sur-Mer, on the route from Boulogne to Paris. Murray describes it in recent times as 'an uninteresting country town, on a hill crowned by a citadel.'*I*It owed its origin to a monastery, of which some vestiges remained, and at that time there was also an old Chartreuse, since destroyed and rebuilt, in the immediate vicinity of the town. ' The fortifications were partly constructed by Vauban on older foundations.' And the same account adds: ' It is now principally known to Englishmen as the spot in which Sterne laid one of the scenes in the " Sentimental Journey."' When Scrope Bernard visited the locality it contained evidently some English residents; he went, perhaps, because he had friends there, but probably did not remain for the whole of his vacation. It must have been during this excursion that he went on to Paris, and, as I have heard my father say, attended the court of Louis XVI., where he beheld Marie Antoinette in her glory. This experience made a lasting impression, partly no doubt by reason of those subsequent events which imparted a tragic interest to the recollection of scenes dazzling by their beauty and splendour. Mr. Bernard must have often spoken on the subject to his children.

I have no notes of this visit, but a letter from Scrope's friend, H. G. Quin, written at Geneva, in the spring of the following year, probably conveys the ordinary impressions of a travelling Englishman at that period. He says:

A letter from Paris would 1 imagine have been little else than an echo of the Ideas which that City had impressed on your ownmind, I therefore wave the subject, observing only that the actual appearance of things there wonderfully corresponds with the Nature of the Government; in fact they are an Epitome of it; everything connected with the King is great, superb, costly, magnificent, and colossal, whilst the very reverse of this is the Condition of the People. I do not suppose there is another city in the World in which the contrast between the mean and the magnificent is more strongly marked. Paris seems to be a heterogeneous mixture of Marble, Dirt, Gold, Filth, Splendor, Poverty, spacious Gardens, blind Alleys, Palaces & Hovels. As to the King, a man need only walk through the streets to be convinced of the nature and extent of his Authority, from the frequency and magnitude of the different*Hotels du Eoi,*he will conceive him to be a very Argos and Briareus.

1Murray,*Handbook for France,*vol. i., 1886

No hint is given that Mr. Quin had any suspicion of the changes that were coming. I do not know whether Scrope felt doubtful, but probably not, since an older friend to whom he wrote for information as to the provision made for the poor in France, and who was resident in the country, does not appear to have harboured any misgivings. This was Mr. Kobert Browne, who had married the widow of General the Hon. John Barrington, next brother of the Viscount then living. It was probably his presence at Montreuil which had attracted Scrope thither, partly if not wholly. As to the young man's interest in Poor Law questions, it is evident that he cherished the wish to become a country gentleman and magistrate, and in time a member of Parliament. But he may also have asked them for the sake of his brother Thomas, who was then preparing the ground for his future philanthropic career. Perhaps the brothers often conversed on this and kindred topics.

It will be observed that Mr. Browne's letter hardly depicts the condition of the lower classes about Montreuil as steeped in the wretchedness so generally ascribed to the whole of France. Besides the curious lack of apprehension for the future which it shows within a very few years of the great catastrophe, this letter is noticeable by reason of the light it throws on the difficulties and deprivations ofCONDITION OF THE POOE IN FRANCE 65

the English colony at Montreuil,1barely thirty miles from Boulogne:

Montreuil, Deer. 6,1784.

I sit down, my dear Bernard, to acknowledge the receipt of your pacquet, with the money &c. I sent your letter and gazettes to Williams who I have not seen for a few days, but I suppose tomorrow or next day shall have that pleasure. As to your question about the Poor Laws, I shall inform myself as soon as possible; all I know at present is that at Montreuil there are none; but a voluntary subscription monthly provides the Indigent with bread and a small sum of money; the collectors are some of the first and most respectable characters here, who gave a certain quantity of bread and money weekly to the Rectors of the 6 parishes with directions to distribute it to such persons as are on the poor list in their respective parishes; but as the subscriptions were voluntary they frequently failed, and the Bureau was obliged to be shut in the month of March last, when the Poor were in the most deplorable condition. I spoke to several of the Collectors and recommended them to go to every house in Montreuil and beg the Noblesse and the Bourgeois respectively to write their names on a list with the sum they would engage to subscribe monthly for a year, which I find they have done, and the poor are now tolerably comfortable at a time when bread is so extraordinarily dear; but whether this will continue another year I cannot answer for.

There was one great abuse in the first Institution, which I hope they have reformed; when a family gave liberally, they recommended people to be put on the list who, very often, were not proper objects of charity, which was one principal, or at least first ostensible reason for the failure of the monthly contributions, as people cried out at the abuse of the charity, &c.

Some years ago, Government opened Hospitals or Asylums in the principal towns of France, where they obliged all the vagrant poor to reside; but this was at the expense of the King, or the Princes of the Blood in their different appanages. At first the officers appointed to take up the vagrants kept a strict hand, but when those places were full and they found there were still many left, they relaxed; and lately I am informed they let the poor beg in the different parts of France without molestation, however, I will this week make inquiries about this affair, and willwrite to you as soon as I hear anything satisfactory. The Abbayes are not obliged to give any specific charity, but are supposed to assist the poor of their cantons; you know there are Nuns who take a vow to educate children gratis, but they live themselves on charity. There are also poorhouses for the reception of Foundlings in every town almost, where the children are kept till they are four or five years old and then sent to Paris, which saves the lives of many infants, as formerly they sent young creatures of a week or a month old, and one half died before they reached the capital.

1 There can be no doubt that the Montreuil in which Mr. Browne resided and which Scrope Bernard visited was Montreuil-sur-Mer, though not so distinguished in my MS. letters; the other Montreuils in France are mere villages.

VOL. III. F

The rest of the letter refers to other topics, personal and public – ' Will you forgive me if I beg you to send me a North Wiltshire cheese of about 20 or 30 Ibs. weight, two more guinea bottles of the same medicine for my friend & to send them by the Paris Diligence.' And the writer then goes into other particulars, such as the disposal of an unnecessary watch; the repair of an old violoncello – for these negotiations a friend in London was exceedingly useful.

After which the writer continues:

Many thanks for the newspapers; they are a great comfort to us; pray are you determined to keep an exact neutrality in case of a war? I find by the papers your Ministry strengthens daily – does Lord Carmarthen come Ambassador here? and does Lord Shelburne take Mr. Pitt's place First Lord of the Treasury? Some officers have orders to join the 15th January, and to have two horses to camp, but many people think there will be no war.

Adieu, Mrs. B and Louisa desire many kind compts, and believe me to be Dr Sir
Your sincere and
Aff Humble Servant
R. Browne.

On his return journey Scrope had the vexation of losing a trunk, probably of some value in itself and also for the property it contained; and this had led to a correspondence with a Monsieur Degros, apparently a wine merchant, in whose house he had perhaps lodged. I doubt if the trunk was ever recovered; nevertheless, Mr. Browne hoped that the sojourn in Montreuil had been sufficiently agreeable to induce a second visit, in spite of this*contretemps.*In the beginning of the next year he wrote to announce theCONDITION OF THE POOR IN FRANCE 67

results of his inquiries on the old subject. The letter*l*is dated Jany 20,1785':

I have done everything possible to find out if there existed any Poor Laws in this country, and have never been able to succeed. I am informed they attempted to tax the Estates in Artois for that purpose & oblige any Village to support their own poor, but they were obliged to desist; I consulted several persons on the subject of our system; they admire the idea exceedingly but are of opinion that it [is] very difficult to put into execution without great abuses arising, & a general remark is that wherever in France there is an ample provision for the Poor, there are a greater number of the Poor than in the other parts; about Mon- treuil, where there are spacious Commons, the Villagers are poorest, as they content themselves with a Cow or two which cost them little or nothing, & tho' there is work for twice the number of inhabitants they will not trouble themselves to gain a shilling, whereas in those places where they have no advantages you never meet any poor but those who have really bodily infirmities; this is a proof to me that our own poor are too well taken care of, as perhaps there is not a country in the world where there are so many of that class, & I should imagine the Poor Laws are one cause, as every one I have ever talked to says, that no one should be admitted on the parish list but by the unanimous consent of the Farmers, as they are the best Judges whether their neighbours are really Poor or only lazy, as it is I believe a self-evident proposition that in so commercial a country as England there should be no poor but the Aged & Infirm, as certainly it is not too populous.

Mr. Browne then proceeds to expound his views as to the right way of administering relief; which, with more or less modification, no doubt were shared by many other persons.

I believe that another abuse is that, once a family is put on the list from sickness, they continue after tho' the cause is done away, which is abominable; they do not seem to agree whether Poor Houses are a prudent scheme, as the Poor with a weekly allowance would live as comfortable and I believe much happier than they do at present, as I fear the officers and directors of such houses enrich themselves too often!

1MS. Letter at Nether Winohendon.

' They,' which word means of course Mr. Browne's informants, are all of opinion that voluntary contributions in every parish under the direction of the Parson & the principal Inhabitants would be infinitely preferable to a tax imposed by Government, as in the former case everyone would be interested to prevent improper persons from being on the list, & at the end of the months, those who were there for mere local reasons (when they should no longer exist) would be struck off by those people who would be most in the situation to judge of these matters.

This is everything that strikes me on that subject; if there is any objections and you would let me know them, I will inform myself about them and let you know what I have heard.

I hope you do not forget my favourite Tax on Travellers into this country & I confess I could wish to see an Absentee Tax not only on Estates but on Interest in the Funds, money lent on Mortgages &c. I know Englishmen would cry out, as an attack on liberty, but between you & me that is all nonsense & we should all contribute to assist government; we for instance spend $400 a year here & live as well as on 7 or 8 in England, & pay no kind of Taxes. I should certainly not murmur to be obliged to pay 2 or 3 per cent as I know my friends in England pay 5 times as much, & I hope every Englishman has the same way of reasoning.

The amazing number of Horses & Hounds sent over here would certainly bear a tolerable tax, as a french nobleman who pays 50 guineas for a horse & 12 guineas for 2 dogs would not feel two guineas more on the former & half a guinea on the latter.

In a postscript the writer adds:

You have no conception of the rage for English Dogs & Horses – at present.

This letter is not entirely composed of such grave topics; it returns thanks 'for a ' handsome pocket book,' which had been much admired, and which was a present from Scrope Bernard, brought over by ' Mr. Littleton' – probably it should be ' Lyttelton ' – Scrope's friend. He was only passing through Montreuil on his way to Paris, and could not be persuaded to alight, though pressed to partake of Mrs. Browne's*sonpe.*English cheeses were evidently in great request: a Cheshire cheese is desired for Mr. LeME. WILLIAMS 69

Gaucher and a small Gloucester for Mr. Browne himself, and there are various details about such matters, including the medicine bottles.

In March, Mr. Browne wrote again, and as he himself intimates, this correspondence was greatly encouraged, to his satisfaction, by the fact of their having a topic in common, which necessitated frequent communication. The letters contain allusions more or less lengthy to Mr. Williams. This young man was the only son of Sir David mentioned in a previous volume as the husband of Rebecca Rowland. He had recently come of age, and was visiting France with the object of learning French thoroughly, and perhaps of being introduced to good French society. This at least must have been the view his friends took, and his mother had written to Scrope Bernard,1begging him to watch over her son, as she considered him peculiarly exposed to temptation. When Scrope returned to England, Mr. Browne evidently succeeded to the office of mentor, and did not spare himself trouble in the cause. With reference to Mr. Williams, he wrote:2

Montreuil is really not a place for a young man to learn French at unless he has as much constancy as your honor or Gapt. Young,&that he will not absolutely live entirely with the English, which is difficult as there are no public amusements, and you know how shy the French are.

I hope this will not discourage you from coming over this summer as you are known & esteemed by the French society, and therefore are sure of turning everything to your advantage. I need not assure you how sincerely happy we shall be to see you and to offer you our humble fare. Mrs. B. desires to say everything kind to you on this occasion and will not give you her blessing unless you come to see her & him who is sincerely

Dr Sir

Your faithful friend

Rob. Browne.

Notwithstanding this pressing invitation, it is not likely that Scrope Bernard visited Montreuil in 1785. He must have been engaged with other projects. For some time hehad been the only unmarried member of his family – excepting the brother who was battling against adverse fate in America. In 1783, the year of Scrope's return from Ireland, his sister Amelia had married Captain Benjamin Baker, of the 5th Foot Regiment, who appears to have been quartered at Stamford, within reach of Lincoln. Of his family I only know what I have heard, that he was descended from the Baker of the siege of Derry. Amelia Bernard was at this time in her 29th or 30th year; her husband must have been some years older, since he had a son by a former marriage, a lieutenant in 1790. For the advancement of that son Scrope Bernard afterwards exerted himself, as appears by family letters on the subject. But the marriage had not been a topic of congratulations to Amelia's brothers – it was another impecunious alliance; but Amelia was of age, and apparently as determined in her way as Fanny. Though perhaps less aggressive, she was, as I have heard, firm in the belief that Providence would assist her and her children. It is curious that this quiet daughter of the family should have become the wife of a warrior, her livelier sisters respectively having married two clergymen and a barrister.

1MS. Letter at Nether Winohendon. *Ibid.

Already towards the end of 1783 – that is, soon after the return from Ireland – rumours had begun to be rife in Buckinghamshire to the effect that Scrope Bernard was about to marry a lady of fortune and reside at Nether Winchendon.1These floating reports were not always presented in the same form; for some reason, now forgotten, Halton was sometimes named as the intended residence. It is also probable that the lady's name varied in the different versions. In one of Scrope's letters to his sister Julia he chides her for bantering him on the subject, and disclaims the idea; whereupon she had to apologise, assuring him that she had heard the news confidently announced by a person she had every reason to believe well informed. Her intelligence indeed was not altogether ill-founded, but it must have been premature, and possibly there was some1Information contained in MB. Letters at Nether Winchendon.

SCROPB BERNARD'S PLANS 71

confusion as to the person, since Scrope endorsed her letter ' Congratulations on a mistake.'

Whatever may have been the real state of the case at that particular moment it is clear that Scrope was full of plans during this year (1784) of comparative leisure; he harboured the idea of entering Parliament, as appears by two letters written for him by Mr. Robert Thornton in April from ' King's Arms Yard.' They were addressed to Mr. Terry and Mr. Eennard of Hull,1soliciting their votes and interest on behalf of Scrope as a candidate for the representation of the city of Lincoln, where a vacancy had occurred through the death of Lord Scarbrough. The Nettleham property, it will be remembered, was still in the family, and the sons of Sir Francis Bernard were freemen of Lincoln. I have no means of knowing whether a contest ensued, but I think it probable that Scrope never went to the poll, from a conviction that he had no chance in that locality. Had Mr. Bernard become member it is likely that he would have resided part of the year in his father's old home, notwithstanding the counter attractions in Bucks. The result perhaps saved the old Manor House at Nether Winchendon from subsiding into a farm house, which has been the fate of many venerable homes of our

English gentry; for it was to this forsaken place that the young man now turned his thoughts, with all the eagerness which habitually characterised his movements.

The house and land had been left by Sir Francis Bernard amongst his children, with instructions that it should be sold. Scrope now aspired to become its possessor. For this purpose he must have been compelled to enter into a long correspondence with other members of the family, especially Mr. White and Thomas Bernard, the executors; but I do not possess many of their letters. In one Thomas alludes to the plan with disapproval, as an undertaking which would 'hamper' his brother, though, on finding Scrope resolute, he did his utmost to make it work smoothly. In truth the house appears to have required a large expenditureto render it a desirable residence, and this outlay, in addition to the purchase money, was scarcely within Scrope's means. Possibly Charles White, whose wife had an affection for the place, may have been more accommodating than Thomas Bernard. Richard King, some of whose letters remain, certainly was; and it may be inferred from the correspondence that he was a good man of business.

1MS. Letters at Nether Winehendon.

Mr. King's affairs were prosperous, since he had been presented by New College to the Rectory of Worthen in Shropshire, a parish ' twelve miles W. S. W. of Shrewsbury'laccording to the ' Gazetteer,' and continued to hold Steeple Morden in Cambridgeshire also, an arrangement then considered perfectly correct, except, perhaps, by a few persons of extremely strict views. In this case indeed the arrangement worked fairly well for some years; Mr. and Mrs. King would seem by the dates of their letters to have divided their time between the two parishes, allowing for occasional holidays besides; they perhaps gave the larger share to Worthen, as the more important and populous parish, and also because it provided a better house for its incumbent than Steeple Morden. Mr. King writes to Scrope in glowing terms of his new residence:3

I shall be very happy when you shall be able to make it convenient to be a personal judge of our habitation, country, and neighbourhood; I think I told you in my last that the country was the finest I ever saw – the neighbourhood also, what we have hitherto seen, is very agreeable and respectable. Our habitation is large and commodious though irregular; we have three good parlours, one as good a room as I should wish to see in any house – and when I have finished some intended improvements, the house will be fit for any private gentleman.

The population of Worthen is given in the 'Parliamentary Gazetteer' as 1,602 in 1801; Steeple Morden had fewer than 500 inhabitants. In both parishes Mr. King appears to have kept a curate. Judging from the customs of the age it might be supposed that these assistants undertook other duty also, but certain passages in the family letters tell1MS. Letter at Nether Winchendon." *Ibid.*

LIFE IN A COUNTEY PAEISH 73

against this assumption. The prospect of retaining the Winchendon home in the family rejoiced Fanny King, and her husband was evidently thus influenced to smooth the way for Scrope. The minute business details of the transaction it is unnecessary to quote; but in the course of the correspondence an illustration occurs of the difficulties and privations then attendant on life in a country parish, which should make all but the most devoted of the present clergy pause ere they condemn absentees and pluralists of the eighteenth century. Mr. King writes,1on 'October 11, 1784 ':

I fear my last letter in answer to yours sent by the coach never came to you, as you do not mention the receipt of it in yours from London dated Oct. 2, and I expect it would have been in London by the 30th of Sept., and I regretted much that your letter which you intended should come to me with great dispatch by the coach, did not come to me till some days later than I should have received it by the post, but I immediately sat down to answer without a moment's delay, and sent it off by a person who was going immediately to Ludlow, who promised not to neglect putting it in the post the moment he came there; but I fear he was either careless or unfortunately lost the letter, as it does not appear by your last that you have received it. I have often reflected of how great importance is the regularity of the post, for it sometimes, if neglected, may be the occasion of great uneasiness and vexation, and in some matters the cause of real distress. The only unpleasant part of our situation at Worthen is that we have communication with the post only once a week (Saturdays) both to receive and send letters, though some few years ago the post used to go by the door on its way to Shrewsbury. I wish to God it could be brought back again into the old channel, for I cannot find out any good reason why it was ever altered.

In spite of delays and mistakes, however, the affair was carried to a successful conclusion, and Scrope attained his wish; he became lord of Nether Winchendon Manor. It is tolerably certain that his anxiety to come out as a country gentleman must have been connected with matrimonial projects, as will appear by the result; but it is also certainthat Scrope Bernard had imbibed a taste for antiquarian lore of the mediaeval type, which was uncommon at that period, and that the Winchendon idea owed much of its charm to this taste.

1MS. Letter at Nether Winchendon.

Some particulars of Scrope's courtship will be mentioned in the next chapter. In the meantime his dreams were probably somewhat rudely interrupted by the following letter1 from William Grenville, flattering as it might be in some respects. It was dated ' Whitehall, 23rd of December.'

My dear Bernard, – Pitt has just been with me to desire that I would mention to you the following idea. You remember that during the Coalition Government he proposed a bill, and carried it through the House of Commons for obliging the Commissioners of Accounts to enter upon an inquiry into the establishments, business, and emoluments of the several Public Offices, in order to judge what reform could be made in them. The bill was thrown out, but he feels himself bound not to drop the idea, although he thinks it inexpedient now to put it into the hands of the Commissioners of Accounts. He has therefore ordered a Commission to be made to three persons, who are the two Comptrollers of Army Accounts and Mr. Baring, a considerable merchant, who are to execute this business. What he wishes to know is whether you would like to take the Secretaryship to this Commission. He imagines the business will employ about six months (I think more), and he states that such an investigation could not fail of giving you an insight into the nature, constitution, and practice of all the offices of Government, besides bringing your name forward as a person employed or to be employed.

It is not his intention to give any salaries in the first instance, either to the Commissioners or to the Secretary, but that they should be paid (as the Commissioners of Accounts and their Secretary are) by vote of Parliament when the business shall be done.

While this lasts it will be an office of extreme labour. It is left entirely to your option whether you choose to undertake it or not, but it is material that he should have your answer soon. I have not written to my Brother on the subject; the event which would render it impossible for you to accept this offer is, I think, not likely to happen. But you will certainly be understood to be at liberty to cross the Channel, should that happen. I shouldA DISTASTEFUL POST 75

1MS. Letter at Nether Winohendon.

think you would do well to ride over to Stowe, and to let me have your answer from thence.

I have written so far without giving you any opinion upon it; but on reflection I think you have a right to my advice, provided you will accept it merely as advice, subject to your own opinion.

In that light only I state my own sentiments to be in favour of your accepting the offer, both on account of the thing itself, from the insight it will give you into the business &c. of office, and from the advantage of accustoming Pitt to have recourse to you on similar occasions, and to look upon you as a man whom he may employ with credit and advantage to himself. Molleson, who was Secretary to the Commissioners of Accounts, and is now a Comptroller of Army Accounts, got that appointment solely on that ground – it being thought a creditable thing to appoint to that office, in these days of reform, a man trained in that sort of school.

Ever most afftely yours

From a letter/of the Rev. Richard King it would seem that the office was accepted by Scrope with reluctance; he probably yielded to the advice of many friends. Scrope could achieve much in his own way, in this, which was his idle year; besides his work as the Marquess's Secretary he had been to France, studied the language of the country, and since obtained information about its provision for the poor, a subject which he probably talked over with Thomas – the two brothers comparing the English system with the French voluntary methods – and he had purchased Nether Winchendon. But such work as he was now asked to undertake was hardly of a kind likely to interest him, and it was to be unremitting for six months or more – how much longer it was perhaps difficult to say, nor did there seem any certainty of adequate compensation. Possibly the likelihood of his courtship or honeymoon being interfered with by this troublesome Commission strengthened his determination to win the lady of whom he had been thinking, and precipitated the declaration; it also gave him, on the other hand, the opportunity of coming forward as a manof more importance, selected by William Pitt for a task of some magnitude. Fortunately the Commission, as might perhaps have been expected, took some time to organise, so that Mr. Bernard's services as Secretary were not required till late in the following year (1785) leaving the interval free for courtship, marriage, and visiting.

1M3. Letter at Nether Winchendon.

4

SECTION 4

SCROPE BERNARD'S COURTSHIP 77
   CHAPTER V
   BRIDAL VISITS TO LINCOLN AND NETHER WINCHENDON
   The Norlands of Woolwich – Sir Samuel Morland – Scrope Bernard's Engagement
   – Samuel Gillam – The Marquess of Buckingham's Testimony to Sorope Bernard's
   Character – Scrope's Marriage with Harriet Morland – They Visit Worcester and
   Lincoln – The ' Stuff and Colour Ball ' – They Visit Nether Winchendon – The State
   of the Manor House – Friendship with the Lees of Hartwell – Sorope Bernard's Last
   Appearance as a Public Speaker in Oxford – His Work as Secretary to the Commission
   – Birth of his Eldest Son, William – The Nether Winchendon Estate – The Knollys
   Family – Portraits at Nether Winchendon – Mrs. Beresford's Burial.

   Thelady to whom Scrope Bernard paid his addresses was Harriet, only child of
William Morland, banker. The firm was then known as Eansom and Morland, but
the actual partners were, I believe, the seventh Lord Kinnaird, who had married Mr.
Eansom's daughter, and Mr. Morland.

   Mr. Morland was the grandson of another William Morland, styled a ' master
shipwright' of Woolwich, who would now, I suppose, be called a shipbuilder;1he was
chosen by the body of ' master shipwrights ' to present an address to William III.

on the occasion of a royal visit to Woolwich. His wife was Alice Leving, daughter of John Leving, another master shipwright, and described in an epitaph in the Old Church at Woolwich as son of ' Eichard Lewing of Bridgen in the parish of Bexley, Kent, Esqre, and also of this parish.'2I have some difficulty about thename of the son of this couple who became the father of the second William Morland. They had a son John, whose portrait in a red coat, with a dog by his side, is at Nether Winchendon; he died at the age of twenty-seven, and three sons of his are buried at Woolwich in the church of St. Mary Magdalen, the old church but then rebuilt; it is not likely that he had any more children, and I do not know the name of any other son. I have some reason, however, to think that the second William's mother was Elizabeth Pratt.

1Some of this information concerning the Morlands I heard from my father Sir Thomas Tyringham Bernard. A licence from the Heralds' College, authorising Scrope Bernard, as he then was, to quarter the Tyringham arms, also exemplifies the Morland bearings, and describes the second William as grandson of William and Alice, but does not name his father.

2The entries of the Morland and Leving burials are at Winchendon, on a scrap of paper, showing the position of their tombs, which must have been marked by slabs on the pavement.

I have lately obtained the following information about the Morland graves from Mr. William Norman of Plum- stead: ' The old church stood much nearer to the river-side than the present one, which was erected in 1733, about which time the old one was rased to the ground, and the space utilised for burials. In 1893-4 the whole churchyard was laid out as a public garden, and most of the old stones and tombs removed – among them the Morlands' tomb, the inscription upon which had at that time become illegible.'

In that same year an old clerk, John Walker Moore, whose father and grandfather had been clerks of the church before him, gave Mr. Norman the information that 'the Morlands' tomb formerly bore an inscription to the effect that the vault which it covered was under the chancel of the old church.'

There seems to have been a tradition that those Morlands were related to Sir Samuel Morland, son of an incumbent of Sulham, Berks, the great engineer and scientific inventor, who had been Cromwell's ambassador to the Duke of Savoy, sent specially to intercede for the persecuted Vaudois. A possible link between Sir Samuel and the Woolwich Morlands may be found in the person of ' Joseph Morland, M. D., F. R. S.,' who, in 1713, published a book entitled 'Disquisitions on the Force of the Heart,' illustrated by a number of diagrams. The book is at Nether Winchendon, and the name ' William Morland ' is written on the title page. By the date Joseph might have been aHARRIET MOELAND 79

brother of the first William, and he was clearly a*protege*of Sir Samuel and admitted to his friendship. He was the editor of the great man's posthumous work on ' Hydrostatics,' and states in the preface that Sir Samuel left him all his mathematical papers.1

Mary Ann, the wife of the second William Morland, was daughter of Austen Mills, a merchant residing at Greenwich; he was twenty-two and she seventeen when they were married at the church of St. Benet Finck, London, 1762. He was brought up to the surgical profession, whether by transmission from Dr. Joseph, I do not know; but he must have left it somewhat early, for he was well established as a banker when his daughter became engaged to Scrope Bernard, and he was then only forty-five. At a later period, from 1786 to 1796, he represented the borough of Taunton, Somerset, in Parliament. His portrait by Northcote, though it presents him as a fine man, is too commercial in its character to do him full justice; he was a man of refined mind. His younger grand-daughter, when recording his death, wrote, with pardonable pride: ' He had travelled in France, Italy, and Germany, and was reckoned one of the most accomplished gentlemen of his time.' In the course of his wanderings he had acquired a small but choice collection of pictures, and various articles then rare and valued as curios and works of art.

Mrs. Morland was a bright, lively woman, as her letters show; she was not apparently what would now be called intellectual, and as her husband objected to her burdening herself with the management of her house, she must haveled a leisurely life; but she was a genial hostess and tender mother, and in due time a devoted grandmother, and looked up admiringly to the husband who was supreme over all his surroundings, receiving in return unremitting attention from him. Her daughter Harriet inherited her amiable disposition, but perhaps with less lightheartedness.

1Dr. Joseph norland's own book is entitled '*Disquisitions Concerning the Force of the Heart, the Dimensions of the Coats of Die Arteries, and the Circulation of the Blood, by*Joseph Morland, M. D. and K. K. S. Printed for John Lawrence at the Angel in the Poultry, 1713.' It was sixteen years earlier that he had sent Sir Samuel Norland's last work to the same publisher. This is called: '*Hydrostatics or Instructions Concerning Water Works,*collected out of the Papers of Sir Samuel Morland, containing the Method he made use of in the Curious Art. London: Printed for John Lawrence at the Angel in the Poultry, over against the Compter, 1697.' Sketches of Sir Samuel Morland's career will be found in the*Dictionary of National Biography,*the*Biographie Universelle,*and many other works.

Mrs. Mills, the mother of Mrs. Morland, came in her widowhood to live in Mr. Morland's house, and was an honoured member of the family. She had several children, and was grandmother of Charles Mills, the historian of the Crusades, Chivalry, and ' Muhamedanism.' Her maiden name was Gillam, a Rochester family; and a brother of hers became for a moment noted in the history of England. Samuel Gillam was a London magistrate at the period of the Wilkes Rlots, about the time when Governor Bernard's troubles were beginning in America, 1765. It was Mr. Gillam who, seeing that the reading of the Riot Act had but inflamed the passions of the mob, that the magistrates were hooted and pelted, and the soldiers assailed with stones and brickbats, gave the order to fire – the first result being that five or six persons were killed, and fifteen wounded.1

It is always a distressing alternative to resort to such measures, but in this case there is little doubt that the resolution of the magistrates, and of Mr. Gillam in particular, saved many lives. ' Happily,' writes Mr. Jesse, ' the terrible chastisement which had been inflicted in St. George's Fields had the effect, for a time, of restoring peace to the metropolis.' Only the day before this event King George III. had written to Lord

Weymouth, Secretary of State: ' I cannot conclude without strongly recommending the justices, ifSCROPB BERNARD'S MARRIAGB 81

1Jesse,*Memoirs of the Life and Reign of George III.,*vol. i., chap. xx. A most unfortunate occurrence had exasperated the mob. The soldiers, it is said, in pursuing a ringleader, bayonetted a young man who was an innocent spectator, mistaking him for the culprit. This catastrophe goaded the rioters to frenzy, and Mr. Gillam's order, which was subsequent, prevented a general massacre of the troops, and perhaps the general wreck of London. Mr. Jesse has in this account spelt the magistrate's name erroneously ' Gillman,' but on another page it is correctly given as ' Gillam.'

they call the troops to their assistance, should show that vigour which alone makes them respected.' And in other letters he had used still stronger language; Mr. Gillam, however, was put on his trial for murder, but acquitted, and lived many years longer, apparently in peace and honour.1

Scrope Bernard's courtship of Harriet Morland must have been well advanced when the Marquess of Buckingham wrote the following letter,2advocating his suit, to her father:

Wotton, April 13, 1785.

Sir, – Although I have not the honour of being personally known to you, yet the affectionate interest which I take in whatever concerns Mr. Bernard will I hope apologize for this liberty. He has detailed to me the conversation which you was so good as to hold with him, & I owe it to him to bear that testimony to his character and conduct, which the most intimate knowledge enables me to give, & in giving it I feel that I discharge a debt of gratitude to him. I will not presume to add anything further upon a subject, which I could not venture to mention to you, but for the confidence which he puts in me, & for the affection which I bear him; if however he should be fortunate enough to be the object of Miss Morland's choice & of your approbation, I will answer for him that he will discharge to her & to you the duties of his new situation with that attention to his character & conduct, which has so warmly recommended him to his friends.

May I hope for your excuses for this trouble; I owed it in favour of one whom I sincerely love & esteem, I will therefore only detain you to assure you of the regard with which,

I have the honour to be

Sir,

Your obedient humble servt

NugentBuckingham.

It is almost superfluous to state that such a recommendation was not thrown away, and that Scrope Bernard became the accepted suitor of Harriet Morland. They were married, from Mr. Morland's house in Upper GrosvenorStreet, at St. George's, Hanover Square, on July 26, 1785; the officiating clergyman was Dr. Price. My father used to say that a portrait by Hoppner, now at Winchendon, represented his mother in her wedding-dress, but he may have drawn upon his imagination. There is a church in the background, but it is a country church amongst fields and trees.1There is also a blue sash to the white dress and a blue ribbon to the white ' Gainsborough ' hat. It is an especially pleasing picture.

1The King wrote to Lord Weymouth on July 8: ' Though averse in general to signing a respite previous to conviction, I think it my duty in the most public manner to show my countenance to those who with spirit resist the daring spirit that has of late been instilled into the populace.' Mr. Gillam was tried and acquitted July 11.

'MS. Letter at Nether Winchendon.

VOL. III. G

Mr. and Mrs. Scrope Bernard appear to have gone first to Worcester; at least it was to Worcester that a business letter was addressed. Whether they visited Hagley is not stated. Wedding tours could then hardly be said to exist; the newly married pair often remained some time with the bride's parents; and then perhaps visited relations, or went to their own home. In this case I know incidentally of the letter to Worcester; and that they were in Lincoln at an early date after their departure from thence. A family gathering took place at the house of Mr. and Mrs. White. The other members of the family there assembled were apparently Fanny and Julia with their respective husbands. These made up the 'party of four brothers and sisters,' mentioned in a letter from Scrope to Mrs. Morland. Emily and Captain Baker must have been in Ireland, and Thomas Bernard was evidently not there, nor his wife, since allusion is made to them as absent members resident in Lincoln's Inn Fields. Another allusion to friends in Southampton Row, I cannot verify; it perhaps refers to some of the Mills family, Mrs. Morland's relatives.

The letter is dated ' Lincoln, August 10, 1785,' and after some preliminary messages, and an announcement of the completed purchase of a house in Bolton Street, Mayfair, from Mr. Pulteney; it continues:l

We arrived here to a minute of the time appointed on Saturday last, and we had not been in Mr. White's houae many minutesSCROPE BERNARD'S WEDDING TOUR 83

1These particulars are partly derived from my father, partly from the diary of an aunt, 4e.

*The Letters in this Chapter are in MS. at Nether Winchendon.

before our arrival was discovered, and the Minster bells struck up, to the great danger of the steeple, which is out of repair, insomuch that the Dean sent the ringers word after half an hour's ringing, that they had done enough for a compliment, and that he was sure the new-comers would be sorry to occasion any harm to the Cathedral. At dinner the City Musick waited upon us and played their whole store of airs and marches, &c. There was an Assembly in the evening which we were told was more fully attended than usual, in expectation of our party making our appearance there; but the ladies were too late and too tired to get themselves dressed, so that we contented ourselves with a domestic party of four Brothers and Sisters, which is a larger family set than has met together this many, many years. At our meals as well as upon the road we have never forgot Upper Grosvenor Street, and as frequent repetition brings on abbreviation, we soon began to toast that, with Southampton Row, and Lincoln's Inn Fields, under the appellation of ' the Row, the Street, and the Fields,' and within these few days have reduced it to ' Row, Street, Fields,' which the little children in their eagerness to emulate us in drinking toasts, have converted into ' Roasted Fields.'

On Sunday morning we went to the City Church, below Hill, and took our places among the Aldermen and Aldresses, which is the title given here (not ludicrously) to their ladies. In the afternoon we went to the Minster, where Dr. Gordon, the Chanter, was so good as [to] interest himself that we might have a good anthem. That evening we spent *en famille,* excepting only a short walk upon the Minster Green, which is the Mall of this place.

On Monday Mr. White had a select Lincoln party to dinner, with cards in the evening – Harriot and I at the commerce table; and yesterday the Dean favoured us with a grand dinner, to which we sat down nineteen in number, were very sociable, and had a pleasant drawing-room party afterwards. Harriot seems to take very well to the good people of Lincoln, and I am sure they do to her. In a little time she would be quite at home here; but upon so short an acquaintance with them, it is perfectly natural that she should be willing to return to Upper Grosvenor Street for the present, and come some other time to improve her acquaintance with the card parties of this place. She is gone out this morning to see the Assembly Rooms, and call at one or two places; she would have staid at home to write, but that I told her my letter would be sufficient, and that she might write another to-morrow, which may accordingly be expected.,

We propose being in town on Sunday or Monday, but her letter to-morrow will inform yon. I beg my affectionate and dutiful remembrances to Mrs. Morland and Mrs. Mills, and my best respects and thanks to Lord and Lady Kinnaird, if you are still with them. The whole Brotherhood here have desired me to present their united love and compts to you and family.

A letter from the Rev. E. G. Bowyer, of Willoughby, followed Scrope Bernard to town, having missed him at Lincoln, and is a good specimen of the ceremonious style of the day. It refers to the ' Stuff and Colour Ball,' which was instituted in that very year for the promotion of Lincolnshire manufactures:

Willoughby, August 16, 1785.

Dear Sir, – Much flattered as I am by the honour of your very obliging letter, I think myself unfortunate that my distance from Lincoln and the shortness of your stay in our county deprives me of the still greater pleasure which you give me reason to think you intended me. Permit me, Sir, to hope that some future opportunity will be more favourable to me and that I may look upon your letter as some kind of earnest for a share of the next visit you will pay these parts.

Mrs. White, whose approbation has been a great encouragement to my endeavours for the employment of the poor, has probably given you some account of the success of our plans, which is really satisfactory for the time.

Mrs. Bowyer and I are not without hopes that we may be honoured with Mrs. White's company at Willoughby Parsonage in November, if she still holds to the kind intention Miss Fellowes told us she entertained of honouring with her presence the little festivity we have announced for the seventeenth of this month, in behalf of our infant manufacture, by an advertisement which perhaps you have seen. The ground of this our hope is that the company then expected will be too numerous for the accommodations of the town of Alford, which is within half an hour's drive of our house.

Allow me to express my regret that so necessary a step as the revision and amendment of the Poor Laws should be for the present laid aside, and to indulge a hope that your abilities will yet be efficaciously exalted in a cause to which your inclination seems to point so strongly, that I shall make no apology for the freedom I mean to take from time to time of communicating to you anything that may seem to me worthy of your notice on thisTHE 'STUFF AND COLOUR BALL' 85

subject, desiring only that such communications may lay by you, till your leisure permits you to peruse them, and though the transactions of this obscure little corner are not important enough to claim much of your attention, yet I shall so far avail myself of the partiality you was pleased to profess for the first account of them, as to transmit to you, as soon as it is published, an appendix I am now preparing.

I have the honour to present my respectful compliments to Mr. and Mrs. White, and to remain most faithfully

Your obliged and

obedient humble servant

Bowyeb.

The announcement of an intended ball having called attention to the subject of the woollen industry, it was resolved to found a manufactory for the employment of the poor, and efforts were made to induce persons connected with the county to assist the scheme by taking shares. Mrs. White appears to have thrown herself energetically into this project. She writes/from Lincoln, ' Nov. 8, 1785 ':

Dear Brother, – I received a message from you in Captain Baker's letter which I understood, I flatter myself, right, & thank you for your acquiescence in case I should wish it. – I forget whether my answr, that we would wait a quarter of a year&I would then let you know how we went on, ever was committed to paper or sent to you, & I am ashamed to say that only on your slight permission, I have since ventured to set down your name & even given Lowrie leave to draw on you at a mouth's date for

*$30*Since which I have paid $20 on the same acct to make

up yr 50. I hope it will not at the present be particularly disagreeable to you, & conclude you will wish me to take the first opportunity of selling it again. This is the time for the Manufactory's having a large stock in hand, both of goods & Wool, but if you permit us to retain your name a quarter of a year*I shall hope*to give you by that time a good account of the money again.

The writer observes satirically:

As it is professedly begun for the good of the Poor, several People we are acquainted with*are waiting to see*if anything is to be*gained by it,* &will then be very ready to enter.1MS. Letter at Nether Winchendon.

She then continues:

It goes on exceedingly well and with a quiet steadiness that does it honour,&will during this winter have the effect of introducing the Parish Spinning Schools in the manner recommended by Mr. Bowyer, so earnestly desired by us all, & they will be independent of the Factory&almost in opposition to it, which is for particular reasons still more desirable, as nothing can hurt it but too great a load of poor, which lay heavy on the fund last winter, but is now removed without detriment to them, & the City

Jersey School taken up to assist in the great work of making the poor*industrious & comfortable.*

She then mentions that ' SrJohn Nelthorpe will have two shares, and perhaps another gentleman or too of [position?] in the county who have behaved handsomely with regard [?] to the public Warehouse plan, which the Dean wishes to see carried into execution.' The festive part is not forgotten. Jane White says that she is ' going in a few days to the Ball. & shall be busy now in preparing the dress, which is an Uniform & very pretty. Mr. White is recovering from the gout but will not venture to go, & I am to accompany another Lady & be at Mrs. Bowyer 's house which will make it very agreeable.' She ends: ' I believe Sister Scrope will think me a little crazy, but desire she will suspend her judgement a while till the event of these things justify ye eager attention.'

By way of resuming the history of this movement I anticipate the course of time. Jane White wrote to Scrope Bernard in the following year, 1786, enclosing 25*Z.* and promising another remittance as soon as she received it. She adds ' if you please to give my Sister Scrope the odd 5s. to lay out in a new song for me, when she meets with a pretty one in English or Italian,' intimating that all claims would thus be satisfied. ' Mr. Bowyer's ball went off very agreeably this year & we had a great meeting the week after at Lincoln,' adding with a thought of Buckinghamshire: 'Will this French Treaty hurt our friends the Lacemakers? I hope not.'

A SCHOOL OF INDUSTRY 87

Mr. Bowyer afterwards wrote a paper for a publication edited by Thomas Bernard, entitled:1 ' A School of Industry for Sixty Girls.' This was one of the institutions founded by the will of Lord Crewe, Bishop of Durham,2 but organised by trustees. Whether Mr. Bowyer had studied this scheme before he came forward in the Lincolnshire plans of improvement, or whether he helped in the Bamburgh organisations a few years later, I am not able to state.

Bishop Barrington wrote to Scrope Bernard, in 1788:

The first specimen Mr. Bowyer gave of his talents in that line which he has pursued with so much credit to himself and so much utility to his neighbours, will make me read his second with equal eagerness and pleasure. I beg that you will thank him in my name, and request that he will never come to London without calling upon me.

Bishop Barrington was translated from Salisbury to Durham in 1791, and Bamburgh Castle was in that diocese; but whether Mr. Bowyer became incumbent by his appointment I cannot say.

The Lincolnshire scheme probably succumbed to the introduction of steam. A recent guide writes of it, in somewhat depreciatory terms:3

This ball was originally established at Alford in 1785, with the view of encouraging the Lincolnshire manufactory of woollen stuff, and was removed to Lincoln, where it has been since regularly held, in 1789. It owes its origin to the Society of Industry, for the Southern Division of the parts of Lindsey, who, August 5, 1785, issued cards for an assembly at the Windmill Inn, Alford, at which free admission was given to all ladies appearing in gowns and petticoats of woollen stuff spun and woven in Lincolnshire, and gentlemen appearing without any cotton or silk in their dress except stockings. The manufacture having been taken up in high circles, it became fashionable for ladies to spin the yarn for their own dresses. Those who did so were distinguished at the ball by white ribbons; their less industrious sisters wearing blue. One of the ladies of rank of the county was each year chosen aspatroness. A colour – that chosen at the first Alford ball was orange – was declared by her at the commencement of the year, in which all ladies were to appear, thus ensuring the wearing of new dresses on the occasion. Lady Banks, the wife of Sir Joseph Banks, was patroness of the first ball held at Lincoln.

1*Reports of the Society for Bettering the Condition of the Poor,*vol i. 'Translated from Oxford in 1674.'Williamson's*Guide to Lincoln.*

Notwithstanding the ' laudable zeal shown by the county ladies in support of their infant manufactory' at the outset, woollen stuff proved to be too heavy a garb to be tolerated in a ballroom; and, in 1803, a compromise was made, by which ladies were admitted free ' on taking 6 yards of stuff of the first quality or ten of the plain,' while those ' who had not less than 4 yards could have tickets 5s. each, gentlemen 10s.*6d.*as usual.' But the manufacture proved a complete failure, and died out in spite of this adventitious aid, and almost the only memorial of its existence is the title of the' Lincoln Stuff Ball,' and the traditionary rule – still nominally enforced – of the choice of a colour for the ladies' costume.

Not later, I believe, than two or three years ago, I noticed a paragraph in the ' Times ' vouching for the continuance of the same ball, which must, however, have lost much of its pristine interest.

From the wording of Scrope's letter to Mr. Morland, written at Lincoln, it is evident that he intended to travel with his wife direct to London, and the plan was apparently carried into effect, since the young couple took possession of the house in Bolton Street about this time. In the autumn they went to Nether Winchendon. No record is left of their welcome to the deserted homestead; but it may be assumed that the bells of the village church rang merrily, though not sonorously like the peal of Lincoln Minster, and that the villagers were treated to some festivities in honour of the occasion.

It is said, however, that the bride, accustomed as she was to town life, and knowing little of the country beyond the civilised neighbourhood of Lee, was discouraged by the forsaken appearance of the place. The Manor House had indeed all but sunk into a farm-house; Kichard Plater, who held the land in its immediate proximity, was living in the house as caretaker; another tenant, Gurney, had beenNETHER WINCHENDON MANOR HOUSE 89

allowed to occupy a far end of the building. By this means it had been kept more or less aired, bnt at the expense of its refinement; and it must have been difficult to make the reserved portion of the home comfortable, according to London ideas, without a thorough renovation. In an age when the prevailing taste in architecture, gardening, and all their accompaniments, was quite anti-mediaeval, the venerable aspect of the place afforded no compensation for its shortcomings; at least, so its new mistress is said to have thought. Possibly, also, the sights and sounds – the rats making their rounds all through the night; the hooting and screeching of the owls, and the dashing of the bats against the windows, ready to enter at the first opportunity – may have affected her nerves; for during this first residence she contracted a feverish indisposition. Mr. Morland wrote in distracted terms to Scrope, praying for full information; but no serious consequences ensued, and ere long Harriet Bernard was restored in good health to the society of her devoted parents.

One pleasant reminiscence of this visit apparently is a note from Hartwell, written according to the fashion of the day, in the third person, but most friendly. It evidently refers to the difficulties of locomotion in Bucks; perhaps the Bernards had no suitable vehicle, but it is also possible that they could not make use of any on the cross road between "Winchendon and Dinton, which was their way to Hartwell – at least at certain seasons. I have heard that Mrs. Scrope Bernard had to ride pillion for some years after she made acquaintance with Winchendon, and of course with a manservant when her husband was not there. The note is as follows:

Sir Wm. and Lady Eliz. Lee return oompts to Mr. & Mrs. S. Bernard, and beg that they will give no attention to formalities; they will be glad to see them in any dress and in any manner or on any day most agreeable to them, and hope shd it be agreeable to them to accept of their carriage they will be so good as to send order for it at what Hour may be convenient to them.

Hartwell, Sept. 10th.

Various kind notes were written from the same quarter – in successive years it would seem – showing that the old feeling of friendship was kept up. The intercourse with the Lees of Hartwell had never been dropped by Scrope; he had even acted as tutor to young William Lee for a short time, residing in his father's house but refusing all remuneration. This youth was a subject of much anxiety to his father, and probably to his mother also, and Scrope had not been able to continue the tutorship so long as Sir William would have wished; his pupil had written to him afterwards from Oxford consulting him about his studies, in an affectionate tone, but somewhat free and easy, considering the difference in their ages.

During the autumn of this year, in which Scrope Bernard had entered upon a new phase of life, he received a letter from France, apparently the last on William Grenville's side of their college or bachelor correspondence. Mr. Grenville did not marry for some years, but he soon became immersed in political business, and the careless freedom of early times was succeeded by the tone of a man who had commenced the struggle of life in right earnest. The letter is here given:

A Nancy en Lorraine.

Ce 20-eOct" 1785. Longos

Cantando memini puerum me condere soles.1

Nuric oblita mihi tot carmina, or you should not have received a letter in English prose to follow the clouds of Epitaphs, Epigrams and Odes which used to be the production of our evenings at an English Inn. You must attribute this entirely to my stupidity and by no means must imagine that Nancy of Lorraine is less adapted to poetical images than Marazion or Penzanza's hold. If there were in me any *veteris vestigia fiammcB*they must have been called out by our journey of this day, through a valley watered by the Moselle, and enclosed by the most beautiful hills, crowned with woods which have just received the first tints of autumn, while the sides are covered with vineyards. The vintageA PRETTY SCENE 91

1The writer has not quoted this passage quite accurately. It runs:

' Stepe ego longos
Cantando puerum memini me condere soles;
Nunc oblita mihi tot carmina.'

is but just begun here, and forms the prettiest moving picture that can be imagined; the whole villages, men, women, and children, gathering the grapes and bringing them in baskets to the houses where they are pressed. I am astonished that this scene has not furnished more images to the Roman poets; perhaps it was too familiar to them, tho' the same thing might be said of our harvest which has however been a constant topic.

It will, I am sure, not be indifferent to you to know that you made a considerable part of our conversation in the course of our journey, and that I took up my pen principally, to express to you what I have not yet done since your going to Chateau Bernard, our sincere wishes for every sort of happiness that can befall you.

If I calculate right this letter will reach you in the midst of your Oxford glories. I would by no means interrupt the consideration of so important a personage as 8rThomas Bodley, and therefore give you no direction for writing to me, for which indeed another reason may be assigned, which is that till we get to Paris we shall never be stationary above two days in any one place, having found that time amply sufficient for acquiring a full and perfect knowledge of the manners, customs, language, laws, manufactures and commerce of the different cities of Europe. I remember a French President in London who had allotted a week for a journey which he had undertaken to England for the sake of acquiring information on these points, and we were told at Brussels of a man there who, having infinitely more capacity for gaining knowledge in a short space of time, had returned there, after sleeping one night in London,*coeff& d I'Angloise.*It is true this*coeffure*did not require much application or labour, as it consisted in untying his queue and letting his hairs hang about his ears. So that you may justly expect to see me return accomplished*in omni scibili atque acquisibili*in France, Switzerland, or Flanders.

After telling Scrope that the travellers had not yet passed through Montreuil, but intended to do so on their way home, and expected to find his friends tenderly remembered, Grenville alludes to friends wbo were apparently travelling in England. The ' King' mentioned in the following paragraph was not Scrope's brother-in-law, nor apparently related to him; his father was Dean of Baphoe. The Moss alluded to was probably son of the Bishop of Bath andWells, and must have taken Holy Orders soon after this tour.

If you see Moss pray tell him that he must live in daily expectation of a new Episoopo-pastoral. I had one letter from King during this tour. But it reached me in the midst of East India dispatches. I beg you will collect from Moss a just and complete account of all their calamities. How often, while he was reading, King fell asleep (as well he might) and the horse turned aside to graze in the bottom of the neighbouring ditch. How often the buggy broke down

'And laid the Bishop's mitred head in dust.'

How often they were splashed by stage coachmen, and how often run over by Phaeton, with a long list of other misfortunes. Our journey has been uncommonly prosperous, and*les Milords Anglais*have come off with flying colours.

I have left no directions for any mortal to write to me. If anything very remarkable happens, of which it is absolutely necessary that I should be immediately informed, you will write to me*d la Poste Restante a Paris,*by which means I may probably get your letter by the beginning of December. You will however write with a due regard to the Inspector General of Foreign Letters.

Believe me ever most afftely yours

The ' Oxford glories' to which Mr. Grenville alludes in this letter, as connected with the memory of Sir Thomas Bodley, I cannot further explain; George Barrington, a son of the General,1and eventually fifth Viscount Barrington, has, however, alluded to this occasion evidently in the following paragraph:

I went to Oxford yesterday to vote for the Camden Professorship, and calling upon the Dean I took an opportunity of mentioning your speech. He said it did you great credit on the whole but he lamented you had not come to Oxford a day or two earlier and shown it to him, that he might amend the exceptionable parts where you had now and then offended against a regimen of grammar which only marked your desuetude of writing Latin.

1See vol. i., chapter x., pp. 215,216, for some account of the Barrington or Shnte pedigree; it may also be found in Burke and Debrett's*Peerages.*

A NEW PHASE OP LIFE 93

This was probably Scrope's last appearance as a public speaker in Oxford. He was there again the following summer, but I do not know for what reason; and he never entirely lost his connection with the University; but in this respect, as in many others, he had entered upon a different phase of life. On his return to London in this year of his marriage it would seem that the work offered him by Pitt commenced in right earnest, that it was continuous and severe, and that Scrope when he found that there was no probability of its coming to an end at the expiration of six months, as at first suggested, began to have thoughts of flinging it up. This I gather from a letter sent by a friend whose name I cannot give, because I am unable to identify the handwriting, and the second portion of the letter containing the signature is not to be found; but there is enough on the first sheet to show that the writer was one who thought he had a claim to address Mr. Bernard in a paternal or semi-paternal tone, and remonstrate seriously against his project of relinquishing a post that might lead to further advantages, before he had given it a fair trial. He comments on the desponding strain in which Scrope had written to him, as unintelligible from one so fortunately placed and, as he supposes, happily married. Thereupon he enters into a dissertation on the evil results of marrying without affection – a folly which he believes Scrope incapable of committing. He then alludes to the expected birth of a first child, and thus fixes approximately the date of the letter.

No doubt the simple explanation of this dolorous mood, into which Mr. Bernard appears to have fallen, was the protracted drudgery of his occupation as secretary to the Commission. All through life the routine of office work was most distasteful to his nervous, excitable nature – unluckily – for he was constantly being driven into it by circumstances.

William, the eldest son of Scrope and Harriet Bernard, was born on July 17, 1786,1at Mr. Morland's house in Upper Grosvenor Street, and it may be hoped that this1Pebrett and Burke,*Baronetages,*' Bernard Morland.'

event had some effect in raising his father's spirits and inducing him to take a more hopeful view of life. This precious child was apparently sent to his grandparents at Lee while his parents were settling down at Winchendon in August, and then went to stay with his uncle Thomas and aunt Margaret in London who had no children of their own. This appears from a letter written by Thomas to Scrope in that month.

My little nephew arrived in Town yesterday, and is I hope in a fair way of being a great and good man. I need not tell you that any attention we can pay you and yours, is ever contributed with the utmost pleasure.

The child was probably sent on to the country; but in the same letter Thomas Bernard continues:

We were obliged to defer our Winchendon visit for many reasons; one, that I thought that under present circumstances it would make an unpleasant hurry to Margaret, and prevent her giving a few hours to her Aunt and Sister this week. We do not go to Wilton Park till the afternoon, and I am obliged to return to town on Tuesday morning. Could you conveniently fix Saturday for the Kings, and let us come to you on Friday which we will make a point of doing? I mention that time, because it is the only time that I am sure of commanding. Mrs. Stainforth comes to us on Saturday. If that suits you we shall sleep at Wilton Park on Thursday, breakfast at Wendover, and get early to you at Winchendon.

Wilton Park, near Beaconsfield, was the seat of Josias Du Pre, Esq.,1a late Governor of Madras. Mr. and Mrs. King were staying with the Smiths at Wendover Vicarage, whence Mr. King wrote to Scrope in anticipation of their visit: 'Fanny in particular promises herself no small gratification.' She had perhaps never seen her childhood's home since the day when ' Monsieur Le Roi' declared his love in a bower.

That the accommodation at Nether Winchendon Manor House was not extensive is clear from this correspondence, since the Kings could not be received the same day as1Burke,*A. Dictionary of the Landed Gentry:*'Dn Prg of Wilton Park.'

HILLSBOEOUGH 95

Thomas and Margaret Bernard; yet there is no mention of the Whites attempting the long journey from Lincoln, while Amelia and Captain Baker must have been still in Ireland, whence the Kings had but recently returned; neither is any other guest mentioned. Possibly Scrope had already begun his work of renovation, which became a hobby, and had workmen in part of the house.

The only long letter*I* possess written by Amelia is dated from Carrick-on-Shannon, and was written on July 25 in this year, just after she had received the news of William Bernard's birth. After congratulations, and thanks for a present to her son Frank – evidently of a silver knife and fork in case – she continues:

Tom seems to thrive best in his native country, is grown very stout. Frank tho' very well at present has not been quite so well since we left England, but is what is called a fine Boy: for myself I am pretty well & so much pleased with some parts of Ireland. I do not know whether we shall not settle in Belfast and the country about it is very enticing; the town well governed and the inhabitants uncommonly well behaved and civil to strangers.

Hillsborough belonging to that Earl is a most charming place. Mrs. King & self & our Husbands spent two days there on our way to this place; it is a few miles out of the way and after the Gentlemen had seen the men settled in quarters they walked on to meet us; the town consists of his own house, a very good Inn & a few small houses, a very handsome church, the whole surrounded by beautiful woods with pretty walk; the Inn is kept by an Englishwoman, the servants & furniture all English brought over at the Earl's expense; in short it has all the luxuries of an Inn with the quiet&comforts of a private house. We saw many other pretty places on the road, but the Inns were miserably bad.

This is a tolerable place, but at first we were much at a loss&but for the better sort of people we should not get on,&what we cannot get for money we do for love; every one milks his own cow, kills his mutton, & grows his garden stuff &c &c,&if I do but send for anything I happen to want, they seem to think it a favour I do them; the mistress of the Inn made aserious complaint that I did not send for anything, so to pacify her I was obliged to send next day for a rosting*[sic]*Pig she had promised me; not a day but presents of Pease, Beans, new Pottaties&o.come in; we live cheap and comfortably&the place is very healthy – The Regt. is in four differl quarters. Baker commands two Companies here. Grenard is head quar". I wish to know where we shall be sent next; country qrs. are generally more agreeable than Dublin. I have filled the Barrack yard with chickens for which I gave 4d& 5lia couple & that was too much, a couple of young Turkies for 8cl& hen & 12 eggs for 51.*,. I call this my retirement & expect in the course of two or three years to come amongst you all & cut a dash, but must now cut some fine Trout 6 of which cost lgweighing between 4 & five Pounds altogether. Adieu, dear brother let me hear from you soon.

1MS. Letter at Nether Winchendon.

In this year, also, Scrope Bernard extended his views beyond the homestead, and endeavoured to reduce the Nether Winchendon estate to some kind of order. He was in correspondence with the Eev. Charles Cave, owner of the ' Hill Farm' portion of the Tyringham estate; and an appointment was made in order that they might examine the contents of an old chest. This arrangement may have brought Mr. Cave to Nether Winchendon, but after the relatives had departed. No practical result, however, came of their interviews at this time; Mr. Cave declined to part with any of his Nether Winchendon property, one portion of which lay so near the Manor House as to interfere with the convenience and pleasure of its owner. Three years later, in 1789, something was achieved. Mr. Bernard was able to purchase 'a messuage and two closes.' This1messuage' was probably a house rather above the size of an ordinary labourer's cottage, which may possibly have been the village inn at the time, and was called the Bear Inn during Scrope Bernard's ownership, which name it still retains; it stood near a gate leading from the village to the ' Hill Farm,' and a small field near by was probably one of those transferred at the same time.

Another matter which the new Lord of the Manor had much at heart was to buy that moiety of the advowsonTHE PUECHASE OF AN ADVOWSON 97 which had gone to the Cave family at the same time as the land, and he wrote to Dr. Andrew, the actual holder of the perpetual curacy, for information upon the subject of his clerical income derived from Nether Winchendon. The doctor, who, it need hardly be stated, was not a constant resident in that parish – (Mr. Newborough was apparently his assistant curate) – wrote' from Ashford as follows:

I had the pleasure of your letter last post, and am puzzled how to set any value at all upon a living, the fixed income of which is not sufficient (and hereafter will be less so) to pay any gentleman that shall serve – I pay Mr. Newborough 20, i' p. ami., the fixed income is about 19$, so that what is strictly purchase- able is*1$*minus. I presume it would be frivolous to suppose you would take into your consideration the trifling and precarious contributions of 4 or 5 farmers, none of whom subscribe more than 15s. a year – Lady Knollys, indeed, subscribes 5 guineas; but 'tis possible that good lady may die some time or other, and we may not perhaps after her decease, be blessed with a successor so well disposed. My particular acquaintance with the late Mr. Knollys, and my laying hold of the*Mollia Tempora fandi.*was the foundation and rise of that beautiful subscription. I always considered it as a lucky hit, and it must be allowed to stand very ticklish in future. In short I look upon the subscriptions (amounting, after deducting the Tithe Feast and subscription to the widow and orphans, to about*8$*)to be what the algebraists call an evanescent quantity. Besides, I take it, the subscribers would disdain to be sold and would fly off at a tangent, were the subject ever so gently touched upon.

This last phrase is obscure, but it probably refers to Mr. Bernard's project of buying the moiety of the advowson, which transaction, according to Dr. Andrew, the subscribers were likely to resent, as a sale of their souls, or at least as an indignity of some sort. It is curious to find such sensitiveness in these Bucks farmers about a practice so fully permitted, if not even encouraged, at that time in the Church of England as by law established. The reverend gentleman further observed that, as he had been appointed by Mr. Cave, the next presentation would fall to Mr. Bernard orhis heirs, and it was therefore scarcely worth his while to purchase.

1MS. Letter at Nether Winchendon. VOL. III. H1See Lipsoomb,*llixt. of Bucks,*vol. i.,' Nether Winchendon.'

The transaction was not effected at this time. Dr. Andrew died in 1790, and was succeeded by Mr. William Lloyd. Before these events, however, the living had received*WOl.*from Queen Anne's Bounty. The*19l.*per annum reckoned by Dr. Andrew as the only settled income of the incumbent was partly derived from a tithe rent charge of*10l.*13s.1paid by Scrope and by Sir Francis before him with the proceeds of former grants in the Tyringham time. Of tithes the Bernards never received any; their privileges as lay rectors have always consisted solely in the obligation to keep the chancel in repair. Scrope Bernard, however, had resolved to become sole patron, and he achieved his object in 1804. Successive attempts to improve the living at last raised it to the magnificent income of*80l.*per annum.

The Mr. Knollys2who had been on terms of friendship with Dr. Andrew was probably Francis Knollys, at one time M. P. for Oxford, who died in June 1754, not quite three months after his nephew, the last Sir Francis, had been created a baronet. The title died with that Sir Francis in 1772. Lady Knollys, daughter and heiress of Sir Eobert Kendall, later of Kempson, co. Bedford, still occasionally resided at Winchendon; one business letter * from her to Scrope Bernard, preserved at the Manor House, is however, presumptive evidence that she had ceased to occupy the house some years later. It is dated: ' Soho Square febryye 26, 1789,' and is written in a fine bold round hand:

Lady Knollys's Compts to Mr. Bernard is very happy to accommodate him vith the ground he desires to have; when he goes to Winchendon her tenant will settle the business with him. She will sign the lease when ready, desires the rent may be paid to her tenant as she does not chuse to alter the account, is sorry she could not acquaint Mr. Bernard before, but did not hear from Mrs. Quartermain till yesterday.

'*Ibid.*,'Pedigree of Knolljs.'

'MS. Letter at Nether Winchendon.

PICTUEES AT NETHER WINCHENDON 99

With this letter the history of the Knollyses of Nether Winchendon ends; at least I have no means of tracing it further. Lipscomb states briefly:

The remains of the mansion of the Knollyses, with certain lands here, after the death of the last Lady Enollys, passed to the family of Longmire, and from them to the Rev. John King Martyn, Rector of Fertenhall, co. Beds, and are now the property of his son the Rev. Thomas Martyn, the present Rector of Perten- hall.

Since Lipscomb's time the house and land have been sold more than once, and the land has been divided; the house, which has been chiefly inhabited by its owners, I have recently purchased. '

For some years Scrope Bernard, who visited Winchendon whenever his other avocations permitted, was in occasional correspondence on family matters with his sister Jane White; in the course of which time several pictures, in the custody of Mrs. White at Lincoln, were transferred to her brother at Nether Winchendon. She enumerates' ' Mr. and Mrs. Terry and Miss Winlowe.' These pictures were probably Mrs. White's property, left her by her father's cousin Jane Hastings, daughter of Mr. and Mrs. Terry, whom I suppose to have been one of her godmothers. There is also mention of a miniature of Mrs. Beresf ord's father, ' which is so strong a Likeness and so good a Painting that I hope you will think it worth accepting as Mrs. Beresford valued it so much.' The miniature really, I believe, represented Francis Tyringham, Mrs. Beresford's grandfather. He died before her birth, and her father died so soon after that she can scarcely have remembered him; nevertheless it was probably Mrs. White who made the mistake, as Mrs. Beresford would have inherited a tradition. I find no mention of any other Tyringham portrait; the rest of the family paintings had probably hung undisturbed on the walls of the Manor House through all its vicissitudes.

Another portion of the correspondence referred to thedates of Mrs. Beresford's birth and marriage. The first was easily ascertained 1; of the second I am not so sure. A third point concerned her burial. Jane White wrote soon after her stay at Winchendon to Scrope, then in Ireland:

1This letter and the rest of the correspondence are in MS. at Nether Winchendon.

I don't know whether the enclosed will [be] of any use to you in Ireland, but you will have the option of forwarding them to any person that is employed for you in these things.

What was the nature of these documents – for such they evidently were – does not appear; but the writer continues:

It has led to a discovery that my Father's sudden seizure, just after Mrs. Beresford's interment, prevented his paying that respect to her memory he wished, for I believe there is not even a*Tombstone.*If you wish me to make any further enquiry, I will go over to Leadenham&examine if the report is a mistaken one. Having gone there in person with great sorrow to attend her funeral, I should be sorry to find it quite true.

When I visited Leadenham there was certainly no appearance of a tombstone or tablet; the sole mention I could find of Mrs. Beresford was in the epitaph to her son. Nor has any monument been erected to her especially at Nether Winchendon, though she is to a certain extent commemorated on a tablet, which includes her father, John Tyringham and Sir Francis and Lady Bernard in its inscription, and which was of course placed there by Scrope. This and the words underneath the clock to some extent perpetuate the memory of the last Tyringham.

1From the register at Nether Winchendon.

5

SECTION 5

THE VICEROYALTY OP IRELAND 101
   CHAPTER VI
   THE SECOND VICBROYALTY OF IRELAND
   Scrope Bernard appointed Usher of the Black Rod and Private Secretary to the Marquess of Buckingham-Death of his Son Thomas – His intention to contest Aylrs-bury – His post of Private Secretary – Debates in the House – William Grenville and the appointment of Master of the Rolls in Ireland – Lord Nugent – Scrope Bernard's departure for England – The Trial of Warren Hastings – Disagreement between the Marquess of Buckingham and the King – The King's illness – Thomas Grenville – Birth of Margaret Bernard – The Opposition to the Viceroy.

   In1787, two years after Scrope Bernard and his bride had made a prolonged stay at Winchendon, and the year after the first family gathering had taken place – William Pitt being still Prime Minister – the Viceroyalty of Ireland became vacant by the death of the Duke of Eutland, and the Marquess of Buckingham, the former Earl Temple, attained the goal of his hopes. On November 2 Scrope Bernard wrote 1 to Mr. Morland, who was then at Bath:

   I have just time to write a line by this post to inform you and Mrs. Morland that Lord Buckingham has this day been declared in Council Lord Lieutenant of Ireland;

and that he has nominated me Usher of the Black Rod and Private Secretary, which office, with the approbation of my friends, I propose to accept. I imagine we shall set off by about the end of this month, but cannot yet be certain. In the meantime I shall have a great deal to do in making family and other arrangements; in which I shall want Mrs. Morland's and your assistance. I should propose the nursery to be stationary in this country for the present; but of this and other subjects I shall write more particularly when at leisure.

Another son had been born to Scrope and Harriet Bernard on October 15, and was named Thomas, having, nodoubt, bis good uncle for a godfather. Whether the agitation into which his mother was thrown both before and after his birth by the changes in the family prospects, or some less obvious cause, affected her nurseling, I do not know; but he died on December 18, the only child his parents lost in infancy.

1MS. Letter at Nether Winchendon.

Scrope Bernard had apparently left England before his son's death. His second period of office as a viceroy's private secretary was, it will be seen, if somewhat longer than the first, so disturbed and broken up by absences from Ireland as to be by no means a satisfactory record; possibly it would not have been more satisfactory had it been further protracted. The accounts of the Marquess's viceroyalty in the volumes compiled from the family archives read of course differently from those written by an independent historian. Mr. Lecky ushers it in with the following remarks 1:

His short viceroyalty in 1783 had given him some Irish experience, and it was thought that the fact that his wife was a Catholic might give him some popularity. With considerable business talents, however, the new Lord Lieutenant was one of those men who in all the relations of life seldom fail to create friction and irritation. Great haughtiness, both of character and manner; extreme jealousy and proneness to take offence, had always characterized him; and before he had been many months in Ireland we find him threatening his resignation, bitterly offended with the King, angry and discontented with the Ministers in England, and very unpopular in Dublin.

In the ' Memoirs' 'the account is of course more favourable:

On the 1st of January 1788, Lord Buckingham transmitted to the Ministry a copy of the speech be proposed for the opening of the Irish Parliament on the 17th. He threw himself at once into the labours of his Government, which, judging from the multitude of topics that pressed upon his time, and the conscientious consideration he bestowed upon them, were onerous andLORD BUCKINGHAM'S EECEPTION 103

1Lecky,*History of Irelaud in the Eighteenth Century*(Edition 1892), vol. ii. chap. v., p. 463.

* *Memoirs of the Court and Cabinets of George III.,*vol. L

absorbing. The correspondence of this period is very voluminous, and embraces in detail an infinite variety of subjects. The universal reliance which was placed in his justice and toleration, drew upon him petitions and complaints from all manner of people.

I leave the reader, after perusing these accounts, to form his own opinion, as far as may be, from the glimpses afforded in this chapter of the second Grenville viceroyalty. To gain a just estimate of the Marquess it is of course necessary to compare him with other leading men of the time, for it is only by such comparisons that he can be fairly judged either in his public or private character.

The first letter addressed by Scrope Bernard after his arrival in Ireland to William Grenville is lengthy, but it relates so much of his own personal movements – they cannot be called adventures – that, although it has already been printed,11 give it in full:

1787, December 27, Dublin Castle, – I have not written to you sooner, because I knew that you would be as well informed of Lord Buckingham's landing and reception here by the Gazette and newspapers, if not better, than I could describe it to you. But as we have now been here for above ten days, it is time I should commence my correspondence.

There seems very little prospect of any difficulty in the approaching sessions here; no opposition is as yet announced. The principal leading interests in opposition have mostly declared their favourable dispositions, and wishes to support; and nothing is to be feared but from their jealousy of the comparative attentions shown to one another, which must end in producing an Opposition sooner or later, as the market is overstocked. Lord Charlemont put himself forward to be one of the two noblemen sent to conduct the Lord Lieutenant up the Castle stairs to the Council Chamber, and sat next him yesterday at the Lord Mayor's dinner, where there was a very pleasant party, and your brother was in high spirits, and gave the greatest pleasure to those around him. Chief Justice Carleton, who sat next me, observing Lord Charlemont's assiduities, whispered that he wondered how long this would last. I think it, however, possible that an old man like him may be tired of volunteering and opposition, and may beglad to seize a moment when he may think he can support, with safety to his popularity. Fitz-Herbert seems a man of very pleasing and taking manners, and to judge very prudently and discreetly in the instances which have been yet seen and, what gives me the most satisfaction, does not manifest the least jealousy of your brother's monopoly of the business. Cuffe lays unremitting siege to him, but I trust will be repulsed, though I know not how it happens, but he seems to be a man much considered here, and of political weight. With respect to myself, I go on very pleasantly in my own quiet way, more sought than seeking, which is the only plan for a private secretary. Lord Buckingham means to give me one of the vacant houses in the Phoenix Park, not far from the Lord Lieutenant's lodge, which will be very convenient for my wife when she comes over, as I should not have had room or conveniences for her at the Castle. As far as I can see, the household is likely to be very well managed under Griffith's and my joint government. I really am satisfied Griffith is as fit a man as could have been found. Young was expected before this, and it was wondered why he did not arrive, when the observation was (not mine) that without doubt he would contrive to arrive accidentally at the Head at the same time with Lady Buckingham, and make himself her Excellency's squire in the yacht to Dublin. I was offered a bet of this, but would not take it, as I am satisfied it is his plan, and it accounts for his delay. I hope you will find questions enough for him, which will require his attendance when the business of your sessions is resumed, at the end of January.

i*The Manuscripts of J. B. For fescue,*JEsg., vol- '> P' 1"-):i-

The next paragraph evidently refers to Scrope's intention of standing for Aylesbury at the next election:

I forgot when I took leave of you to state what passed at the
interview which it was agreed I should seek with Lord
previous to my departure. He held the same explicit language that he had used to your brother, declared that he should not put up anybody himself and would give me no impediment; adding that he had no doubt I should succeed, if I did not mind creating so many troublesome neighbours. I am however more fortified by the deep clays and ruts than his lordship; and if it should come to that, I am not so tied down but I should always have my remedy. Accordingly as I passed through Aylesbury finding Chaplain in all the rest of the secret, I told him this remaining part, and how he was to proceed in case of a vacancy. I called on Sir William Lee as I went on, who, to my surprise, remindedSCEOPE BEENARD'S EMOLUMENTS 106
me that I was to have written to him when I was last in Ireland, bnt I had forgot it; and asked me whether he might expect an occasional letter from me this time; which pleasure I certainly shall not deny him; and Lord Harcourt's picture at the Mansion House suggested itself to me yesterday as a topic for opening the correspondence.

Something passed in a conversation when your brother was with you at Whitehall at which I was hurt, and which I think it necessary for my credit that I should explain. When you were talking of the Lord Lieutenant's emoluments commencing, in the present instance, from the day of his declaration in Council, you added that, what was a better thing, his private secretary's emoluments also commenced from the same date. Now as my present emoluments (those of Usher of the Black Eod) are a sessional grant, I thought you could mean nothing else by that expression but the emoluments of private secretary, which I declared from the first moment of my being appointed Black Eod I would not accept; and it would be highly to my discredit if, with an office of that degree of profit, I could have thought of taking any salary as private secretary, which, being an allowance out of the pocket of the Lord Lieutenant, could not with any propriety be taken where there is such ample compensation from another office. I did not make this observation at that moment, lest your brother should have thought me ostentatious of what was no matter of ostentation. But I own I was uneasy, lest by what you said at the time, that I was the only officer whose profits were not affected by the early commencement of Lord Buckingham's government, you should have thought me a pluralist in so improper an instance; though perhaps in some instances, where the public were sure to be at the expence whether I accepted it or not, I may have shown myself not averse to pluralities.

I must conclude this letter here. I have so full a confidence that none of these letters, particularly to friends of Government, are pried into at the Post Office, that I have written without reserve on all subjects; and beg a hint if you think I do wrong in using this freedom. I little thought that it would ever fall to my lot to have the honour of franking a letter to you, but it is an instance of what odd things happen. If you would prefer to have my letters sent under cover to Anderson, I will beg an intimation to that effect. The objection would be the delay in the receipt of my communications, particularly if he should be out of the way, or accidentally in the country. but of that you will be to judge.

Long as this letter is, the writer added a lengthy postscript:

I was delighted to find by one of your letters that you intended paying some attention to Lyttelton. I have taken the greatest pains on that subject, and have been continually afraid lest he should be lost for want of common attention. He is very many degrees above his father in point of political weight, character, and abilities. If there were nothing else in his favour but his name of Lyttelton, I should be sorry not to see it reunited to those of Pitt and Grenville in political life; but when, in addition to this circumstance, he is a young man of uncommon value, I should have been grieved to have seen him enlisted under any other banners. I meant before I left town to have told you where he lived, and to have requested you to call upon him, but it escaped me. He is very shy, and feels any inattention shown to his father as much as if it was to himself. Upon my making an appointment, at Lord Wescote's desire, for his lordship to call on Lord Buckingham the Friday before he left town, Lord Buckingham would hardly at first consent to receive him, but did at last; and I understand expressions of civility passed between them. You however will have ample opportunities of placing all this on a better footing in the course of the winter. In case Mrs. C. Macartney dies, which is daily expected, Lyttelton will come to Ireland to settle his affairs; and in that case I shall see him often at the Castle, and have opportunities of putting him in Lord Buckingham's way. In such a situation I think nothing could prevent him from becoming intimate with, and attached to your brother.

In my letters (in case you approve of my writing on at this rate) you will find many expressions of self-importance, which arise out of the nature of the subject, and which I must beg you to excuse, whenever they occur. I stated your wishes for William Bisset, when the list of chaplains was made out, and he is appointed 7th Chaplain.

Apparently Mr. Grenville approved of Scrope's communications, for the letters are continued, although they were not so diffuse as the first, or are perhaps curtailed by the transcriber. On January 17 Mr. Bernard wrote:

After having gone through my duty in the House of Lords today, I attended the debates of the House of Commons. Your brother has written to you, and will have informed you of Mr. THE DUKE OF RUTLAND'S ADMINISTRATION 107 Parsons' motion respecting the Duke of Rutland's administration, which missed fire. Indeed the feelings of the House were strongly against him, and seemed to join in the sentiment of *de, mortuis nil nisi bonum.* The Attorney-General, in answering Parsons, asked him whether he would persist in putting *his absurdities* to the vote. After the House adjourned, Parsons went off in a great hurry, and it was said that he meant to challenge Fitzgibbon, and that they would fight before morning. But I take this to be mere talk, and that it could not be meant seriously even by those who suggested it. Nothing has been said of it since. Lord Delvin spoke very well, was very collected, clear, and distinct. Packen- ham, who seconded, spoke but one short sentence to your brother's disappointment, who expected him to discuss foreign politics and abuse the French. I have not time to state further particulars, and therefore conclude.

On February 14, Mr. Bernard writes, 1 as before from ' Dublin Castle':

Grattan's long expected motion respecting a commutation for tythes comes on this evening in the House of Commons, when there is expected to be a late sitting. If I get home time enough, before the post goes out, I will let you know the issue of the debate; and the numbers, if there should be any division.

The rest of the letter is occupied, for the most part, with strictures on a Mr. Young, who was ' at times, in my own confession, very entertaining,' and therefore generally liked; but presumptuous in his familiar mode of designating persons of rank and importance, and his habit of glorifying his own family and himself. Of this habit Scrope says:

It sometimes makes my blood boil to hear the pitch of extravagance and absurdity to which he carries this kind of conversation. My emotions, however, on the occasion proceed from a cause peculiar to myself. I was not aware that I should have been put to this scene of trial. It has left me in a feverish state of mind, which two days since has hardly diminished. It will, however, pass off in a short time, I trust. It is hardly fair to trouble you with all this, but it is a relief to me, and you will excuse me.

This over-sensitiveness seems to point to some personal1 *The Manuscripts of J. B. Fortescue,.* fc'sj., vol. L, p. 303.

reason for dislike, but no hint of such is given; and it may have been only the effect of political agitation and anxious work upon a nervous temperament.

The next day Mr. Bernard writes *I* to correct a mistake he had made in the numbers of a division, notes some parliamentary facts, and continues:

I have settled the point of attendance with the Lord Chancellor, who says I may as well humour Sir H. Cavendish by attending the delivery of all money bills, but I need attend on no other occasion. Some of the members told me that, if what Sir H. Cavendish said had appeared to make the smallest impression on the House, they would have risen to say a word on my part; but as it passed off without further observation, they thought it wiser to let it drop.

Grattan's motion about tithes did not come on till February 24; on this occasion he made ' a wonderfully able and animated speech, which lasted three hours.' The Attorney-General and Mr. Parsons opposed, Curran supported the measure, which was lost by a large majority. This letter concludes with: ' Sir H. Cavendish, very ill-naturedly, took notice of my not coming up with the Bills from the House of Lords, which has always latterly been done by the deputy usher. Not a person followed him in the observation.'

On February 29, Mr. Bernard wrote 2 an account of ' Mr. Forbes's motion for limiting the amount of pensions' and 'his second motion for an address to his Majesty on the subject of pensions,' both of which were lost, in spite of Curran's eloquence. After some notice of the discussions, Scrope continues:

You see we keep up somewhat above the proportion I mentioned of 5 to 2. There have been some curious debates about lowering the interest of money, in which Government were neuter, though brought forward by Sir John Parnell. Neutrality on any question produces relaxation of discipline, and Mr. Fitz Herbert is a little too much inclined to slacken the reins, but all the restTHE MASTER OF THE BOLLS IN IBELAND 109

1*The Manuscripts of J. IS. Fortescue, Esq.,*vol. i., pp. 308, 304.1*Ibid.,*vol. i., pp. 306, 307.

of us are so much for a tight hand, that I trust we shall open and go through with the next campaign very well in that respect. There is no other question of any consequence in this. The last messenger went off before I was aware of it, else I should have sent your seal.

There are no letters by Scrope Bernard in the Fortescue Collection for some weeks after the one just quoted. In the interim occurred a negotiation for obtaining William Grenville's appointment as Master of the Bolls in Ireland. The subject bears on this volume by reason of the great friendship between Mr. Grenville and Mr. Bernard; and the slur which in some persons' estimation this negotiation threw upon Mr. Grenville's reputation. Mr. Lecky writes/on this subject:

I have mentioned the anxiety of all parties in Ireland to bring back to the country the great offices which were held by absentees. Eutland, shortly before his death, had tried to induce Pitt to make an arrangement for the restoration of the Vice Treasurers to Ireland. It would, he said, be ' an object of great utility to his Majesty's Irish Government, both as a measure calculated to fasten on popularity, and at the same time as uniting the more solid advantage of crediting new objects for ambition of the first men and the most extensive connections in this country.' Pitt was unable or unwilling to consent, but shortly after the appointment of Buckingham, the death of Eigby made it possible to bring back the important office of Master of the Bolls. The office, however, was coveted by William Grenville, the brother of the Lord Lieutenant, who was now President of the Board of Trade in England. His letters on the subject are curious, and far from edifying. He found that part of the revenue which Bigby had received was derived from an illegal sale of places. He doubted whether the office could be legally granted for life, and whether the performance of certain duties might not be required, and for these and some other reasons he at last determined to relinquish it to the Duke of Leinster, but asked and obtained for himself the best Irish reversion – that of the office of Chief Eemembrancer, which was held by Lord Glanbrassil. An appointment so flagrantly improper completely discredited Buckinghamat the outset of his administration, and it was well fitted to exasperate equally both the most selfish and the most disinterested of Irish politicians. The unpopularity of the Lord Lieutenant was, however, chiefly personal, and confined to a small court or political circle. The country continued perfectly quiet.

1Lecky,*History of Inland in the Eighteenth Century*(Edition 1892), vol. ii., chap. v. p. 464.

And the historian enumerates several signs of contentment and prosperity. But the letters of William Grenville undoubtedly afford a sad instance of a frank and generous nature warped by the exigencies of a political career. In his mind at this time the idea of office appears to be wholly unconnected with any recognition of consequent duties. Even more might "indeed be said. The compiler of the 'Memoirs,' however, sees nothing amiss in the incessant schemes of promotion which formed a great part of the correspondence between the Marquess and William Grenville. He says of Mr. Grenville:*l*' The letter in which he unfolds all these plans to his brother is affecting in its appeal to those feelings of implicit trust and attachment which existed so warmly between these distinguished men.'

It must also be admitted that Scrope Bernard showed no dislike to these manoeuvres; he was perhaps not in a position to do so, and his warm attachment to William Grenville led him to rejoice in anything that rejoiced his friend. But he does not appear to have been mixed up in any intrigues. His next letter – or the next in the collection – is dated from the house in the Phoenix Park, indicating that his wife had joined him in the interim.

On May 19, he dates a letter 2 from ' Phoenix Park':

I do not know whether you will have taken any notice of my silence for this last month or two; or, if you have, whether you will have put any unfavourable construction upon it; but it has been owing to my expectation, for many weeks past, of coming over to England, and consequently having reserved my observations on what was going on here to the time of seeing you. As it would be a convenience to me to spend a few weeks in Buckinghamshire, I had proposed to your brother to be there whjle the militia wereIRISH AFFAIRS 111

1*Memoir* * of the Court and Cabinets of George III.,* vol. i.
2*The Manuseripts of J. B. Forteacue, Esq.,* vol. i., p. 829.

out, which he had intended should be in the month of May, and as there is little necessary business here in my line at present, he had not disapproved of my plan. From some omission, however, in forms and notices, the militia cannot now be out till the autumn; and while this point has been under consideration, I have remained in uncertainty respecting the time of my coming over. I still think of crossing the water soon, though without the pretext above mentioned; but not being now tied to any particular time, I may be led to continue here longer than I imagine; and, accordingly break the interval by writing a few lines to say, that though so long silent, I am still in the land of the living, and that in a little time you may see me, or perhaps may not see me, for having fixed no day it does not become me to speak very positively.

The matter of the Rolls has remained so much in uncertainty, that I did not follow up my short congratulations with others more diffuse, and suited to the occasion and my feelings upon it, as had been my intention. From what, however, Lord Buckingham has hinted to me, I shall soon have matter of ample and more permanent congratulation to you in this kingdom; and in the course of time, be able to wish you joy of the improvement of your situation on your side of the water.

Mr. Fitz Herbert, who left us about a fortnight ago, will have informed you of the state of things here. We are very quiet, but are told by all the little men that the great men hate us, and are threatened with much opposition next winter; which we shall have, but it cannot be to a degree which will be material, or which has not been foreseen from the first. The leading Government men are, I am told, offended with his Excellency for not forming personal intimacies with them; but, on the other hand this circumstance pleases the jealous feelings of those who are in opposition, or in a state of indecision between both; at the same time that it accords with his own inclination and judgement. Mr. Longfield who has persisted in supporting us, though your brother would give him no encouragement, has shown us a proof of his kind dispositions by producing your silver box with the freedom of Cork, which had been so long missing; a circumstance which may have appeared to you rather suspicious; but, when I tell you the reasons, you must own yourself not only satisfied, but very much flattered, for he said that *you was so little in Dublin when Secretary, that they had not a proper opportunity of presenting it; and, since that time, they have not known where to send it to you.* I have had it many weeks in my possession, and shall not fail to bring it with me to England, as I know it will be a valuable acquisition to your shaving apparatus.

Lord Nugent arrived here in good health on Friday last, and rather opportunely for the family in one respect, it having been somewhat melancholy since Tompkins's death, which your brother and Lady Buckingham took much to heart. They have of late been a good deal out on parties, and, by way of a little change, they purpose living for the next month or two at a house belonging to Mr. Lees at the Black Rock, which they have taken for that purpose; where they will have the advantage of being near Lord Nugent's house called Glare Hall, which he built about twenty years ago; and at which he will now reside. Lady Buckingham has had a swelled face for a day or two past, and your little niece is just recovering from the smallpox. In other respects the family are all very well.

In this case of the young Lady Mary, the smallpox must be understood to be the kind produced by inoculation, then the best known means of minimising the risks of that scourge. To which of many political mysteries the Marquess alludes in a letter of the following day, May 20, I cannot say. He writes 1:

I had talked with Bernard upon a certain speculation long before it was even probable, so that I am sure that the very little which I have been able to say to him has given him certain suspicions. He will, however, be in London for a month, in about ten days, having made up his mind to attend our militia meeting which we expected in June.

Mr. Bernard's departure for England must have taken place about the time specified; I bave no particulars of the event, but it must have been on this occasion that his wife also left Ireland. Her sojourn there must have been in some respects a pleasant time, from the varied society, the occasional festivities, and the constant kindness of the Lord Lieutenant and the Marchioness, who was a lady of a bright and lively disposition. Among the guests at the Castle, as I have been told, was Lord Mornington's brother, Arthur Wesley – so the name was then written – and Lady BuckingTHE TRIAL OF WARREN HASTINGS 113

1 *The Manuscripts of J. B. Fortescue, Esq.,* vol. i., p. 330.

ham is said on one occasion, when he was late for breakfast, to have gone with the ladies then staying with her to call him. This is not unlikely, as such practical jokes were at that time not uncommon. 1It is, however, quite likely that considerations of health induced Mrs. Bernard to give up the comparatively brilliant life of the Viceregal court for a quiet sojourn amongst her friends in England.

A question arose about a picture which Scrope Bernard had ordered to be sent to "Winchendon from Dublin. The agents at Chester sent to know if the picture was by an Irish or English artist; if by the former, it was liable to duty. The sequel does not appear; but there is very little doubt that the portrait is of Scrope in his picturesque dress as Usher of the Black Kod – a full length portrait in pastel or crayon, though much smaller than life-size, and it may be assumed that it is by an Irish artist.

The first intimation of Scrope Bernard's presence in London I have found in a letter dated ' Bolton Street, June 10, 1788'; it is on the subject of the trial of Warren Hastings, late Governor-General of India, ' for high crimes and misdemeanours' alleged to have been committed by him in that capacity. The trial had begun on February 13, and had been brilliantly opened by Sheridan's speech for the prosecution. This effort had perhaps exhausted the orator for a time, since the third day does not appear to have been remarkable. The compiler of the ' Buckingham Memoirs' 2remarks on Mr. Bernard's letter, that ' the point, naturally enough, which made the deepest impression on him was the exhibition in evidence of the private letters that passed between Mr. Hastings and his Secretary.' He writes to Lord Buckingham:

My Lord, – I have been this morning at the trial; it was Sheridan's third day. It was near one o'clock before he began. There was nothing very striking or brilliant in his oratory; he continued for about an hour and a quarter, and then retired. Mr.

1This story I heard from my stepmother; it was probably transmitted to her through some Buckinghamshire relative.

'*Memoirs of the Court and Cabinets of George III.*

VOL. III. I

Adam assisted him in the reading parts, and continued reading after he retired. Presently he made a lame apology for him, saying that

he had a very trifling without specifying what, whether illness,

agitation, or want of due preparation. Mr. Fox soon afterwards made a more complete apology for him, and the Court adjourned; but till what time I have not heard.

I was gratified with the sight as an object of curiosity, but not as affording either pleasure or entertainment. It would seem preposterous to me, if, upon any charge against the Government of Ireland, the Lord Lieutenant's, or his secretary's*private*and*separate*letters were to be subjected in a Court of Justice to the acrimonious, malevolent and palpably strained comments that forty of the ablest men of an opposite party could put upon them, particularly without having an equal number of persons of a similar description in point of talents and political weight to defend them. And yet this seems to be the case in the instance of the present tribunal; for the letters read and commented upon to-day were chiefly of the above description: the letters absolutely official were very little dwelt upon.

Your Excellency's most faithful and affectionate servant,

S. Bernabd.

Possibly Mr. Bernard's criticism was hypercritical, as regarded Sheridan's management of the case. Lord Bulkeley wrote to the Lord Lieutenant on the 14th,1' Sheridan finished his summing-up yesterday on the Begum charge, and has certainly throughout displayed the greatest and most artful abilities.' Whether Scrope had any further opportunity of attending the trial I do not know; but it ifa not improbable, since it lasted till April 23, 1795.2

Apparently Mr. Bernard left London very early in July, for Mr. Grenville, dating from 'Whitehall, July 1,' says to his brother: 3 ' I shall write to you again to-morrow and it is not impossible that you may receive that letter before this, as I think I shall avail myself of Bernard's offer to be the carrier of it' – a sentence which implies that the private traveller could reach Ireland more quickly than the mail. On July 5, the Marquess writes from Black Rock:4

1*Memoirs of t)1e Court and Cabinets of George III.,*vol. i. 2 Haydn,*Dictionary of Dates,'*Hastings' Trial.13*Memoirs of the Court and Cabinets of George III.,*vol. i.1*The Manuscripts of J. B. Fortescue, Esq.,*vol. i., p. 342.1*Memoirs of the Court and Cabinets of George III.,*vol. i.

LORD BUCKINGHAM AND THE KING 115

I have only time to say, in three words, that I received yesterday yours of the 1st, referring me to another which I was to have through the hands of Bernard. The mail of the 2nd is just come in and brings no letter from you, but as no mail leaves Dublin tomorrow, I was unwilling to leave you unanswered for three days, though I can say nothing decisive, till I see the sort of solution which you propose.

The Marquess was at this time in a restless, irritable state, probably intensified by the dangerous illness of his only son, which, however, ended in a complete recovery. But his mind was especially disturbed by an insult which he considered that he had received from George III.:1

The King's personal interference in appointments and promotions had produced, on several occasions, remonstrances and complaints from Lord Buckingham, and the judicious zeal of Mr. Grenville was in constant requisition to prevent an open rupture between the Lord Lieutenant and the Government. Calm and enduring as he was, Mr. Grenville frankly stated to his brother that, although he could never tire of the employment of serving him, his patience was almost exhausted by finding that one case was no sooner settled or compromised (for it generally ended in that way) than a fresh one came upon the *tapis.*At length the tenacity of the King on these points wounded Lord Buckingham so keenly, that it very nearly led to the most serious consequences. Lord Buckingham wished to appoint his nephew, Colonel Nugent, to a vacant lieutenant-colonelcy within his own patronage, and through some friendly channel notified or expressed his desire to do so; but the King without communicating his intentions or waiting to go through the ordinary official forms, which usually founded such appointments on the recommendation of the Lord Lieutenant, appointed another person to the vacancy – Colonel Gwynne. Lord Buckingham felt the slight so acutely that he threatened to resign.

From this step he was strongly dissuaded by his brother and also by Mr. Pitt; and the affair, like others, ended in a compromise; but it rankled in the Lord Lieutenant's mind, although thrown into comparative oblivion before the end of the same year, by the King's terrible illness, which had been coming on apparently for weeks before it was definitelyannounced. This calamity, which dismayed the British Islands, was in some respects most acutely felt by loyalists in Ireland on account of the complications brought about by its possession of a Parliament distinct from England and Scotland, and of various Acts differentiating it from the other two countries. The chronic irritations of Ireland, and the critical state of foreign affairs which might not improbably lead to an attempt at enlisting Ireland against England rendered the situation of Lord Lieutenant unusually arduous. The Marquess also had domestic anxieties – his father-in-law, Lord Nugent, died that autumn, and left, of course, succession business to be gone through; and the expectation of a third child troubled the Marquess, who was doubtful whether it would be best for his wife to go to England for the birth, in which case he would accompany her, or to remain in Ireland. The latter opinion prevailed,1and her son George was born in Ireland on the 31st of the following December.2

Under these circumstances Scrope Bernard probably had a troublesome time as the Marquess's secretary, but there is hardly any notice to be found of the work achieved. On October 18, Lord Buckingham writes to William Gren- ville:

As to my own affairs, on which head you complain so much of my neglect, I do not really recollect any point which I had left unanswered, either through my letters or through Bernard, except that of my bond to you for the l000i. advanced to Tom.

Mr. Thomas Grenville was the second brother of the family – between the Marquess and William; he had often differed in opinion with them both, especially with the Marquess, whose views he withstood not unfrequently when they did not coincide with his own.

It would seem that Scrope Bernard had been sent to London on the Lord Lieutenant's business that autumn, sinceLOED BUCKINGHAM'S NAVY ACCOUNTS 117

1The Lord Lieutenant states, in his letter of December 1, that his wife had declared to remain in Ireland.

*Debrett, Burke, and other*Peerages*.

the great man writes1to William Grenville, under date ' December 1, Dublin Castle':

Bernard has heard from me on the subject of my navy accounts, which hang heavy on my mind; and on the subject of a purchase which I am negotiating for W. Fremantle.

Close on that letter, which is twice adorned with cipher figures, like other letters written during this crisis, follows another, which states that:

Bernard wrote me the enclosed letter, very unexpectedly, by which I see that he is probably at Holyhead. I shall write to him by this messenger to re-dispatch him to London, for he may be of great use to me by writing, when you are too much engaged in the House for that purpose; and you must be sensible that every communication must be most interesting. I enclose his letter that you may see how cruelly I have been used by Eose's carelessness on the subject of my navy accounts.2

And then follow some lines of lamentation and exhortation to exertion.

It seems, indeed, that Mr. Bernard went on to Dublin, which apparently the Lord Lieutenant did not expect; but perhaps he had almost been persuaded that his Secretary would be best by his side, since he writes to his brother on December 13:

Your letter of the 9th was put into my hands an hour after Bernard left me. I wished very much to have kept him, partly indeed because I may want him for the same reasons as those which induce you to wish him in England; but I feel that he can be so much more useful with you that I have acquiesced. He will state to you a great deal of general observation which I have detailed to him upon my situation, and the state of this kingdom, and much of what I have entrusted to him is an answer to your proposition in your last letter. It is fitting upon every consideration, that you should know that I cannot think of making myself responsible in the slightest degree, for any one thing which the Parliament of this kingdom may do if I should meet them*after my friends are dismissed in England.*

1*The Manuscripts of J. B. Fortescue, Esq.*(Letter of December 1, 1788), p. 377.

Ibid.(Letter of December 2,1788), p. 379.

Towards the end of this letter, which is a long one, the writer adds, after expounding his views as to restrictions in case of a Eegency:

On this point I have explained myself with Bernard, and must refer you to him, and he will tell you why I am so little sanguine in my expectations from the virtue of our Parliament. I must again repeat that Pitt or Fox are equally uninteresting, and that no testimony will be given by them except to the Minister actually in office.

On the 18th the Marquess writes again*l:*

Your letters of Sunday and Monday have arrived this morning by the same mail; the north wind having detained them at Holyhead, while the north-east winds kept Bernard in Dublin exactly a week beyond the time which was fixed for his departure. I mention this, as I would wish you to believe that I would not have detained him where he can be of so little use compared to the services which you can entrust to him in England. His mystery was a desire to save a year's absentee tax and to avoid his wife's lying-in; and for these ridiculous reasons he had left London, proposing not to return.

The absentee tax was certainly a serious matter to a man of small income, which, perhaps, the Marquess did not realise. The second reason could hardly have approved itself to him, seeing that he had determined to remain with his own wife even if he had to cross the channel on purpose. However, Mr. Bernard was at last compelled to encounter another comfortless journey by sea and land, in a very bad season; only a few days before, Lady Fortescue, the Lord Lieutenant's sister, and her husband, had been compelled to put back to Kingstown, after an eight hours' attempt to cross, and to wait for a favourable opportunity. I have, indeed, no records in letters of this stay in England; but only the negative evidence of no Dublin letters being quoted before February 1789.

His daughter Margaret was born on December 21,1788, apparently in South Park Street, because the Bolton Street house had been let.

The first letter in the Fortescue collection, of the followingIRISH POLITICS 119

1*The Manuscripts of J. B. Fortescue, Esq.,*p. 387.

year, from Scrope Bernard to William Grenville, is dated: ' 1789, February 6, Dublin Castle.' In it allusion is made to a previous letter which is not in the printed collection; neither is the whole of this letter, nor of the succeeding one. The extracts given, are here quoted: 1

I was obliged to close my letter of yesterday before I had finished what I had to say, else I meant to have added that, notwithstanding the appearance of temper and coolness in the Houses yesterday, the opposite party seemed very confident of their strength and sanguine in their expectations of success. My hopes are that the first question or two may be such as to induce some of the great interests to divide with us; and a division or two in our favour in the outset would soften the effects of a contrary event upon the main question; and would deter the party from afterwards attempting any question of violence towards Lord Buckingham, which has at times been whispered. Yet after all, what I am most anxious about is, that people in England should know how it is that the same majority does not follow Lord Buckingham's government here that has followed Mr. Pitt's in England; and that this is owing to the disposition of the great men and placemen here, always to follow the English party in power, be it what it may, so as to secure to themselves the patronage of the country and a continuance in their offices. I am told, that the Speech is very generally approved of, as saying just as much as it should, and no more. Some persons thought that their particular hobby horses whatever they might be (Charter Schools, Linen Board) ought to have been mentioned, but should have known that this could not have been with propriety. It is thought that there will be long debates in both Houses to-day, and that there will be divisions in each. I own I wish there may so long as the questions are of the nature I have above alluded to. No packet is at present on this side of the water, but one may come in before evening; and in that case the Mail will go at an early hour, 7 o'clock; so that you may probably hear no account of to-day's business by this post.

The sequel of the story was told by Scrope to his friend Grenville the very next day:2

The hopes which I expressed to you in my letter of yesterday of a preliminary division in our favour are, by the event of lastnight, entirely vanished; as, on a question respecting the day of taking the physicians' reports into consideration, we were beat by a majority of 54, the numbers being 128 to 74. We had much the greater share of the independent members with us, and were beat solely by the combination of the Shannon, Ponsonby, Loftus, and Leinster interests against us, which interests are guided by the Prince's party in England. I wish this matter may be fairly represented on your side of the water, and may not reflect any discredit on your brother's conduct in the eyes of people there. Some people spoke with great violence, particularly Sir J. Blaquiere, who delivered a studied invective with the greatest possible bitterness, being incensed by pique and disappointment. But he was very well answered by many of your brother's friends, particularly Toler, Fitz-Gibbon, Parnell, Coote, Hewitt, and Mark Beresford, as you will see in the 'Freeman's Journal.' The Addresses came up to-day; a respectable but not a very full attendance. Our situation begins to grow very unpleasant, but we consider ourselves as suffering for the common cause.

1 *The Manuscripts of J. B. Foriescue, Esq.,* p. 408.

*' 1789, February 7, Dublin Castle.' (From the same Collection).

I am told that in the House to-day, the triumphant party would not permit any public business to be brought forward; and they talked of adjourning till Wednesday, when the Committee sit on the state of the nation.

I have been told that some people were against us on this question (being averse to delay) who will be with us on the main question of the limitations; but I do not know how to credit such language.

6

SECTION 6

RECOVERY OF THE KING 121

CHAPTER VII

ScropeBernard'sPoliticalCareer

Recovery of the King – Scrope Bernard's Election as Member for Aylesbury – Friction between the Marquess of Buckingham and the King – The Thanksgiving for the King's Recovery – Scrope' Bernard appointed Under-Seoretary of State for the Home Department – The Marquess of Buckingham resigns the Viceroyalty – Election Riots at Aylesbury – Scrope Bernard's Degree of Doctor of Civil Law – British Slaves in Algeria – The Family Name of the Duke of Wellington – Colonial Questions of the Day – Ministerial Changes.

Thecountry was now more pleasantly excited by the gradual recovery of the King, of which the Lord Chancellor's visits to Kew, mentioned in the last quoted letter of Mr. Grenville, were a consequence. It came opportunely to the rescue of the Lord Lieutenant, as will appear by Scrope Bernard's description of the situation in a letter' to William Grenville. The same letter contains his simple and natural account of his own sensations during a time of suspense. It is dated February 21, 1789:

I scarce ever spent a day that was so uncomfortable in the preceding part of it, and so pleasurable in the close of it as yesterday. My anxiety on the subject of the Aylesbury election was at its height, and added to late sittings up for some nights past either at the House of Commons or writing despatches, had produced the most unpleasant effect upon my nerves, which was not mitigated by the croakings of everybody about me respecting the consequences to be expected in the two Houses that evening, from Lord Buckingham's having refused to transmit their Address.

This Address requested the Prince of Wales whose ' virtues' it stated ' have been so matured as to enable' his * Eoyal Highness to discharge the duties of an important trust,' to take upon him ' the government of this realm. underthe style and title of Prince Regent of Ireland,' during the continuance of the King's illness. The Lord Lieutenant explained to Lord Sydney, Home Secretary, the reasons of his conduct.1' I bless God,' writes Mr. Grenville, to his brother, ' it is yet some time before these*matured and ripened virtues*will be visited upon us in the form of a Government.' Such an event seemed, however, but too probable at one moment. Mr. Bernard continues, referring to the Marquess's refusal:

1*The Manuscripts of J. B. Fortescue, Esq.,*vol. i., p. 416.

No one of his Cabinet here would have thought of suggesting to him that step; and of those to whom he mentioned it, only the Chancellor and the Attorney-General were hearty in it. And when he talked of it to me, I was only restrained from murmuring at it by knowing that it was an object to English party, and that you had advised and pressed it. When Lord Buckingham delivered his answer on Thursday last, great chagrin manifested itself on the countenances of those who had acted with Mr. Grattan; and if a succession of English news respecting the King had not damped their spirits, I believe this chagrin would have shown itself in the most unpleasant and violent manner. Your brother delivered his answer with dignity, and great appearance of temper, and will have acquired immortal honour by his firmness throughout this business, in which he has met with every discouragement from people here, and has I believe only been supported by the decided opinion contained in your letter; excepting indeed that the Attorney-General has on this, as on every other occasion, stood by him in a very decided and honourable manner. The good news, however, which arrived from England, and the dislike which the House seem to have to any personal attack upon him, prevented their going the lengths that were talked of last night. And as on every question which they tried they lost ground in proportion as it was directed more against him, I should think that they would venture to go no further, and would not take up the subject of your reversion, and that of the arrangements hi the revenue, which Grattan had shown an intention of bringing forward, by moving for papers respecting them. The same ground will be gone over in the Lords, but I apprehend they will be very tame upon it, and the Archbishop of Cashell and others mean to shirk it.

Thus all their threats came to little or nothing. And as for their resolutions, though the last is strongly worded, nobodySCROPB BERNARD ENTERS PARLIAMENT 123

1*Memoirs of tin- Court and Cabinets of GeOrge III.,*vol. ii.

regards it, or lays any stress upon it; and, as a consolation, it has been a means (with the help of the good news) of making a difference in the divisions of above 20 members. In addition to my satisfaction on this head, I had the pleasure in the evening to receive your letter, with one from Aylesbury, announcing the favourable event of that election, with which I am extremely gratified. Lord Buckingham says that my setting off immediately is out of the question, I must therefore defer it for a week or two. I think however that I ought to behave in the handsomest manner, both in regard to personal attendance and expense to the Borough as well with a view to my next election, as for the general benefit of the party in that quarter.

A fortnight had just elapsed from the date of the preceding letter, when, on March 9, the Marquess of Buckingham wrote1to his brother:

Bernard will leave me on Tuesday next, and by him you will be more informed of my ideas and wishes than you can from volumes of correspondence.

And three days later Mr. Bernard himself wrote2 to Mr. Grenville:

1789 March 12 Dublin Castle.

Though I have not written to you myself for some time, you have seen such frequent accounts in my handwriting of what is going on here, that I have thought it unnecessary to intrude upon you with letters from myself particularly as nothing occurred to me to mention beyond what either your brother's letters or the newspapers would detail to you. We all remain in good spirits, being confident that our adversaries can do us no mischief; for although we may be beat in the House of Commons on most popular questions, yet we feel strong enough there to carry through any material business, and prevent personal attacks, as we showed you on the night on which Mr. Grattan moved his resolution against your reversion.

Besides the Pension Bill, there remains another question,*videlicet,*the Repeal of the Police, upon which we are likely to be beat in the House of Commons. But one half of the Opposition would not vote as they do on these measures if they were not sure that they would be thrown out in the House of Lords, in whichHouse we shall have a majority of about ten or a dozen, and perhaps more, if the Irish Ambassadors do not bring over some fresh proxies with them from England, for which I hear they have been canvassing, though I am not aware of any Peers that have taken their seats, who have not already been applied to, by one party or the other.

1*The Manuscripts of J. B. Farteseue, Etq.,*vol. i., p. 427. **Ibid.,*Tol. i., p. 432.

William Fremantle returned about ten days ago, and I should have set off before this, but I could not be spared immediately; and I have had a good many concerns of my own to attend to previous to my taking leave of this country, to which it is probable I may not return again. I have fixed to sail next week, probably on Wednesday the 18th and shall come to town immediately to take my seat, and then go down to pay my compliments to my electors.

*The Morning Herald*says*that the Castle is surrounded 1vith guards to protect the Marquis from the fury of the populace.*

There are no other guards than the usual sentries, and your brother drives out in his coach continually without any other attendants than an aide-du-camp and two footmen.

*The Public Advertiser*says that he shuts himself up from the world. The fact is that he sees all sorts of people from eleven o'clock till five every day; and has either had company to dinner, or dined out, almost every day for some day[s] past.

When Scrope Bernard penned this letter, expressing his belief that he should never revisit Ireland, he must have been aware that the Marquess was not likely to remain

Lord Lieutenant for many months. The King's recovery, however favourable to the prospects of the party, had one serious disadvantage; it revived the friction on the subject of appointments, especially in the Nugent case. Lord Buckingham became chronically irate with George III., and ere long with Lord Sydney as the King's agent. He complains, on April 3, to his brother, that Lord Sydney:*l*

is quoted for having said that the persons interested in the question of the promotions recommended me in June last might be at ease, for that*he had stopped my jobs.*This agrees with Nepean's strange speech to Bernard, recommending me to send over another list*omitting them all.*Now I have neither temper nor spirits for such a battle, and therefore I have determined never to send overTHANKSGIVING FOR THE KING'S RECOVERY 125

1*The Manuscripts of J. B. Fortescue, Esq.,*p. 442.

another list till those of May and June are returned to me, and if this is not done I shall insist on being relieved*immediately,*and shall leave to the whole world the full right of deciding on the conduct towards me from the King, and from his Lordship, and this too at the time when the whole army of Great Britain ones shame on the two most iniquitous jobs of Major Burrard and Captain Lenox; to which this of Major Taylor, junior to almost every English cavalry major, and junior to three Irish cavalry majors, is a proper counterpart, even if the name of Colonel Nugent was out of the question.

Scrope Bernard was perhaps glad to be out of all this; he certainly went to England this time in improved spirits. Even if his chief's Viceroyalty was to be cut short, with perhaps untoward results to himself, his name was now before the public as member of Parliament for Aylesbury. No doubt he accomplished all that he had intended – took his seat, and met the borough electors; but the first news I have of him relates to the Thanksgiving for the King's recovery. Lord Temple, mentioned in the letter, was the Marquess's eldest son, a boy of twelve, who must have accompanied the Marchioness to England some time before.1

London, April 23rd 1789, Two o'clock, P. m.

My Lord, – The ceremony of this day has been gone through exceedingly well. The procession from the House of Commons began at eight o'clock, and the King reached St. Paul's between eleven and twelve. The arrangement of the cathedral, particularly the dome, presented a beautiful sight. The King seems much reduced by his late illness – was remarkably composed during the service, and attentive to the music. His Majesty, as well as the Queen, seemed much affected with the solemnity of their first entrance, as were many of the persons present. Lady Uxbridge was near fainting away.

As the King went out of the church, he seemed to be in good spirits, and talked much to the persons about him; but he stared and laughed less than ever I knew him on a public occasion. He returned to the Queen's House between three and four o'clock. Mr. Fox and most of his party were there. He and Colonel Fitzpatrick were stationed in front of the altar, and directly opposite the King being the part of the cathedral for PrivyCouncillors and Peers' sons. Mr. Pitt sat near them, but not in the first ranks. I saw Lord Temple in a very good place, in that part of the church. I did not see Mr. Burke there, and therefore suppose he continues ill. The trial was deferred yesterday on account of his illness, which people say was occasioned by his working himself into too great a passion the day before. I have the honour to be ever, my Lord,

1*Memoirs of the Court and Cabinets of George III.,*vol. ii.

Your Excellency's most faithful and affectionate servant,

S. Bernard.

' The trial' in this letter means, of course, the protracted ordeal through which Warren Hastings had to pass. It was then only in its second year.

In the ensuing month of May, William Grenville was appointed Secretary of State for the Home Department. True to his early friendship, he offered Scrope Bernard the post of Under-Secretary of State. It was accepted, but, as will be seen, rather as a matter of necessity than of satisfaction; and what is more singular, Scrope's father-in-law, Mr. Morland, seems also to have disliked the prospect. The following letter endeavours to make the transaction clear, by smoothing some complications which had evidently resulted from the delivery of a former letter by a servant.

Fludyer Street. Sunday Evening 7th Jane.1

My dear Sir, – I find that Mrs. M. and you have been so good as to call on me this morning, and am sorry I was not at home, particularly as I wished to say a word to you in consequence of yours of Friday, which was perfectly intelligible, but it seems by the purport of it, that I am the person, who have written unintelligibly.

I meant to explain to you that, in order to set myself right with the world after my late expenses and enable Harriet and myself to settle quietly on this side of the water, I intended taking a permanent office here, superior in emolument, but less pleasant in point of labour and confinement in London, in lieu of the temporary office held in Ireland on much easier and more comfortable terms.

In doing this I thought I consulted the interests of one part

1MS. Letter at Nether Winohendon.

SCEOPE BERNARD'S NEW OFFICE 127

of the family, and the wishes of another part, more than my own personal gratification. But you tell me on this occasion that it will be consulting my own comfort to take the office in London – I can only say that I had originally determined never to take an office, which would confine me so much to London as the Under, Secretaryship of State. And when it was once before proposed as an arrangement for me (before those reasons operated which have occasioned my present determination) I said that I did not wish it for the reason I have mentioned – a reason which now gives way to the considerations above alluded to, as, however little I might like the office, I should not get one of equal emolument and advantage if this opportunity was suffered to pass by.

I thought these circumstances so obvious, and so decisive, that I wrote rather to communicate my intention, than to consult upon it, and, before I got your letter, I had accepted – If, however, you really are perfectly indifferent on the subject, and Harriet can be prevailed on to be the same, it will make a material change in my sentiments and conduct.

I should have waited on you to dinner agreeably to your obliging invitation; but, exclusive of other business, that of Mr. Grenville's re-election detains me at home. In the meantime I wished not to delay making myself understood as I seem not to have done it before. Or perhaps, from the hurry you mention yourself to have been in at that moment, it might happen that the interruption of intermediate business prevented your perfect recollecting the letter at the time you wrote the answer. – Mark had no instructions to wait for an answer, and there was no occasion for his pressing you to write one at such a moment. I am, my dear Sir, very faithfully,

and affectly yours

S. Bkknaed.

Love and remembrances

to William and the ladies.

' William' was no doubt the son of Scrope and Harriet Bernard, who seems from an early age to have been almost appropriated by his grandparents. This letter reveals the fact that the period of attendance on the Viceregal Court and the missions undertaken on its behalf, had not proved a financial success, and it must be supposed that Mr. Morland admitted the force of his son-in-law's reasoning, since Scrope Bernard entered upon the duties of his office. Possibly his father-in-law had not realised how near the Marquess of Buckingham's Viceroyalty was to its end.1The Lord Lieutenant, who had become really ill from the vexations of his exalted position, spent the summer in England by the King's permission; and, after being enabled to make an elaborate settlement of claims advanced by his friends and followers to peerages, posts, and pensions – with which he was fairly well satisfied – he resigned the Vice- royalty towards the end of the year.

While Scrope Bernard had been making up his mind to accept a position for which he felt no vocation, he had been involved in some unpleasantness with respect to his other piece of promotion, the representation of Aylesbury. Within three months from the election the neighbourhood had been disturbed by lawless proceedings; the popular excitement being stimulated by the prospect of a General Election in the following year.8' On the 16th of May a large concourse of electors went to meet Colonel Lake on the Aston Clinton road,' writes Mr. Gibbs. ' On their return they came into collision with a party of Bernard's supporters, and Bernard's men are reported to have behaved very badly.' Further particulars are, however, noted in a letter3of the Rev. Joseph Smith to his brother-in-law, Scrope Bernard:

The Meeting at Aylesbury on Monday had some serious consequences. The 4 returning officers with a few friends met at Ivatts' to have their share of conviviality. A riot somehow ensued. About 148 went*en cavalier*to meet Lake and accompany him in. He was attended by Little Barker and his brother Warwick Lake, and afterward joined by Ld Geo. Cavendish, I understand that about a third of the Number were not voters. – Sellers, the Chimney Sweeper, in his full Professional Hue, mounted on a white horse – with Moll Smith behind him – graced the Colonel's Cavalcade and*Entr6[e]*.Upon the whole I know not whether the Col has not lost as much interest as he has gain'd Renown by the Event of the Day.'

1*Memoirs of the Court and Cabinets of Oeorge III.*

*Gibbs (Bobert),*History of Aylesbury,*Chapter xxv. ' Parliamentary Representation (resumed).'

* MS. Letter at Nether Winehendon.

AYLESBUEY ELECTION EIOTS 129

It must have been this demonstration which exasperated the Bernardites, and led to violence. Mr. Gibbs continues: ' So great was the disturbance that Edward Terry was called upon to read the Riot Act, and it is recorded that he got a black eye for his pains. The riot led to a prosecution.' Which prosecution, it may be briefly stated, came to nothing. The accused persons were brought before the Rev. Joseph Smith; he granted warrants against four men who had ' insulted and assaulted' the constables in the execution of their duty; but after going through certain formalities, such as appearing at Quarter Sessions, &c., they escaped scot free: even Budd, who had given the black eye, was acquitted.

The historian of the town next expatiates on the ' benevolences' – so called – which both parties dispensed to their supporters from time to time; in these practices, however, they kept within the bounds then traced by custom, and were considered blameless. The conclusion was rather tame; Mr. Wrighton, the former colleague of Sir Thomas Halifax, retired; consequently Lake and Bernard were both elected without further contest in 1790.1

On June 7 in that same year, 1790, Scrope Bernard became the father of another son, who received the ancestral name of Francis.2In connection with this event it may be noted that Lord Valentia writes, on June 25, to Mr. Bernard: ' Lady V. will wait upon Mrs. B. on Sunday morning if agreeable, to drink caudle.'3

Amongst all his calls in various directions, it would seem that Scrope clung even at this time to the idea of professional life. During his visit to England, in the autumn of 1788, he had taken the degree of Doctor of Civil Law at Oxford. Out of this occurrence a controversy arose on the question of precedence between Scrope Bernard and another Doctor, Maurice Swabey, which forms the subject of the following letters:

1The letters on this subject are all among the MSS. at Nether Win- chendon.

*Debrett, Burke, Lipacomb. * MS. Letter at Nether Winchendon.

VOL. nl, K

Oxford October 25 1789

Sir, – I have no other idea than, that as being superior in every sense in the University you must take your rank before DrSwabey and DrCoote. There is, if you recollect, no admission to Regency, and I think with you that, as you all commence Regents at the Act whether you were admitted on this or that day, procedure will not be at all affected by it. It will be however necessary that you have a certificate of the day of your admission to the Degree, which I will transmit to you if required, and in what form you please.

Sir,

Yr faithful & obed1hb>= Serv1.

S. FOKSTER.1

Dr. Swabey was apparently not disposed to let the matter drop, and Dr. Bernard gave him the following letter

for the Dean of Christ Church:

Whitehall 29th Oct 1789

Dear Sir, – I am to be admitted an advocate at Doctor's Commons on Tuesday next at the same time with DTM Swabey & Coote, and there is a doubt whether Dr Swabey or myself rank as Senior in the University, as according to such seniority will be the order of our admission on this occasion.

I am of longer standing & took my degree first, but DrSwabey was presented on the first day of October and took out his Regency in person, when I was admitted (as I am told) by a Dispensation passed after he was presented; and I did not attend myself till two days afterwards – I imagined that the admission to Regency was a matter of course, & did not affect our rank in the University. He understands that the respective rank of Doctor depends entirely on the time of their presentation to the Vice Chancellor – What therefore we wish to ascertain is which of us ranks first in the University, and in what order our names appear there as Regent Doctors of Law, if we are entered as such. And I hope you will excuse my requesting you to take the trouble of ascertaining this point with the Vice-Chancellor on my part.

We both rank before DrCoote, as being Grand Compounders. I am

Dear Sir,

Your very faithful

& obedt servt

S. Bernard.

Dr. Forster was Registrar of the University of Oxford.

A WEIGHTY CONTROVERSY 131

This letter is marked ' (Not delivered).' It was returned by Dr. Swabey in a letter dated ' Commons, 31st Octr1789,' and addressed ' Dr. Bernard,' in which he explained his reason for so doing:

Finding on my arrival yesterday in Oxford, from the information of a friend, that the question had been already put to the Vice-Chancellor, in consequence of your application to Dr Forster, in whose sentiments He had coincided, and that custom is said to have sanctioned a different opinion from that which I had been led to entertain on the subject, I did not think it necessary further to stir in a matter, I dare to say, not settled with1 sufficient consideration; and I shall be happy to acquiesce on Tuesday in your right of seniority.'

So ended this weighty controversy. The certificate transmitted to Scrope was expressed as follows:

It appears by the Register of the University of Oxford, which is in my custody, that Scrope Bernard of Christ Church was regularly admitted to the degree of Doctor in Civil Law on the twentieth Day of November, in the Year of our Lord 1788; Which said Degree of Doctor in Civil Law was not conferred on him by Grace or Favour.

SamuelForstbk,*Bea'*.

Oxford Nov. 20 1788.

Tied up with the foregoing letters is a most respectful and apologetic epistle from ' Wm. Child, Eobe-maker, (Nephew and Successor to the late Mr. Mark Child) No. 78 Corner of Bishop's Court, Chancery Lane,' requesting the honour of supplying Mr. Bernard with ' Doctor of Laws' Kobes.' It is addressed: ' The Worsh1Dr Barnard.'

There is another record of this episode still extant. In the gallery at Nether Winchendon now hangs an oval wooden shield painted with the arms of Bernard quartering Tyring- ham and Winlow, with an ornamental border – partly of oak leaves; and beneath, the inscription – ' Scrope Bernard LLD, NoV 3rd1789.'

It was in this same year that Mr. or Dr. Bernard, after some correspondence with the Heralds' College,1succeededin having his arms and pedigree registered; the arms being differentiated by order of the college – the bear was to be represented with a collar as well as a muzzle. He further obtained the Heralds' licence to quarter the arms of Tyringham as well as Winlow.

1These statements are found in the correspondence and other papers on the subject, and the arms are blazoned on a parchment,also those of Morlnnd, setting forth the permission of Garter King at Arms, with his own shield displayed and elaborate seals attached.1MS. Letter at Nether Winchendon.

And now came the trial – how far the new UnderSecretary would learn to take an interest in the duties of his office, and look upon the career thus opened to him as his appointed vocation in life. If there was some chance that he might become reconciled to it as a road to eminence, there was perhaps more likelihood that he would in time become extremely weary of its drudgery.

The early days of Scrope Bernard's Under-Secretaryship were marked by difficulties respecting a troublesome claimant. Mr. Evan Nepean, who appears to have been Mr. Grenville's Private Secretary, writes from Bath – where he was probably enjoying a holiday – on November 10, 1789:1

Dear Bernard, – Mr. Murray has never been watched by the people employed under the direction of the Secretary of State. The object he has in view is that of getting a Pension, which he has tried a variety of methods to obtain. He represents that he is a natural son of the late Prince of Wales by one of the Atholl Family; (who never existed). That his mother had a pension on the Irish Establishment of $140 per ann., and that in the early part of his life*100$*or*20Q$*per ann. had been allowed for his Education and Maintenance, which allowance has been discontinued about 20 years. – I made a particular enquiry into these matters, and found that the account[s] he gave of his mother and of himself were entirely without foundation, and that he is nothing more or*[sic]*less than an impostor. He has I understand frequently obtained money from the King, has had some from the Prince of Wales, and I believe he has also had supplies from the Treasury.

Why, when so many persons were hanged for almost nothing, this objectionable man could not have been arrested long before, it is difficult to understand; but this does notA TROUBLESOME CLAIMANT 133 seem to have been thought of, the first idea was simply to guard, by elaborate precautions, against the risk of his injuring, or even alarming, the King, his alleged half-brother, since the writer continues:

It does not appear to me that any danger is to be apprehended from him, but I would nevertheless advise his being watched and prevented from visiting St James – that can be done by sending*Clarke,*who knows his person, and Macmanusor Townsend to the door where the King enters from the Park whenever His Majesty comes to Town. They should be directed to keep him off, if he should attempt to get near His Majesty, and while the Lev6e continues*Clarke*should be stationed at the bottom of the stairs to prevent his going up. Neither Macmanus or*[sic]*Townsend will be suspected as they are frequently there, looking out after the Pick Pockets who infest the Palace at these times. The Equerries will take care of him, if he appears on the Terrace at Windsor.

I settled with Mr. Grenville before I left Town to employ a trusty man constantly at Windsor, and I thought that I should have been able to have got a proper person for that duty, but I found upon talking to him (Catmeer) [?] that he was obliged to be twice or thrice a week in town to attend to his duty. I then had an idea of employing a man whose name is*Parker,*but I could not find his address.

Until we can meet with a suitable person, It may not perhaps be amiss that Clarke should be at Windsor when the King is there, and that Macmanus or Townsend, after Murray's person has been ascertained, should be stationed at St James when the King comes to town, and be directed to take Murray into Custody, if he should be in the smallest degree troublesome

Yours faithfully

EvanNepean.

The sequel of Mr. Murray's story I do not know.

Many of the memoranda of this time are of a monotonous description – the mere routine of office indeed; but they illustrate the life of Scrope Bernard at this period, and a sample of them is therefore given.1

Desire Fawkenor to summon the Council for Tuesday at 2 o'clock. We need only send the letters to the Lord Chancellor – D of Leeds, Ld Chatham, Lord Kenyon, Ld Westmorland, & Pitt – He should however know whether the D. of Leeds will be in town, as, if not, somebody else must attend.

1From MSB. at Nether Winchendon.

Let Millbanke know that he will be wanted at that time, and that I should wish to see him at my office on Tuesday at*eleven.*

I enclose a draft to the Lds Justices, wh. you will send me for signature early to-morrow.

Send the inclosed to the Ld Chancellor – He will be either in town or at Knight's Hill.

It is not an interesting occupation to wade through shoals of letters begging for introductions, compensations, posts and promotions, and many other things, down to free transmission of parcels beyond the seas – a favour which peers and peeresses did not disdain to ask; and I do not profess to have performed the task thoroughly. A large proportion of missives received by Scrope Bernard as Under-Secretary are of this description. There are, however, some letters and other documents in the collection relating to matters of wider interest, such as the exportation of provisions from Ireland – or, rather, the prevention of any such heinous act; the arrival of ships, and their condition, &c. &c.

That the treatment of convicts and the arrangements for their transportation when respited from capital punishment should occupy considerable space is, perhaps, not surprising; but there must be many persons who are not aware that British subjects were – a little more than a hundred years ago – exposed to the perils of Mohammedan slavery in Algeria. I have found a letter*l*from a British Consul, touching the redemption of a slave, which tells its own tale, and is here given at length to illustrate the insecurity of navigation at that period:

Copy Algiers 24th Feby 1790,

(Private)

Sir, – I had the Honour on the 9th Instant to be favored with your Letter of the 25th November last, with this inclosed Copy of a Letter and Attestation, signifying to me Mr. Secretary Grenville's Wishes respecting Charles Colvill a Slave in Algiers. I have theA BRITISH SLAVE IN ALGERIA 135

1MS. Letter at Nether Winchendon.

greatest Pleasure and Satisfaction, in acquainting you, for Mr. Grenville's Information, that strictly following the Line of Office he has prescribed me, I have this Day, in Consequence of some private Commission I had lately with the Regency, prevailed upon them to use their Influence with the Dey to release Charles Colvill upon moderate Terms, and through them, have released him from Slavery for the low Sum of $330. 8. – no Slave taken by Sea, has for the last three Years been released under the Sum of between 5 & $600. I paid the Ransom Money immediately, and took Colvill Home with me, where he will remain until his Friends pay the $330. 8. – to MessTM Drummonds & Co Bankers at Chaining Cross, who have my Authority to receive it, as I have not the Pleasure of being acquainted with either of the Gentlemen mentioned in the Copy of the Letter you inclosed me.

I have, from authentic Documents produced, every Reason to believe that Charles Colvill was shipwrecked, and that his entering into the American Service, was owing to his Distresses at the Time, and not meeting with a British Vessel that wanted Men in Philadelphia; during his Captivity no man could have acted with more Credit to his Country. I have great Pleasure in having executed Mr. Secretary Grenville's Wishes so expeditiously, and shall esteem myself highly honored when he is pleased to command either my public or private Services.

I am &c

CharlesLogie. Scrope Bernard Esqre

One incident in the official correspondence, which has acquired value by the subsequent course of history, is the difficulty about the first commission of Mr. Wesley – that is, of the future Duke of Wellington. The two following letterslconfirm the fact that, although the second title of the Earl of Mornington was Viscount Wellesley, the family name was then Wesley – a fact since carefully suppressed in the Peerage.

Dear Sir, – I have spoken to Major Hobart with regard to the Ensigncy designed for Mr. Wesley; and we have enquired respecting it & fear some mistake. I recollect his speaking to me on the subject, and I think that he was recommended to SrG. Yonge to have the Ensigncy in the 9th which was to be opened by the Promotion of Lt. Beresford to a Company in the 27th. Icannot find that the succession to Beresford is filled; nor have I the Eecollection or Copy of a Letter on the subject. Will you be so good as to have Enquiry made at the War Office & we will search further here

1MS. Letters at Nether Winchendon.

Yours most faithfully

E. CookbDublin Castle. 6 Aug. 1790

This letter is addressed to Mr. Bernard.

The second runs:

Dear Bernard, – -Many thanks for your kind attention to my letter respecting Lieut Walsh: – A letter is sent this evening to Messrs. Freemantle &c., with regard to Wesley's Commission

Ever yours
most sincerely
E. Cookk. Dublin 27 Oct. 1790

In one of his undated sheets of memoranda, Mr. Grenville writes: ' Remember to give me Cooke's letters and the Comms to carry to the King.' It is stated, in Debrett's ' Peerage,'*l*that the Duke of Wellington ' first entered upon active service in 1794, when, with the rank of Lieut.-Col. in the army, he commanded a brigade in the unsuccessful expedition to Holland under the Duke of York.' His promotion was therefore rapid, and he had risen to the Lieutenant-colonelcy without risk to life or limb.

Some of the colonial questions of that day were of considerable public interest, but they are topics of allusion rather than discussion in the correspondence I possess. The dispute with Spain about ' the Nootka Sound '2trade, and settlement 'in Vancouver's Island, though trivial in itself, involved wide issues. The Quebec question culminated in the Quebec Government Act of 1791, which established representative government in Canada.'3This last subject is not only noticed in several letters from Grenville to Bernard, but was also the occasion of Mr. Bernard receiving threeTHE QUEBEC QUESTION 137

1Debrett,*Peerage of the United Kingdom,*vol. i.' Wellington (Duke of).' * Lecky,*Hist, of England in the Eighteenth Century,*vol. iv., chap. xvii. '*Ibid.*

letterslfrom Sir William Scott, afterwards Lord Stowell, which are here given. The first is remarkable for commencing in the third, and concluding in the first person; the second for its abrupt termination.

Sir William Scott presents his compliments to Mr. Scrope Bernard, and will be much obliged to him for a copy of the Instructions to Lord Dorchester, dated August 1768, referred to in official letter of Lord Grenville respecting the lands belonging to the Ecclesiastics at Quebec, as neither the Attorney nor myself have it.

I have written upon the Honduras Case, and what I have written is now with the Attorney, for his consideration of the

subject.

I am dear Sir

Yours very truly Thursday W. ScOTT.

The second letter is altogether without a date, but is endorsed by Mr. Bernard – ' K. 29th Novr 1790.'

Dear Sir, – I forgot to mention to you when I first saw you, that we have looked into the business of the Monastery of S'Sulpice in Canada, and are perfectly disposed to report in behalf of the Crown, upon any Eeference however general that Lord Grenville may think proper to send us.

The third letter is dated at the end of the letter. Commons Deer 1st 1790.

Dear Sir, – The Attorney sent to me a Report from the Crown Officers at Quebec, which he said Mr. Grenville had desired us to look over, in order that we might consider what opinion we were likely to form upon the same Subject;*and particularly for the purpose of pointing out what should be the Nature and Terms of the Eeference to be sent to us;*And we agreed; And we agreed upon Conversation that any general Eeference to us upon the Eight of the Crown would be sufficient, as we were clear in the affirmative. That is all that I know of the Matter excepting that He is positive no Eeference has been sent to Him.

The Mode therefore of sending it, if any should be thought necessary, is for Lord Grenville's own Determination.

I am dear Sir

Yours very faithfully

Wm. Scott.1MS. Letters at Nether Winchendon.

Another letter of interest is from the restless and unfortunate Theobald Wolfe Tone, then about twenty-seven years of age.1Born in Dublin, after leaving Trinity College he had come to London to study for the Bar, but threw up his profession to take up politics – that is, to agitate for the repeal of the Penal Laws; though himself a member of the Established Church, he felt deeply the degraded position of his Roman Catholic fellow-countrymen. At this time, however, he had not avowed himself an enemy of England, but was striving to induce the Government to carry out certain plans to which this letter2refers. It is, of course, addressed to Mr. Grenville, but passed through Scrope Bernard's hands.

Sir, – A very short time since I took the liberty to transmit a plan for military establishment at the Sandwich Isles to the Duke of Richmond, to whom I am utterly unknown. His Grace with a condescension utterly unexpected by me, answered my letter immediately and informed me that I should have addressed myself to you. My ignorance of the etiquette of office must excuse my mistake which however his Grace has been so kind as in some degree to rectify, by offering to lay the plan before you, which, in a letter by this post, I have requested him to do.

You will perceive, Sir, that it is but a sketch. The number of men, the times of service, in short the whole arrangement is but for an example and may be altered at your pleasure; but I hope and trust that you will find the general scope of the design worthy of your attention. I have thought of it so long and with unceasing ardor for its execution that I should doubt my own judgement, were it not in a degree corroborated by the manner in which the Duke of Richmond has received my proposal.

If you should think the plan worthy of your notice, I shall be proud of your permission to go more into detail, either by letter or personally. If you should think it fit for adoption, I trust I shall be allowed my utmost and most earnest wish, permission to devote myself wholly to its execution.

It is a proof that I am, myself at least, satisfied of its merit when I stake my whole future success in life, as I would my life itself, on the event.

The Duke of Richmond's condescension to me emboldens meWOLFE TONE 139

1*Memoirs of Tiieobald Wolfe Tone,*written by Himself. Edited by his son Wm. Th. Wolfe Tone.*Biographic UniverseUf,* 'Tone (Theobald Wolfe).'- MS. Letter at Nether Winchendon.

to hope that my present application to you will not pass without your notice. I therefore take the liberty to subjoin my address I am Sir, with great respect

Your most obedient humble servant

TheobaldWolfeTone. Oct. 1st 1790 No. 5 Great Longford Street, Dublin.

This letter is endorsed ' answered S B – If any steps are taken respecting his Plan, he will hear further on the subject.' I have not found any statements of the purpose or details of this plan. But in the following year, a letter from the author was intercepted1 – declaring his' unalterable opinion' to be against the evil influence of England, and in favour of separation – which must have effectually put a stop to all chance of its adoption. The unquiet career of Wolfe Tone came to a close in 1798. He was captured in the*Hoche,*2a French vessel sent to invade Ireland – being then an Adjutant-General in the French service – and committed suicide to avoid the ignominy of the gallows.

In 1792, the Home Secretary, who had been elevated to the Peerage as Lord Grenville, was transferred to the Foreign Office, and the Eight Hon. Henry Dundas, who was President of the Indian Board, became Home Secretary. From sundry notes, written by Lord Grenville at this time, it is evident that Scrope Bernard ran the risk of being left out altogether, which his friend was anxious to prevent. In the result he remained at the Home Office with the new Secretary.

Of the short period during which Mr. Dundas held the Secretaryship I have few records.3Occasionally he writes from Wimbledon to make appointments with the UnderSecretary, or to express his intention of not coming to town unless it is absolutely necessary. On this subject Mr. John King, who was also in the Home Office, writes:

There is no reason in the world why you shd come before thetime you propose. Mr. D. is gone to Wimbledon, & does not return before tuesday. – By the by this going to Wimbledon, & doing business at his own House in Somerset Place is playing the old soldier with us.

1Leoky, Hist,*of Ireland in the Eighteenth Century*(Edition 1902), vol. v., chap. xi.
*Ibid.

*The following references are all from MS. Letters at Nether Winchendon.

The communication, formally worded, decides that the Under-Secretary is not justified in complying with 'the requisition made by Colonel Lowther, of the Whitehaven correspondence.' At another time Mr. Bernard is directed to ' summon a cabinet to meet to-morrow at $ past two o'clock.' Then there are letters from and to him about hopes and grievances, from various quarters, as in Grenville's time. The letter, endorsed by Mr. Bernard March 23,1792, is from the Solicitor-General 'J. Scott,' afterwards Lord Chancellor, and Earl of Eldon, stating that it is impossible for him to leave the House of Lords; it continues: ' If you can slip down here you will find me at the Bar; if the subject of Mr. Dundas's Letter can be so communicated.' There is a postscript ' perhaps the Attorney General will, who I understand is to be with Mr. D.'

In September 1791 the Duke of York married the Princess Frederica of Prussia. The following note relates to the Duchess's formal reception of the Ministry and the Royal Households – the word ' famille ' signifying household. It is endorsed ' Copy of a note from General Bude ' to General Grenville.

Le Due d'York m'envoye pour vous prier d'informer les Ministres de sa Majest6 que la Duchesse les recevra en particulier domain a St. James. – Us doivent lui etre presentes d'abord apr6s la Famille du Eoi et avant celle de la Eeine – autant qu'on peut fixer le moment ce sera & 1 heure et demie.

Lundy a Midy.

On receiving this Mr. Dundas wrote to his Under-Secretary from Wimbledon the same evening:

Dear Bernard, – I have just received the enclosed. I am at a loss to know whether it is a copy sent to me for my own information, or sent to me by Lord Grenville, as more properly belonging to my Department, that I may inform the rest of his Majesty's Ministers. The subject is in truth one which belongs to neitherHBNEY DUNDAS 141 of our Departments, but the intimation ought to have come to each of us from the proper officer of the Duke or Duchess of York's Household. That is however of no moment, and care must be taken that the information at any rate is conveyed.

You'll therefore take care to enquire at Lord Grenville[s] office how the fact is. If a copy of the enclosed has been sent to all the Ministers as well as to me, you have no occasion to take further trouble about it, but if it is meant that I am to give the Intimation, take care that it is accurately done.

Yours

Eventually, as appears in a communication from Mr. Aust, who was probably Lord Grenville's Under-Secretary, that gentleman was desired by his Chief to forward the important notice to all members of the Cabinet.

The straggling, unformed handwriting of Mr. Dundas presents a strong contrast to the neat, almost feminine calligraphy of Lord Grenville, of his brother, the Marquess of Buckingham, and of several other more or less distinguished correspondents of the Under-Secretary. Some, indeed, wrote more clerk-like, others – as, for instance, Sir William Scott – bolder hands than the Grenville brothers; but scarcely any even approximate to the Dundas scrawl.

In 1792, Mr. Dundas resigned his secretaryship, with the expressed intention of devoting himself entirely to his duties as President of the Indian Board. Whether Mr. Bernard was compelled to retire, or left, in disgust at the continual changes, a post he had reluctantly accepted, I do not know. His friendship for Lord Grenville had doubtless lightened the burden of uncongenial work at first, but the last months of office were not thus cheered. Mr. Dundas could never of course have been to him the same as his former chief, though his letters are civil and pleasant, when not hampered by formalities; but it is known that he, like his great leader Pitt, had a weakness for strong potations, without the extenuating circumstances which might be urged in Pitt's case.

Whatever may have been the reasons, Scrope Bernard now retired from public life, except so far as his county andParliamentary position kept him in touch with the questions of the day, in which it is evident that his interest continued to the last. His friend John King remained in the official groove, and was for some years Under-Secretary.1He married the sister of another friend, Charles Moss, who became Bishop of Oxford in 1807.2

1Burke,*A Dictionary of the Landed Gentry,* 'King, ol Chadshunt,' and ' King, of Preston Candover.'

Abbey,*The English Church and its Bishops,*1700-1800, vol. ii. Haydn,*Book of Dignities.* THE FRENCH REVOLUTION 143

CHAPTER VIII

INCIDENTS OF A STORMY TIME

The French Revolution – News from Paris – Birth of Thomas Tyringham Bernard – The Manors of Great and Little Kimble – Trespasses of Villagers – Purchases of

Land by Scrope Bernard – Chequers – Emigration from France – The Deseoeulles – War with France – Petitions for Peace – Death of the Second Viscount Barrington – Birth of Richard Scrope Bernard and Mary Ann Bernard – Scrope Bernard re-elected for Aylesbnry – He becomes a Partner in Ransom and Morland's Bank.

ScropeBernard'speriod of office as Under-Secretary coincided with the first startling manifestations of a momentous Revolution, which convulsed France, and shook Europe to its centre. England was of course not free from peril; she had her own discontented and dangerous classes, who were more to be feared than a foreign enemy; and even some of her ablest men hailed the outbreak of the French struggle as the commencement of a better era; but the extremes to which it was carried, the fearful excesses which marked its progress, eventually checked the outburst of this feeling, and even caused a strong re-action.

The quiet life of an English family like the Bernards was but little affected by the strong movement in France; there were no near relatives in the army or navy.

In this chapter, however, while relating the story of my grandfather's private life, I have noted such indications of the crisis as can be found in the papers at Nether Winchendon. They are, of course, fragmentary; but a more extended view belongs only to general history and biographies of men conspicuous in the great contest.

A letter 1 signed ' C. M.' (Charles Moss) and dated ' Spa, August 28,' seems to belong to the year 1790. It relates the impression received in an outward journey:

1MS. Letter at Nether Winchendon.

At Dover the packet did not sail for Ostend for above three days after our arrival, &, as we met with an acquaintance who had just passed thro' France without difficulty, we took our course for Calais – & I am glad we did so, because it gave us an opportunity of seeing to what a pitch of absurdity the people were arrived. – The waiters, nay the very postilions & the labourers talk politics, of dethroning the monarch, of his violability or inviolability &c with as much importance, and as much appearance Of the object being within their power, as you wd talk of sending your son to school, & selling your estate.'

Two letters from another correspondent belong to the spring of 1791, when England was apparently waking to the consciousness of the tragic aspect which the great French drama had assumed. Scrope Bernard then had a friend in Paris, who does not sign his name, probably by way of precaution. I am unable to identify the writer, although it is quite possible that there may be other letters from him, not on the subject of France, in the collection at Nether Winchendon. His two Parisian letters contain nothing very striking, but the experience of an intelligent observer in the midst of such exciting scenes cannot be altogether devoid of

interest.

Hotel d'Angleterre Rue de F. St. Thomas' 24 April 1791.

Dear Bernard, – I obey my promise in writing to you, though I am unable to give you any particular news; the difficulties attending a first visit to Paris have so much occupied my time, that it has left me no opportunity of gaining information.

I had no idea, until I became a witness, of the general infatuation of the French people respecting the Revolution; every peasant and every woman and child from Calais to this place wears the cockade, and the people here abandon every other consideration but that which relates to the situation of public affairs; the commonest of the rabble collect in small bodies in the street to consultNEWS FEOM PAEIS 145

1This evidently means ' Bue des Filles St. Thomas.' The date of this letter, which is not very distinct, looks like ' 1790,' but, even*i*f it was so written, the date must have been a mere slip of the pen; it was evidently written just before the letter immediately following, and the events are those of 1791. It it one of the MS. Letters at Nether Winchendon.

on state affairs, and on every pillar and in every street there are stuck up inflammatory publications which they are continually reading. From what I perceive I do really think that Europe united could hardly effect a counter-revolution; they tell me that in the southern parts of France the public are still more violently attached to their new system.

I this day was in the Hall where the National Assembly meet, but unfortunately they were not speaking; there is a gallery, at each end and on the sides, for the public, and the benches below are arranged all round for the Deputies, &c.; in the midst of one of the sides is the President's seat, elevated, and before him a table for the clerks, upon which is placed the bust of Mirabeau. – There has been a considerable ferment, which is not yet subsided, upon the subject of the King's permission to leave Paris. The Assembly have allowed him this liberty, which the people dislike, and Monsieur de la Fayette, displeased with their conduct in objecting to this favour towards the King, has resigned the command of the National Troops, who were all yesterday and to-day attending him, in order to persuade him to resume it, but as yet they have been unsuccessful. This morning the drums were beating in parts of the town to call a meeting of the National Troops at five o'clock, to take an oath to conform themselves to the laws, – which they will do without understanding them, and which will not quiet the disturbance, for everything is actuated by prejudice and by passion.

In looking at the remains of the Bastille, a Frenchman told me, with the highest exultation (which certainly is natural on such an event) that he was one of the first to enter that horrid prison; it is wonderful how totally they have demolished it, there is hardly a stone left, and the workmen who are employed will very soon have removed the remaining few.

I will write to you again before I leave Paris; it is uncertain how long I stay, or which way I shall return, therefore I would not have you write to me unless you have any commands, which you may send me in a letter directed to Mr Perigaux, which in all events will be sent after me.

You will know my hand and therefore I need not add my name in assuring you that I am most sincerely yours

This anonymous correspondent wrote ' again four days later:

Paris 28th April 1791

My dear Bernard, – Since my last nothing new has occurred. The National Guard have prevailed on Monsr de la Fayette toresume his command, but without accepting the system which he had pointed out for their future conduct; however he has reprimanded the Company of Grenadiers who behaved so improperly towards the King and Queen, though it was his intention (if practicable) to have cashiered them, but he did not think proper to put this latter intention into execution.

1MS. Letter at Nether Winehendon. VOL. III. L

I was yesterday at the National Assembly, and I was never witness to such a scene of turbulence and violent contention; several speaking at the same time, and each endeavouring to be heard in spite of the President's bell, which was continually ringing, to keep order, without effect; whenever a few sentences could be heard, they were received either with the clapping of hands or the groans of the members; in short I had no belief of such want of order until I beheld it.

There has been a riot respecting the departure of a regiment from Versailles, but disturbances are so frequent, that they pass without consideration or noise; I understand however that it is settled.

I am considerably amused at Paris with the spectacles?] [part of the word was evidently torn off in breaking the seal] and variety of sights, but the people, having mistaken liberty for licence, render it necessary to be very discreet and prudent in one's behaviour, and often when I wish to laugh, I am obliged to refrain from fear- You can have no idea of the want of subordination, of the total abolition of all order, it is liberty to the fullest extent, and whilst such liberty prevails this kingdom can never profit by its Revolution.

Very truly yours

I am unable to pronounce with certainty as to the letters of which the signature is composed, or the name it is intended to suggest. The writer must have been a person of strong nerves if he could keep up an inclination to laugh amidst his perilous and distressful surroundings. But I doubt whether he fully realised the approaching horrors of the great crash.

The King and Queen, with their children and Madame Elisabeth, weary of a scarcely disguised captivity, attempted flight in the following June, but were recaptured at Varennes. Scrope's previous correspondent had probably left Paris before that time, but Mr. Morland appears to have been there, and, since he was a man of observation and knowledge of the world, it is to be regretted that no letter of his, DOMESTIC TRIFLES 147

describing the situation, is extant. Possibly he may have considered it prudent to reserve the narrative of his experiences till his return. The only allusion I can find to this visit is in a letterLfrom Mrs. Scrope Bernard to her husband, dated ' Winchendon Bower, July 2nd,' a heading which may mean either that she was writing in the ' Courting Bower,' or that she gave the old house a pet name to show how entirely she had overcome her original prejudice against it.

I was wishing to hear from my Mother, in order that I might learn a little of what is become of my Father at Paris, – and am much surprised to hear from you that he and Paris are in a quiet state. I was afraid he was in a dangerous situation, being among the French.

I imagine it will be a very long while now (if ever) before their troubles are over. I pity degraded Monarchy exceedingly. – I have lent the newspapers, with the affecting account, to my neighbours to read.

The rest of the letter, with its allusions to home life, forms a contrast to the beginning. Willy's birthday – ' next Thursday ' – had begun to be a subject of consideration; he was apparently in town with his father, and the writer expresses

her satisfaction that' Greatgrandmamma' – Mrs. Mills – had taken tea with them. '
Madge,' or Margaret, was of sufficient age to send ' her duty ' to her father, and had
some ' pretty curls ' to show him when he came to the country. Sundry other matters
of domestic interest fill up the sheet of paper. Harriet Bernard considered that the
opera box – her husband either had one of his own or, more probably, shared it with his
brother – should be lent a second time to a young lady, Miss Hamilton, who had sung
at their concerts. Then follow some items of country news – the safe arrival of a mare,
' but without a saddle,' the low state of the ale, and the desirableness of unpacking
and tasting ' the new cyder,' the whole finishing up with an important postscript: '
We have got all our hay in.'

On the 15th day of the following September another son was born to Scrope and
Harriet Bernard, in Bolton Street. He was baptized in London by the name of Thomas
Tyring- ham, his uncle Thomas, and, I believe, also his aunt Margaret, standing
sponsors on the occasion. His father wrote on this occasion to the perpetual curate of
Nether Winchen- don, desiring that the child's birth and baptism might be entered in
the register of that parish, which was accordingly done.1This circumstance, and the
double Christian name, which was at that time uncommon, suggest that he may even
then have entertained the idea of making the boy his successor at Winchendon. His
eldest son William had been virtually adopted by Mr. Morland, and was recognised
heir, after Mrs. Bernard, to the bulk of his property. Moreover, earlier in the year
1791, Scrope had been buying land which he may have intended for Francis, his second
surviving son. In March, William Bridges Ledwell, ' together with his Mother. and
others, conveyed all their interest and title to the estate and Manor of Little Kimble,
to Scrope Bernard, Esq.'!

1MS. Letter at Nether Winchendon,

It was probably about the same time that Mr. Bernard bought the adjoining ' Manor
of Great Kimble,' with ' the Manors of Marshal and Fennel's Grove, comprising the
hamlets of Marsh and Kimblewick,' of ' the Right Hon. George John, Earl Spencer,
K. G.' 3The new possessions were situated about twelve or thirteen miles from Nether
Winchendon by road, and formed a more important estate.

These purchases, while they gave fresh scope to Mr. Bernard's energies, did not
diminish his interest in Nether Winchendon, for it was also about this time that he
must have built the stone bridge near his house, for which purpose, as I have heard,
he diverted a small portion of the channel of the river Thame in order to render the
situation and appearance of the new bridge more suitable and picturesque. It would
seem to have been in consequence of the facilities afforded by this change that, in
the following year, one ' W. Bray' complained of a path made by theVILLAGE
LAWLESSNESS 149

1MS. Letter and entry in Begister of Nether Winchendon.'Lipscomb,*Hist, of
Bucks,*vol. ii., ' Little Kimble.'2*Ibid.,*vol. ii.,' Great Kiinble,'

villagers through his tenant's land in Cuddington parish, which was divided by the
river from Nether Winchendon. Possibly Mr. Bray may have been lessee of the Dean
and Chapter of Rochester, who long held certain fields inconveniently wedged into
other people's property. He suggested that Mr. Bernard should stop the trespass ' by
putting a roller with iron spikes on the top of the gate and guarding the sides.'/But I

have no evidence that this was ever done. In the matter of making new paths wherever it suits their convenience, regardless of other folk's rights, the present inhabitants of that country are not very much behind their forefathers. Scrope Bernard had to suffer, like his neighbours, from their lawlessness. Richard Plater, a Winchendon man belonging to a family of small farmers, who became his factotum about the land, wrote,* early in 1791:

I have given it out in the town amung the poor that you was greatly a frunted at there caring your posies and Eails a way, but am a fraid it will not make very little difference, for they have cared the greatest part of the post and rails in Mr Bainton's cloas a way.

Plater wrote a good hand, but his composition was not perfect and his spelling most peculiar. A large number of his letters have been preserved.

A further illustration of the aggressiveness of the surrounding population, is to be found in a letter from Dr. Littlehales, Perpetual Curate of Brill and Boarstall – written from the old gatehouse known as Boarstall Tower, the only remnant of a mansion pulled down some years previously – to Mr. Bernard in London, enclosing the following statement:

Bucks to wit

The Information and Complaint of Elizabeth Jessop of the parish of Lower Winchendon in the County of Bucks widow taken upon oath before me J. L. Littlehales Doctor of Laws one of his Majesty's Justices of the Peace for the said County the 13th day of June 1792

Who says that she lives in the same parish together with Elizabeth Blake, another widow of the parish, and that frequentlythey have been disturbed in their Beds all hours of the night by William Goff and Eichard Smith Labourers belonging to the said parish by knocking at the door and breaking the viz. door down – iind particularly on Wednesday last the Sixth Instant about Twelve o'clock at Night as they were in their beds – they were disturbed by a most violent knocking at the door – and upon the Deponent calling out ' who is there' one of the two men above mentioned answered ' Come down,' when this Deponent said Go about your business or else I will fetch the Constable to you. But they still kept beating at the door, and upon this, Deponent & the said Elizabeth coming down to go to the Constable, Mr. Gurney, and calling out to him, Mr. Gurney came to the window and told her he had no business unless she brought a warrant; upon which she went towards her own door again. – Eichard Smith struck her a blow in the face with his fist – and smasht a wooden Bottle full of Beer about the said Elizabeth Blake's head.

1MS. Letter at Nether Winchendon.

*MS. Letters and other papers at Nether Winchendon.

The Mark of

before me Elizabeth Jessop

J. L. Littlehales

The result of the magisterial inquiry does not appear. It may seem surprising that Scrope Bernard should not have had enough of such petty annoyances at Winchendon, and should have cared to involve himself with more land. But at the time of this outbreak he had not only become the lord of the Kimble manors, but had also taken a lease of a mansion in the adjoining parish of Ellesborough. There was no gentleman's house on his new property – a manor- house and another old residence had been almost demolished in the course of the eighteenth century. The mansion taken by Mr. Bernard was called Chequers,1and was to be let during the minority of its owner Sir John Russell. Mr. Bernard's reasons for occupying the house are stated in a letter,2written from Salisbury to a Mr. Powlett, two years later, when he was already thinking of sub-letting the place:

When your letter arrived I was absent on the duty of escortingTHE CHEQUEES 151

1It is now generally called Chequers Court, but was then known as Chequers, Checkers, or Chakers,' &c.

2MS. Letter at Nether Winchendon (Rough Draft).

some French prisoners to Warminster; else, I should have answered it by return of post. The house in question (Checkers near Missenden and Wendover) is not my property, and I am the more particular in letting it on that account. My own house in Bucks (Winchendon) being situated at a less convenient distance from London, I lett it to another person, and have taken this of Sir John Russell's Executors upon a lease during his minority. There is some account of the House and Pictures in the 2nd Vol. of the Memoirs of Cromwell's family under the head of Russell.

If I may trust to the statement of my uncle Frank, or Francis, who was under two years of age when my father took Chequers, Winchendon was let to a man who wished to start a paper-mill there. This was a hobby of the day, intended to develop the resources of the country; but it was very soon stigmatised as an injury to the poor, on account of the number of corn-mills it suppressed – probably the hobby was over-ridden. At Winchendon, as I have heard, it did not succeed, and the paper-mill soon gave up business, which must have had the accompanying result of throwing the manor house at Nether Winchendon once more on Mr. Bernard's hands. During the period of the paper-mill enterprise, I imagine that the old corn-mill in the Grove/was demolished; as I learned from an old inhabitant, both existed for some time together and gave employment jointly to the parishioners. In all likelihood the corn- mill was out of repair and paying badly when the idea of a rival was started; and, when that project failed, the new building became the village corn-mill. It stands at the end of the Grove nearest the manor house.

Scrope Bernard's new residence at Chequers was naturally a subject of much curiosity amongst his relatives. The mansion at that time still preserved its Tudor appearance, but has since been much modernised. It was situated in the romantic region of the Chilterns, and Velvet Lawn, the well-known resort for picnic parties, is on the estate within a short distance of the house. Lipscomb describes2thismansion as ' situated in a little valley S. S. E. of the parish church, and surrounded by irregular eminences, clothed to their summits with beech trees, interspersed with box, larch, and holly, in a very picturesque manner.' Like many old houses it was not so placed as to command a distant view, as it easily might have been. The most marked feature of the interior was a gallery seventy-five feet long, with mullioned windows; and it contained many portraits and other memorials of Oliver Cromwell, his family, and connections, brought there by the Russells. Altogether the excitement in the Bernard family was fully justified.

1See vol. i., ch. vii., of this Family History. " Lipscomb,*Hist. Bucks,*vol. ii., ' Ellesborough.'

Thomas Bernard wrote1in 1792, expressing his fears that business might prevent him from paying it a visit: ' unless we were to run to you with posthorses, take an early dinner, and return the same day.' Jane White writes also from London, thanking Scrope for his offer to meet her and her daughter Amelia at Chalfont:

We will be there on Wednesday before one o'clock, (no very extraordinary accident preventing,) and in case you should find your whiskey horse lame, or anything should hinder your meeting us, we will come quietly on to tea. Shall be exceedingly glad to spend two or three quiet days with dear Sis, and get thoroughly acquainted with our pretty cousins.

A ' whiskey ' was then a favourite kind of carriage. The letter concludes:

If you have an opportunity of acquainting the good folks at Wendover that I bring down Julia's commission I shall be obliged to you.

The Kings appear to have been staying at Wendover about the same time; and Mr. King writes his regrets at being prevented by a severe cold from accompanying Fanny in her walks to Chequers. Then – after expressing his disappointment at missing Mr. Bernard in town – he adds:

I was also not a little mortified in not having the opportunity

The family letters here quoted are all in MS. at Nether Winchendon.

A LANDOWNERS ANNOYANCES 153

to hear your grand debate 1 on the Reform, when I find Mr. Pitt spoke as never man spoke before in that house.

The people of the Chiltern district were not an ideal race, and Mr. Bernard encountered on his Kimble property annoyances of the same description as in the Thame valley. The following epistle illustrates this statement:

Sir, I made bold to trouble you with afue lines to let you no*[sic]*that I & my Servant man have catched John Delifield your Hous keeper furiting in my warren with Several nets at Cooms: it was within the bounds of ragelton's halloway. I asked him what business he had furiting there; he told me he wanted some Rabbits and would have some Let them be whose the would, he was very impertint indeed to me & said it was not my warren.

I thot it best to Let your Honrno of it that I might have your advice in it before I purseed any further it was yesterday the 26 of Decrhe was there great part of the day.

SrI am your HorHumble St

JoshWard.

Kimble Warren – Wendover – Backs

27 Dr 1792.

As to the rights of the parties in this controversy I am unable to form an opinion. Occurrences of this description, no doubt, took place on both estates year by year; but the details already given may suffice.

How far the anarchy in France, combined with the gradual rise in price of many necessary articles, especially bread, in this country, had disposed the minds of the lower classes to lawlessness, I cannot say; but there was much alarm in England, and a royal proclamation had been issued on May 21, 1792, requiring all magistrates and civil officers to exert themselves, ' for the Suppression of divers wicked and seditious Writings, published and industriously dispersed with a view to excite Discontents, Tumults, and Disorders, in this Kealm.' But, whatever may have been the momentary effect of this proclamation, the treasonable practices were very soon resumed, and a printed admonition was sentby the Home Secretary, dated November 4, addressed apparently to all the Lords Lieutenant of counties. The copy sent to the Marquess of Buckingham ' informs him of:

1For particulars of this debate, see Belsham,*Memoirs of the Reign Oj George III.*,vol. iv., book xxiv. (Sixth Edition).

His Majesty's directions that it should be given in charge to the Grand Jury, at the next ensuing General Quarter Sessions of the Peace for the County of Buckingham, diligently to enquire and true Presentment to make of all such wicked and seditious writings so published and industriously spread as aforesaid within the said County, as shall be given to them in charge, or shall otherwise come to their Knowledge; in order that the Authors, Printers, Publishers and Distributors of all such wicked and seditious writings as aforesaid, may be severally dealt with according to Law.

This severe injunction the Marquess of Buckingham qualified with a few gracious words; perhaps he really thought it inapplicable to his county. In any case he addressed the magistrates as follows:

Stowe, November 26th 1792

Sir, – I have the Honor of sending you a Copy of a Letter which I have received from the Secretary of State, notifying to me the King's Commands, respecting the charge to be given by the Magistrates at the ensuing Quarter Sessions for this County to the Grand Jury. And I am happy at the same time to express, from a long and intimate knowledge of the Magistracy, and of the Inhabitants at large of this respectable County, my fullest persuasion that no District in the King's dominions stands less in need of this Proof of his Majesty's paternal solicitude for the Security and Happiness of his People, exciting us to the faithful Discharge of our judicial Duties, and to every exertion for the support of our happy Constitution

Your very faithful

and obedient Servant

NugentBuckinghamBy order of the Gustos Kotulorura Acton Chaplin

Clerk of the Peace.

The stream of emigration from France had begun in 1791; the refugees at that period consisted chiefly of the*noblesse,*but as time went on many persons of less preEMIGEATION FEOM FEANCE 156

1All the documents referred to in the text are at Nether Winchendon.

tension were thankful to escape. In 1792 Lille was besieged by the Austrians, armed against the French Republic. This war appears to have driven to England a family, named Descoeiille, who had been intimate with Scrope Bernard when he stayed at Lille, and who seem to have now quartered themselves on the Bernards. In virtue of their acquaintance with the Hon. Mrs. Storer, no doubt, they were received by the Marquess and Marchioness of Buckingham, and possibly they may have been persons of some importance in their own neighbourhood, but their letters are not calculated to impress the reader with an idea of high culture.

In a letter from Wivenhoe, written in March 1794, Madame Descoeiille reminds Scrope Bernard of an offer he had made them of Winchendon for a few weeks, and asks if they may now go there, because Wivenhoe is full of visitors to the baths, and all lodgings still vacant, very dear – or, if it is possible, they would prefer to stay in the Bernard's London house, supposing it to be empty, as more convenient for lodging-hunting. Probably they did not visit Winchendon, which was let, but were invited to the London house, though it was not empty, since Mrs. Scrope Bernard writes to her mother, after mentioning that a harper had been to her house to hear ' Madge ' play, with a view to deciding whether she should take lessons:

The Descoeiille family hanging on us is not a pleasant affair when things are so dear – washing, meat,&etceteras – to people that have a family of their own; and they, poor creatures, can't pay for anything themselves.

The Descoeiilles professed an intention of returning to Lille, where their property was situated, when both armies should have left the neighbourhood, and no doubt they meant what they said, but they were hindered by the course of events, and remained in England many years – not, it may be hoped, in the same helpless condition.

It was natural that great difference of opinion should exist in England as to the expediency of going to war with France – that is, with any of the Governments of the Eevolution. But, ' the English Ministers,' says Lecky, ' still carried their desire to be neutral in French affairs to the verge, if not beyond the verge, of inhumanity,' until, in February, 1793, immediately after the execution of King Louis XVI., the Republic declared war on England. If this was to be the final result, it does seem a pity that the English did not arm in time to prevent the first series of atrocities, and when armed did not act with sufficient skill and vigour to check a continuance of massacre. Some illustration of this campaign, under the Duke of York, and of the*beauties*of war, is found in a letter forwarded by Jane White to her brother Scrope. She writes:

A tenant of Mrs. Whetham's has received a letter from his son in the 2nd Dragoons; it is penned with such simplicity and spirit that I send you a copy of it. You may take an extract for the news, if you like it, leaving out the name. Miss Crawford was here this morning (with Lady Lincoln) – her brother is in the same Reg1, and she was much pleased with it. The letter is as follows:

Ghent Jan. 19th '94.

Honoured Father and Mother, – This comes with my very kind love to you and hopes you and Brother and Sister is well, as this leaves me. I bless God for it. We are in winter quarters at present, and we shall remain here until we take our quarters in the field. We have 30,000 French lies within 15 miles of us now, they be under Hedges or any where they can get; they are almost starved to Death. We have 25,000 of the Turks to join us on the 1st of Feby. I should have wrote before but we have not been settled long. All the Summer after retreating from Dunkirk, we was marching about, but will be at Dunkirk again betimes at Spring and give them a proper dressing, and Lyle too we will have, for we have got a fine army for them, and we are the Boys thats not affraid to face them though they send their Cannon Balls ever so hot. We gave them several good dressings before we left Camp. We went within two miles of Lyle and cut 280 all to pieces, we did not leave one to tell tales, that's bravo. We lost 3 men that day all shot through the head; 2 died instantly, the other came to the Hospital and died there in 3 days. I have a great deal of news what has happened this autumn, but I cannot have time to send any now. We have got as good meat as any inTHE BEAUTIES OF WAE 157

England and cheap. T.', pr pound; and all kinds of garden stuff very reasonable. The best Beer is no better than good English small Beer; Gin we have got plenty, and very cheap. Please to let me have an answer as soon as possible, and direct to me 2nd Dragn. Gds. with the Duke of York's army Ghent French Flanders.

I am your Son

W. P. N. B. This is far more plentiful place than England.

From the tone of Mrs. White's letters it would seem that she and Scrope Bernard were both in favour of keeping up the contest, a point still warmly debated. In the same letter she writes:

Mr. Grey has made a foolish piece of work at Nottingham, & we have just got a copy of a letter he directed as I understand to be written to his Party there, & then, by a mistake of the Xtian name in his Frank, it was sent to a person of sentiments totally different, & they had it printed in a Handbill & circulated about the Town; the chief purport of it to desire they will get petitions against the war signed as quickly as possible, & that further instructions should be sent next post; it is understood here that he wants to provoke Ministry to arrest him. Lady Lincoln was so anxious to show it Lord L. that I could not ask to keep it, but her LadyP will return it on Saturday.

I scarcely need tell you Mr. White and My young folks are very well; I should hardly be so bad a wife as to be here if they were not.

This letter was written from Mrs. Whetham's ' beautiful place' at Kirklington, while on the way from Lincoln to London. The lady of the house apparently required the presence of some friend owing to her weak state of health, for Mrs. White had previously written:

I am going home on Tuesday next, on which day I hope Mrs. Manners Sutton will meet me at Newark and return here in Mrs. Whetham's coach. Mrs. Whetham has been extremely ill.

In another letter it appears that this lady required a house in town for three months, ' somewhere towards Piccadilly, Berkley Square, Grosvenor Square, or Hanover Sq.'

In due time Mrs. White forwarded the erring document to her brother. Her letter is dated ' Kirklington Feby '94.' She writes:

The paper I mentioned to you as printed at Nottingham is returned to night & I send you a copy of it. I believe Sir R.

Sutton has sent one to the Speaker of H. of C or some friends.

I don't know any one who has seen the original letter. The document as made public at Nottingham was headed

'Hebeis

NottinghamAllOnAnUpeoab – Ob

AChangeInThePostmen – BeingAGeneralMistake

ForTheGoodOfTheCountby

Copy of a Letter sent to Citizens S y W g & W m

*dc. – of Nottingham*Citizens

Charles G y Esq M P requested me to inform you –

That he could wish all societies or as many Towns as*cmdd be got,*to petition again for Peace. But not to petition the*King*(except you petition the Commons at the same time) for petitions to the King would only be lodged in the Secretary of State's office, & the Ministry would advise the King to return no answer!!

P. S. – On Monday between 1000 & 1400 of the London corresponding Society met at the Globe Tavern; they passed very spirited Resolutions, which you will receive to-morrow.

Note, 500 dined at the above Tavern

I am, Citizens, a Friend to Freedom No 9 PiccadillyJohnHarSon'

On February 1, 1793, in the midst of the agitation consequent on King Louis's violent death, died William Wildman, second Viscount Barrington, whose name has been often mentioned in these pages. He had been a kind friend to Sir Francis Bernard and his family, and in his private capacity apparently continued such to the last. His political influence had no doubt waned, since he had lived many years out of office.1Of his public reputation it is unnecessary to speak; his untiring devotion to the Crown, under all circumstances, led to much animadversion. Lecky, however, gives him full credit for purity of motive.

With the nephew who succeeded him as third Viscount,

1According to Burke,*Peerage, &c.,*he bad been out of office ever since 1778.

SECTION 7

the eldest son of his deceased brother, General John Barring- ton – with the General's two younger sons, who became successively fourth and fifth Viscounts, and with their sister, Mrs. Tristram, afterwards Mrs. Cooke, the 'Louisa' of Mr. Browne's letters – the Bernard family continued on terms of social intimacy for many years longer; but the passing away of that generation and the course of events at last broke the tie.

In 1793, Scrope Bernard's fifth son, Richard Scrope, was born; and on February 11, 1797, his second daughter, Mary Ann. Unfortunately Mrs. Bernard never recovered her health after the birth of this child; she continued to watch over her family, and to entertain her friends, but always with more or less effort.

Another General Election took place in 1796. There was no contest at Aylesbury, where Scrope Bernard and Colonel Lake were re-elected.

During these years Scrope Bernard evidently practised to a certain extent as an advocate, but, owing to the fact of his having started late, I do not think that he ever had a large business. The author of an ' Obituary Notice' – who was perhaps a relation – suggests that he entered this profession in order to qualify for the post of Judge of the Episcopal Court of Durham. Bishop Barrington, however, was not translated to that See until 1792, three years later than Mr. Bernard's call. He did eventually obtain the office, but I am uncertain how soon after that date. He retained his chambers in Doctors' Commons until 1800, at least, as appears by a boyish letter from his eldest son, William, asking leave to go and see him there. Eventually his calling in life was settled by the offer of a partnership in Ransom and Morland's bank.1

During this period, his elder brother Thomas was commencing his course of philanthropic labours; but before proceeding to relate any details of his work, it seems desirable to state the few particulars known respecting the unfortunate head of the family, Sir John Bernard.

1 The style of the Firm in 1788 waa ' Ransom, Morland &Hainmersley,' as appears by a letter so signed.

CHAPTER IX

SIR JOHN BERNARD

Sir John Bernard's Prospects – The First Massachusetts Act of Confiscation – Proscriptions in New York – Poverty of Sir John Bernard – The American Loyalists – Ministerial Changes – Sir John Bernard's Claims upon the Government – Sabine's unsympathetic Account of Sir John's Life – Contrast between his Situation and that of Thomas and Scrope Bernard – Sir John's Return to England – The alleged Restoration to him of Mount Desert Island – Efforts of the Family to dissuade him from Returning to America – His Visit to France – He is appointed to an Office in Barbados – He receives tardy Compensation for Losses in America – His Life in Dominica – His Death.

SirJohnBernard'shistory is a melancholy record of a life with a bright dawn, gradually darkening until, after the midday storms, it set in persistent gloom. In his youth welcomed and courted as the Governor's son he had every prospect of becoming – as a large landowner and successful merchant – one of the most important persons in the Province of Massachusetts. A few years saw him beggared and outlawed.

It has been stated that Sir Francis, notwithstanding his experience of American character, did not believe the revolutionary governments to be capable of carrying into execution acts of arbitrary confiscation; and even if John's apprehensions were roused, he, as well as the Governor's other children, may have refrained from urging his own view of the situation on a father who was evidently sinking, since it was not in the power of any member of the family, or of all the members collectively, to avert the blow.

The first Massachusetts Act of Confiscation,1was published in the ' London Evening,' of July 18, 1779, and no doubt in other papers. How long previously John BernardLOYALISTS IN MASSACHUSETTS 161

1 Hutehinson,*Diary and Litters,*vol. ii., chip. vi.

had known of its promulgation in America depends on his abode at the time, whether in Boston or the neighbourhood, or far away, in or near Mount Desert; but it must have been soon followed by the news of his father's death, which made him a baronet, but completed his ruin, because Sir Francis, supposing that he had provided for his eldest son as amply as his means allowed, by bequeathing to him the greater part of his American property, had left him very little besides. The war, indeed, still dragged on, and upon its issue depended the ultimate result of the American Acts; for this reason, apparently, Sir John resolved on returning, to hold his own, if possible, in the face of all obstacles.

In Massachusetts (writes Sabine)1 a person suspected of enmity to the Whig cause could be arrested under a magistrate's warrant and banished, unless he would swear fealty to the friends of liberty, and the Selectmen of towns could prefer charges of political treachery in town meeting, and the individual thus accused, if convicted by a jury, could be sent into the enemy's jurisdiction. Massachusetts also designated by name, and generally by occupation and residence, three hundred and eight of her people, of whom seventeen had been inhabitants of Maine, who had fled from their homes, and denounced against any one of them who should return, apprehension, imprisonment and transportation to a place possessed by the British, and for a second voluntary return, without leave, death without benefit of clergy. By another law, the property of twenty-nine persons, who were denominated ' notorious conspirators,' was confiscated. Of these, fifteen had been appointed ' mandamus councillors,' two had been governors, one lieutenant-governor, one treasurer, one attorney- general, one chief justice, and four commissioners of the customs.

The county committees received power to pass sentences of imprisonment and banishment on suspected persons.

It has been mentioned that Governor Sir Francis Bernard possessed 30,000 acres in the Province of New York.2There measures of proscription and confiscationsoon followed. Governor Hutchinson writes, on February 6, 1780: '

1Sabine,*The American Loyalists; Preliminary Remarks or Historical Essay,*p. 78.
' See vol. i. of this Work, chap. xiv., p. 316.
VOL. III. M

A newspaper from New York of Dec 15thcontains an Act of the new State, confiscating the estates of a great number of persons beginning with Lord Dunmore, their former Governor, Tryon, their last Governor; and goes on with Watts, and four or five more of the Council, and a great number of others; and concludes with Sir Henry Clinton, and banishes them all upon pain of death.

It is probable that news of this further deprivation – for it is almost certain that the Bernard estates would be among the first annexed – reached Sir John before he left England. Sabine states2that' the effects of fifty-nine persons, of whom three were women, and their rights of remainder and rever- sion. were to pass by confiscation, from them, to the "people."' The loss was lessened, perhaps, in the Bernard case, by the fact that Sir Francis had not begun to settle these lands.3In New York the liberty of suspected persons was at the mercy of the ' County Committees.' In most of the other states analogous regulations were made.

Mr. Hutchinson4wrote on this subject:

I have read the histories of most of the civil dissentions of which we, in the present age of the world, have any knowledge; but I have not met with an instance equally arbitrary, revengeful and severe, with the Acts of the new State of Mass Bay.

Mr. Jay, a distinguished adherent of the new Governments, who a little later was appointed, with Franklin and John Adams, one of the plenipotentiaries in the peace negotiations, wrote, in a letter to Governor Clinton, dated Madrid, May 6, 1780:

An English paper contains what they call, but I can hardly believe to be, your Confiscation Act. If truly printed, New York isTHE CONFISCATION ACTS 163

1*Diary and Letters of Governor Hutchinson,*by Peter Orlando Hutchinson, one of his great-grandsons, vol. ii., chap. viii.

2Sabine,*The American Loyalists; Preliminary Remarks,*p. 79.

'*Ibid.,*p. 78.

4Hutohinson,*Diary and Letters,*vol. ii., extract from ' The Governor to J. Putnam, Aug.*3,*1779, in Letter Book.' Given in a Note to chap. v.

Note to Sabine's*The American Loyalists: Preliminary Remarks,*p. 98.

disgraced by injustice too palpable to admit even of palliation. I feel for the honor of my country, and therefore beg the favor of you to send me a true copy of it; that if the other be false, I may, by publishing yours, remove the prejudice against you occasioned by the former.

Contrary to Mr. Jay's belief, the copy seen by him was authentic; he never changed the opinion here expressed to Governor Clinton. Elsewhere Sabine states that: '

Mr. Jay's disgust was unconquerable, and he never would purchase any lands that had been forfeited under the Confiscation Act of New York.

Dr. Ryerson, a Canadian, descended from American Loyalists, and, writing in the nineteenth century, puts the matter in a strong light: *

The Draconian Code or the Spanish Inquisition can hardly be said to exceed in severity and intolerance the acts of the several State Legislatures and Committees above quoted, in which mere opinions are declared to be treason, as also the refusal to renounce a solemn oath of allegiance. The very place of residence, the non-presenting oneself to be tried as a traitor, the mere suspicion of holding loyalist opinions, involved the loss of liberty and property. Scores of persons were made criminals not after trial by a verdict of a regularly empannelled jury, but by name in Acts or Eesolutions of Legislatures; and sometimes of Committees. No modern civilized country has presented such a spectacle of the wholesale disposal by name, of the rights, liberties, and properties, and even lives of citizens, by inquisition and various bodies, as was here presented against the Loyalists guilty of no crime against their neighbours except holding to the opinion of their forefathers, and the former opinions of their present persecutors, who had usurped the power to rob, banish, and destroy them – who embodied in themselves at one and the same time, the functions of law makers, law judges, and law executioners, and the receivers and disposers, or, as was the case, the possessors of the property which they confiscated against the Loyalists.

1*The American Loyalists: Preliminary Remarks,*p. 94.

2Byerson (Dr. Egerton), Chief Superintendent of Education for Upper Canada from 1844 to 1876.*The Loyalists of America and their Times,*vol. ii., chap. zxxvi. (Toronto and Montreal, 1880).

That Sir John Bernard should have escaped persecution under this Draconian Code is almost impossible. I have, however, very little information concerning his life at this period. His brother Thomas stated, in words already quoted, that he*l'*underwent a series of confinements and sufferings in America,' but the particulars do not appear; and the short biographical article which Sabine has allotted to the Governor's ill-fated son makes no mention of any arrest or even threat of imprisonment; but he writes of course with an American bias. He merely says of Sir John:2

Soon after the Revolution he was in abject poverty, and the misfortunes of himself and his family seem to have unsettled his mind. When, in 1769, Sir Francis was recalled from the government of Massachusetts, he possessed a considerable landed estate in Maine, of which the large island of Mount Desert, Moose Island (now Eastport), and some territory on the main, formed a part. John, at or about the time of his father's departure had an agency for the settlement of these and other lands; and probably until the confiscation of his father's property in 1778 was in comfortable circumstances. His place of residence during the war appears to have been at Bath, though he was sometimes at Machias.

The only ' Bath,' on Massachusetts territory, which I have found in a ' Gazetteer,'3is described as ' a village in Lincoln County, 165 miles N. E. from Boston.' ' Machias,' which, according to Sabine, had been formerly called ' Mechisses,' was much further north, now in Washington County, Maine, ' situated in a bay of its own name. There are two considerable villages of this name within the township, one at the falls of the east branch of Machias river, the other at the falls of the west branch.'

In Sir John Bernard's time these villages can scarcely be said to have existed. There seems to have been only a fierce population of ' loggers' and ' sawyers,'4whose habitationsSIR JOHN BEENAED'S POVERTY 166

1*Life of Sir Francis Bernard.*(By one of his Sons.)

*Sabine,*The American Loyalists:*' Bernard 'Sir John).' p. 156.

2*The Edinburgh Gazetteer:* 'Bath,' 1822.

4Sabine,*The American Loyalists: Preliminary Re/marks.*These ' loggers,

were no doubt very straggling, and who were not favourable to English rule. Machiaslis ' 339 miles from Boston, and 300 by water.'

The mansion of Governor Bernard, on Jamaica Pond, later occupied by the younger Sir William Pepperell, became the quarters of the Rhode Island Colonel Miller for a while, and later was used as a camp hospital.8

In the ' Life of John Adams, by his Son,' much stress is laid on the exertions he made to reach Pownalborough, on Kennebec River, to plead a cause in 1765. The biographer speaks of the ' obstructions of nearly impassable roads, through an inhospitable region,' and notes that his father ' fell sick on the way '; he, however, arrived in time, and this cause, won under difficult circumstances, was the starting-point of his fame. But Pownal, or Pownalborough, although Mr. Adams described it as being ' at almost the extreme verge of civilisation,' was only about half the distance of Machias from Boston; and this long journey Sir John Bernard had to travel without gaining any fame. The roads are scarce likely to have improved in the interval, and latterly what population there was must have been more or less hostile.

Perhaps he sometimes tried a sea voyage by way of improvement; but the service, judging from its organisation on more frequented routes, must also have been tedious, comfortless, and perilous. Whether he travelled by sea or by land he must have arrived at his destination only to find his title to the land impugned, and his right to remain on it denied.

If this was his situation during the continuance of the war, it must have been much aggravated by the conclusion of peace. Great Britain, after an attempt to obtain compensation for her own adherents from the now ' United States,' as a condition of that peace and of the recognition of American Independence, gave way upon that point, as on others.1Defeated and humiliated, she was unable to obtain her own terms, and when, on September 3, 1783, a treaty was signed, the American Loyalists were left to their fate.

and ' sawyers,' began the sea warfare with England soon after the battle of Lexington. Armed only with such weapons as they used in their daily work, they seized the royal schooner ' Margranetto,' mounting fonrRuhrand fourteen swivels.

1*The Edinburgh Gazetteer,* 'Machias,' 1822.

2Winsor,*Memorial History of Boston,*vol. iii., ' The Revolutionary Period,' chap. 2.*The Siege of Boston,*by Rev. Edward E. Hale, D. D.

The part of the treaty with England which excited most severe criticism2(writes Mr. Lecky), was the abandonment of the Loyalists. These unfortunate men had, indeed, a claim of the very strongest kind to the protection of England, for they had lost everything in her cause. Some had simply fled from the country before mob violence, and had been attainted in their absence. Others had actually taken up arms, and they had done so at the express invitation of the English Government and of English Generals. Their abandonment was described by nearly all the members of the Opposition as an act of unqualified baseness, which would leave an enduring stain on the English name. ' What,' said Lord North, ' are not the claims of those who, in conformity to their allegiance, their cheerful obedience to the voice of Parliament, their confidence in the proclamation of our Generals, invited, under every assurance of military, parliamentary, political, and affectionate protection, espoused with the hazard of their lives, and the forfeiture of their properties, the cause of Great Britain?'

It had hitherto nearly always been the custom to close a struggle, which partopk kutoly of the nature of Civil War, by a generou:u.'t of amnesty and restitution. At the peace of Miinster a general act, of indemnity had been passed, and the partisans of the Spanisl overeign had either regained their confiscated properties, or- been indemnified for their loss. A similar measure hlH a'ed in favour of the revolted Catalans by France at the peeee of the Pyrenees, and by England at the peace of Utrecht, and Spain had frankly conceded it. The case of the American Loyalists was a still stronger one, and the Opposition emphaticallyTBuiRMed that the omission of any effectual provision for them inR Treaty of Versailles, ' unless marked by the just indignation of Parliament, would blast for ever the honour of this country.'

1Sabine,*Tlie American Loyalists: Preliminai-y Remarks.-* Lecky,*A History of England in the Eighteenth Century*(Edition 1890), vol. iv., chap. xv., p. 264.'

SIE JOHN BEENAED'S CLAIMS 167

Fierce debates' took place in both houses, and led to the resignation of Lord Shelburne,2the Prime Minister, some months before the peace was concluded. A coalition ministry was formed by Lord North and Charles James Fox; it did not last quite to the end of the year, and William Pitt then became Premier.

The Government had already begun giving assistance to some of the exiles before the close of the war,3believing that only temporary assistance would be required.

It now found a crushing number of these unhappy people thrown upon the national generosity, or rather sense of honour. How soon Sir John Bernard's brothers began to plead his cause I can but guess from Mrs. White's letter of April 29, 1782,4in which she speaks of hopes from an expected change of ministry. From time, to tkute his father's executors, Thomas Bernard and Charles "Wjhilie; Advanced money for the purpose of pushing forwarcfrhis ease. But it appears that Sir John had not only thejlmitory action of the Commissioners appointed for the cwvsiderKion of loyalist grievances to contend with; his claims were altogether disallowed.

In the ' Life of Sir Francis Bernard, by his son Thomas,' privately printed in 1790, it is stated that Sir John, after the ' series of confinements and sufferings ' already mentioned, was ' almost the only person precluded from participating in that relief which British justice and liberality had provided for the sufferers by the American War.' In a note he adds:

I had intended to have inserted Sir John Bernard's case in the Appendix to this work – but I have thought it better to wait for some minutes of evidence, which I have applied for to the American Board.

There is reason to doubt if the case ever appeared in any book or pamphlet; it is not mentioned in the lists I haveseen of Thomas Bernard's writings,1and no copy seems to have been preserved in the family, but the motive for withholding it has not transpired. Possibly the minutes were never obtained; and a hope may have been held out to the relatives that their requests might at some future period obtain attention, while in the meantime silence was desirable, if not indispensable.

1Sabine,*The American Loyalists: Preliminary Remarks.*

*Lecky,*A History of England in the Eighteenth Century*(Edition 1890), vol. iv. chap. Xv.

' Sabine,*The American Loyalists: Preliminary Remarks.*

< Given in Chapter ii. of this Volume. The Executors, according to a memorandum in my possession, advanced money for the purpose stated above.

The narrative of Sir John's experiences is therefore lost – which is to be regretted; as, in addition to its domestic value, it must have afforded some insight into the life of the time.

The family considered that Sir John had claims in respect: (1) Of his loss of the post of naval officer to the port of Boston. (2) Of the annihilation of his business as a merchant. (3) Of the confiscation of his land. But some pretext was found for ignoring every one of these wrongs. Yet the qualification for redress was far from rigid, as will appear from the following list of classes, given by Sabine,2into which the claimants were officially divided:

First Class. – Those who had rendered services to Great Britain.

Second Class. – Those who had borne arms for Great Britain.

Third Class. – Uniform loyalists.

Fourth Class. – Loyal British subjects resident in Great Britain.

Fifth Class. – Loyalists who had taken oaths to the American States, but afterwards joined the British.

Sixth Class. – Loyalists who had borne arms for the American States, but afterwards joined the British navy or army.

These six classes were eventually – in consequence of popular clamour – placed on the same footing, a proceeding not consonant with ordinary ideas of justice. There were many other points on which the Commissioners' decisions were open to cavil. Sir John Bernard's difficulty I at firstAN UNSYMPATHETIC SKETCH 169

1There ia a complete list – or intended to be complete – of Sir Thomas Bernard's writings at the end of the biography by the Rev. James Baker. The case is not there, nor is it in the catalogue of the British Museum, I believe; it is certainly not under the head of ' Bernard.'

'Sabine,*The American Loyalists,*note to*Preliminary Remarks,*p. 105.

supposed to be, that he was ' a loyal British subject,' and yet not ' resident in Great Britain,' and so did not come within the letter of any one of the definitions. Yet surely he had ' rendered services to Great Britain,' as naval officer, and in sundry other ways. Scrope Bernard indeed ascribes his exclusion to ' the nature of his losses.' This is an incidental mention of the subject in a letter to Scrope; and I cannot attempt to explain the phrase. In his ' Sketches of American Loyalists,'*I*Sabine has given short notices of both John and Thomas Bernard, and in both of these he terms Sir John ' a Whig,' which, in American parlance, meant a favourer of independence. This, also, I have no means of explaining; certainly, all that is known of him up to the time of his visit to England, in 1779, is inconsistent with this epithet; but it is possible that, at some later period, when he found that England had cast him off, he may have been willing to make his peace with the revolutionary government. Such a concession would, in ordinary circumstances, have been completely overlooked, on repentance, as the list of classes shows; whether the case of a Governor's son was different it is impossible to say without further evidence; but Thomas Bernard gives no hint that his brother's exclusion was attributable to any such cause.

The very unsympathetic account given by Sabine of Sir John's troubled life, is continued as follows:

Not long after the peace he lived at Pleasant Point a few miles from Eastport in a small hut built by himself, and with no companion but a dog. An unbroken wilderness was around him. The only inhabitants at the head of the tide-waters of St. Croix were a few workmen, preparing to erect a saw-mill. Robbinston and Perry were uninhabited. Eastport contained a single family. Yet, at the spot now occupied by the remnant of the tribe of the Passamaquoddys, he attempted to make a farm. He had been bred in ease, had hardly done a day's work in his life; and yet he believed that he could earn a competence by labour. He told those who saw him, that ' other young men went into the woods, and made themselves farms, and got a good living, and he saw no reason why he could not.' But he out down a few trees, became discouraged, and departed.

1Sabine,*The American Loyalists,* 'Bernard, Sir Thomas, Baronet' – ' Bernard, Sir John.' Thomas is placed first, out of the regular order, for some reason which doe!; not appear.

His abject condition in mind and estate rendered him an object of deep commiseration; and his conduct during hostilities having entitled him to consideration, the legislature of Massachusetts restored to him one half of the island of Mount Desert. Of his subsequent history, while he continued in the United States, but little is known to me. He came to Maine occasionally, and was much about Boston.

Sabine, writing from an American point of view, has probably exaggerated Sir John's helplessness and want of perseverance. That he was unfit to struggle single-handed against the forces of nature in a bleak northern latitude is quite likely; but he had never been an idler, and, for some years previous to the Confiscation, he must have lived more or less the life of a settler, though, no doubt, with men under him. His situation, after that event, an outcast in a howling wilderness, presented a strong contrast to the position of Thomas working in Lincoln's Inn Chambers and dining in the Middle Temple Hall, and to that of Scrope in Doctors' Commons and Lord Temple's mansion – both latterly possessing comfortable homes of their own, both mixing in cultivated and sometimes in brilliant society. But the younger brothers were most anxious to effect some change in the life of the unfortunate bead of their family, and I gather from a letterlwritten by Thomas to Scrope, that the chief obstacle was Sir John's own determination. Easily as Sabine represents him to have been turned from his purpose, he did not return to England until 1786,2where he was really wanted to assist in winding up his father's affairs, and yielded to the remonstrances of his relatives, and possibly also to the prospect of ever increasing severity on the part of the United States Government, and especially of the Massacbusetts authorities. John Hancock was then Governor, Samuel Adams Lieutenant-Governor, of that State.5RESULTS OF CIVIL WAR 171

1MS. Letter at Nether Winchendon.

-This also appears from Letters and Memoranda at Nether Winchendon.

3Winsor,*Mem. Hist, of Boston,*vol. iii.

As to Sir John's frequent visits to Boston, I do not know what business or how often it may have called him there. He can hardly have gone for pleasure.

Military occupation, pestilence, and the Sight of the Tory party, had done their work (writes Dr. Lodge), and had more than decimated the people. Commerce, the main support of the inhabitants, suffered severely in the war, and had been only partially replaced by the uncertain successes of the privateers. The young men had been drawn away to the army; both State and Confederacy were practically bankrupt; and the disorganisation consequent upon seven years of Civil War was great and disastrous.1

Of Sir John's own friends scarce one would be left, and strange men had taken their places. Mr. Curwen2probably understated the case when he wrote, in 1779:

Two or three persons, I am told, who had not money enough for shoes for their feet, are now riding coaches of their own in Boston. Solomon says, ' I have seen servants on horseback, and Princes walking on foot.' I really think the royal preacher was a prophet, and pointed at the events of our day; at least the present state of English America verifies the remark.

As to the restoration of half the island of Mount Desert, no tradition has been preserved in the family; if such a restoration ever took place it cannot have been for long; the authorities in Massachusetts must speedily have resumed possession, and possibly some fresh persecution accompanied the resumption. Thomas Bernard evidently did not realise the ' commiseration ' and ' consideration ' which, according to Sabine, characterised the behaviour of the victorious Americans to his brother, for he has spoken of nothing but cruelty.

From the time when the Bernard family welcomed Sir John, on his return to England, there is no doubt thatits members made every effort to dissuade him from ever setting his foot in America again. Yet his position in England, as a ruined man, was distressing and humiliating; and the exertions of his brothers seem to have been directed to obtaining for him some official post – they could only hope for a small one – and this is some evidence that the excitement of brain to which Sabine alludes, must, whatever its previous extent, have passed away. Had it remained and amounted to insanity there would have been nothing very surprising in the fact – it was no uncommon result of the sufferings and hardships of the unfortunate Loyalists; as will be shown in the next chapter. But, though not driven absolutely mad, Sir John's nerves were more or less shattered by his late experiences, and he remained all his life to some extent a crushed and broken-down man.

1Lodge (Henry Cabot, Ph. D.),*The Last Forty Years of Town Government,*1782-1822. In Winsor's*Mem. Hint, of Boston,*vol. iii.*The Last Hundred Tears,*part i.

*Curwen (Samuel, Judge of Admiralty, &c.),*Journal and Letters from*1775to1784, 'Letter to Bev. Isaac Smith, Sidmouth,' dated 'Exeter, Feb. Ill, 1779.'

At this period, 1786, he was turned forty; it was therefore not easy to procure a post for him in a new and untried line, nor would it be easy for him to adapt himself to the circumstances. It would seem, however, that as soon as the family affairs were settled he went to France; the first news I have of him is contained in a letterlhe wrote to his brother Scrope, on August 8,1788. In this epistle he thanks both his brothers for remittances, including seven magazines and a newspaper – and proceeds:

I understand that there are two portrait painters here; one of which being well recommended, I went in quest of him, and was informed by his landlady that he was absent on a journey, and that she did not expect his return in less than six weeks. After twice to-day calling, I found the other at his lodgings, where I saw three pieces of his performance, one of which (a pretty good likeness) I immediately knew. As you are very desirous that I should lose no time in sitting for my picture, and send it by the captain of the vessel who delivered me your two packets, it is with pleasure I acquaint you that I conceive it will be in my power early to comply with your request, and to which I shall give due attention, thanking you for your civility and notice of me in preferring to number my portrait amongst your collection. I have been for some time past, (as I still continue to be) very seriouslyA SOJOUEN IN FRANCE 173

1MS. Letter at Nether Winchendon.

indisposed, oppressed with a very bad settled cold, &c., upon which account, had not your orders forbad any delay, I should have been inclined to have postponed my sitting, to have given time for the recovery of health and spirits, that my picture might have afforded a better countenance, than I can expect it will at the present.

The result, no doubt, is to be seen in a small oil painting at Nether Winchendon, which has preserved only too faithfully the woebegone appearance produced by a severe cold accompanying an aggravating nervous depression. It is a stiff front-face representation, possibly a good likeness in some respects, but certainly verging on caricature.

I have no information as to the reason of Sir John's stay at Dunkirk. France seems hardly a country he would have chosen for pleasure, having regard to the part the

Government and people had taken as allies of the American Revolu- tionists; at one time I thought he might have obtained some small consulship, or vice-consulship; but in the sequel he appears rather as a free man. He probably economised by living out of England, besides escaping from a galling position; and as he seems to have lingered in the country he may have possessed some of his brother Francis's talent for languages, and made friends as he wandered. In the beginning of 1791 he was still in France, though in a part very distant from Dunkirk; and this, notwithstanding the agitated state of the country, which may perhaps have reminded him of America. I can bring forward nothing to show where he had been meanwhile.

In February 1791, Mr. William Grenville wrote to Lord Buckingham:

You probably know also that Selwyn's death gives me the disposal of his office in Barbados, of between $400 and $500 per annum; but it can be held only by a resident. I feel myself bound, in the first instance, to offer to Nepean, who is killing himself by his labour here, to give it to any proper person who will vacate anything for it here. If that fails, you know I have no other idea of patronage than that of consulting your wishes, or serving our joint objects.'

1*Memoirs of the Court and Cabinets of George III.,*vol. ii., 1791.

Mr. Grenville's first idea must have failed, since the rough draft of a letter' from Scrope Bernard to Governor Parry, dated Whitehall, July 5, 1791, shows that Sir John Bernard was appointed to this office, for which there may not have been much competition:

Sir, – A Patent having passed the Great Seal dated the fourth of June last, appointing Sir John Bernard (my eldest Brother) Register in Chancery, & Clerk of the Crown & Peace in Barbados in the room of the late Mr. G. Selwyn, I take the liberty of mentioning to your Excellency this appointment, & of requesting your friendship and good offices towards my Brother after his arrival in the Island. He is at present in the South of France;&proposes going immediately to Bordeaux, & embarking from thence to the West Indies without coming to England. I therefore send his Patent & a few other things to meet him at Barbados, & hope you will excuse my consigning them to your care till the time of his arrival, which will probably be in the course of August. And in the meantime I will trust to your taking such steps respecting his Office as may be proper and for his benefit, preparatory to his arrival.

Sir John having been a great sufferer in America, without having been able from the nature of his Losses to obtain any compensation for them, his wish at Barbados will be to live in a moderate scale, & if you could assist him with your advice respecting the proper advantage and plan of life at Bridgetown consistent with propriety, you would be of considerable service to him, & this & any other instance of your attention & kindness would be thankfully acknowledged by

Sir

Your Excellency.

The Governor's reply is dated ' Barbados, August 29th 1791':

Sir, – I am honoured with your letter together with Sir John Bernard's, and take the earliest opportunity of assuring you that nothing shall from my part be wanting to promote his interest, and to render his situation in this country as pleasing to him as the nature of things will admit of.

The full amount of the profits of his office I very fairly statedA NEW CAREER 175

1This letter and Governor Parry's reply are copied from MSS. at Nether Winchendon.

some time since to my friend Nepean, and as this is by far the cheapest island in the West Indies, I think his expenses need not exceed his receipts, provided it will be consistent with his rank in life to execute the office himself. But this and every other difficulty you may rest assured I shall endeavour to remove, and be happy upon all occasions to testify my readiness to comply with your wishes, and to assure you of the esteem with which I am,

Sir

Your most obedient and

most humble servant

D. Parry.

The appointment was evidently not one to marry on, but Sir John had probably looked upon himself, for some years, as destined to a single life. At the age of forty-six, he now commenced a new career, without the hope and spirit of youth or the well-balanced tone of a serene middle-age. The transit to his new home was tedious, if not stormy, since he had not reached Barbados when the Governor wrote to his brother. There were disturbances amongst the ' Malottos ' of the nearer French islands, Guadaloupe and St. Lucia, which, in the following October, culminated in massacres; but I do not know whether Sir John's arrival was at all delayed by this rebellion. When once settled, his life was probably untroubled by calamities for some time; his biography now, indeed, is a blank, since I have no letters throwing any light on the period.

In 1799, Sir John was in England; this date is fixed by an entry in one of his sister Julia's manuscripts. My father had some recollection of him, derived, no doubt, from this visit. It may have been at this time that he was transferred to a post in Dominica, which apparently included work in St. Vincent and Martinique, and perhaps improved his position. Moreover, the persevering efforts of his brothers at length wrung from the British Government thirty thousand pounds, as compensation for the losses in America,1and this sum, allowing for inevitable deductions, went, I believe, entirely to Sir John, whose presence in England was probably desired for this settlement.

1This information I derived from my uncle, Sir F. Bernard-Morland, and my father.

During this visit his second portrait was in all likelihood painted. It bears no great resemblance to the first, but is equally characterised by a gloomy expression.1Good fortune had come too late.

Three letters written from ' Roseau, Dominica,' to Scrope Bernard, throw some light on Sir John's history four or five years after his return to the West Indies. They are chiefly on business, and it is evident that the writer was fond of buying and selling houses and land – a very natural hobby in one who had made the settling and improving of a new country part of his business during the years of his youth, and had then been deprived of all power to follow this or any other outlet for his energies. It may be assumed that his official work left him time for this recreation, but it may have been pursued somewhat recklessly; and I am afraid that the compensation grant was frittered away in unfortunate investments of this sort.

Sir John's principal residence appears to have been at Roseau,2the capital of Dominica, but a small town; it was situated ' on a point of land on the south-west side of the island, which forms two bays.' Occasionally he seems to have visited the other two islands, and in his last years he was evidently once more involved in the troubles of warfare, to an extent that was at least annoying and was near leading to serious consequences. The French were endeavouring to recover Martinique, which had been wrested from them nearly twenty years before. It would seem that Sir John was suspected of being in communication with them, although his American experiences had afforded him no reason for courting their alliance. But this is the only construction I can put upon one of his letters.3' Lord S. made representations to the English Government,' inCONVULSIONS OF NATURE 177

1Now in the possession of Scrope Bernard's great grand-daughter, Mrs. Walton.

*Bees'a*Cyclopadia,*'Roseau – now Charlotte Town.' ' MS. Letter at Nether Winchendon.

relation to some rumour concerning his conduct, which appears to have arisen, so far as I can judge, from his having bought a house and land in the island, and gone to look after them at this critical time – a result perhaps of his old habits of determined resistance to circumstances and disregard of danger.

That there was some danger appears from his letter*l*of July 9, 1803, written in Dominica:

I am yet far from having recovered from the excessive fatigue occasioned by a precipitate retreat from Martinique, attended by a long and tempestuous passage on a crowded vessel across the Channel to this island.

The charge, which Sir John indignantly denied, was apparently dropped, and he remained at his post. On the point of land between two bays he had opportunities of observing those convulsions of nature which added to the troubles of war. In a letter2of September, 1804, he says:

The Packet by which I forwarded mine of the 28th ulto. to you, was drove on Shore and totally lost at St. John's, Antigua, during a storm of long continuance; the mails on board, as I am informed, were saved, and therefore it is probable that such Letter will reach you with this. Of the losses sustained during the Storm of Persons who had property afloat in the different Bays of all the Islands in these Seas you will have better information from Newspapers than it is in my Power to give you. Several Vessels in this Bay were saved by going to Sea at the commencement of the Gale: all others remaining in this Bay were drove on the Shore and totally lost, except one Ship and one Brig, belonging to London, who rode out the Storm. Every Tree near the Sea, and within reach of the Spray of it was blasted; some were blown down and some torn up by the Eoots.

The struggle with France which cut Dominica off from St. Vincent, and other islands probably, was a source of great inconvenience. The last letter31 can find in Sir John's handwriting, dated from Roseau, ' Novemr4th 1804,' about two months after the previous epistle just quoted, states that:

1MS. Letter at Nether Winchendon.2*Ibid.* * *Ibid.*

VOL. III. N

This is a horrid war for the West Indies; its effects are extreme scarcity of all necessaries, and consequently enormous prices. Our seas swarm with French privateers, who are very active and not unsuccessful. Whilst I am writing, a French Row-boat with sixteen oars has been plainly discovered to have boarded and taken possession of a Mail-boat on her passage from Antigua to Barbados, and to have hoisted French colours over the English. All here is motion and commotion.

This day (Sunday), which with you is a day of rest, is here a day of tumult, drunkenness, and riot. As the plantation negroes have this day to themselves, it would indeed be very difficult, if not impossible, to preserve that order and decorum, which is most devoutly to be wished.

This unfortunate war had probably a disastrous effect on Sir John's improvement schemes. Whether he was subject to any personal danger in the ensuing years there are no letters to show. That he was grateful for the exertions of his brothers on his behalf there is no reason to doubt from his correspondence, but it is doubtful whether he ever attained to a cheerful view of life. Sir John Bernard died on August 25, 1809, aged sixty-three, at Roseau.[1]Communication with the West Indies must have been very imperfect at that time, since the news did not reach England till the following January (1810).[2]

[1]From various Family Records.

The interval between the death and the reception of its announcement in England is recorded in the Diary of Mary Ann Bernard-Morland.

8

SECTION 8

Distressing Cases of Insanity – EiohardKing – The Fate of General Lyman and his Family – Fate of Colonel Robinson and his Family – Atrocities in the Northern Provinces – Sufferings of the Episcopal Clergy – The Retaliation exercised by Loyalists – The Share of John Adams in the Policy against the Loyalists – Treatment of the Exiles in England – Dr. Peter Oliver – Parson Peters – Captain Fenton – Peter Van Shaaok – Action of the Commissioners in England – Timothy Ruggles – Jonathan Sewall – Daniel Leonard – Samuel Quinoy – John Adams, Ambassador of the United States – John Hancock – Samuel Adams.

Thenarrative of Sir John Bernard's ruined career seems to require as its accompaniment some mention of the trials endured by the great body of American Loyalists, although the subject is but indirectly connected with the history of the Bernard family. It must have been often in the thoughts of its members, notwithstanding that I possess only occasional records of their continued interest in the common cause.

Compared with some of this faithful and persecuted band, Sir John might almost be termed a happy man. Name after name in the pages of Sabine's book 1 is followed by the words, ' Proscribed and banished, suffered much at the hands of the Sons of Liberty.' The plundering and burning of houses, the wounding or even killing of their inmates, seem to have been matters of everyday occurrence.

It has been stated, in commenting on Sabine's intimation that Sir John's troubles had affected his head, that undoubted insanity, of a permanent nature, was sometimes the result of the miseries and terrors of the times. Two distressing cases of this kind may be mentioned.

1Sabine,*The American Loyalists.*

Eichard King was a prosperous merchant of Scarborough, Maine, ' with a leaning towards the Government,' to whom many persons had become indebted beyond their ability to pay. In consequence, apparently, of this circumstance his troubles began early, soon after the attack on Mr. Hutchinson's residence, of which the outrage now to be related appears to have been an imitation; and the story has been handed down by no less a person than John Adams:

Taking advantage of the disorders occasioned by the passage of the Stamp Act, a party, disguised as Indians, on the night of the 16th of March, 1766, broke into his store, and his dwelling-bouse also, and destroyed his books and papers containing evidence of debts. Not content with this, they laid waste his property and threatened his life if he should venture to seek any legal mode of redress. Many of the perpetrators were, however, detected and brought to justice.1

John Adams was Counsel for King in the suit which followed; and he, who had no pity for Hutchinson, but rather rejoiced in the impunity of his assailants, writes:

The terror and distress, the distraction and horror, of his family, cannot be described by words or painted on capvas. It is enough to move a statue, to melt a heart of stone, to read the story.8

The popular bitterness thus engendered did not, however subside, and in 1774 a slight incident occurred which soon caused it once more to break out. A vessel of Mr. King's was found to have delivered a load of lumber in Boston by special license, after the port had been closed, and the materials had been purchased for the use of the troops. On this occasion forty men from the neighbouring town of Gorham came over and compelled Mr. King, in fear of his life, to make a disavowal of his Opinions. These repeated shocks seem to have been too much for Mr. King's constitution. He became distempered in mind, and died in the following March.3

The story of another family is still more distressing. General Lyman4belonged to Connecticut, where he wasFATE OF THE LYMANS 181

1John Adams's Letters to his Wife, Note to No. 9.

*Ibid.*No. 9.' *Ibid.*

4Sabine.*The American Loyalists,*<$c.' Lyman (Phineas).' An additional notice, headed ' Lyman,' commemorates the fate of the General's sons. Atthe end of the war the property was confiscated and the family, shipwrecked on the way to Jamaica, lost everything, and barely escaped drowning.

distinguished both as a lawyer and as an officer. His misfortunes began with a voyage he made to England to ask a grant of lands for a company, chiefly military. Through official neglect and intrigues he was detained eleven years; and meanwhile his affairs in America went to wreck and ruin. The grant was at last obtained in 1774, just as the changes in his native land rendered it useless; he returned to find his family in want and to encounter political agitation. General Lyman died imbecile and his eldest son a lunatic.

The widow, her brother and daughters, made their way to the dearly purchased land amid perils and hardships which continued after their arrival. They fled before the Spaniards in 1782, and one division of the party was imprisoned by the Americans. A younger son of the General, who had been a brilliant officer in the British Army, worn out by successive troubles, ended his life in a state of melancholy madness. Three sons remained, of whom Sabine records only that they lived and died in obscurity.

Most of the violent acts which are recorded in this chapter were perpetrated in the northern provinces, but many, no doubt, took place in every colony, though perhaps with less frequency in some than in others. One instance may here be mentioned of cruelty in the south, which will suffice, as this history is concerned chiefly with Massachusetts.

Lieutenant-Colonel Joseph Robinson,1 from Virginia, resident in South Carolina, was marked as a Loyalist and a price was set on his head; his house was fired by rebels, after his escape, but while his wife and children were still there. The lady had but just time to drag her little girls out of the flames; she placed one child before her on horseback; a negro, her sole attendant, carried the other in like manner; and they travelled thus several hundred miles across a disturbed country, till she joined her husband in East Florida, where their troubles, though much mitigated, were probably by no means over.

1 *Ryerson,* vol. ii., chap. xli. Letter from Hon. E. Hodgson, a grandson of Colonel Robinson, Chief Justice of Prince Edward's Island.

It certainly seems, however, as if the northern provinces were specially notorious for atrocities. A horrible story is told of General Putnam forcing two boys to hang a man named Jones, of Eidgefield, Connecticut, on a charge of carrying provisions to British soldiers, although he denied this charge to the last.1 The boys executed their dreadful task with sobs and tears, while the General ' compelled them at the sword's point to obey his orders.'

The cases of the two Dunbars of Halifax, Massachusetts, which actually occurred before the beginning of the war, are instances of refined cruelty without palliation.

Daniel Dunbar,2

of Halifax, Massachusetts, was an officer in the militia, and in 1774 a mob demanded of him the surrender of the colours of his company. He refused; when the multitude broke into his house, took him out, forced him to get upon a rail, where he was held, and tossed up and down until he was exhausted. He was then dragged and beaten, and gave up the standard to save his life.

Jesse Dunbar3

bought some fat cattle of a Mandamus Councillor in 1774, and drove them to Plymouth for sale. The Whigs soon learned with whom Dunbar had presumed to deal, and after he had slaughtered, skinned, and hung up one of the beasts, commenced punishing him for the offence. That punishment was cruel in the extreme. His tormentors, it appears, put the dead ox in a cart, and fixed Dunbar in his belly, carted him four miles, and required him to pay one dollar for the ride. He then was delivered over to a Kingston mob, who carted him four other miles and exacted another dollar. A Duxbury mob then took him, and, after beating him in the face with the creature's tripe, and endeavouring to cover his person with it, carried him to Councillor Thomas's house, and compelled him to pay a further sum of money. Flinging his beef into the road, they now left him to recover and return as he could.

1 Sabine, *The American Loyalists,* 'Jones, of Ridgefteld, Connecticut.'

=*Ibid.,*' Dunbar, DanieL'

2*Ibid.,*' Dunbar, Jesse.'

DESCENDANTS OF THE PILGRIM FATHERS 183

Such were the noble descendants of the Pilgrim Fathers – or, if not their descendants, the men who were brought up amid their traditions and educated in their principles!

The subsequent history of Jesse Dunbar is not given. Daniel recovered his injuries sufficiently to reach the British lines, and accompanied the Eoyal forces to Halifax, Nova Scotia, in 1776. These outrages, it should be remembered, are chronicled by a writer who sympathises with the insurgents, though not with all their deeds. He records some cases of cruelties committed by the Loyalists and the British, but chiefly by leaders of armed forces, and, for the most part, measures of retaliation.

The Episcopal clergy, whose position can never have been very comfortable in the northern provinces, fared badly during the war. Many escaped to England, and many could not escape. Dr. Seabury, 1a prominent and representative man, has left some account of their troubles in a letter to the Society for the Propagation of the Gospel, written from Westchester, province of New York, in 1775. ' Dr. Cooper and Dr. Chandler have been obliged to quit their community, and sailed for England last week.' 2Dr. Myles Cooper, president of King's College, the first-named clergyman, was saved from the violence of the mob only by the presence of mind and ready wit of a collegian named Hamilton, who harangued the assailants while he escaped. Dr. Seabury had since been concealed in the Wilkins mansion on Castle Hill Neck, Westchester, with Cooper, Chandler and Isaac Wilkins. They were secreted in or about a chimney, and supplied with food through a trapdoor in the floor. Dr. Seabury continues:

I have been obliged to retire a few days from the threatened vengeance of the New Englanders who lately broke into this Province. But I hope I shall be able to keep my station. The charge against the clergy is a very extraordinary one – that theyhave, in conjunction with the Society and the British Ministry, laid a plan for enslaving America.

1 See vol. ii. of this Family History, chap. xxiv., pp. 181, 182.

'Beardsley (E. Edwards), D. D., LL. D., rector of St. Thomas's Church, New Haven, Conn.,*The Life of Samuel Seabury, D. D., First Bishop of Connecticut, and of the Episcopal Church in the United States of America.*

Beardsley, the Doctor's biographer, proceeds to state that

The fears which Seabury had expressed in his letter to the Secretary were soon realised. He had been serving, as beat he could, his two diminished congregations, and working in another way to obtain a partial support for his family, when an armed force from Connecticut invaded the territory of New York, seized him at his schoolroom, and carried him to New Haven. The particulars of his arrest, and the recital of his wrongs and of the cruelties inflicted upon him, were well stated in a petition to the General Assembly, asking for relief from ' the heavy hand of oppression and tyranny.'

Dr. Seabury obtained his release, and lived on at West- chester, in considerable discomfort, until another invasion, after the Declaration of Independence, drove him to seek refuge with the King's troops in Long Island. When they left he retreated to New York, then in British occupation and in a country which was ravaged by both armies. From thence he wrote to the Society various particulars of the unfortunate clergy.

His biographer states that he noted the death of Mr. Avery, missionary at Rye, but does not give any particulars, beyond the assertion that

He detailed the sad circumstances as he had received them, and placed the cause of his death, whether justly or not is uncertain, among the barbarities of civil war.

Then follows another sad case.

In the same letter he reported the death of another missionary, the Rev. Luke Badcock, who for six years had been stationed at the manor of Philipsburg (now Yonkers), and, like himself, was a sincere and active Loyalist. From his allegiance to the King sprang the calamities which hurried him to the grave.

The latter end of October (wrote Seabury) he was seized by the rebels at his house, and carried off to the Provincial Congress at Fishkill. His papers and sermons were also seized and examined, TREATMENT OF WOMEN AND CHILDREN 186

but, as nothing appeared on which they could ground any pretence for detaining him, he was asked whether he supposed himself bound by his oath of allegiance to the King; upon his answering in the affirmative, he was deemed an enemy to the liberties of America, and ordered to be kept in custody. About the middle of February he was taken sick, and, as his confinement had produced no change in his sentiments, he was dismissed with a written order to remove, within ten days, within the lines of the King's army, being adjudged a person too dangerous to be permitted to continue where his influence might be exerted in favour of a legal government. He got home with difficulty, in a raging fever, and delirious. In this state he continued about a week (the greatest part of the time delirious), and then died, extremely regretted. Indeed I know not a more excellent man, and I fear his loss, particularly in that mission, will scarcely be made up.

Over one portion of Dr. Seabury's statements his biographer has drawn a veil:

His description of the treatment of women and children*is too painful to be re-peated.*This treatment must be ascribed to that spirit of lawlessness which, unhappily, in times of great excitement and disorder, is somewhat beyond the control of magistrates and military commanders. New York was their place of refuge, where they found protection, if not support. ' Many families of my parishioners, said he, are now in this town, who used to live decently, suffering for common necessaries. I daily meet them, and it is melancholy to observe the dejection strongly marked on their faces, which seem to implore that assistance which I am unable to give. To pity and to pray for them is all I can do.'

As regards the clergy, one more extract from the same biography is here given, which sums up the case:

The Rev. Thomas Barton, a missionary of the Society in Delaware, was forced to surrender his loyalty or find protection within the British lines; and in a letter to the Secretary, dated New York, January 8th, 1779, he said: 1 – ' The clergy of America, the missionaries in particular, have suffered beyond example, and, indeed, beyond the records of any history, in this day of trial. Most of them have lost their all, many of them are now in a state of melancholy pilgrimage and poverty; and some of them havelately (from grief and despondency, it is said), paid the last debt of nature. We may exclaim,*Quis furor, 0 cives!*What have we done to deserve this treatment from our former friends and fellow-citizens? We have not intermeddled with any matters inconsistent with our callings and functions. We have studied to be quiet, and to give no offence to the present rulers. We have obeyed the laws and government now in being, as far as our consciences and prior obligations would permit. We know no crime that can be alleged against us, except an honest avowal of our principles can be deemed such, and for these we have suffered a persecution as cruel as the bed of Procrustes.'

1*Historical Collections,*Delaware, p. 181, quoted in the Life of Bishop Seabury.

With regard to the cruelties practised on the general body of the Loyalists, none has spoken more forcibly than Sabine, himself a patriotic American; he exclaims:

Did the cause of America and of human freedom gain strength by the deeds of the five hundred who mobbed Sheriff Tyng, or by the speed of the one hundred and sixty on horseback who pursued Commissioner Hallowell? Were the shouts of an excited multitude, and the crash of broken glass and demolished furniture, fit requiems for the dying Ropes? Were Whig interests promoted because one thousand men shut up the Courts of Law in Berkshire, and five thousand did the same in Worcester, and mobs drove away the judges at Springfield, Taunton, and Plymouth? because in one place a judge was stopped, insulted, and threatened; in another the whole Bench were hissed and hooted, and in a third were required to do penance, hat in hand, in a procession of attornies and sheriffs? Did the driving of Ingersoll from his estate, of Edson from his house, and the assault upon the home of Gilbert, and the shivering of Sewall's windows, serve to wean them, or their friends and connexions, from their royal master? Did Ruggles, when subsequent events threw his countrymen into his power, forget that the creatures which grazed his pastures had been painted, shorn, maimed and poisoned; that he had been pursued on the highway by day and night; that his dwelling had been broken open, and he and his family had been driven from it? What Tory turned Whig because Saltonstall was mobbed, and Oliver plundered, and Leonard shot at in his own house? Was the kingly arm actually weakened or strengthened for harm, because thousands surrounded the mansions of high functionaries, and forced them into resignation – or because sheriffs were told that they would perform their duties at the hazard of their lives? Which party gained by waylaying and insulting at

BITTER PEESECDTION 187

every corner the ' Rescinders,' the ' Protesters,' and the ' Addressers '? Which by the burning of the mills of Putnam? Had widows and orphans no additional griefs, because the Probate Courts were closed by the multitude, and their officers were driven under cover of British guns? Did it serve a good end to endeavour to hinder Tories from getting tenants or to prevent persons who owed them from paying honest debts?

On whose cheek should have been the blush of shame, when the habitation of the aged and feeble Foster was sacked and he had no shelter but the woods? − when Williams, as infirm as he, was seized at night, dragged away for miles, and smoked in a room with fastened doors and a closed chimney-top? What father, who doubted, wavered, and doubted still, whether to join or fly, determined to abide the issue in the land of his birth, because foul words were spoken to his daughters, or because they were pelted when riding, or moving in the innocent dance? Ibthere cause for wonder that some who still live should yet say, of their own and their fathers' treatment, that' persecution made half the King's friends '? The good men of the period mourned these and similar proceedings, and they may be lamented now.1

From Mr. Sabine's conclusions I venture to differ. The patriotic persecution did not, of course, advance ' the cause of human freedom,' but it was, I must believe, a great success from the American point of view. If it made Loyalists, it crushed them also, old and new alike. Numbers of persons whose convictions and feelings were, and always had been, in favour of allegiance to England, were driven by terror, often as the only way of saving their children's lives and their own, to acknowledge the new Government. Some, no doubt, took refuge in England or Nova Scotia who might in other circumstances have settled down quietly as citizens of the United States; but America probably does not to this day regret their loss, although a voice may here and there be raised speaking a kindlier feeling.

As to the amount of retaliation exercised by Loyalists, it must have been in the early stages of the struggle very slight. Few were in a position to assert themselves. General Ruggles was an exceptional man, who weathered the stormand became Attorney-General of Nova Scotia, no very brilliant post in those days, however; but what he did, or had the power of doing, cannot have had any appreciable effect on the other party. And the same may be said of the acts of any other Loyalist who attained office in the recently settled colony of Nova Scotia, or elsewhere. Before quitting this subject it may be observed that some of the instances of persecution to which Sabine alludes acquire fresh force when the details are given. Ropes, for instance, was lying in the agonies of small-pox when his house was wrecked;1he died the next day.

1Sabine,*The American Loyalists: Preliminary Remarks, or Historical Essay*,pp. 76-7.

The same author asserts that 'the good men of the period ' mourned the proscription of the Loyalists; but one whom the United States reckon amongst their ' good men,' and also amongst their greatest men, was a chief persecutor.9' Perhaps no one did as much to promote the cruel policy against the Loyalists as Mr. John Adams, who was the ruling spirit in all the proceedings of Boston for years,' writes Dr. Ryerson; and he quotes from a letter written by John Adams, when Ambassador from the American Congress to Holland, addressed to Thomas Gushing, then Lieutenant-Governor of Massachusetts, in which he adverts to the Loyalists as ' thorns indeed to us on both sides of the water,' and continues: ' but I think their career might have been stopt on your side if the executive officers had not been too timid on a point which I strenuously recommended at the first, namely, to fine, imprison, and hang, all inimical to the cause, without favour or affection.'

John Adams did not stand alone in advising strong measures. Of Josiah Quincy Hosmer says: ' In unwise fervour he could counsel assassination as a proper expedient. Warren, too,' he adds, ' could rush into extremes of rashness and ferocity. wishing that he might wade to the knees in blood.'3ENGLAND'S TREATMENT OF LOYALISTS 189

1Ward (G. A.),*Biographical Notices of many American Loyalists, ttc.,*' Judge Ropes.'

2Ryerson (Dr. Egerton),*The Loyalists of America and their Times,*vol. ii., chap. xxzvi.

' Hosmer,*Samuel Adams,*chap. xxi.: ' Character and Service of Samuel Adams.'

Even the American idol, Washington, was scarcely more moderate; exulting over the hardships of the Boston refugees, he wrote deliberately:

One or two have done what a great number ought to have done long ago – committed suicide. By all accounts there never existed a more miserable set of beings than these wretched creatures now are. They were at their wits' end, and, conscious of their black ingratitude, they chose to commit themselves, in the manner I have above described, to the mercy of the waves at a tempestuous season rather than meet their offended countrymen.1

There can be no doubt that the lot of the exiles was in most cases a hard one. Severed from old friends and old surroundings, in some cases from near relatives, they escaped the dangers of the sea only to meet with scant welcome in the land to which they had fled for refuge. It might have been expected that in old England her unfortunate children would have found sympathy and support; but, on the contrary, they appear to have been disliked, as reminding the inhabitants of defeat and adding to the burdens of the people, and therefore by no means entitled to assistance, but rather the contrary.

Governor Wentworth,2of New Hampshire, having by degrees lost his popularity, had been driven to seek safety in his fort at Portsmouth, and from thence fled to Boston, where Gage then governed, and finally to England. He wrote in May 1783, from Hammersmith, to Captain Cochran of Portsmouth:

As to your coming here, or any other Loyalist that can get clams and potatoes in America, they most certainly would regret making bad worse. It would be needless for me to enter into reasons; the fact is so, and you will do well to avoid it.3

In the following year Dr. Peter Oliver, who was labouring at the thankless task of starting afresh as a physician in a strange land, complains of the conduct of a landlord or lodging-house keeper, adding:

1Sabine,*The American Loyalists: Preliminary Remarks,*p. 14.2See vol. ii. of this Family History, chap. xxiv., pp. 193, 194.2Sabine,*The American Loyalists,*' Cochran, Captain John,' of Portsmouth, New Hampshire.

We are obliged to put up with every insult from this ungrateful people, the English, without any redress. If this nation does not make the refugees compensation for the losses they have sustained, so far as it is in their power, a curse will befall them sooner or later.1

The English Government was at this time supposed to be doing something for the Loyalists, but Dr. Peter Oliver, son of Chief Justice Oliver, writing in the same year, probably expressed the feelings of many sufferers who had petitioned, and attended again and again – all in vain.

I stayed in London above three weeks, and returned, heartsick of it, without effecting my business with the Commissioners of the American Department.2

Jonathan Sewall, the ' Philanthropos' of former days, who had been Attorney-General, under Sir Francis Bernard from 1767, wrote to Curwen:

The situation of American Loyalists, I confess, is enough to have provoked Job's wife, if not Job himself; but still we must be men, philosophers, and Christians, and bearing up with patience, resignation, and fortitude, against unavoidable sufferings is our duty in each of these characters.3

Curwen himself exclaims that ' the gratitude of Courts ought to be reckoned among the nonentities of Lord Rochester's list.'

In the course of his stay in England he met with many pitiable cases. Early in December 1775, he writes:

Thence to Heralds' Office, where Parson Peters, with his friend Mr. Pinderson, lodges; the latter has lately arrived from Boston, having escaped by rowing himself in a cock-boat eighteen miles into the sound from his native place, Norwich, Connecticut; and being taken up by a vessel and put on board the*Rose*man-of-war, Capt. Wallace, and conveyed to Boston.4

These events happened in 1775, and General Gage hadPARSON CLAEKB 191

1Eutchinson (Governor),*Diary and Letters,*vol. ii., chap. ix.' *Ibid.,*vol. ii., ohap. ix.

= Curwen,*Journal and Letters,*ohap..,dated Bristol, Dec. 18, 1778.*b1 'i,.*chap. i.

taken military command of the town when Mr. Pinderson returned. Curwen continues:

It seems he was harshly dealt with by the Sons of Liberty; being obliged to make two confessions to save his life; notwithstanding which, he was hunted, pursued, and threatened, and narrowly escaped death (or the Simsbury Mines, to which he was finally adjudged, and he thinks with the loss of his eyes), which would have been his fate, but for his seasonable and providential retreat.

Sabine mentions that ' Many Loyalists were confined in private houses, some were sent to jails, and others to Simsbury Mines.'1

On another occasion (February 13, 1781), Mr. Curwen was visited by ' Parson Peters,' who was really a man of some note, and was admitted to preach at Lincoln's Inn Chapel, and a

Parson Clarke,2late a townsman; from a cold taken on board a prison ship in Boston harbour, to which he was consigned by the patriots in punishment of Toryism, he has lost his voice, and is scarce able to articulate. This, added to his deafness renders him a lonely, pitiable object; he has received twenty pounds per annum from the Society for Propagating the Gospel – Government declining to give him a settled stipend, though it has once and again presented him with a scanty gratuity.

About a year and seven months later (July 16,1782) the same writer records the partial recovery of ' young Parson Clarke,' who could ' speak articulately, and with some degree of clearness.'3He stated that he had recovered the power of speech suddenly, on the seventh anniversary after losing it. In spite of depressing circumstances his nerves had recovered their tone, no doubt. In London he was at least free, and could meet friends.

In some instances, comparatively few, no doubt, the misfortunes of Loyalists were directly traceable to the action of the British army, but were not for that reason more speedily alleviated by the Government. This appears in the case ofCaptain Fenton,1who from Dublin petitioned Earl Temple, then Lord-Lieutenant of Ireland, in 1783. He was probably not a native of America, but the same Captain Fenton who is mentioned by Sabine1as having a commission in the British army, although settled in New Hampshire, where he held several appointments. When the troubles came he expressed his views too openly, and was attacked by a mob, who pursued him to the Governor's house ' with a field piece, which they threatened to discharge unless he was delivered up. Fenton surrendered.' Apparently he lingered some time in Boston, where he was tried and imprisoned, finally being allowed to escape and go to England.

1Sabine,*American Loyalists,*' Note to Preliminary Romarks, p. 84.- Curwen,*Journal and Letters,*1781, chap. xv.'*Ibid.,*chap. xvi.

The appeal to Earl Temple states that the Petitioner had ' lost a large property in House and Lands in America, over and above May Place on Bunker's Hill, which was burned by order of General Gage, and a Fort built thereon for his Majesty's service, to the utter ruin of said place. having also his employment taken from him.' A copy of this Memorial is amongst Scrope Bernard's papers; he was no doubt commissioned by Lord Temple to bring the matter before Lord Shelburne, then Prime Minister,3though it appears from Mr. Bernard's letter to' John Morris, Esq.,' that Captain Fenton 'not long since was dismissed by Lord Shelburne from the government of Fort William in New Hampshire,' and therefore had little chance of favourable consideration. The reason of his dismissal is not stated, but too much zeal in the Royal cause is not unlikely to have been a ground of offence to Shelburne. In his Memorial the Captain prayed to be appointed Consul-General to the United States, then just recognised by Great Britain; but whether he obtained that post, or any other, I know not. Lord Shelburne decided that the matter did not belong to his department, and must be referred to Lord Sydney; and so, in that time of excitement and changes of Ministry, it may have gone on*ad infinitum.*

1This Memorial is amongst the M88. at Nether Winchendon.

* Sabine,*The American Loyalists,*'Fenton, John.'

3Beatson,*Political Index,*1788, vol. i. Haydn,*Dictionary of Dates.*

REFUGEES IN NOVA SCOTIA 193

Many Loyalists, as already noted, fled to Nova Scotia, where their fortunes were various. Some were sent to colonise the wildernesses of Upper Canada and New Brunswick, where they encountered terrible difficulties, and were neglected by the British Government, which had enticed or driven them thither.1The enterprise proved fatal to a certain number. Even those who remained in Halifax, a recently settled town, must have had a hard time, for some years at least, if not for life. The following letter,8dated ' Strand, London, 1791,' and addressed to Scrope Bernard as Under-Secretary of State, relates to the painful case of a refugee in Nova Scotia:

Sir, – A Petition to the Lords of the Treasury was transmitted to me by Mr. James Stewart, son of the late Mr. Anthony Stewart of Halifax, who died of a palsy, leaving five infant children totally unprotected and unprovided for, their Father having lost his all in Maryland, in consequence of his attachment to Government during the War – and the pension of 150$ p. annum given him in consequence of these losses, now ceasing with his. Mr. James Stewart, the Petitioner, being at an age to take care of himself, claims nothing – but he is married & has a Family who [sic] he can hardly maintain – much more support his Brother and Sister. He informs me that Mr. Strange, Chief Justice at Halifax, has written to you upon the case – and therefore in case you have the means or the desire to promote the prayer of the Petition, which is for a part of the Pension to be continued to the children of Mr. Stewart, I take the liberty to inform you I have transmitted the petition to Mr. Bose but it would be very presuming and useless for a Humble Individual as I am to solicit for such a favour being granted.

Sir

Your most obedient

& most humble Servant

ThomasCoutts.

I do not know the result of this application. In some instances the refugees in England were driven by desperation to make their peace with the revolutionaryGovernment and return to America after the conclusion of the war. The sad case of Mr. Van Shaack has been epitomised by Sabine from the unfortunate gentleman's own narrative.

1See Ryerson,*The Loyalists of America,*vol. ii., chap. xli. especially.

2MS. Letter at Nether Winchendon.

VOL. III. O

In 1778 his sick wife desired leave from the Governor to enter her native city of New York, then held by the British, but beleaguered, in the hope of being cared for during her illness; this boon was refused, and she then applied to Lafayette to implore the services of a skilful British surgeon, Dr. Hayes, then his prisoner. This request the General at the instigation of the Committee of Safety, refused; she sank under the effects of her disease and its aggravations, dying with words of forgiveness on her lips. Her loss was the first of a series of misfortunes. Within eight years the widower lost his father and six children, from causes largely due to the war and its consequences; he was, moreover, destitute and an outlaw, had lost the sight of one eye, and was in dread of total blindness.1

' Of overt acts against this country' (writes Sabine) ' Van Schaack had committed none: his sole offences were his opinions. That he was a pure and noble man there is sufficient proof.' Unable to make a home in any other country, Mr. Van Schaack eventually made his way back to the States. Sabine asserts that he was received with honours and became eminent in the law after his return. If so, he was a man of marvellous vigour and nerve. He died in outward seeming a dutiful son of the Kepublic, but he must have been more, or less, than human if he could really love it and rejoice in its success.

Such cases of return were, however, the less frequent that they were generally discouraged.

At the peace (says Sabine) justice and good policy both required a general amnesty, and the revocation of the acts of disability and banishment, so that only those who had been guilty of flagrant crimes should be excluded from becoming citizens. Instead of this, however, the State Legislatures generally continued in a course of hostile action, and treated the conscientious andLOYALISTS' CLAIMS 195

1Sabine,*The American Loyalists,*'Vn Schaack, Peter, Esq.'

pure, and the unprincipled and corrupt, with the same indiscrimination as they had done during the struggle.1

He specially characterises New York, Massachusetts and Virginia as ' neither merciful nor just.'

That the Mother Country did admit a certain amount of responsibility for the welfare of the American Loyalists has been shown in the previous chapter, and some work was done.

On the 5th of April 1788, the Commissioners in England had heard and determined one thousand six hundred and eighty claims (besides those withdrawn) and had liquidated the same at $1,887,548. Perhaps no greater despatch was possible, but the delay caused great complaint. The King, his Ministers, and Parliament were addressed and petitioned, either on the general course pursued by the Commissioners, or on some subject connected with the Loyalist Claims. Letters and communications appeared in the newspapers, and the public attention was again awakened by the publication of essays and tracts, which renewed the statements made in 1783 of the losses, services, and sacrifices of the claimants.2Two years previously (1786) the agents of the Loyalists had invoked Parliament to hasten the final action upon the claims of their constituents, in a petition drawn up with care and ability. ' It is impossible to describe, (are words which occur in this document) the poignant distress under which many of these persons now labour, and which must daily increase should the justice of Parliament be delayed, until all the claims are liquidated and reported. ten years have elapsed since many of them have been deprived of their fortunes, and with their helpless families reduced from independent affluence to poverty and want; some of them now languishing in British gaols, others indebted to their creditors, who have lent them money barely to support their existence; and who, unless speedily relieved, must sink more than the value of their claims when received, and be in a worse condition than if they had never made them; others have already sunk under the pressure and severity of their misfortunes.

Sabine insinuates that this picture may be overcharged, but he quotes the statement of Galloway,3' a distinguishedLoyalist of Pennsylvania,' made in 1788, which is quite as strong:

1Sabine,*The American Loyalists: Preliminary Remarks,*pp. 86, 87.

'*Ibid.*pp. 107-8.

' Galloway':; tract was entitled:*The Claims of the American Loyalists Renewed and Maintained upon Incontrovertible Principles of Law and Justice.*Galloway is mentioned in vol. ii. p. 324 of this Family History.

It is well known (says the writer) that this delay of justice has produced the most melancholy and shocking events. A number of the sufferers have been driven by it into insanity and become their own destroyers, leaving behind them their helpless widows and orphans to subsist upon the cold charity of strangers. Others have been sent to cultivate a wilderness for their subsistence, without having the means, and compelled through want to throw themselves on the mercy of the American States, and the charity of their former friends, to support the life which might have been made comfortable by the money long since due by the British Government; and many others, with their families, are barely subsisting upon a temporary allowance from Government, a mere pittance when compared with the sum due to them.

Many victims were not included in the first measures of compensation. ' Mr. Pitt' (says Sabine) ' had introduced and carried through in 1785 a Bill for the distribution of $150,000 among the claimants '; but, he adds, ' that sum, it was held, was to be applied to a distinct class, to those who had lost " property," and neither to those who had lost " life- estate " in property, nor to those who had lost " income."'*l*

How many subsequent Bills were passed I know not; but I have in my possession a pamphlet entitled ' The Case of the Uncompensated American Loyalists' – these being fifty-five persons – ' whose claims (arising on debts owing them in America, previous to the Revolutionary War, and lost during that period by allegiance to his Majesty), were established under the Commission appointed by the Act of the 43 Geo. III., but who from particular circumstances have not obtained the benefit of the Act of the 23 Geo. III., chap. 80.'2There is no date on the title-page, but the documents are brought down to 1816. Many claimants are represented by executors, &c. ' John Lane' appears ' for Paxton Commissioner and Governor Hutchinson.'

1Sabine,*The American Loyalists: Preliminary Remarks,*p. 109. *Ibid.*pp. 86-87.

TIMOTHY RUGGLES 197

Mr. P. 0. Hutchinson/doubtless alludes to this effort at obtaining justice when he says:

Such were the delays that even so late as 1821, thirty-eight years after the war had ended, and forty-three years after the passing of the Confiscation Act, the subject was again mooted in Parliament.

He does not state the result. The Eev. John Inglis, afterwards Bishop of Nova Scotia, alludes to the subject in a letter2of the following year (1822), addressed to Scrope Bernard, then Sir Scrope Bernard-Morland. What was the end, or whether there ever was one, I know not.

Although the fate of the exiled Loyalists was in all cases probably a hard one, it is not denied that in some cases they partially regained their position, though always as the result of a severe struggle. These successes must be attributed to exceptional mental and physical vigour, and perhaps also to the assistance of influential friends.

Foremost among the Loyalists of Massachusetts, after as well as before the final outbreak, was ' stalwart Timothy Kuggies.'3In 1774, when his home was rendered uninhabitable by the ill-treatment of his cattle and attacks upon his house by night, he took refuge in Boston, where he formed an association of Loyalists for mutual defence. When the British army evacuated the town, he accompanied it to Halifax, Nova Scotia, but left a little later for Long and Staten Islands, New York, where he organised a force of three hundred loyal militia.

' After many vicissitudes incident to his position in so troubled times,' writes Sabine, ' he established his residence in Nova Scotia. Of the beautiful site of Digby, in that colony, he was a proprietor and a settler.' The development of this property was apparently a principal occupation of his later life. ' He died in 1798, aged eighty-seven years.'

Jonathan Sewall,4who, under the signature of ' Philanthropos,' had defended Governor Bernard in the newspapers, and became Attorney-General in 1767 and Judge of Admiralty for Nova Scotia in 1768, was also a refugee in Boston after his ' elegant house at Cambridge,' as it is called by Sabine, was injured by the mob. He was one of the proscribed, and went on to England; after some years of weary waiting he emigrated to New Brunswick, and was appointed a Judge of Admiralty in that partially reclaimed wilderness. It was a poor post for one of the rising men of Massachusetts. His wife was a Quincy, sister of John Hancock's wife; and he was also the bosom friend of John Adams, whose regard survived the separation brought about by politics. Sewall lived to see both these men in high places; Adams, indeed, had nearly attained the highest, when Sewall, who had sacrificed a brilliant career for conscience' sake, died in 1796. His son Jonathan was more fortunate; he became Chief Justice of Canada.

IHutchinson,*Diary and Letters, vol.*ii. chap. ix.

*II*MS. Letter at Nether Winohendon.

9Sabine,*The American Loyalists,*'Ruggies (Timothy).' **Ibid.,*'Sewall, Jonathan.'

Sewall,*l*when Attorney-General, was concerned in a transaction which ought to have won him lasting honour in the land of his birth; but he was a Loyalist.

He commenced the suit in May, 1769, in favour of a negro against his master for his freedom, by James Eichard Lechmere, of Cambridge. The late Chief Justice Dana was counsel for the defendant. The suit terminated the following year in favour of the negro; and I believe it was the first case where the grand question was settled, abolishing slavery in that State. The case of the negro Somerset, which Blackstone commends so highly, and which has been matter of self-gratulation in England, was not settled till 1772, two years after the decision in favour of James.

Daniel Leonard,2another barrister, is known chiefly in connection with Governor Hutchinson, whom he defended in a pamphlet as ' Massachusettensis,' but he appears to have been a political writer for some time previous to Sir Francis Bernard's departure; in any case he was a Loyal representative for some years. Leonard ran the usual course: bullets were fired into his house, he went to BostonSAD STORIES 199

1Cnrwen,*Biographical Notices*(by Ward?),' Hon. Jon. Sewall.'

2Sabine,*The American Loyalists,*'Leonard, Daniel.'

then to Halifax, and to England, and was finally Chief Justice of the Bermudas,1a cluster of four hundred rocky islands in the Atlantic, whose population in 1822 was little over ten thousand, nearly half blacks.

Samuel Quincy,2the successor of Jonathan Sewall as Solicitor-General, who visited Sir Francis Bernard in Ayles- bury, may be said to have given up more than other exiles. His family had one and all embraced the cause of the revolution, and on leaving America he bade, unconsciously, a last adieu to all his family save his wife. She appears to have joined him later, probably when he obtained the modest appointment of ' Comptroller of the Customs' at the port of Perham, in Antigua. Here she died; he married again, but died on a voyage to England to recruit his health, within sight of land. His widow re-embarked, only to die on the return journey.

Many other sad stories might be told; and I do not forget that there were Loyalists who did not leave the States, in some cases could not, but lived on in a constrained position, objects of suspicion and dislike to their neighbours and the authorities, and liable at least to petty persecutions, sometimes to more stringent measures of repression. But they lost their connection with England, and necessarily became by degrees identified with their surroundings. If not effected at once, a generation or two must have seen the change.

That the leaders of the successful party – the insurgents – throve on revolution is almost a foregone conclusion. James Otis3is the most marked exception. Weighted by incipient brain disease, and uncongenially married to a lady of Loyalist opinions, whose views influenced their children, his mind gave way altogether after a quarrel with Eobinson, the Commissioner of Customs; he spent the remainder of his days under care in a farmhouse, at the door of which he waskilled, some years later, by a flash of lightning. Hawley, whose tendency to depression has been noticed, retired early from the strife and led the life of a private gentleman. Warren died young.

1*The Edinburgh Gazetteer,*1823, ' Bermudas or Homers' Islands.' * Sabine,*The American Loyalists,* 'Quincy, Samuel.' Curwen,*or*Ward,*Biographical Notices,*'Samuel Quincy.' Tudor,*Life of Otis.*

John Adams/stands forth pre-eminent as having attained the highest possible position in the United States. His early career in his native land, his missions to France and Holland, have been the subject of some pages in these volumes. After the peace he became ambassador of the United States to England, and was received by George III., reluctantly, indeed, but with magnanimity. Unhappily, many Loyalists were then, perhaps, perishing from want. The wrath of John's wife, Abigail, the daughter of William Smith, Congregational minister of Weymouth, United States, was, however, excited by the coldness of Queen Charlotte's manner.2Her first reception was civil, though, perhaps, scarcely cordial; but on subsequent occasions – whether the Queen's anxiety about public affairs and her husband's health or the self-assertion of Mrs. Adams was the immediate cause – the ambassadress considered that she had not received the measure of courtesy due to her exalted position, and she did not forget this omission. At a much later period, when the French Revolution seemed to have shaken the Throne of England, she wrote to her daughter:

Humiliation for Charlotte is no sorrow for me. She richly deserves her full portion for the contempt and scorn which she took pains to discover.3

John Adams was distinguished as a political writer, an orator, and a statesman; he became Vice-President of the United States under Washington, and his successor as President. In his declining years he was harassed by opposition, which led to his retirement from public life, and he was not exempt from domestic bereavements; but on the whole his life was singularly fortunate. He survivedJOHN HANCOCK 201

1*Life of John Adams.*See also various American histories.

2'Memoir of Mrs. Adams,' by Charles Francis Adams, prefixed to the Collection called*Familiar Letters of John Adams and his Wife, Abigail Adams, during the Bevolution.*

'Memoir prefixed to*Familiar Letters.*

to see a son his successor in the Presidency, and died in his native land of Massachusetts in high honour. Like Hancock, he loved display as well as superiority; in age as in youth he was an aristocratic partisan of popular rights.

John Hancock's career up to the time of Sir Francis Bernard's departure has been sketched in the previous volumes of this History. Together with Samuel Adams, he escaped from Boston to Philadelphia in order to avoid arrest by General Gage's order, joined Washington, John Adams, and others, and became first revolutionary Governor of Massachusetts in 1780. In 1773, while Governor Hutchinson was still in Boston, Hancock was elected Treasurer of Harvard College. The result is told by the revolutionary historian of Harvard, Josiah Quincy, and curtly summed up by Birkbeck Hill:

George III. was down, but Governor Hancock was up. In an evil day for the University that favourite of the people had been appointed Treasurer. He would neither discharge the duties of his office nor resign his post. The Corporation, after patiently waiting two or three years, appointed his successor. To conciliate the great man, they asked for his portrait, to place beside that of his uncle, who had been a benefactor. He neither sent his portrait nor settled his accounts. So powerful was his position that the Corporation did not dare to bring him before a court of law. They could scarcely have been worse off had they had to deal with George III. himself. It was not till full eleven years after their first demand that he condescended to state the amount of the balance still owing by him to the College. On being pressed for payment he would do nothing more than give a bond and security. It was in vain that the distress of the Professors was laid before him. Their salaries were unpaid, but neither interest nor principal could be got out of the great man. He died in 1793, leaving ample means, but the debt still owing. It was not till eight years later that his heirs discharged it.

Ward charges Mr. Hancock with similar conduct towards Mr. Harrison Gray,1 Treasurer or Receiver-General of Massachusetts, to whom he owed ' a large sum for borrowed money, no part of which would he pay in his lifetime, and of which a small part only was received from his executors,' and he contrasts this callous conduct with Mr. Gray's high sense of honour. That gentleman, when he departed into exile, left the books and files in his office in exemplary order, although they might have proved valuable against his own actual losses and the impending confiscation. He calls Mr. Gray ' the model of a faithful Treasurer,' and both Ward and Sabine describe him as a model man in all respects.

1 Ward, *Biographical Notices,* 'Harrison Gray.'

Hancock's money was spent on ' grand living,' and his hand was open ' to every object coinciding with his views or his interest;. it suited both his interest and his policy to postpone debts and gratify friends.'

Hosmer records his brilliant entertainments to the French officers in Boston. Thirty or forty dined with him each day, whom he dazzled with his liveries and plate. At Concert Hall, too, he gave them a great ball, and stimulated other Whigs to similar hospitalities.

Probably the restless Samuel Adams, the wirepuller of all agitations in Massachusetts, was, of all the revolutionists in that State, the least satisfied with his success. It must have been undoubtedly galling to behold his ' puppets,' as they had been called, in several cases exalted over his head. He continued throughout the course of the revolution to be the life and soul of political intrigues, but, as might have been expected from his antecedents, he was too much of a revolutionist to be in his right element when organising a constitution, and had to give way to the colleagues from whom he differed. For many years he was a member of Congress, but eventually lost his seat when opposed by a young and popular orator.

' The would-be Cromwell of America,' as he is called in the pamphlet of a refugee American printer, and perhaps justly, he saw men whom he had introduced to public life, and, as he probably believed, moulded to his ideas, rising above him. The brilliant fortunes of John Adams could scarcely fail to affect him with a sense of undeserved inferiority. He became Lieutenant-Governor of Massachusetts, in succession to his former tool, Thomas Gushing, andSAMUEL ADAMS 203

under John Hancock, once styled his ' dupe.' In Hutchinson's time he had been at variance with Hancock, and they were again while in office at variance for some years; but a reconciliation was eventually brought about, and on Hancock's death in 1793 Adams, at the age of seventy, was elected Governor.1

It was a grand position for the former maltster and tax- collector, but can hardly have satisfied all his longings. The revolution, moreover, had brought about some changes which he had not contemplated, and certainly not desired: religious toleration was making rapid advances, and recreations distasteful to Puritans were recognised. Samuel Adams resigned his government after three years: it had probably come too late and developed too many uncongenial elements to be enjoyed; he lived five years more in retirement. The great grief of his later life had been the death of his only son, who is said to have succumbed to his exertions and hardships as a surgeon during the war. By his wife and daughter he was carefully tended, and he survived to be eighty-one, dying – it may be said to his credit – a comparatively poor man, in 1802.

1*Memoir of J. Qwncy Adams,*by C. F. Adams, vol. i. Note to p. 38.

9

SECTION 9

CHAPTER XI

THOMASBERNARD, TREASUREROPTHEFOUNDLING
HOSPITAL

Cordial Relations between Thomas and Scrope Bernard – Retiring Disposition of
Thomas and Margaret Bernard – Their Circle of Friends – ' The Clapham
Sect' – Thomas Bernard purchases a House at Iver – Serjeant Adair –
Thomas Bernard retires from Practice at the Bar – His Disposition towards
Philanthropic Efforts – Neglect of Officers charged with the care of the Poor –
Addison's Denunciation of the Prevalence of Infanticide – The Founding of
the Foundling Hospital – Infant Mortality in the Hospital – The Trade in
Carrying Children – Indiscriminate Admission to the Hospital stopped –
Suppression of the Branch Establishments – Jonas Hanway promotes an
Inquiry into the Condition of Children in the Workhouses – Thomas
Bernard's Connection with the Hospital – He Supports the Suggested
Admission of Exposed and Necessitous Children of Soldiers and Sailors –
He is elected Treasurer – His Administration of the Hospital – The Mothers
of the Foundlings.

Forthirteen years after his marriage Thomas Bernard was a diligent worker in the profession he had chosen. There is not much to be related about this portion of his life. Some few allusions have already been made in previous chapters, in connection chiefly with his brother Scrope's career; what little remains to be said will find a place here.

The intercourse between the two brothers was always cordial, and Thomas was of use to Scrope in many small matters of business, especially while Scrope was in Ireland. One of the arrangements to which several of Thomas's letters refer was the insertion of certain paragraphs in newspapers, apparently to forward the views of the Lord Lieutenant.1

It is possible that Thomas and Margaret Bernard remained with her father after the marriage; but whateverTROUBLES OF IRISH PROPERTY 205

1MS. Letter at Nether Winchendon.

was the reason, they were domiciled in Soho Square for a year. He writes 1 on January 8, 1783: ' We get into our new house in Lincoln's Inn Fields – South Side – in the beginning of April, but not on the first of April.' Some years later, apparently, a letter is dated from Great Russell Street; but it was probably a temporary residence only, since they seem to have made Bloomsbury Place8their next abode. Mrs. Bernard's sister, Miss Adair, is mentioned a little later as living in Lansdown Place.3

Margaret Bernard apparently had property in Ireland; it must be hers that is referred to in several letters, but, according to the custom of the time, Thomas writes of it as his. It was not long before he experienced the trouble and vexation attendant on Irish property. In the letter of January 8, 1783, he continues, with reference to an attack on the property:

As to the Proclamation, if it is little or no expense, I shall be glad of it; by little expense I mean not above 4 or 5$.That Estate gives me a good deal of Trouble, and would, I think, be better for a resident Irishman than for me. Nothing but Mr. Smith's being so good as to take the Care of it has reconciled me to keeping it, & now, if a tolerable offer was made me, I*would*sell it and willingly leave the greater part of the Purchase Money in the Purchaser's hands.

The Proclamation came out, disclosing the fact that his house had been violently attacked; apparently as part of an organised system of annoyance and intimidation. The original document has been mislaid, but a letter4from ' Rich. W. Talbot,' asking Scrope Bernard to apply to his brother ' for his interest in the County of Dublin upon the approaching election,' dated February 5, 1790, may almost be said to determine the locality of the property within certain limits.

Thomas and Margaret Bernard probably moved little ingeneral society; he had his profession, and she appears to have been of a retiring disposition; but they had a wide circle of friends. In early days, it would seem, he wrote to Scrope:

1MS. Letter at Nether Winchendon. *Life of Sir Thomas Bernard,*by the Bev. James Baker.'Miss Adair's address appears in a list of subscribers to the Society for Bettering the Condition of the Poor.4MS. Letter at Nether Winchendon.

This is written at the close of a business evening, & not the more legible or intelligible for that. Mrs. B. is gone a routing, she is very well. I am returning home expecting to meet her at supper.1

At all times, however, the old intercourse with relatives was kept up; not only did Mr. and Mrs. White visit Thomas from Lincoln, but Mrs. Edmunds also; and he speaks of going to Norton with young Shore, who had succeeded his mother in 1781, and expecting to meet Bishop Barrington's wife there; he is glad ' our Bishop has arrived safe ' – apparently in Ireland, for the letter is addressed to Scrope in Dublin.

On another occasion he – perhaps his wife also – dined in Cavendish Square with the Bishop of Salisbury (Shute Barrington), Mrs. Barrington – probably the Bishop's wife – and Mr. Price,2a nephew.

The name of Pownall is more than once mentioned in letters, and refers apparently to the Under-Secretary of State, the friend of Sir Francis Bernard. Of the American refugees, Sir William Pepperell is the only one who can be traced. He remained in London, and his name appears in a list of subscribers to a society3which owed its origin to Thomas Bernard, so late as 1805.

But Thomas Bernard's marriage apparently introduced him to a circle which must have strongly influenced his after-life. His wife's uncle, James Adair, the King's Serjeant, was a man of some importance, and having only one child of his own, a daughter, who married Admiral SirTHE 'CLAPHAM SECT'207

1MS. Letter at Nether Winchendon. It is dated ' Jan. 21,' and probably refers to 1783. The following extracts are also from MS. letters at Nether Winchendon, but without the date of any year.

2The son of a sister of the second Viscount and the Bishop. See Debrett and Burke,' Barrington, Viscount.'

1*Reports of the Society for Bettering the Condition of the Poor,*vol. ii. List of Subscribers.

John Colpoys, K. B., he bestowed much affection on his brother's daughters.1The Serjeant loved politics; he was a warm friend and admirer of Fox. Already in 1769 he had come forward at a meeting of Middlesex freeholders; ' to instruct Wilkes and Glyn, their representatives; he moved the resolution concerning the tumult in St. George's Fields, the riot at Brentford, and the commission of the Peace.' Successively member of Parliament for Cockermouth and for Higham Ferrers, he was of course opposed to the war with America, and disapproved of Lord North, but his general views appear to have been somewhat modified by time.

There was, indeed, a liberal set, of a different type from the followers of Wilkes, with which the Serjeant had become intimately connected. On February 17 he spoke in favour of the abolition within a limited time of the slave trade. ' Politics ' (wrote Wilberforce) ' are said to harden the heart and pervert the understanding. In this instance it seems not. Sergeant Adair's speech I like the best of all, comprehensive, strong, clear.' And a little later they were working together for the redress of Quaker grievances, and Wilberforce notes:2' March 25 – Got Adair to put off his motion,' being himself too unwell to attend. He was in the House of Commons the following day, when the Serjeant's Bill was brought forward, and was partially successful.

Long before these entries were penned in the Diary of William Wilberforce, Thomas Bernard had probably been introduced to him by Serjeant Adair, and through him to the society of those friends whom the Kev. Sydney Smith had jocosely described as ' the Clapham Sect,' and whose social life Sir James Stephen, the nephew of Wilberforce, has made known.3

From Sir James's own account it would seem that this ' Sect' or ' Coterie,' was pre-eminently remarkable, but ina good sense, for what has since been called ' making the best of both worlds.' It consisted chiefly, if not entirely, of men prosperous alike in their pecuniary and domestic affairs – singularly fortunate in their exemption from most of the sorrows of life, indeed – and in some cases in the public reputation which they achieved. William Wilberforce and his connection, Henry Thornton, owned adjoining properties and pleasant residences at Clapham. They had some congenial neighbours and many visitors from London and more distant localities, but, while thoroughly enjoying the blessings of their own lot, they strove in many ways to brighten the lives of those less happily placed.

1 Woolrych, *Lives of Eminent Serjeants,* vol. ii.

2 *The Life of William Wilberforce,* by his Sons, vol. ii., chap. xii. (Second Edition).

' *Essays in Ecclesiastical Biography,* by Sir James Stephen, K. C. B.,' The Clapham Sect.'

It does not appear that Thomas Bernard was ever one of the inner circle, although he must have been on cordial terms with many of its members. Two of them – besides Wilberforce – took part in subsequent philanthropic schemes suggested by him; these two were the Eev. Thomas Gis- borne,1of Yoxall Lodge, Staffordshire, a thoughtful writer and exemplary pastor, but one of the most retiring of the band; and Sir John Shore,2afterwards Lord Teignmoutb, who had been Governor-General of India. Other names appear in letters and other illustrative documents occasionally, showing the many ties which drew Mr. Bernard to these pious and agreeable gentlemen, while at the same time his own life remained distinct.

During this period he bought a house with grounds at Iver, near the southern extremity of Buckinghamshire, and also ' the Eectory and Eectory Manor,'3besides certain tithes. Here he apparently spent a portion of his vacations. The Bar was not then so exacting a profession, in point of attendance, as it has been since, and there were many intervals of relaxation.

In and about Iver there were several gentlemen's seats, and Thomas Bernard there formed some lasting friendships. STONE'S TRIAL 209

1 Author of *An Inquiry into the Duties of Men, $c.,* and *A Familiar Survey of the Christian Religion, $c.*

2 Created an Irish Baron in 1797, see Debrett and other *Peerages.* He was President of the British and Foreign Bible Society.

' Lipscomb, *Hist. Bucks.,* vol. iv.,' Iver.'

He writes to his brother Scrope, September 23, 1788, from Lincoln's Inn:

I received yours just as I was leaving Ivor this morning. If the weather continues fair I hope to see you and your Company on Saturday next. Mrs. Du Pre, her son, three of her Daughters, &Mr. Bateson Harvey (who has purchased Langley and takes possession next Monday), will be of the Party.

I wish to show my Clients the magnificence of Stowe, our Lord Lieuten's Residence. We lye at Aylesbury on fryday, & proceed to Stowe time enough to order dinner & take a previous peep on Saturday. Will you send a hint to the Inn at Stowe to be ready to receive us, & a few Lines of Advice to meet us at the George at Aylesbury?*

Mr. (afterwards Sir Eobert) Bateson Harvey continued on intimate terms with Thomas Bernard during the rest of his life. Another gentleman of the neighbourhood, Mr. Sullivan, of Kichings Park, Iver,[2]was a fellow-worker in schemes of reform. As a guest the name of Stephen occurs twice in letters,[3]and that gentleman was probably the brother-in-law of Wilberforce.

In 1796, the year in which Serjeant Adair is mentioned * by the biographers of Wilberforce, he appears to have been especially prominent, he was counsel for a Mr. Stone, who was accused of high treason – that is, of having given traitorous information, when in Ireland, as to the state of England to a clergyman named Jackson, who was an emissary of the French Government and had since poisoned himself in prison.

It appeared in the course of the trial that Stone had discouraged the idea of invasion; and after deliberating three hours, the jury returned a verdict of ' Not Guilty,' which was received in court with loud applause, echoed by the Hall. One unlucky gentleman was caught in the act ofshouting and made an example of; he was fined $20, and, his cheque being refused, taken into custody. The Serjeant's speech, which was much admired, is given at length in the ' State Trials.'

1MS. Letter at Nether Winchendon.

*The names of these two gentlemen will frequently appear again in connection with Poor-Law reform and the Society for Bettering the Condition of the Poor.

*MS. Letters at Nether Winchendon from Thomas to Scrope Bernard.4Woolrych,*Lives of Eminent Serjeants,*vol. ii.

VOL. III. P

Serjeant Adair had declined to be classed as an unreasoning partisan of Mr. Fox, and when the latter proclaimed his unqualified admiration of the French Revolution, notwithstanding its excesses, he withdrew from the Whig Club, but did not renounce all friendship with his late leader. Eadical as some persons may have considered him, he really fell a victim to his loyalty, or perhaps his patriotism, by joining the volunteers raised in London and the neighbourhood to repel the threatened invasion, at an age when he was no longer fit for such work. On July 21, 1798, after returning with his corps from a shooting-practice, and while walking by Lincoln's Inn, he was seized with paralysis, and being carried to his house in Lincoln's Inn Fields, died there in a few hours.

Woolrych adds that ' he was buried in Bunhill Fields, on the 27th, by his father and mother.'

Before this event took place Thomas Bernard had retired from the practice of his profession, and commenced to devote his time to other objects. His biographer says little about the step; merely that by ' marriage and by assiduous attention to his profession for fifteen years he acquired such a competence as satisfied his desires, and led him to withdraw himself from the law and look out for some useful occupation of his future life.'1And from that period it was devoted to ameliorating the lot of his less favoured brethren and sisters. He had a wife like-minded with himself, and they were childless; the accumulation of money was therefore no object; although, indeed, Thomas extended an almost paternal care over his nephews and nieces, and especially over the children of his deceased sister, Amelia Baker.5Margaret Bernard, who had no young relativesTHE FOUNDLING HOSPITAL, 211

1*Life of Sir Thomas Bernard.*

* These assertions are verified by numerous passages in letters and other papers at Nether Winchendon.

so near, as her only sister never married, seconded all his efforts, and they were much beloved by the rising generation.

Probably Mr. Bernard had always had a disposition to philanthropic efforts, which had been intensified by companionship with a wife who is said to have been a worker among the poor, and also by his introduction to the circle at Clapham. He would seem to have begun by some attempts to improve the domestic habits of the lower classes. He also took an active part on the Committee of the Foundling Hospital, its nearness to his residence in Bloomsbury Place allowing him to attend even while he was in full work at the Bar; and his election to the office of Treasurer, or Resident Governor of the Hospital, in May, 1795,1apparently decided the next move; he must have ceased to practise in the course of that year.

At this period France and several other European countries possessed institutions for the rescue and support of deserted and destitute children.2If nothing of the sort had been established in England, it was – as we are told – because this work of mercy was included in the functions of the Poor Law passed in the reign of Elizabeth. But it had been scandalously ignored, probably from the very beginning. Perhaps matters had grown worse by degrees; I only know that early in the reign of Queen Anne public indignation was aroused.3' The officers whom the laws had charged with the care of the poor had been so negligent that some infants had been suffered to perish with cold and hunger in the streets, without any attempt for their relief.'

The movement, headed by certain benevolent merchants, to raise subscriptions for building an asylum met with opposition on the ground ' that it might seem to encourage vice, by making too easy a provision for illegitimate children,4and it was dropped for a while; but several persons left legacies for the hospital – whenever it should be founded. lu 1713 Addison called attention to the subject in the ' Guardian,' denouncing the prevalence of infanticide; and ten years later Thomas Coram, master of a vessel trading to the American coast, and a man of remarkable benevolence and still more remarkable disinterestedness, came forward as the champion of the cause, in which he enlisted the sympathies of twenty-one ladies of rank as well as of sundry noblemen and gentlemen.

1*Life of Sir Thomas Bernard.*

2*An Account of the Foundling Hospital,*by Thomas Bernard.

' Pugh,*Remarkable Occurrences in the Life of Jonas Hanway.' Ibid.*

In the Ladies' Memorial it is stated that:

No expedient has yet been found out for preventing the frequent murders of poor miserable infants at their birth, or for suppressing the inhuman custom of exposing new-born infants, or the putting out such unhappy foundlings to wicked and barbarous nurses, who, undertaking to bring them up for a trifling sum of money, do often suffer them to starve for want of due sustenance or care; Q$r, if permitted to live, either turn them into the streets to beg ar&teal, or hire them out to loose persons, by whom they are trained up in that infamous way of living; and sometimes are blinded, or maimed and distorted in their limbs, in order to move pity and compassion, and thereby become fitter instruments of gain to those vile merciless wretches.

Captain Coram himself stated that he had been a witness ' to the shocking spectacle of innocent children who had been murdered and thrown upon dunghills.' His petition for a charter, sent to the King with the two memorials from the Ladies and from the Noblemen and Gentlemen, was successful, and the good work was commenced in 1737. After a modest beginning in Hatton Garden, an estate was purchased from the Earl of Salisbury, on which the present palatial building was erected, the architect being Theodore Jacobson.1

And now some of the eccentricities of English charity came into full play. Several of the most eminent painters and sculptors of the day volunteered to adorn the principal rooms of the new institution with more or less appropriate works of art; the most inappropriate of all being, perhaps, A FASHIONABLE LOUNGE 213

1Brownlow (J.),*Memoranda, or Chronicles of the Foundling Hospital, in- eluding Memoirs of Captain Coram, &c.*

Hogarth's ' March to Finchley,' unless the spectacle of vice in many phases was intended to act as a deterrent. Perhaps, as the picture was placed in the committee-room, it was supposed to be out of the way of the children. Hogarth was really interested in the new foundation, as many of his acts prove. Handel organised an entertainment of vocal and instrumental music from his own works, some of it composed for the occasion, which the Prince and Princess of Wales attended; and for several years he superintended an annual performance of his' Messiah ' for the benefit of the institution. The King (George II.) contributed $2,000 to the chapel and $1,000 for the services of a preacher, of whose sermons the children probably understood not a single word, except when he may have alluded to their desolate condition.

It is scarcely surprising to learn that with all these attractions the Hospital soon became a fashionable morning lounge; a quaint print of the time*l*represents a parade of beaux and belles in the enclosure on the south side of the edifice. The artists not only gave some of the works, but they also held exhibitions in the Hospital – an arrangement no doubt suggested by convenience, there being then no rooms elsewhere suitable for the purpose. They also held their annual dinner there, and that festival and the governors' anniversary dinner must have been lively gatherings. But all the gay doings and the munificent patronage did not remove the difficulties inherent in the administration of the new establishment.

Although the theoretical completeness of the English Poor Law had been held not to preclude the necessity for a Foundling Hospital, the somewhat illogical belief prevailed that it ought to modify the new arrangements, and, consequently, the foreign system of receiving the children in a ' turning-box' was not adopted; yet numbers of children were brought to the Hospital, and several branch establishments were opened in the country,' with large rolls of county governors and county committees,' amongst which may be noted one in Aylesbury.

1In Brownlow's*Memoranda.*

But in 1756 the London committee was already short of money, while its success in other respects was not brilliant, since at the close of 1757 it was found that 2,311 infants out of 5,618 received had died. There were probably many causes for this mortality, but it appears to have been attributed partly to want of funds; and having regard to the fact that institutions of a similar character abroad received assistance from the State, the committee applied to Parliament for a grant, as indispensable to the maintenance of their foundation. The grant was promised, but on condition that all children left at the gate were to be admitted indiscriminately. And the publication of this new rule was the signal for a rush to the Hospital, many of the children brought there being in the last stage of disease or inanition, sent, it would seem, to save the expense of burial; and there were instances in which they did not live to be carried into the wards, and the numbers were so overwhelming as to threaten ruin to the whole scheme of the foundation, especially as the announcement of the Parliamentary grant checked the flow of private charity.

The new rule of unrestricted admission opened the door to another evil – a trade in carrying children.

A man on horseback, going to London with luggage in two panniers, was overtaken at Highgate, and being asked what he had in his panniers, answered, ' I have two children in each; I brought them from Yorkshire for the Foundling Hospital, and used to have eight guineas a trip; but lately another man has set up against me, which has lowered my price.1

This was not the worst phase of the traffic.

At Monmouth, a person was tried for the murder of his child, which was found drowned with a stone about its neck! when the prisoner proved that he delivered it to a travelling tinker, who received a guinea from him to carry it to the Hospital. Nay, it was publicly asserted in the House of Commons that one man who had the charge of five infants in baskets, happened in his journey to get intoxicated, and lay all night asleep on a common; and in the morning he found three of the five children he had inJONAS HANWAY 215

1Brownlow,*Chronicles of the Foundling Hospital.*

charge actually dead. Also, that of eight infants brought out of the country at one time in a waggon, seven died before it reached London, the surviving child owing its life to the solicitude of its mother, who, rather than commit it alone to the carrier, followed the waggon on foot, occasionally affording her infant the nourishment it required.1

It may be added that such children as did reach the Hospital alive, were frequently stripped of every particle of clothing; thereby not only were their lives imperilled, but all clue was lost to their origin; whereas the governors, at the first outset of the institution, had expressly desired that persons leaving children there should also leave some token by which they might, if desired, be afterwards identified. Some of these deposits and the clothes of sundry infants showed them to be children of at least one parent in good circumstances.

In the course of the fourth year of its operation the House of Commons passed a resolution annulling the order for indiscriminate admission – none too soon; also, however, withdrawing the Government grant.

About the same time an inquiry into the management of the country branches established by the committee of the Hospital showed that it had been often victimised in another manner, the parish officers and their allies having, for reasons of their own, sent children to the Houses who were neither deserted nor destitute, and this discovery led to the suppression of these branch establishments.

The institution now certainly stood in need of some good friend willing to go thoroughly into the consideration of its difficulties, and to reflect on the best means of overcoming them; and such a one was found in Jonas Hanway,2who in 1758 was already a governor. His father was ' an officer in the naval line, and for some years storekeeper to the dockyard at Portsmouth,' who had died prematurely from the effects of an accident, leaving his children to be reared by their energetic mother. Jonas became a merchant andtravelled much; as superintendent of the Caspian trade he went through multifarious experiences and adventures in Persia; then, finding himself in middle age a bachelor with a good fortune, he determined to spend some of his time and money in helping his fellow-creatures.

1Brownlow,*Chronicles of the Foundling Hospital.* 'Fugh, Some*Passages in the Life of Jonas Hanway.*

Mr. Hanway soon formed a strong opinion against indiscriminate admission, especially as there was in England no provision for making the Foundling boys serviceable as soldiers or sailors, and apparently no effectual supervision, as in France, over any of the children after their departure from the Hospital. The chances of reclaiming infants thus admitted, weighted as they mostly were by hereditary tendencies to degradation, were therefore minimised; and it was found, on inquiry, that those who had already left the institution had in most cases rejoined the ranks of the vicious and criminal population.

An idea which struck Mr. Hanway while investigating this perplexed subject was, that the provisions of the Poor Law ought no longer to be ignored, but that the workhouses and the Hospital might work together, perhaps in different departments, for a common object; and this led to an inquiry into the condition of children in workhouses. The following statements form a portion of the report:*l*

During the year 1765, in the workhouse of St. Clement Danes, one nurse, Mary Poole, had twenty-three children committed to her care, and on the 25th of January, 1766, eighteen were dead, two had been discharged, and three only remained alive.

Of seventy-eight children received into the workhouse of the united parishes of St. Andrew and St. George, Holborn, in the year 1765, sixty-four were dead before 1766.

Of forty-eight received into the workhouse of St. Luke, Middlesex, 1764, for nurture, – died within the year, thirty-seven.

Of nineteen received into the workhouse of St. George, Middlesex, in 1765 – died before 1766, sixteen.

In some other parishes not one child was living of all that were received in the course of twelve months.

Mr. Hanway took especial pains to verify these state- ' Pugh,*Some Passages in the Life of Jonas Hanway.*

POOR LAW CHILDREN 217

ments, and he extended his inquiries into the country, where things were not nearly so bad, although there was plenty of carelessness. The anecdote here given refers apparently to London:

He observed that a certain overseer refused to allow the mother of a new-born infant more than one shilling and sixpence a week for nursing it, and remarked to him that this pittance was less than he gave to strange nurses. ' Yes,' said the conscientious officer, ' but you don't consider that this woman will take care of her own child, and it may be on our hands a long time, whereas we shall, perhaps, hear no more of the others.'

Mr. Hanway and his colleagues in the investigation now formed the idea of receiving children from the unhealthy London workhouses into the Hospital with parish payment; but the Poor-Law authorities having, in consequence of the revelations just noticed, resolved to put the pauper children out to nurse in the country, this plan was dropped. And the final result of the committee's deliberation was to restrict admissions at the Foundling Hospital to the first children of girls who up to the time of their seduction had borne a good character. Great attempts were now made at economy; which was, indeed, rendered necessary by the withdrawal of State aid. During the few years that such aid was extended it had averaged $33,530 per annum; and the committee does not appear to have shown much skill in reducing its expenditure, although the change in the system produced such a diminution in the number of applications as to assist its efforts materially, while, on the other hand, this result exposed the institution to the reproach of comparative uselessness. That it had departed to some extent from the original intention of its founders and benefactors is evident, and the uncertainty of its aims cannot have tended to an advance in public favour.

Thomas Bernard's connection with the Hospital must have commenced soon after his call to the Bar; he was one of the fifty governors, or members of the managing committee, in 1785, and must have been acquainted with Jonas Hanway, who lived till the following year. It is not unlikely that he may have heard of Thomas Coram in Massachusetts; the good Captain had spent some years of his life there, where he was a great benefactor, and the memory of his good works must have survived until Governor Bernard's administration; also, it may have formed a link in the chain of events which turned his attention to the Hospital.

The institution was still in pecuniary difficulties, and about this time took into con-sideration a project of meeting expenses by letting some of its land on building leases. This idea had been previously mooted; but the scheme had been strongly opposed, on the pretext that the children, if surrounded by buildings, would be deprived of air and exercise; though, as a matter of fact, the founders had been originally compelled to buy much more land than they intended in order to secure a site. This outcry had effectually hindered any arrangement from being carried out. Mr. Bernard now pro-posed that twenty acres should be secured to the institution, the remaining thirty-six being let for building, on conditions which ensured a due regard for health, and even for appearance. Some difficulties raised by neighbouring owners and occupiers had to be adjusted, and eventually Brunswick and Mecklenburgh Squares rose on either side of the Hospital, with several wide streets about them, according to Mr. Bernard's plans. The rest of the governors and other persons interested in the institution were so well satisfied with this result that the whole committee of management determined to bestow the name of the governor who had brought this matter to a happy conclusion on one of the new streets, and it is called Bernard Street to this day.

These facts are related by the Rev. James Baker.1Mr. Bernard himself gave particulars of an alteration in the internal arrangements of the Hospital effected under his management in an account which he published of its history. This is cautiously worded, as it might otherwise have affected the reputations of certain persons who were1*Life of Sir Tlwmas Bernard,*by Eev. James Baker.

THE FOUNDLING INFIRMARY 219

his fellow-workers. It appears that the governors as a body, and perhaps none more so than those who deprecated the effects of building on the children's health, had been most negligent as to the accommodation and care of the sick.

The infirmary of the Hospital had, by a resolution of June 1753, been directed to be placed in the western wing, at the south end of the upper floor.1

Apparently there had been objections raised to this position, but it does not seem to have been bettered.

By subsequent resolutions different situations were appointed for it; and as is usual where there are various measures and various directions, without any fixed or particular attention to the subject, it had at length sunk into a low, damp, confined building near the Hospital gate, incapable of separate accommodation for the sexes, and bidding defiance to medical skill to restore the inhabitants to the free air and healthy apartments of the Hospital. Hopeless labour is generally void of exertion. In the present instance the unfavourable situation of the infirmary seems to have produced an extraordinary effect of inattention and want of cleanliness in those who had the care of it, and this and the other evils attending the scite [sic] of the Infirmary being increased by two epidemical disorders in December, 1789, the Quarterly Court referred the whole to the investigation of the General Committee; the result of which was a systematic regulation as to the cleanli-. jaess, management, and diet of the children, which has been since very well observed: the establishment of a regular visitation of the Hospital and the restoration of the infirmary to its original scite*[sic]*,a change which has operated as a charm on the sick- list of the Hospital, and reduced it to half its former average.

Apparently the institution was at this time by no means flourishing; there was perhaps a dread of the new regulations, by which the mothers had to appear with their infants, and to state their case. In January, 1794, a court was summoned to consider the propriety of making all the ' exposed and necessitous children of soldiers and seaman who are, have been, or shall be, employed in the service of their country during the present war eligible to the Foundling Hospital.' Mr. Bernard was a strong supporter of thisproposition, because he considered that these children had exceptional claims on the public, and that their case might be reasonably construed as coming within the scope of the work for which the institution had been originally founded; moreover, there was apparently no other charity prepared to receive them, except, perhaps, in very small numbers. He was sorry that only a qualified resolution was passed, declaring the children admissible up to the age of five, so far as the funds would allow, 'consistent with a proper degree of attention to the other deserving objects of the charity.' And he quotes Adam Smith on the topic of soldiers' marriages, that

1*Account of the Foundling Hospital,*by Thomas Bernard.

So far from recruiting their regiment, they have never been able to supply it with drums and fifes from all the soldiers' children that were born in it. A greater number of fine children, however, is seldom seen anywhere than about a barrack of soldiers. Very few of them it seems arrive at the age of thirteen or fourteen.

After enumerating the dangers, moral and physical, to which a soldier's child is exposed, even when the parents are living, Mr. Bernard continues:

But for the child whose father, or perhaps both his parents, have perished in the field, his settlement or connections distant or unknown, where can the poor orphan look for preservation and instruction but to some national establishment like the Foundling Hospital? If this is not an exposed and deserted child, entitled by its own distress and its father's services to the peculiar protection of its country, it should seem that no such case can exist.

A letter from Thomas Bernard to his brother, written in 1792, evinces a desire to ease off the work of his profession; in 1795, as already stated, he resolved to give it up altogether, and during the year, carried this determination into effect. His election to the Treasurership of the Foundling Hospital1in the May of that year gave him the opportunity of carrying out his views of improvement in the internal administration of the institution. It has been shown that the architectural and decorativeA NEW PROJECT 221

1*Life of Sir Thomas Bernard,*by Rev. James Baker.

arrangements bad not been carried out originally on an ascetic or even a simple scale; the Treasurer was therefore provided with a residence at one extremity of the Hospital buildings, containing large and comfortable rooms. In these Thomas and Margaret Bernard made their abode for eleven years, allowing for holidays and unavoidable absences, and devoted a considerable portion of their time to the superintendence of the establishment.

Mr. Bernard's biographer says that

He began by adopting Count Eumford's plans as to food and fuel, and fitted up the kitchen and fireplaces of the Hospital on the Count's principles, and with his personal assistance, a similarity of pursuits having produced great intimacy between them, which continued many years. This new project succeeded, reducing the consumption of coals in the kitchen from thirty-five chaldrons a year to ten, saving the labour of one of the two cooks, rendering the labour of the remaining one more easy, and dressing the food better than before.

Changes were also made in the diet of the children. When the institution was founded, the enormous allowance of one pound of butcher's meat a day for each child was given. This had since been apparently modified, so far that suet puddings, made with an admixture of flour, were substituted for meat on two days in the week. Mr. Bernard altered this to rice and treacle; in both cases milk was used, but less in the rice pudding; and the rice went further than the suet and flour – the last having been a serious item in a time of scarcity.

Moreover, the difference was found beneficial to the children, whose constitutions were wholly unprepared for a heavy diet. The meals were carefully superintended. Day by day, as I have heard my father state, Mr. Bernard took his place punctually at the head of the boys' table, Mrs. Bernard, in like manner, presiding in another room over the girls during the one o'clock dinner; thus ensuring not only that the food should be properly served, but also that the children should be trained in good habits.

In less than a year after his appointment Mr. Bernardwrote the ' Account of the Foundling Hospital,' from which extracts have been made. A second edition was printed in 1799, with a supplement; it was dedicated to the governors, or rather to those who had co-operated in reforms and improvements, ' by their affectionate friend and faithful servant, Thos. Bernard,' and contained seventy-three small octavo pages, besides the preface, &c. In the supplement he wrote:

There was a period when the proportionate mortality in the Hospital had been very considerable, and the children were neither healthy in constitution nor promising in aspect; but that period is, I trust, entirely passed by. I question whether any public establishment, or even if private families, can show better effects of care and attention in this respect than what is exhibited in the Foundling Hospital.

The children were generally admitted at about the age of six weeks, and forthwith baptised; wet nurses were procured from the country to meet them, and they were sent in charge of these women to their homes, where they remained about four years, under the eye of an inspector, and liable to surprise visits from friends of the institution.

At the age of four years [continues Mr. Bernard] the children are returned to the Hospital. They are then (if not sooner) inoculated and placed in the school, when they are gradually accustomed to regular and early habits of order and attention; the lesser children being occasionally let out to play during the school-hours. They rise at six o'clock in the summer and at daylight in winter; part of them being employed before breakfast in dressing the little children, in cleaning about the house, and the boys in working a forcing pump which supplies all the wards and every part of the Hospital abundantly with water. At half-past seven they breakfast, and at half after eight go into school, where they continue, the boys till twelve, the girls a little later. At one o'clock they dine, and return to school at two, and stay till four in the summer and in winter till dusk; except on Saturday, when they have a half-holiday. They are also instructed in singing the Foundling hymns and anthems, and in their Catechism, and are occasionally employed in and about the house during play-hours. At six in the evening they sup, and at eight go to bed.

THE MOTHERS OF FOUNDLINGS 223

It appears from other paragraphs that the girls learned needlework, house work, laundry-work and cooking; the boys were instructed in several trades, and also attended to the garden, and kept the large courtyard clean. In an article written by Mrs. Bernard for a series of reports/instituted by her husband, it is incidentally stated that a lending library was formed for the use of the Foundling children. The greatest care was exercised in the selection of places for the young inmates when old enough to leave the Hospital. This was made a special point, in consequence of former negligence having led to deplorable results. The children were apprenticed, and frequently visited during their term of service, the girls by the matron, the boys by the schoolmaster, and very few disappointed expectation.

In resuming the subject, Mr. Bernard attributes the amelioration of the Foundling children

To the removal of an ill-placed infirmary to its present airy and healthy situation; to an increased cleanliness in the children and in the house; and to some improvement in their diet, and (which I conceive to be very important to children) a more unrestrained liberty during their hours of play and recreation.

He adds:

I repeat with a confirmed and most satisfactory experience what I have stated in the former instance, that' an happier, a more healthy or a more innocent collection of beings does not exist in the world than is to be found within the walls of the Foundling Hospital.'

One word must be said, in conclusion, concerning the mothers of the foundlings. The eighteenth century was a time when society, always hard upon women, was, in England, especially severe on the victims of seduction, while continuing very lenient, and even gracious, to the seducer. In this state of things Captain Coram thought he had discovered the main cause of infanticide: *

He found that it arose out of a morbid morality then possessing the public mind, by which an unhappy female, who fell a victim to the seductions and false promises of designing men, was left to hopeless contumely, and irretrievable disgrace. Neither she nor the offspring of her guilt appear to have been admitted within the pale of human compassion; her first false step was her final doom, without even the chance, however desirous, of returning to the road of rectitude. All the consideration which was given to her condition, was the enactment of laws to bring her to punishment, after she had been driven to the commission of the worst of crimes: for the error of a day, she was punished with the infamy of years; and although her departure from the path of virtue, so far from being the consequence of a previous vicious disposition, might have been brought about by an awful scheme of treachery, she was branded for ever as a woman habitually lewd.

1*Reports of the Society for Bettering the Condition of the Poor.*

-Brownlow (John),*Memoranda, or Chronicles of the Foundling Hospital.*

In other words, he believed that despair, sometimes amounting almost to insanity, led to many of the cases of infanticide, though not of course to all.

The system of admission without any attempt at inquiry had, however, been abandoned before Thomas Bernard became connected with the institution, and the new arrangements required those mothers who sought entrance for their children to attend in person, and submit to the interrogatories of the governors – a plan which seemed doubtful as a check to infanticide, since it involved the exposure of their shame, and, before a tribunal of men, must – even if it so far succeeded – have a tendency to harden these unfortunate women.

Mr. Bernard's endeavour was, evidently, to soften this rule. He wrote/some years later:

The preserving and educating of so many children, which, without the Foundling Hospital, would have been lost to that society of which they are calculated to become useful members, is certainly a great and public benefit. The adoption of a helpless unprotected infant, the watching over its progress to maturity, and the fitting it to be useful to itself and others here, and to attain eternal happiness hereafter, these are no common or ordinary acts of beneficence; but their value and their importance are lost, when compared with the benefits which (without any prejudiceMAEGARET BERNARD'S DISPOSITION 225

1*Reports of the Society for Bettering the Condition of the Poor,*vol. iv. No. 4 of the Appendix. Note to p. 38.

to the original objects of the charity) the mothers derive from this Institution, as it is at present conducted. The preserving the mere vital functions of an infant cannot be put in competition with saving from vice, misery and infamy, a young woman, in the bloom of life, whose crime may have been a single and solitary act of indiscretion. Many extraordinary cases of repentance, followed by restoration to peace, comfort, and reputation, have come within the knowledge of the writer of this note. Some cases have occurred, within his own observation, of wives happily placed, the mothers of thriving families, who, but for the saving aid of this Institution, might have become the most noxious and abandoned prostitutes. Very rare are the instances, none has come within notice, of a woman relieved by the Foundling Hospital, and not thereby preserved from a course of prostitution.

In this work of mercy I have no doubt that Margaret Bernard was a most efficient worker – very privately no doubt – for the opinion of the age must have been against a lady's name being divulged in connection with such a mission; and, moreover, such efforts are best made privately, when it is possible. But the veneration which my father always entertained for this aunt – who was, I believe, also his godmother; the affectionate feeling with which he selected the New Testament she had given him in his boyhood, to read in his old age, seldom opening it without making some reference to her virtues – is to me evidence of her holy and beneficent life; although his mention of her attendance on the Foundling children is the only fact I can call to memory. This view is, indeed, corroborated by Julia Smith's allusions to her sister-in-law's self-denying and charitable disposition.

In conclusion, it may be admitted that the London Foundling Hospital, though no doubt an efficient school, is not really what its name implies. The workhouses are, as they were originally intended to be, the real Foundling Hospitals, since it is to them that waifs and strays are carried, and are received as a matter of course. Many recent institutions are indeed more easy of access than the foundation of Thomas Coram. What different steps ought to have been taken it is not easy to say. The turning-box system of

VOL. III. Q

indiscriminate admission has, I believe, been abolished in France and some other continental countries, and other modes of combating the evil have been adopted. But infanticide is not extinct anywhere; and I do not know that the problem, how to reconcile the claims of humanity with the duty of repressing vice, has – as yet – been satisfactorily solved anywhere.

10

SECTION 10

COUNT RUMFOED'S GRATES 227
  CHAPTER XII
  THE SOCIETY FOR BETTERING THE CONDITION OP THE POOR

Count Rumford's Orates – The Establishment of a Ramford Eating-honse on the Foundling Estate – Thomas Bernard's Projects – The General Object of the Society for Bettering the Condition of the Poor – Thomas Bernard requested to Arrange the Publication of Extracts from the Communications Received – The first General Committee of the Society – The Reports of the Society – Thomas Bernard's Views as to the Wants of Agricultural Labourers – The Parish Windmill on Barham Downs – Thomas Bernard is instrumental in Forming a School for the Indigent Blind in London – Houses of Recovery for Fever Patients – Lord Winchelsea's Experiments with Small Holdings.

ThomasBernard'sactive mind could not long rest content with the limited sphere of activity presented by the Foundling Hospital. He was accustomed to a busy life, and the nature of his new occupations left him many intervals of freedom. His first idea was apparently to diffuse the benefits of Count Rumford's grates amongst the charitable institutions of London, and eventually of the whole country. And he began with the Marylebone Workhouse, either because it was one of the largest, or by reason of some connecting link not now discoverable.1

At one of the meetings of the Proclamation Society, on the 20th of April 1796, Mr. Bernard produced a proposal, to be offered to the Select Committee of Marylebone Parish, for introducing into their workhouse, under Count Rumford's inspection, all his improvements, the Society, as the proposers, undertaking to defray all the expenses incidental to the alterations, and to give the parish the full benefit. For this object a subscription of one hundred pounds each from Mr. Bernard, the Bishop of Durham, Mr. Eliot, Mr. Wilberforce, and some others, was raised to commence operations; but this proposal was not acceded to.

1*Life of Sir Thomas Bernard.*

In the meantime, however, he (Mr. Bernard) had succeeded in two other attempts to disseminate these plans of economy – the one by the establishment of a Rumford Eating House on the Foundling estate; an account of which he afterwards published in the Reports of the Society for Bettering the Condition of the Poor1in the name of the person who had undertaken the management of it; the other by introducing them under his own immediate inspection, on a considerable scale, near Rippon*[sic]*in Yorkshire.

It must have been about this time, or very little later, that the Governors of Christ's Hospital applied to Mr. Bernard2for assistance in introducing the Eumford arrangements. This he willingly undertook:

at the same time asking that they would either appoint a Select Committee to direct the management of the new kitchen, or put it entirely under his directions. He was told that their officers were persons of such respectable character, as not to require any interference of that kind; and upon inquiry, it was found that the cook had the perquisite of the dripping, and her husband (who had some appointment about the house) the perquisite of the cinders; and that these two persons were to have the direction of the new experiment. As a considerable saving was to be made in these two articles, it might be supposed that there was little prospect of success beyond the period of the personal attendance of the cook from the Foundling Hospital – and so it happened: the new kitchen spoiled and wasted the meat, and increased the consumption of coals.

During the course of these experiences, Mr. Bernard,3who had already the sympathy of three influential friends, was evidently revolving the possibility of enlisting public feeling in favour of his projects.

The partial success of these his new occupations encouraged further exertion, and suggested to him the advantages to be derived from the formation of a Society of Benevolent Individuals who should unite their labours for promoting and disseminating all improvements and proceedings relative to the poor, and thus byA SOCIETY FOE THE POOE 229

1*Reports of the Society for Bettering H1e Condition of the Poor,*vol. i., No. 28. 'Extract from an Account of a London Soup-shop.' By William Hillyer.

'*Life of Sir Thomas Bernard.* ' Ibid.

drawing to a centre every information of this nature which could be collected from various quarters, might render their operations more public and more extensive than could be done by private individuals.

In the beginning of November, 1796, after several previous conferences with the Bishop of Durham on the subject, he produced an outline of his plan for the formation of a ' Society for Bettering the Condition of the Poor.' No objection was made except impracticability; at the same time he was requested to prepare a circular letter on the subject, which might tend to show how far the objection was surmountable. For this purpose he prepared the following, which was an address to a few friends, who, it was conceived, would interest themselves in the measure:as well as for the most important improvements in fuel, food, and in the mode of assisting the poor, the world is indebted to the philanthropy and abilities of Count Rumford.

' December 17,1796

' Sir, – The purport of this letter is to propose the formation of a " Society for Bettering the Condition and Increasing the Comforts of the Poor; " an establishment which we trust, may be the means of adding much to the general mass of national happiness. In other liberal pursuits the joint labours of intelligent and active men have never failed to produce considerable effects. Models, inventions, and experiments have been improved and applied to purposes of great importance. The same degree of success may reasonably be expected from a Society, formed for the improvement of the most beneficial of all sciences, the promotion of the welfare of our fellow-creatures.

' Its object would be everything that concerns the happiness of the poor, every-thing by which their comforts can be increased. To remove the difficulties attending parochial relief, and the discouragement of industry and economy by the present mode of distributing it; to correct the abuses of workhouses, and to assist the poor in placing out their children in the world; in this, and in the improvement of their habitations and gardens; in assistance and information as to the use of fuel, so as to give them more benefit from it; and in adding to and meliorating their means of subsistence, by public kitchens and by other means – much may be done by the union of liberal and benevolent minds – much by the circulating of information, and by personal assistance and influence.

' It must afford a strong additional inducement to efforts of this nature to consider, that in proportion as we can multiply domestic comforts, in the same degree we may hope to promote the cause of morality and virtue. For a very gratifying illustration of this,

'It is not however merely the increase of the comforts and morals of the poor, great as that benefit would be, that may be effected by the proposed establishment; its improvements and experiments will be more or less applicable to farms, manufactories, private families and to every situation of life. But, supposing it otherwise, were its object confined to the poor only; yet to add to the plenty of a nation, by encouraging its means, and to strengthen by increase of happiness the attachment which every true Englishman feels to his country and its invaluable constitution, must be deemed at any time objects of no trifling consideration.

' If you should so far concur with us, as to give a general approbation of the plan, we shall hope to be honoured by your attendance at Mr. Wilberforce's, Old Palace Yard, on Wednesday the 21st instant, at a quarter before two o'clock; in order to consider of the formation of the Society, and of the outline of the necessary regulations.'

This letter was approved and signed by himself, Mr. Wilber- force, and Mr. Eliot – the Bishop of Durham being absent in the country; and a meeting was accordingly held on the day proposed. Mr. Bernard then gave some explanation as to the proposed objects and plan of the Society; a unanimous resolution was adopted for its establishment; and a Committee was appointed to prepare a draft of Regulations for the Consideration of the Society.

His Majesty, being informed of the plan and object of the Society, was graciously pleased to declare himself the Patron of it.

At a subsequent Meeting the following Resolution, declaratory of their Plans was passed:

' Resolved, that the general object of the Society be to collect information respecting the circumstances and situation of the poor, and the most effectual means of meliorating their condition; in order that any comforts and advantages which the poor do now actually enjoy in any part of England may eventually be extended to every part of it, with as much improvement and additional benefit as may be to the poor; and with a tendency gradually to diminish parochial expenses. For the attainment of these ends, it appears to the Society, that the circulation of useful and practical information, derived from experience, and stated briefly and plainly, so as to be generally read and understood, may be ofA SOCIETY FOE THE POOE 231

very great national and individual benefit, and may induce and enable all well-disposed persons to unite in the promotion of an object so important to the happiness and welfare of the community at large, and particularly of that valuable branch of it, the labouring poor.'

In order that the papers might be made interesting, and all the necessary information comprised in as small a compass as was consistent with the objects of the Society, it was resolved rather to make extracts from the communications which should be received, than to publish the whole; the present plan was therefore adopted, and Mr. Bernard was requested to arrange and superintend the publication, and the first number came out in May 1797.

When the first volume of these collected extracts was published, in 1798, the General Committee ' was headed as follows:.

'*President*
TheLobdBishopOfDurham
Vice-Presidents
WilliamMobtonPitt, Esq., M. P.
ThomasBebnabd, Esq.
Eich. JosephSulivan, Esq.2
TheEablOfWinchelsea.'

Then followed a list of thirty-four members, many of them distinguished in various ways – all indeed, probably, men ofsome mark in their day. The Bishop of Durham was Shute Barrington, who had been translated from Salisbury in 1791. The name of Wilberforce appears as a member of the Committee; he sent one paper, which was published in the first volume of Reports,1and devoted such time and attention as he could spare from his own special objects to the work of the Society.

1Some perplexity has arisen from the variations in different editions of the Ueports. I possess two volumes of what appears to be the first edition, published respectively in 1798 and 1800; from which the above-given list of Vice-Presidents is taken. From the London Library I have had the use of the same two volumes – the fifth edition, 1811. In these Mr. and Mrs. Bernard are called Sir Thomas and Lady Bernard, which they were in 1811, but not in 1798 or 1800. The King is announced as Patron, the Bishop of Durham as President; but the Vice-Presidents are Lord Dynevor, Sir Thomas Bernard, Bart., the Bev. Dr. Glasse, and John Hinckley, Esq. I cannot explain this discrepancy, but it cannot represent the original list. The names of the Committee also vary. The Committee did, no doubt, vary from time to time, but I do not see how there could be more than one original list. Vols. iii. and iv., obtained from the London Library, appear to be first editions; Vol. v. might be second, as the Preface is dated 1805, but it was not published till 1808.

' Afterwards Sir Bichard Joseph Sulivan, M. P. See vol. of Reports (iii.) dated 1805.

Another gentleman is mentioned as having co-operated with Mr. Bernard, the Bishop of Durham, and Mr. Wilberforce, in launching the Society; and also, shortly before, in the attempted reforms at the Marylebone Workhouse. This was the Hon. Edward James Eliot,2eldest son of the first Lord Eliot of St. Germans, Cornwall, and brother-in-law of William Pitt, the Prime Minister. He never recovered from the shock of his wife's death, and himself died so soon after the formation of the Society that his name is not found in the list of members; but he is mentioned in a note, evidently by Thomas Bernard, with regret, affection, and even admiration.3

There were in course of time changes in the Committee, and also among the Vice-Presidents – who never indeed exceeded the number of four – Mr. Bernard being always one. Lord Teignmouth, John Sulivan, Esq., the Rev. Dr. Glasse, the Duke of Somerset, Dr. Grartshore, Lord Dynevor, John Hinckley, Esq., were, at various stages, his colleagues.

To describe all the ground covered by the Society's publications would be difficult and tedious; some idea of the whole will be formed from the chapters in these volumes which treat of the Society's work. Its reports extended over nearly eleven years, from February 17, 1797, to October 19,1807, and are one hundred and forty-two in number.4THE SOCIETY'S OBJECTS 233

1*Extract from Oxley's Account ofthe)Poor and Strangers' Friend Society, at Hutt,*by William Wilberforce, Esq. The ' Observations' following the ' Extract' are probably by Wilberforce.

*Note to vol. i. Appendix No. V. of the Society's Beports. For Mr. Eliot'e parentage and office, see Debrett, Burke, and other*Peerages,*'Earl St. Germans and Baron Eliot.'

3These names are in the list of Vice-Presidents in the various volumes of Beports.

1These figures have been ascertained from the volumes of Beports.

The Appendices to the five volumes, eighty-eight in all, were in many cases amplifications of the subject treated in the Reports.1Mr. Bernard wrote – ostensibly – forty Reports, and two of the appended papers; but is known to have been responsible for many more, and also for the Prefaces to all the volumes, which gradually developed into careful and suggestive essays.

In one of the appended papers in the first volume * I find some attempt at classification; and the list there given is consequently quoted here:

The following are selected as the subjects of information upon which the Society is desirous of obtaining and circulating information.

Parish Eelief – how it may be directed for the benefit of the poor.

Friendly Societies – their good effects and how they may be best encouraged.

Parish Workhouses – the amendment of them.

Cottages – the increasing the comfort and neatness of them.

Cottage-gardens – and the means of enabling the cottager to keep a cow, or of supplying him with milk.

Parish Mills for corn; and Parish Ovens.

Village Shops, for better supplying the Poor with the necessaries of life.

Village kitchens, and Soup Shops.

Cottage Fire-places and Chimnies – the improvement of them.

Fuel – how the poor may be better supplied with it.

Apprentices to Manufacturers, and all Parish Apprentices.

County Jails – the means and effects of reforming them.

Beggars – the least exceptionable modes of assisting them.

Public rooms for the resort of the industrious Poor in cold weather.

The greater number of these headings, it will be observed, refer especially to the country poor, whose condition at that period Mr. Bernard evidently considered one of great hardship. Other details affecting their comfort were subsequently discussed in the Reports; and many subjects were introduced relating to towns, or to both town and country – such as hospitals and asylums for various descriptions of suffering and privation, schools, church accommodation, &c.

1Mr. Baker states that he wrote most of the Reports; in some cases this may mean suggested and revised. See ' List of the Principal Works of the late Sir Thomas Bernard, Bart.,' at the end of the ' Life,' by Rev. James Baker.

2No. V. in the Appendix to Vol. I. of the Society's Reports entitled:'Acconnt of the Society, its object, subject of inquiry, regulations, Ac.'

Some of these will be noticed in subsequent chapters. This chapter and the next contain an exposition of Mr. Bernard's views with regard to the agricultural labourer's wants. His ideas, and those of his fellow workers, refer to a state of things which has, in great measure, passed away, but which may be advantageously studied as history, even when it cannot be otherwise utilised. Some improvements urged by the Society have long since been carried into effect – often by its agency; others have been brought about by the changes in public opinion; but even in these cases the Society – that is, the men who composed it and brought the power of united action to bear upon the evils of the day – constituted an important factor.

The first paper which Mr. Bernard contributed to the Reports was on the ' Administration of Parochial Belief at Iver'; and will be noticed in the next chapter on account of its connection with Buckinghamshire. It was immediately followed by an account of ' A Parish Windmill on Barharn Downs, in the county of Kent," which begins in the following terms:

In January 1796, a parish Windmill was erected by subscription on Barham Downs, very near the village of Barbara. The subscribers were eight in number; the subscriptions $40 each. The whole cost of the mill (which began to work on the 5th of April 1796, and contains two pair of stones, one for wheat and one for other corn) was $336; the expense of the scales and utensils of different kinds was $17; the whole together amounting to $353, being $33 more than the original sum subscribed. The surplus of expense was discharged out of the extra profits of the mill that were received between the 5th of April 1796 and the 1st of January 1797.

1Extract from ' An Account of a Pariah Windmill on Barham Downs, in the County of Kent,' by Thomas Bernard, Esq.*Beports of the Society for Bettering the Condition of the Poor,*vol. i., No. VIII.

EXACTIONS OF MILLERS 235

This enterprise was suggested by the exactions of the millers, as a class, which especially affected their customers among the poor – and there seem to have been many of this description; their average ' toll' on grinding Mr. Bernard reckons1 at a fourteenth.

During the late scarcity, corn was in some parts of England, at one time, as high as a guinea a bushel; the toll on which would be one shilling and sixpence; but when it is recollected that the miller's toll is always taken from the best of the meal and from the finer flour that is in the centre of the hopper, the value of that toll cannot be less than two shillings and sixpence a bushel. If, in addition to these circumstances, we advert to the fact, that, during the scarcity of wheat, some millers purchased at half price foreign and damaged corn, which they mixed with English wheat, we shall have reason to believe that five shillings a bushel on grinding wheat is not more than may have been made, in some instances, during that period of scarcity.

The actual price of grinding was ordinarily sixpence a bushel, with a deduction of one pound for waste; at the Barham Mill the charge was fourpence, with a deduction of half a pound only. Persons could, if they pleased, have their corn ground before their eyes – a bushel taking only ten minutes; this regulation attracted many customers. Whole meal was sold on one day in the week for ready money to the poor of Barham and the four adjoining parishes; the person who was employed to buy the corn, and was responsible for its quality, being in attendance on behalf of the subscribers. The rate was fixed by the average price of wheat on the preceding Saturday at Canterbury, with the addition of a fixed charge for grinding, and was generally about a shilling per bushel lower than at the neighbouring mills; the result being that the millers had reduced their prices, and sold their flour ' much nearer to the price of wheat than they did formerly.'

The subscribers had determined that all profits, after recouping themselves, should be appropriated in some wayto the benefit of the Barbara poor; on this agreement Mr. Bernard remarks*l*:

1Note to the foregoing Account. The next quotation is taken from another Note.

*I*hope the proprietors will excuse my expressing a hope that this surplus may be applied in giving aid and encouragement to those labourers, whose industry and economy have enabled them to do without parochial relief; by furnishing the annual premium of a cow, a pig, or the fitting up of a cottage, as the means of enabling them to thrive, and of raising them above the condition of applying for relief under the Poor's rate.

The prime mover in the establishment of Barham Mill appears to have been a Mr. Oxenden, who was well supported. When the report was published, a Parish Mill had just been erected at Chislehurst, in Kent, by the subscriptions of ten ladies and gentlemen; it was built on a site granted by the lord of the manor, consisting of two acres for mill, house, garden, and paddock; and the construction of the mill was superintended by the Rector. This clergyman, the Rev. Francis Wollaston, afterwards contributed a paper on Chislehurst Mill to the Society's Reports.

It was not only in respect of mills that the poor found themselves at a disadvantage. The paper,2on ' A Village Shop at Mongewell, in the county of Oxford,' contributed by the Bishop of Durham, which is the second Report in the first volume, describes an attempt at saving them from the high prices charged by small shopkeepers – themselves frequently at the mercy of larger and richer tradesmen – by placing many articles, but chiefly groceries, within easy reach:

A quantity of such articles of consumption as they use, as bacon, cheese, candles, soap, and salt, was procured from the wholesale dealers, to be sold at prime cost and for ready money. They were restricted in their purchases to the supposed weekly demand of their families. The bacon and cheese, being purchased in Gloucestershire, had the charge of carriage. Most other situaEFFORTS FOR THE POOR 237

' Note on Memorandum appended to the Beport, No. VIII., vol. i.

*Reports of the Society for Bettering the Condition of the Poor,*vol. i., No. 11. Extract from an ' Account of a Village Shop, at Mongewell, in the County of Oxford,' by the Bishop of Durham.

tions would be nearer to an advantageous market. This plan was adopted under the apparent inconvenience of not having a more proper person to sell the several commodities, than an infirm old man, unable to read or write. He received the articles that were wanted for the week; and it has appeared by his receipts at the close of it, that he has been correct. Since the commencement to the present time, there has been no reason to regret his want of scholarship: a proof how very easy it must be to procure in every village a person equal to the task. As he has parish pay, and his house rent is discharged, he is perfectly contented with his salary of one shilling*per*week, having also the common benefit of the shop.

The Bishop then goes into minute details as to the working of the scheme, which had been started in 1794, and supplied three small parishes besides Mongewell. He also deals with the question of the possible injury to small shopkeepers, suggesting that the more deserving among them might be employed in these shops, and that the steady and permanent character of the business would compensate for the loss of their previous profits, which were generally precarious.

Two papers were contributed in this volume by Mr. Bernard, which may be mentioned here, leaving the efforts on a larger scale for other chapters. One relates to the soup shop at Birmingham,1where a bread and meat soup was prepared ' on Count Eumford's principle, so far varied in the cookery as to be adapted to an English taste ';

the bones were utilized by means of a digester, which effectually dissolved them, and the meat seems to have been cooked with some skill. The other describes a ' Parish Dinner for Poor children at Epping,'2in Essex. There was a school of industry in the parish for the employment of children, and ' an ordinary was, on the recommendation of Mr. Conyers, opened in October last,' that is, in 1797,' and a general dinner has been provided on week days for any children of thatplace whose parents desire it.' The charge was sixpence a week, and the dietary resembled that in use at the Foundling Hospital. It was provided by the mistress of the workhouse, in a room adjoining that building, used at other times as a spinning school. The table was nicely laid, grace was said regularly, and the children trained in good habits and manners. In some cases, but apparently not in all, the prosperous neighbours paid for the children.

1*Reports of the Society B. C. P.,*vol. i., No. xxx. Extract from ' An Account of the Manner in which the Poor have lately been supplied with bread and meat soup at Birmingham,' by Thomas Bernard, Esq.

"*Ibid.,*vol. i., No. ixxiii. Extract from' An Account of a Parish Dinner for poor children at Epping,' by Thomas Bernard, Esq.

The situation of Epping, a large market-town, with a surrounding forest the scene and object of petty thefts, and a public road through it, was not very favourable to the industry and regular habits of the poor, nor was their usual dinner of a hunch of bread, part to be swallowed with a little water as they went along (the other part being most frequently thrown away), conducive either to their health, or to habits of economy. It is therefore a most pleasing circumstance to state that within one month after this dinner had been regularly provided at Epping, the appearance and manners of the poor children there were totally altered.

In case of illness the dinner could be sent for. It was also the workhouse dinner, and the overseers sometimes allowed it to the very poor in lieu of relief in money.

The housing of the rural poor was a favourite topic with Mr. Bernard and his friends, and the possibility of surrounding their dwellings with more aids than were then known – unless in very exceptional cases – to comfort and sustenance. An extract from Mr. Kent's book, ' Hints to Gentlemen of Landed Property," is given in an Appendix to the first volume of the Society's Reports, advocating the ' three acres and cow ' which have since become such a prominent subject, and it was followed up.

Mr. Bernard carefully inspected the working of Lord Winchelsea's experiments, which had already formed the subject of a short paper by the Bishop of Durham, andLORD WINCHELSEA'S EXPERIMENTS 239

1*Reports of the Society B. C. P.*vol. i., Appendix No. III. ' Observations on the larger sort of cottages, and the mode of erecting them.' Extracted from'Hints to Gentlemen of Landed Property,' by Nathaniel Kent, Esq. Published in 1775.

described at some length the result of his observations:1

A late visit into Rutlandshire has given me an opportunity of acquiring more minute and correct information respecting the circumstances and situation of the cottagers keeping cows, in the four parishes of Hambledon, Egleton, Greetham, and Burley on the Hill. I give the result of my inquiries, and I give it with more precision and detail than I otherwise should, as I am very desirous of enabling landowners to ascertain whether, in their own peculiar instances, it will not answer for them to follow the example of what has been done in that neighbourhood. At the same time I beg leave to anticipate the observation, that in arable countries where there is a scarcity of grass land, and in those districts where, from vicinage or a peculiar market, grass land bears a rent above its intrinsic value, it may not be practicable to supply cottagers with pasture for a cow, without some sacrifice on the part of the landlord.

The writer then describes the position of the eighty cottagers who keep cows, varying from one to five in number; how about a third part have their lands in severalty; the rest have the use of a cow pasture in common with others.

Most of them possessing a small homestead, adjoining to their cottage; every one of them having a good garden, and keeping one pig at least, if not more. Without any exception they pay for their land the same rent as a farmer would. The cottagers who keep cows are almost all of them labourers in husbandry; there are however among them, some widows and daughters of deceased labourers, and some men who work as country carpenters, or in similar trades. I can add that of all the rents of the estate none are more punctually paid, than those for the cottagers' land. The steward informs me that there has never been an instance of an arrear or of a delay in payment, even for a few days.

But these small holders were provided with well-kept cottages – ' and yet pay no more rent, than the ruinous and miserable hovels in England generally do'; which no doubt greatly helped them on their way. Mr. Bernard narrates how this system of farming was started, assuringhis readers that its results on the character of the fortunate cow-keepers and their families was most beneficial. He says:

1Extract from ' A Further Account of the Advantages of Cottagers keeping Cows,' by Thomas Bernard, Esq.*Reports,*vol. ii., No. LX.

As a proof of the effects of this system in promoting industry and frugality, I give the history of one of them, Christopher Love, of Hambledon, who is now seventy-five years of age, and has for fifty-three years back kept three cows; and nevertheless has gone regularly every summer, for fifty years past to harvest work in Cambridgeshire: because he is in more request there, and receives better wages, than he would at home. He has bred up a family of nine children in great comfort, and is now well and in good health himself, and has been in Cambridgeshire this preceding harvest, but thinks he shall go no more, as the family for whom he went to work are all dead or removed.

I saw one instance among them of a man who was bringing up and supporting nine children, all healthy, well-fed, clean, and neatly dressed. A little child under four years of age was asked if she could spin? ' No, she was too little, but she could knit.' – 'Her sister (said the mother, pointing to another girl, between five and six years of age), spins very well; she got a prize for spinning this year, and brought home a premium of the value of six shillings in clothing.'

Mr. Bernard then points out the valuable training afforded by these small holdings:

The education of their children to husbandry, to the management of cattle and of a dairy, and of every occupation that can tit them for the service of a farmer, is a very important advantage of this system: and if there were no other benefit to be derived from it, but that of adapting, and habitually preparing, the rising generation for the most useful and necessary employment in the island; – this alone would produce an abundant compensation for any effort, or attention, that has been, or may be, directed to the subject. They are not only stout, healthy, clean, well clothed, and educated in regular and principled habits of life, but they are used to almost every part of their business from the earliest period of life, every inhabitant of the cottage being, from infancy, so interested in their cow, their pig, their sheep, and their garden, as to imbibe, at a very early age all the material information in those subjects.

It need hardly be said that the long and compulsory schooling of the present era would stand considerably inBRITTON ABBOT 241

the way of this farm training, and that consequently the pleasant picture could scarcely be realised under existing circumstances. But in Thomas Bernard's day it might be a reality. He had illustrated his views by the true story of Britton Abbot, the occupier of a ' beautiful little cottage situated two miles from Tadcaster, on the left hand side of the road to York, with a rood of land well planted with fruit trees, vegetables, &c., and displaying three bee-hives.' After making the acquaintance of this notable man, Mr. Bernard, in 1797, published his biography, with observations, in the form of a pamphlet; and it was republished, when nearly out of print, at the request of the Society, as an Appendix to the second volume of Reports, where it affords an interesting narrative of a labourer's struggling life brought to a successful issue. His prospects had been once well-nigh wrecked by an enclosure at Poppleton, which drove him, with six children and a seventh expected, from the house and land he had occupied for nine years; only through the consideration of ' Squire Fairfax' did he obtain the rood of land on which he built his new house, and laid out and enclosed his garden. Whether there were many like him I cannot tell. In a paper/contributed to the Society's Reports by Thomas Thompson, Esq., the provision made by Lord Carrington on his estate at Humberston, in Lincolnshire, 'for cottagers keeping cows,' is briefly described. Other instances of the same provision were no doubt to be found in various parts of the kingdom; but it is hardly necessary to remark that the experiments of Lord Winchelsea and Lord Carrington were both carried on under specially favourable circumstances – those noblemen having sufficient means to incur risk without inconvenience, and ample space to carry out the plan with comfort to all parties; but that such schemes could not be urged upon persons of moderate incomes and small estates, without a probability of disaster to the landlord, and perhaps eventually to the tenant.

1Extract from ' An Account of a Provision for Cottagers keeping Cows at Humberston in the County of Lincoln,' by Thomas Thompson, Esq.*Reports of the Society B. C. P.,*vol. ii., No. LIII.

VOL. HI. R

One advantage, indeed, existed for such arrangements in the eighteenth century, and a little later, which has been to a great extent lost. Large tracts of waste land were then far more frequently to be met with than now. ' Five unsightly, unprofitable acres of waste ground would afford habitation and comfort to twenty such families as Britton Abbot's,' remarks Mr. Bernard; and he was a party to the scheme of enclosure at Iver in Bucks, where it was intended to form cow-pastures for the benefit of the poor. But processes of enclosure, whether well or ill-intended or designed, have been continued until in many neighbourhoods there is no waste land available. At the same time, however, some such homesteads as Britton Abbot's have arisen and bettered the condition of the villages, and the system of allotments leaves no ground to complain of want of land, or of the produce of land.

' In June 1798,' writes Mr. Baker,1' the first volume of the " Reports of the Society for Bettering the Condition of the Poor" was completed, and a cheap edition was published for more general circulation.' The soup-house, begun at Iver and on the Foundling Estate, had been established in several parts of the metropolis, and in Birmingham and other places, as a temporary remedy – (of course such establishments should never be permanent) – for the scarcity which then existed.

' The Publications of the Society for Bettering the Condition of the Poor ' soon began to operate. A society on the same principles was established at Cork, in March, 1799; and one in the City of Dublin in the following month. They were both conducted with considerable energy and effect, and were followed, in January, 1801, by an establishment of the same kind at Edinburgh. In the meantime the society at Winston, in the county of Durham, for the aged, had been formed in May, 1798, and a similar society at Wendover in July, 1799; and, in the same year, the Clapham Society for Bettering the Condition of the Poor, and several others.

1*Life of Sir Thomas Bernard,*by the Kev. James Baker.

THE DUBLIN FOUNDLING HOSPITAL 243

The results of Mr. Bernard's management at the Foundling Hospital in London also had roused the attention of some eminent persons in Dublin to the condition of a similar institution in the Irish capital; and not without cause, for it was worse than that of the one in London.

In the beginning of 1798 [writes the Kev. James Baker],1Mr. Bernard was applied to by Mr. Pelham (now Earl of Chiohester) respecting the Foundling Hospital in Dublin, where great inattention and a great mortality had taken place. Of twelve thousand six hundred and forty one children received in six years, ending the 24th of June, 1794, as many as nine thousand eight hundred and four had died; two thousand six hundred and ninety two were unaccounted for, and only one hundred and forty five were to be traced.

In the Infirmary the mortality had been still more shocking. Of five thousand two hundred and sixteen children sent into the Infirmary in those six years, three individuals only came out of the walls alive.

These facts were ascertained on the oath of the culprits themselves; and were occasioned partly by gross negligence, and partly by the radical defect of the system of a general admission of this nature; which has a direct and uncontroulable tendency to encourage the vice, and increase the mortality of our species.

In the endeavours of the Governors to reform these evils, Mr. Bernard supplied them with all the information which his experience could afford; especially by drawing up a statement as to the reception and management of the children in the establishment which he superintended.

At this moment, however, Thomas Bernard's mind seems to have been especially occupied with the subject of the agricultural labourer. He frequently recurs to it, and the following passages are from his observations on the proceedings of an Agricultural Society in Sussex:2

If we would preserve those blessings which Providence has bestowed on this favoured island, it is necessary that the higher classes of society should be*immediately awakened to the duty*ofassisting by every exertion in their power, the prevalence of industry, prudence, morality, and religion among the great mass of our fellow-subjects. To this desired effect, disinterested kindness, and well directed encouragement are indispensable requisites. Without them, words and actions are but empty professions; and the poor and uneducated cottager will never*profitably*receive that instruction, which is not enforced by the example of the teacher.

1*Life of Sir Thomas Bernard,*by the Kev. James Baker.

**Reports of the Society B. C. P.,*vol. ii., No. LI. Observations on 'An Extract from an Account of the Rewards given by the Sussex Agricultural Society to the industrious and deserving Poor,' by Thomas Bernard, Esq.

It is the misfortune of this country, and it has been the calamity, and it*may*prove the destruction of Ireland, that the different classes of society have not a sufficient bond and connection of intercourse; that they want that frequent communication of kindness and benefit and that reciprocal good will and esteem, which (except only in the case of the worst of beings) must always result from rational creatures possessing the means of knowing aTid appreciating each others' good qualities and utility. When that does not take place, the unfortunate consequence is, that neither of the parties does justice to the other. The rich do not sufficiently estimate the virtues of the poor; nor are the latter aware of the real and affectionate interest which many of the higher classes in England feel for their concerns.

But this is not all, the rich become less useful, because they undervalue their own influence and power of doing good; and the poor are often degraded in their own opinion, and debased in character, by the persuasion that they neither possess, nor are entitled to, the esteem and commendation of the other ranks in life.

And in the prefatory introduction ' to the same volume the writer touches at some length on the topic:

The question whether the rich support the poor, or the poor the rich, has been frequently agitated by those who are not aware, that while each does his duty in his station, each is reciprocally a support and blessing to the other. All are parts of one harmonious whole; every*art* contributing to the general mass of happiness, if man would but endeavour to repay his debt of gratitude to his Creator; and by a willing habit of usefulness, to promote the happiness of himself and his fellow creatures. In this way the higher classes of society may, by superiority of power and education, do more service to the other parts of the community than what they receive; the welfare of the poor being then, in truth, more promoted by the gradations of wealth and rank, than it ever couldA PLEA FOE THE POOR 245

1*Reports of the Society B. C. P.,*Prefatory Introduction to the Second Volume dated Nov. 2, 1798. This volume was not published till 1880. It contains the Reports of 1798 and 1799.

have been by a perfect equality of condition; even if that equality had not been in its nature chimerical and impracticable; or (if practicable) had not been hostile and fatal to the industry and energy of mankind. Rank, power, wealth, influence, constitute no exemption from activity or attention to duty; but lay a weight of real accumulated responsibility on the possessor. If the poor are *idle* and *vicious,* they are reduced to subsist on the benevolence of the rich; and if the rich (I except those to whom health and ability, and not will is wanting) are *selfish, indolent,* and neglectful of the conditions on which they hold superiority of rank and fortune, they sink into a situation worse than that of being *gratuitously maintained by the poor.* They become *paupers of an elevated and distinguished class;* in no way personally contributing to the general stock, but subsisting upon the labour of the industrious cottager; and whenever Providence thinks fit to remove such a character, whether in high or in low life, whether rich or poor, the community is relieved from an useless burden.

These remarks are followed up by an earnest exhortation:

If there should be among my readers, any one whose views are directed to himself only, I could easily satisfy him, that his means of self-indulgence would be increased, his repose would be more tranquil, his waking hours less languid, his estate improved, its advantages augmented, and the enjoyment permanently secured, by his activity in the melioration of the condition, the morals, the religion, and the attachment, of a numerous and very useful part of his fellow-subjects. – To the patriot, who wishes to deserve well of his country, I could prove that, from the increase of the resources and virtues of the poor, the kingdom would derive prosperity – the different classes of society, union – and the constitution, stability. – To the rich who have leisure, and have unsuccessfully attempted to fill up their time with other objects, I could offer a permanent source of amusement; that of encouraging the virtues and industry of the poor, with whom by property, residence, or occupation, they are connected; – that of adorning the skirts of their parks and paddocks, of their farms and commons, with picturesque and habitable cottages, and fruitful gardens; so as to increase every Englishman's affection for an island replete with beauty and happiness; – that of assisting the poor in the means of life, and in placing out their children in the world, so as to attach them by an indissoluble tie, and by a common interest, to their country, not only as the sanctuary of liberty, but as an asylum, where happiness and domestic comforts are diffused, with a liberal and equal hand, through every class of society.

11

SECTION 11

CHAPTER XIII

TheSociety'sWorkInBuckinghamshire

Thomas Bernard's House at Iver – Papers Contributed to the Society's Beports by Members of His Family – His Interest in the Working of the Poor Laws – His First Contribution to the Society's Beports – His Decided Opinion in Favour of Boarding-out Workhouse Children – The Village Soup Shop at Iver – The Provision of Fuel for the Poor of Lower Win- ohendon – Resistance to the Introduction of Proper Chimneys into Cottages – The Society at Wendover for Encouraging Prudence and Industry – The Progress of Vaccination for Small-pox – Mrs. Parker Sedding's Interest in the Poor in the Workhouse – Her Work aa an Overseer.

Mentionhas been made of Thomas Bernard's house at Iver, Bucks, in which he probably spent the greater part of his vacations for some years, and where he no doubt matured, if he did not form, some of his opinions on the state of the country poor.

' Iver,' says Lipscomb, the county historian, ' is a parish of large extent, and contains about 2,462 acres, comprising large tracts of heath and waste land.' It was probably the sight of so much ground – unprofitable from more than one point of view – that led to his suggestions for turning such land to good account.

Besides the papers contributed by Mr. Bernard to the Society's Reports, three bear the name of his wife, Margaret Bernard, one of his brother, Scrope Bernard, and two of their brother-in-law, Joseph Smith; in these, of course, Julia Smith may have had a share. Jane White, the eldest sister of the family, contributed part of a Report; Fanny King furnished the subject of one of Mrs. Bernard's contributions, and it will be seen that some years later a Ladies' Branch of the Society owed much to her pen as well as to her powers of organisation.

THE POOE LAWS 247

Other persons, less nearly related, also helped – from the Bishop of Durham, who contributed several papers beginning with the second number ever published, 1 of which the village shop at Mongewell, Oxon, formed the subject – to Mrs. Shore, of Norton Hall, Derbyshire, whose paper2is entitled: ' An account of the manner and expense of making stewed ox head for the poor.' A large proportion of members of the society and subscribers consisted of Mr. Bernard's relations, connections, and personal friends.

Since Thomas Bernard had a house at Iver in Buckinghamshire, Scrope Bernard possessed the Manor House of Nether Winchendon, and Julia Smith inhabited the vicarage at Wendover in the same county, several of the papers in the Society's Reports relate, as might be expected, to work done in that county – though not in all cases by the family. These will form the subject of the present chapter.

In a letter to his brother Scrope, Thomas expresses regrets for not having attended a meeting at which the Marquess of Buckingham was to preside, and returned thanks for the compliment paid him by the Marquess in making him a Deputy Lieutenant for Bucks. The reason for not attending is characteristic; he was previously engaged to a parish meeting on the reform of Iver Workhouse.

The biographer of Thomas Bernard observes, after speaking of his exertions to form the Society:

While Mr. Bernard was thus employed in disseminating throughout the kingdom useful information on the works of charity, he spared not his personal exertions in similar occupations. As Chairman of the Petty Sessions for the Hundred of Stoke, in Buckinghamshire, he was watching over the execution of the Poor Laws with vigilance and discretion. With this objecthe printed and distributed a ' Charge to the Overseers of the Poor' of that district, 1 in which he laid down the principles of their duty, and gave much useful advice in the execution of their office. In his own immediate neighbourhood he was engaged, in conjunction with Mr. Sullivan, in improving the internal discipline, decency, and cleanliness of Iver Workhouse, as well as its external appearance. He found in it fifty-three persons; of whom thirteen were above the age of fifty, three helpless men and women under that age, and eleven children, too young to be placed out in the world. Fifteen of the remaining twenty-six were placed out in service or otherwise, in the course of a month, and the other eleven were only kept till places could be found for them. In this instance (he remarks) it is to be observed that twenty-six of these fifty-three persons would have been better out of the workhouse; but the house had been formed, and on that account it had not been the man's interest to put them out, as that would have occasioned some immediate expense, and it might probably have been the cause of his allowance from the parish being reduced at the end of the year, or of his losing his contract by the competition of a lower offer.

1Extract from ' An Account of a Village Shop at Mongewell, in the county of Oxford,' by the Bishop of Durham.*Reports of the Society B. C. P.,*vol. L, No. 11. The first of the Reports, the one which preceded the Bishop's, was: ' An Account of a Friendly Society at Castle Eden in the county of Durham,' by Rowland Burdon, Esq.

*Extract from ' An Account of the manner and expence of making stewed ox's head for the Poor,' by Mrs. Shore, of Norton Hall, Derbyshire.

Mr. Bernard's first contribution to the Society's Reports is on ' the mode adopted as to parochial relief in the hundred of Stoke.' From this paper his biographer derived the information in the last part of the paragraph just quoted; but a further extract2will explain his views more fully:

In December 1795, when the applications of the poor for relief were necessarily increased, on account of the high price of bread, it appeared to the magistrates of the hundred of Stoke, that a regular book by way of register of the cases relieved in that district, might be put to considerable use, and might tend to put the relief given to the poor, on a more regular system.

With that view a folio book was prepared with four columns; the first containing the name of the pauper and his parish, and whether he (or any other person) was*sworn*to the circumstances of his case, or whether those circumstances were*admitted*by the overseer, on his personal knowledge; in the second column his own account of the condition of his family and of the amount of*PAEISH EELIEF 249*

1The Charge is given in Appendix No. IV. to vol. i. of*Reports.* *Extract from ' An Account of the Mode adopted as to Parochial Belief in the Hundred of Stoke, Bucks.'*Reports,*vol. i., No. VII.

their earnings; in the third, the relief asked; and in the fourth the order or agreement respecting it.

The heads of the four columns occupy the long side of a folio page.

A specimen is then given of the form of the book and mode of entry. Omitting some further details, I insert the notice which, in March, 1796, the magistrates sent round to the different parishes in their hundred:

'HundredOfStoke.

' In order to encourage industry and economy, and to explain their general plan of granting relief for the poor, the magistrates give notice, that particular attention is paid by them to the number of children of any age to require relief; and to the degree of industry of the person applying, and of every part of his or her family; and that, for this purpose, a book is kept by them, in which these circumstances, and any other, entitling the party to relief, are entered before any order is made.

' The magistrates, having hitherto granted relief,*at home,*to persons applying on account of children under seven years of age, have it now in their power, under the provisions of an Act lately passed, to extend that relief to industrious and sober persons, who have in part, though not entirely, the means of comfort and subsistence in their own dwellings: they therefore declare that, in all cases, where any parish workhouse is*farmed out,*they shall consider that circumstance as an additional reason for giving (as far as the law authorizes) relief,*at home,*to the industrious and well- disposed poor of that parish; it appearing that the forming of a parish workhouse sets the interest of the party in opposition to his duty, and prevents the relief, that the poor are by law entitled to, and which they would otherwise receive.

' They also recommend to the parishes not to lessen at all (or at least in a very small degree) the relief to the labouring poor, on account of any allowance the party may receive from any friendly society; or on account of any little portion of property which his industry or economy may have treasured up against an evil day; such a conduct tending to discourage frugality, and increase the parish burthens.'

This notice was signed by Sir Charles Palmer, Mr. Sullivan, Sir Eobert Harvey, Mr. Penn, Sir William Johnston, and myself, acting magistrates for the hundred of Stoke.

Sir Eobert Harvey was the gentleman called in a previouschapter Mr. Bateson-Harvey. Mr. Sullivan, of Richings Park, Iver, was probably an elder brother of the Mr. Sulivanlwho was a Vice-President of the Society; but he, Sir Robert Harvey, and Mr. Penn, were members of the General Committee.

The report concludes, according to the custom observed in the Society's Reports, with some ' Observations'; these may be termed amplifications of the previous topics. The same description applies to the forcible ' Charge to the Overseers,'2which occupies ten pages of an Appendix to the ' Reports,' headed:

'HundredOfStoke*Bucks, to wit:*

*1*To Overseer of the Poor for the Parish of in the said County.'

And begins:

' Sir, – The office, to which you are this day appointed, is of no small importance; inasmuch as the welfare of a considerable part of our fellow-subjects depends upon the due execution of it. It is*your*duty, Sir, to be the Guardian and Protector of the Poor; – and, as such, to provide employment for those who*can*work, and relief and support for those who*cannot;*to place the*young*in a way of obtaining an honest livelihood by their industry, and to enable the*aged*to close their labours and their life in comfort.'

Mr. Bernard held a decided opinion in favour of boarding out the workhouse children, which, however, scarcely touches the controversy of the present day on that subject, because the conditions were so different. There were then no workhouse or district schools, no provision apparently of any kind for discipline and education, and the children simply ran loose in the workhouse, worrying the old people, and,'FAEMING' WOEKHOUSES 251

1Their names are generally spelt differently; but ' Sullivan' is the only spelling in Lipscomb, who gives a pedigree, and in Burke's*Baronetage.*Here the two gentlemen seem to be identified as brothers. John became a Privy Councillor, Richard Joseph a baronet. One portion of the family called itself O'SuUivan.

2*Reports,*vol. i., Appendix No. IV.

it may be assumed, picking up many undesirable notions and practices.

The paragraph immediately preceding the recommendation to board out all children, touches on the practice of ' farming' workhouses; and shows the extremes to which this doubtful practice was carried. After noting some of its bad tendencies, Mr. Bernard continues:

Where, indeed, a principal landowner, or land occupier, of a parish can be induced to contract for the parish workhouse, *he has an interest in the permanent improvement of its condition,* and in the diminution of the distresses of the poor; but where a *vagrant speculating contractor* visits your parish, with a view of making his *incidental* profit by farming your workhouse, we trust you will consider the Christian principle of doing as you would be done by; and that you will not confide the poor whose guardian and protector it is your duty to be, to one, into whose hands you would not trust an acre of your land, or any portion of your own property.

The report on the ' Village Soup Shop at Iver ' ' was written by Mrs. Bernard, and begins as follows:

In October 1796, a village soup, shop was set up at Iver in the county of Buckingham. The most proper person that occurred for the purpose, was the wife of Eichard Learner, an industrious man, who had lost a leg by an accident in the course of his labour; and who, notwithstanding that disadvantage, had brought up a large family decently and creditably, without parochial relief – She was an industrious and notable woman, and had lived in a family as a kitchen maid. She attended by desire, several times, to see the soup made, which she afterwards took home for the use of her own family. She was then informed that if she could make the same kind of soup twice a week during the winter, it would be a benefit to her poor neighbours, and a considerable advantage to herself: that she should be furnished with the receipt, and the necessary utensils and materials to set up her shop; which consisted of a tin pot that contained four gallons, and a bushel of split pease, and that we would purchase of her tickets, or give orders for soup, for her poor neighbours, at threepence a quart, besides recommending to others to purchase of her similar tickets for other poor persons, whom they wished to be of use to.

1 Extracts from ' An Account of a Village Soup Shop at Iver, in the County of Bucks,' vol. i. of *Reports,* No. 18.

The advantages which this proposal held out to her were these; that the soup which she sold for threepence a quart, she could make for half that money; that, therefore, if she could get by the tickets, and by chance customers, a sale of only eight gallons a week (which was about her average) her profit, with very little interruption to her other work, would be not much less than four shillings a week; besides the comfort, of which she seemed fully to feel the benefit, but which it was much easier for her to enjoy than to describe, of being in the midst of a cook shop.

What happened in the present case, is what will hardly fail to happen in similar cases: there were few poor families in the parish, but what, placed on some list or other, received a good meal, to take home twice or oftener each week to their houses.

The soup was strictly vegetarian, consisting of split peas, and potatoes previously boiled and mashed, with a seasoning of herbs, salt, pepper, and onion; the whole boiled in water very slowly. This recipe had been used in the soup kitchen originally established on the Foundling estate, and afterwards moved to Fulwood's Rents, Gray's Inn. In the concluding observations, a strict supervision of the cook is enjoined, as everything depended on her choice of materials and mode of treating them. It is also stated that the plan was imitated in the parish of Langley, adjoining Iver, where Sir Robert Harvey resided.

The paper, contributed by Scrope Bernard, on ' A Provision of Fuel made for the Poor of Lower Winchendon,'¹is specially interesting from a family point of view, because it relates to a parish where a descendant of his still has a home, and affords opportunity for comparing the Winchendon of that day with the Winchendon of the present advanced age. It begins:

There having been several prosecutions at the Aylesbury Quarter Sessions, for stealing fuel last winter, I was led to make some particular inquiries, respecting the means which the poor at Lower Winchendon had of providing fuel. I found thatTHE POOE OF WINCHENDON 253

1Extract of' An Account of a Provision of Fuel made for the Poor of Lower Winchendon,' by Scrope Bernard, Esq.*Reports,*vol. ii., No. LXVII.

there was no fuel to be sold within several miles of the place, and that, amid the distress occasioned by the long frost, a party of cottagers had joined in hiring a person to fetch a load of pitcoal from Oxford, for their supply. In order to encourage this disposition to acquire fuel in an honest manner, and to induce the poor to burn coal instead of wood, in a country very bare of the latter article, a present was made to all this party (eight families in number) of as much more coal as they had purchased, and the carriage of the like quantity was further allowed them free of expense. Having no grates, they had employed the village blacksmith to tack together a few iron bars by an iron rim at each end, which when raised above the hearths by loose bricks, had enabled them to keep up a good fire. I went to see one of those grates; it was a foot square, quite flat, and had been made out of an old scythe by the blacksmith at the expense of one shilling. In this manner some of the poorest families in the village got through the last hard winter.

This article, indeed, carries the mind back to the days of the Tyringhams as well as forward to the present time. If the tradition of Mrs. Mary Tyringham's letter be accepted, in which she suggested that the thick woods of Nether Winchendon would hide the existence of the Manor-house, and probably of the village also, from an invading army, a great change must have taken place in the course of little more than fifty years. That it had not very long affected the parish, at least to a serious extent, is probable, from the fact that the habits of the people were as yet so little adapted to the new state of things. Mr. Scrope Bernard continues his narrative of his attempt to help the villagers by saying:

But they complained of the want of faggots to light their fires, which were not to be obtained by honest means. To remedy this, against the next winter, I had three waggon loads of the small faggots called kindlers, made up from a fall of beechwood, in the Chiltern country, ten miles off, and brought to Winchendon in the summer season. And as, in September, from the state of the harvest, it was foreseen that it would be a trying winter for the poor, a vestry was called and it was proposed, as one mode of relief, that they should allow the poor the carriage of a limited portion of coal; which was then sold at 1* 4dthe hundred, at the Oxford Wharf. At the same time they were informed that elevenhundred faggots were provided out of ihe Chiltern woods, as kindlers, to assist such a plan, which it was intended to sell much under the real value, at a penny a piece.

Scrope Bernard then narrates the distribution of the coal ' with three kindlers to every hundredweight, by a person residing in the centre of the parish.' Twenty-nine families out of thirty-five came to buy, bringing ready money; one person, probably the head of a family, was a man ' who had been lately imprisoned by his master for stealing wood from his hedges.' One hundred and ten persons were thus relieved ' at an expense to the parish, aided by voluntary charity, of about three guineas per month, being the charge for carriage distribution, and occasional excess of price.' The six families who did not buy were ' prevented by some particular circumstances which rendered the supply unnecessary.'

In the ' Observations ' following his article, Mr. Bernard notes that a charity of the same kind had been started the previous winter at Whitchurch, in Bucks, but entirely on voluntary lines; and, that ' one or two of the most opulent' parishioners had refused to contribute. He proposes that, if possible, such schemes should always be adopted as the act of the parish, allowing the sum thus assured to be supplemented by private charity, as at Nether Winchendon.

As frequently happens the persons to be benefited by innovations which they refused to consider as improvements had obstructed Scrope Bernard's previous endeavours at reform. He continues:

I have often wished to bring coal into general use at Winohendon; the poor however being jealous of any new schemes, under the impression that they are more calculated for the benefit of others, than of themselves, and the farmer not being very fond of new expenses, I had judged the attempt to be vain. But the circumstances above recited, having led both parties to make a trial, I believe that the one finds a great addition of comfort, and the other no great increase of expense.

The attempt to introduce proper chimnies into cottages in this neighbourhood, instead of the present spacious and airy ones with seats in the corner, has met with constant resistance, nor is it to beTHE FAMILIAR INGLE-NOOK 255

expected that any impression will be made on the poor inhabitants till they have had full opportunity of ascertaining, by observation and experience, the comforts and advantages of chimnies on a different construction. In the hope of effecting which change in their opinions, two cottage chimnies, on Count Rumford's principles, are now building in this village.

It is not difficult to sympathise with the cottager who was required, by alterations in the general mode of living, to give up his old familiar ingle-nook, and the chimney corner of ancient times died hard. Some specimens remained in my youth, and even after it; but, so far as I know, close kitchen-ranges are now almost universal.

Scrope Bernard's ' Observations' I conclude with a survey of the question in its moral aspect:

If we wish effectually to prevent the poor from stealing wood, and from similar acts of theft, it should be our first aim to put it perfectly in their power to obtain on fair terms the articles necessary to their existence. When the means of life and the acquisition of food and fuel are beyond the attainment of the*industrious*labourer, the inducement to guilt, and to invading the store of his neighbour, becomes so powerful as to put the virtue and integrity of the poor man to a very severe trial. – Persons enjoying the superior advantages of education, with minds formed to habits of honour and virtue, may feel confident in their own powers of forbearance, even under such circumstances; but it will not follow that it is either wise, or just, to expose the cottager to so great a temptation. Where the option is not given them of acquiring in an honest manner, and in exchange for the produce of their labour, the indispensable necessaries of existence (and such is fuel in this northern climate), however we may condemn any crime which may follow, we have no great reason to be surprised at such a result; nor perhaps ought we to consider ourselves as entirely exempt from a share in the guilt.

The following ' Account of a Society at Wend over, for encouraging Prudence and Industry,' by the Kev. Joseph Smith, tells its own tale. The two previous Societies mentioned therein had been formed in the diocese of Durham – the first at the Bishop's suggestion, the secondunder his immediate auspices, near his own palace; and they had been noticed in one of the Society's Reports:l

1The date of these ' Observations' was February 1, 1800.

Upon perusing the account of the benevolent and excellent establishment of Sunday societies2for the aged poor at Winston and Bishop's Auckland, I considered it as incumbent on me, at least to endeavour to form something of a similar nature in my own parish of Wendover; but at that time of the year (the latter end of autumn) I found it impossible to do anything effectual and useful for that purpose in a country parish. I therefore deferred it till a more favourable season. Early in the spring, having first secured the cooperation and assistance of two very worthy and charitable families in the parish, I visited the cottagers, and pointed out to them, in as strong terms as I could, the benefit and comfort which they would derive from such a society; but I found, in my own parish, an insurmountable objection to a meeting of elderly persons, at each other's houses, on a Sunday evening; an objection arising from a circumstance, that the labourers are scarcely any of them resident within the town, but are dispersed in their habitations in all directions, over a very extensive parish, containing a square of about five miles. From the different parts of such a district it would be hardly practicable for the aged and infirm to attend alternately at each other's dwellings; and there seemed to be objections to any common room, in a central situation, being applied for that purpose; or indeed that any fixed place of meeting, except the church, should regularly be used, for reading or expounding the Scriptures.

The last sentence evidently refers to the state of the law respecting conventicles, which forbade more than twenty persons, not belonging to the house, to meet for worship in an uncertified place.3The relinquishment of the Sunday gatherings involved the loss of a pleasant as well as edifying social meeting. It was part of the Winston arrangement, apparently with the hearty concurrence of the old people, A CHEAP SUNDAY DINNER 257

1Extract from ' An Account of a Sunday Friendly Society for the Aged Poor, at Winston,' by the Rev. Thomas Burgess.*Reports,*vol. ii., No. XLVII. In the ' Observations,' the Bishop's Auckland Society is mentioned.

*Extract from ' An Account of a Society at Wendover, for Encouraging Prudence and Industry,' by the Rev. Joseph Smith.*Reports,*vol. ii., No. LIX.

'See Arnold (T. J.),*Summary of the Duties of a Justice of the Peace out of Sessions* – ' Dissenters.'

that they should be regular at public worship; ' they make a point of attending church on Sundays, when not prevented by sickness, infirmity, or some unavoidable impediment, and also on other days, whenever they have opportunity.' Possibly the Wendover members may have been fairly regular also, allowing for distances; but as they rejected the idea of meeting afterwards, they apparently did not reap the benefit of another portion of the scheme:

There*is*a cheap but comfortable Sunday dinner provided, gratis, for all who attend church. It is prepared from one of the receipts in the first volume of the Society's Reports, the expence of it not exceeding three halfpence a head. They dine at the house of one of the members, which from its situation is most convenient for the infirm members. The dinner is dressed at the Rectory, and sent on the Saturday evening to the house where they dine.

The subsequent meeting is called an evening meeting, but the labourer's evenings then began and closed early, and Mr. Smith does not mention the dinner; it probably failed with the other arrangement, of which he writes:

I therefore very reluctantly gave up, for the present, the attempt to engage the old people to meet systematically on the Sunday evening at each other's houses, for their mutual comfort and religious improvement; and I have confined my endeavours at the commencement, to inducing, in all my poorer neighbours, a habit of saving some part of their earnings, during the period of the year when they could best spare it, against a time when they would most want it. To the poor, therefore, both male and female, and of all ages, I proposed that part of the plan only; as the means of laying up, from the excess of the most productive part of the year, that which might procure them comfort and relief at the season the least productive, and the most expensive; and in order to make it generally known, I employed the schoolboys at the writing- school in the parish to copy out the following proposals for a weekly contribution of money during the summer months, to be repaid them with a considerable increase, the addition of one third at least, at the end of the year.

The scheme was called a ' Friendly Society for the encouragement of the prudent and industrious labourers of the parish of Wendover'! ' T. Lovell, Esq., F. P. Bingham, Esq.,

Vol.

and the Rev. Joseph Smith, Vicar,' arranged to receive the contributions of the labourers every Sunday morning at their own houses as the people went to church; the text, 1 Cor. xvi. 2, was quoted as an encouragement to this practice: – ' Upon the first day of the week let every one of you lay by him in store, as God hath prospered him.' The three gentlemen engaged to add, at Christmas, a third to the sum contributed by the poor, if the payments were kept up till then, in some special cases more; and the bounty was not to form any hindrance to parish relief. Donations from parishioners in easy circumstances to the fund were invited. About sixty labourers at once brought their contributions from sixpence to a shilling, although twopence would have entitled them to the benefit of the association; the boys who received a trifle for copying the announcement were eager in making it known.

Such schemes of course seem commonplace now, but were then no doubt new, and received as inestimable boons.

In April 1801 the Vicar of Wendover contributed a paper to the third volume of the Society's Reports/on ' the mode of parochial relief at, and near, Wendover'; the gist of which is that in that locality

the calculation of the relief of the poor has been made on the presumed and*supposed*earnings of the labourer, and not on the actual amount of what he does actually acquire by industry and exertion.

The writer continues:

As the principle on which this has been grounded is the same as that adopted by the farmers at Whelford, I should not have made it the subject of a communication, except to notice two or three variations, which may perhaps, not be undeserving of attention.

Whelford is in Gloucestershire, and the Report in which it is mentioned was communicated by the Earl of WinchelVACCINATION 259

1Extract from ' An Account of the Mode of Parochial Relief at, and near Wendover,' by the Eev. Joseph Smith.

sea;1 but he gives the credit of the scheme altogether to the vestry – that is, the farmers – of Whelford. Both this and the Wendover scheme are on the lines laid down by Thomas Bernard in his address to the Overseers for the Hundred of Stoke – namely, that the industry of the poor should not be turned against them by being made a bar to parochial relief.

These are the only records I can find of the work carried on by the Bernard connection in Bucks; there are other entries in the Reports which refer to the county, and would probably never have been publicly known but for the existence of the Society. One of these refers to the subject of vaccination, which was then making its way, not without opposition, but surely, as the best means discovered for the prevention of small-pox. It will be seen that Mr. Bernard was a friend of Jenner, and an active supporter of his discovery, which is mentioned at length, and strongly recommended, in the fifth volume of the ' Eeports.'2

The paper contributed by the Eev. J. T. A. Reed,3who practised vaccination in the neighbourhood of Buckingham, is, perhaps, more nearly connected with the Society's work than at first appears, as it was probably through that Society that he learned, if not the existence of the new discovery, at least of its value. It begins:

In March 1800, having previously informed myself of the safety and efficacy of the cow-pock, I began to inoculate my two parishes, Leckhampstead and Akeley, near Buckingham. I was induced to do this at that particular time, because the Grand Junction Canal was in its progress in my immediate neighbourhood; and, like every other great work employing vast bodies of men from distant quarters, would probably introduce the smallpox. It was my wish that the labourers of these parishes shouldhave the benefit of the high wages given on auch occasions, without being exposed to the danger of that dreadful pestilence.

1*Reports of the Society B. C. P.,*vol. iii., No. LXXX. Extract from ' An Account of what has been done for the relief of the Poor at Whelford,' by the Earl of Winchelsea.

'- See Appendix xxv. of vol. v., containing the Reports of eminent Physicians and Surgeons.

'*Reports of the Society B. C. P.,* vol. v., No. CXXXVIII. Extract from 'An Account of Vaccine Inoculation in the Neighbourhood of Buckingham,' by the Rev. J. T. A. Reed.

Having been in the habit of administering medicines to the poor, my offer to inoculate them was very generally accepted; and especially, as most of these people are employed in milking. The common answer of such persons to my proposals was, ' we all know that nobody ever died of the Cow-pock, and we all know that nobody ever had the Small-pox after it; but what an odd thing it is, that anybody should think of inoculating with it.'

Mr. Reed originally intended to vaccinate in his own parishes also, but he was induced to extend his operations to the vicinity of Towcester, in Northamptonshire, where those who had been vaccinated by him were enabled to attend with impunity on small-pox patients, and, when the great fair at Towcester was expected on old May-day, one thousand persons were thankful to be thus safeguarded by him. In 1804 the small-pox was raging among the people employed at the Grand Junction Canal, and 570 persons were vaccinated; in the following year 270 in Potterspury only. He speaks with satisfaction of his success in all his cases, amounting to upwards of 4,700, in a period of six years.

There were many amateur vaccinators at this time, perhaps partially instructed, no regular medical organisation existing as yet for the purpose, but inoculation with the small-pox itself was still carried on. I have not anywhere read that the amateurs did any harm, beyond sometimes inspiring misplaced confidence when they had not thoroughly performed the operation. Mr. Reed, it is probable, like many clergymen, had received some medical training, and went to his work advisedly.

The last good work connected with Bucks that will be mentioned owed decided encouragement to Mr. Bernard, if even he was not the instigator of the enterprise; the paperTbears the name of George Brooks, Esq.:

Mrs. Parker Sedding of Stoke Fogies*[sic]*, Bucks, widow, rents a farm of upwards of 400Z. a year. Seeing that the state of the poor, A FEMALE OVERSEEB 261

1*Reports of the Society B. C. P.,* vol. v., No. CXXIX. Extract from 'An Account of a Female Overseer of the Parish of Stoke,' by Oeorge Brooks, Esq.

especially in the workhouse, was in an ill condition, she consented to undertake the troublesome office of overseer; and is now, with the commendation of the justices, serving her third year in that office.

The interior of the workhouse was irregular and dirty, and the poor inhabitants of it filthy and idle; and, as its distance from her own dwelling prevented her going to inspect the orderly and cleanly regulations she would 'establish, with that frequency which their necessity required, she voluntarily left the comforts of her own house, and lived one whole month in the workhouse. She employed the poor to clean the house throughout, and compelled them to observe cleanliness in their own persons, to fumigate the clothes and bedding in the oven, to mend the ragged garments capable of being mended, and to make what new ones were necessary; and, having taken proper measures that the poor should have sufficient and sound clothing and bedding, wholesome food, instruction and employment, she left them in a state of order, cleanliness, and comfort, under the charge of a careful man and his wife, whom she had engaged to superintend the workhouse under her direction. This couple perform the offices of schoolmaster and mistress to the children, read the prayers daily with all the poor, and on Sundays read to them the Holy Scriptures. They also instruct the poor in spinning. Being unable to prevail upon the vestry to establish a parochial manufactory in the workhouse, on a scale adapted to their numbers, Mrs. Sedding has done it at her own charge, and has introduced a little manufactory of worsted. The poor have a portion of their earnings. One little boy in petticoats at the spinning wheel, earned twopence a day, and had it all for himself; and as he knew he was to be put into boys' clothes when he had earned them, he was working very diligently indeed to obtain them. A little girl eight years old earned threepence a day for herself.

Exclusively of these interior improvements, it should not be omitted to be stated, that, when Mrs. Sedding was named overseer she found the poor were *farmed.* She took the care of them into her own hands, made them more comfortable, paid off the arrears of debt owing by the parish, and, notwithstanding this incumbrance, she has reduced the poor's rates. Mrs. Sedding is universally allowed to be one of the best farmers, as well ns best neighbours; she is a most active woman, and is continually doing good among the poor.

I would submit to consideration, whether this valuable *Female Overseer,* in her sphere, is not forwarding the views of the Society, and whether it would not help to promote their human object if the example of such an overseer of the poor were Bono-ticed and recorded by the Society, that it might be generally held out to the imitation of other overseers, where any excitement may be wanting to put the condition of a workhouse into better order especially in some of the country parishes.

The writer continues this topic in the ' Observations,' adding:

The late Earl of Rosslyn, who lived in the parish, and took an active part in the interest of the poor, was so much satisfied with Mrs. Sedding's conduct in her office, as to request her to continue it another year, and she accordingly has served a third year. Many of the circumstances above stated are well known to others as well as to myself. At my request David Pike Watts, Esq., personally visited the workhouse at Stoke, and viewed the state of things there, since the salutary regulations introduced under the direction and through the indefatigable exertion of Mrs. Sedding.

The Reverend Arthur Bold, the Vicar of Stoke Fogies is a frequent observer of these proceedings in the parochial workhouse, warmly commends the zeal and perseverance with which they have been carried into effect, and would, I make no doubt, be ready to allow any references to be made to him respecting them.

The date of this communication is ' 3rd February, 1806 '; there is a note to the paper signed ' B,' and dated the following February 15, which is, of course, by Mr. Bernard, to the following effect:

I have great pleasure in being able to add to Mr. Brooks's, my own testimony of Mrs. Sedding's merit as an exemplary overseer. In attending as a magistrate at Salthill, I have been a witness of Mrs. Sedding's conduct in the execution of her office, and of the success which has attended it, and I have taken an opportunity of recommending her knowledge of her duty, her care of the poor and her attention to the true interests of her parish, as objects of imitation to the other overseers of that district. In consequence of Mr. Brooks's account, and of the corroborative testimony of Mr. Watts and myself, the Committee of the Society for Bettering the Condition of the Poor, at their monthly meeting, last week, came to a resolution: ' That George Brooks, Esq., be requested to convey to Mrs. Sedding, the Thanks of the Committee, for her great ExerA FEMALE OVERSEER 263

tions for the benefit and improvement of that Parish, and that a copy of the Reports of the Society be presented to Mrs. Sodding as a testimonial of the sense which the Members of the Committee entertain of her conduct.'

Why, then, had Mrs. Sedding no successors in office of her own sex? Were there no women in the neighbourhood like-minded with herself? Or were they discouraged by the men?

12

SECTION 12

CHAPTER XIV

LONDON CHABITIES AND THE ROYAL INSTITUTION

Institutions for the Blind – The Asylum for the Blind at Liverpool – The School for the Indigent Blind – Houses of Becoveryfor Fever Patients – Prevalence of Malignant Fever in London – Opening of a House of Becovery in Gray's Inn Lane – Erection of the Cancer Institution – Count Rumford's Career – The Acquaintanceship between Thomas Bernard and Count Rumford – Their Plan for founding the Boyal Institution – The Committee appointed to consider the Plan – The Objects of the Institution – Its Constitution – Count Bumford's and Thomas Bernard's Scheme with regard to Bridewell – Thomas Bernard's Interest in the Casual Mendicant Poor – ' Martin's Act.'

Londonwas undoubtedly a very different city at the close of the eighteenth century from the London we are now acquainted with; the population I find estimated, in 1801,1at 900,000 only, but even this was a sufficient number to include a formidable amount of vice, poverty, and misery of all descriptions. And little had been done to combat any form of evil.

Here, then, the Society, from its first commencement found an ample field for work, and some of the consequent reforms are noted in this chapter.

It must appear singular, for instance, that so little had been done for the blind. A few blind children had been taught music at the Foundling hospital, but there seems to have been no systematic attempt before this time at enabling the blind to gain their own living. It was in the provincial commercial town of Liverpool, then rising into note, but far below the capital in wealth and population, that Mr. Bernard found an institution for this purpose, which he made known for the imitation of other towns, but especially of London.

This was the Asylum or School of Instruction for the1 *The Edinburgh Gaaetteer*(Edition of 1822).

INSTITUTIONS FOE THE BLIND 265

Blind, established in 1790,1which aimed, not at separating the scholars from their families, but at affording them good industrial teaching in comfortable rooms during eight hours of the day; scholars from a distance were provided with lodgings in the town. They received from eighteenpence to five shillings weekly – the supposed value of their work – though, for some time, it was, of course, worth nothing; their friends or the parish were expected to contribute a part of this.

' Upon my visiting the Asylum to-day – (3rd of August 1798) [writes Mr. Bernard] – I found 43 blind persons at work; 16 of whom were females and 27 males.' The principal employment of the women seems to have been spinning yarn for window cords, sail cloth, and linen cloth. The men made baskets, lobby cloths, doormats, whips,2and clock and window cords.

Special advantages were given to scholars who showed musical talent. They might be admitted at the age of eight instead of twelve or fourteen, and if partially instructed before admission might enter after the prescribed age of forty-five. As a rule pupils remained about four or five years only. There were few failures; of certain scholars who might be so considered, Mr. Bernard remarks leniently:

There are ten who have been strolling fiddlers, and have since learnt a trade in the School; but who have nevertheless resumed their former occupation – and who can wonder at their recurring to an art, which habit and want of sight must have made pleasant, and almost necessary to them; when he considers how great is the blank in the mind of a blind person, and how much of that may be filled up by their own music, though sometimes with less delight to their hearers than to themselves? [And he adds]: They have, however, the benefit of having learnt a trade, whereby in future they may add to their other means of support.3

The idea was taken up by a Mr. Houlston, in London, with the result that a meeting was held on January 8, 1800, and ' The School for the Indigent Blind' formed, of which the Bishop of Durham was chosen President. By a paper which the Bishop contributed to the Society's ' Reports ' it appears that the Institution began on a small scale in ' part of the buildings formerly known by the name of the Dog and Duck, in St. George's Fields, and once applied to very dissimilar purposes.' ' For the earlier arrangements and conduct of this establishment' (writes Mr. Baker), 'Mr. Bernard took an active part; and after he had withdrawn his personal attention to it, continued to express much pleasure in observing the degree of zeal and exertion with which it was conducted.' He indeed revisited the Liverpool Asylum in 1806, and wrote another paper on the progress and success of its work.1

1 Extract from ' An Account of the Asylum (or School of Instruction) for the Blind at Liverpool,'by Thomas Bernard, Esq.*Reports of the Society B. C. P.,*vol. ii., No. XLIV.

''Whips were soon afterwards discontinued. It is not stated why.

'Extract from ' An Account of the House of Recovery established by the Board of Health at Manchester,' by Thomas Bernard, Esq. (dated Nov. 1797). It is probable that he had not then visited the Institution.

An undertaking of perhaps greater magnitude was the providing houses of recovery for fever patients, on the plan of one at Manchester which Mr. Bernard visited August 2, 1798, the day before he went over the Blind Asylum at Liverpool. He sent a paper to the Society's first volume of ' Reports ' on this subject, and obtained a hearing for the scheme in the metropolis. A House of Recovery did not signify, as might be supposed, a convalescent home, but a refuge to which persons could be removed whose circumstances rendered recovery in their homes apparently hopeless. In London there were persons in many quarters huddled together in one small room night and day, sick or well, and sometimes dead and living. This had been the case in Manchester, but the House of Recovery had made such a marked difference in the health of the locality, that its benefit had since been extended to places outside the town. Thus London had to take from a remote county the first idea of checking the inroads of disease by isolation. Dr. Haygarth, who had made notes for thirty years on the subject, and had established district fever wards in Chester Hospital,2seems to have been one of the first physicians, ifCHECKING DISEASE 267

1Extract from ' A Further Account of the House of Recovery at Manchester,' by Thomas Bernard, Esq. (dated June 7, 1799).

2' Notes and Additional Observations collected by a Member of the Committee.' Appendix to the*Reports of the Society B. C. P.*vol. ii., No. XIV.

not the first, to realise the necessity of the case. Dr. Fer- riar took the lead at Manchester when the house was established in 1796.

In London, Dr. Murray, one of the physicians to the Carey Street Dispensary, a neighbourhood which had suffered severely from the scourge, at the request of the Society for Bettering the Condition of the Poor, published his ' "Remarks on the Situation of the Poor in the Metropolis, as contributing to the Progress of Contagious Diseases, with a Plan for the Institution of Houses of Recovery, for Persons infected by Fever.'*l*

But the terrible scarcity, which appears to have exercised an influence over every phase of life, retarded the active measures in contemplation until May 1, 1801, when the Committee called a meeting, which was well attended by persons of various classes. The Duke of Somerset, the Earl of Pomfret, the Bishop of London, were present; and at the request of the meeting the Bishop of Durham took the chair. Resolutions were adopted, on the motion of Lord Sheffield:

That it appears to this meeting by a certificate from the physicians of the hospitals and dispensaries in London, that the contagious malignant fever has been for some time past, and now is, prevalent in the metropolis: and that it has been occasioned by individual infection, which, with proper care, might have been immediately checked – or has been produced, or renewed, by the dwellings of the poor not having been properly cleansed and purified from contagion, after the fever has been prevalent in them: – that it also appears that this evil (the injury and danger of which extend to every part of the metropolis) might be prevented, by cleansing and purifying the clothes, furniture, and apartments, of persons attacked by this disease, and by removing them from situations where, if they remain, the infection of others is inevitable; – and that a subscription be immediately set on foot, for the purpose of forming an Institution for checking the progressof the contagious malignant fever in the metropolis, and for removing the causes of infection from the dwellings of the Poor, upon a plan similar to that which has been adopted with great success and effect at Manchester.

1Extract from ' An Account of the Institution to Prevent the Progress of the Contagious Fever in the Metropolis.'*Reports of the Society B. C. P.,*vol. iii. No. XCII.*(Note.* – This Paper was originally prepared for the*Reports,*by Thomas Bernard, Esq.; but its insertion has been deferred on account of its having been printed separately, and distributed by the desire of the Committee of the Fever Institution. It is of considerable length.)

It appears that, in 1750, some agitation had been caused by the prevalence of fever, and sundry measures had been taken which checked its progress for a while, until the increased difficulty of procuring food had so reduced the vitality of the poorer classes as to facilitate a fresh outbreak. Of course distressing cases were reported, such as the increased publicity of later years has rendered familiar to most persons. A husband and wife in Lumley's Rents, near Chancery Lane, were without attendance, in a room of which the windows would not open; the wife's sister took the children to her home, and ran in occasionally ' to set a little whey by their bedside,' but dared not remain lest she should carry the infection back with her – which she actually did. This woman was advised that the man could be received at a certain hospital without notice, as in cases of accident; he was taken there and rejected, reaching his room again only after three hours spent in a hackney coach. For another case, in Clarence Passage, St. Pancras, the parish officers refused to afford any help, except for passing the sick persons to their own parish, a hundred miles from London.1

Many patients no doubt owed their illness to carelessness, induced partly by extreme poverty, in sleeping on infected bedding, and to such ignorance as keeping door and window closed in a room without a fireplace, the room being nine feet square, and inhabited by six persons.

These cases, and others quite as perilous, the Committee did its best to alleviate; but in spite of the titled and wealthy persons who were supposed to take an interest in the matter, the most that could be achieved in the direction of permanent improvement was the opening of one small House of Recovery in Gray's Inn Lane. To obviate the useFEVER PATIENTS 269

1The information here given is chiefly bom: ' Three Reports of the Sub- Committee appointed by the Fever Institution,*&c.,*'vol. iii. of the*Reports of the Society B. C. P.*Appendix No. III.

of hackney coaches – the precursors of cabs – a litter was invented, composed of sacking and oil-cloth, supported on poles, something like those of a sedan-chair;*l*it could be carried by two men, or even women. It is on record that the sight of this unusual conveyance on one occasion collected a crowd which refused to let the patient depart. But as she became worse she was, at her own request, eventually conveyed by permission of the mob to the Institution, and recovered. The prevalent fever was pronounced by Dr. Haygarth and other physicians to be in nearly all cases a form of typhus, by whatever name it was called. It was to a great extent checked by the removal of the patients, followed by a vigorous use of lime-wash in all infected dwellings.

The Parliamentary Grant (says Mr. Baker)2of three thousand pounds voted to this Institution in 1804, aided by a gift of five hundred pounds from the Society for the Poor, and additional subscriptions of one hundred and two hundred pounds each, from some of its original supporters, was applied in 1813 to the purchase and fitting up of the westernmost of the two buildings erected for the Small Pox Hospitals, situate in an airy part of Pancras Road, and admirably calculated in all respects, with arcades and space for the convalescents to take air and exercise; and so separated and secluded from other habitations, as not to leave ground for the least alarm of infection to the most timid mind.

This building contains sixty-four beds, and received within its walls between the 1st of March and 21st of November, 1817, no less than four hundred and seventy patients afflicted with contagious fever.

It is needless to add that Pancras Eoad must have been a very different locality in those days from what it now is. The possibility of appropriating a building intended for smallpox patients indicates a diminution of the number of cases of that disease, probably brought about by the more frequent practice of vaccination.

In all these arrangements (continues Mr. Baker), from the first formation of the Institution to its present establishment, Mr. Bernard principally contributed to its success, both by the unwearied attention which he paid as a Member of the Committee, and the many efforts he made by numerous publications on its behalf to draw the public mind to the due consideration of a measure so important to the health of this vast metropolis.

1The conveyance used in Manchester was a sedan-chair of a special make.'*Life of Sir Thomas Bernard.*

Of Mr. Bernard's interest in the Cancer Institution I cannot write at any length, as his biographer gives scarcely any details of the movement. It arose on the failure of another institution, but in what manner is not explained. There was no connection between the two in their objects.

It has been stated that Mr. Bernard wrote an account of the London Foundling Hospital which was sent to Dublin to assist in the scheme of reformation started for the Foundling Hospital there. In this report he again alludes to the benefits reaped by the mothers of those children who had been admitted to the London institution, in the following words:'

It should not be unnoticed that there occur every year instances of penitent mothers, who, benefiting by the concealment of their shame, have become industrious, respectable, and prosperous in life. Some have been afterwards enabled to marry decently and comfortably, and in some cases to the very person who was the original cause of their misfortune. Of these several have come to the Hospital to reclaim their children, which are delivered to them, if they can satisfactorily prove their ability to maintain them.

There seems little doubt, from the interest which he constantly showed in the rescue of women as well as children, that Thomas Bernard must have been a prime mover in another attempt at furthering the cause, in which he certainly took a part, as mentioned by his biographer:2

In June 1799, the Committee of the Society for Bettering the Condition of the Poor had established an Infant Asylum which had two objects, the preservation of a peculiar class of infants, and the supply of wet nurses for the children of some of the other classes. The irreconcilable enmity and jealousy however of the nurses and female attendants, soon broke up the new establishTHE CANCEE INSTITUTION 271

1*Reports of the Society B. C. P.*
- *Life of Sir Thomas Bernard,*by the Eev. James Baker.
meat, and on its ruins was erected in June 1801, the Cancer Institution.

So far as can be gathered from this concise statement, the Asylum must have been intended for illegitimate children who for various reasons were ineligible to the Foundling Hospital, or had failed to gain admission there. It was so far on a different principle, that the mothers were not entirely separated from their children, and there may have been divergencies in the system. But the institution lasted so short a time that there is no account of it in the Society's ' Reports.' It apparently failed through the lack of devoted women to undertake the task of superintendence and reformation as a labour of love, not merely as a means of living.

Some of the life governors – that is, the principal donors to the Asylum – apparently resolved to transfer their gifts to a new charity rather than take them back; and there were no doubt discussions as to the most pressing calls for benevolent exertion, which resulted in a much needed institution.

In June 1801, there was formed in London an institution for investigating the nature and cure of cancer;' a disease to which the rich as well as the poor are liable; but which seems to bear more hardly on the latter, as wanting that alleviation of pain, and that degree of attention and assistance, which an evil so hopeless and so aggravated must require.

A meeting was called by Dr. Denman, and resulted in the formation of a committee of superintendence, consisting of twenty-one gentlemen, and of a medical committee composed of fourteen eminent physicians and surgeons, Dr. Denman being secretary, and the person to whom all communications should be addressed. The visitation of patients at their own homes was to be speedily begun; and, when the funds allowed, a house was to be hired for the reception of indigentsufferers, who were to be admitted free for some weeks, and then in some special cases to remain on at a small charge.

1Extract from ' An Account of the Institution for Investigating the Nature and Cure of Cancer,' by Thomas Bernard, Esq.*Reports of the Society B. C. P.,*vol. iii., No. XCIX.

A register was to be kept of all cases, and a list of queries sent round to all corresponding members, on the nature, symptoms, and treatment of cancer. The queries were prepared under the direction of the Medical Committee, and inserted in the ' Account,' published by the Society, as a long note. Thomas Bernard wrote or compiled the ' Account' and the ' Observations ' which followed it. And thus a systematic attempt, probably the first, was made at investigating the nature of the disease, which is still a subject of inquiry and research.

I now come to a more cheerful topic, the foundation of the Eoyal Institution, in which the biographers of Count Eumford and Mr. Bernard seem each to claim the greater share for their respective heroes. It does not appear, however, to be denied that it was a subject much discussed between them, and also that the details were left chiefly in the Count's hands by reason of his scientific knowledge and varied experience. To elucidate this view, a sketch is here given of his previous life of adventure – an extraordinary record, even in that disturbed epoch.

The name of Count Eumford has been mentioned more than once as the friend and fellow-labourer of Thomas Bernard, and the originator of valuable improvements. But the talents of this remarkable man extended far beyond the production of model grates and ranges, and his biography' is one of the most curious episodes of his time.

Count Eumford 1 was originally plain Benjamin Thompson, the scion – it is said – of an old family, sprung from one of ' Winthrop's company,' who was located at Charleston, near Boston, in 1630. The boy was born, in March 1753, at a large farmhouse in North Woburn, Massachusetts. HisCOUNT EUMFOED'S CAEEEE 273

1*Memoir of Sir Benjamin Thompson, Count Rumford; with Notices of his Daughter,*by George E. Ellis. (Published, in connection with an Edition of Rumford's complete Works, by the American Academy of Arts and Sciences, Boston, 1871.)*The Royal Institution, its Founder, and its fIrst Professors,*by Dr. Bence Jones. Longmans, Green d- Co

father died the following year, and his mother, by birth Euth Simonds, the daughter of a distinguished officer, took for her second husband one Josiah Price, and moved to another house in the same parish. It has been said that this step-father was a tyrant, but the charge is not proved. Benjamin was, no doubt, a difficult boy to manage, and his genius for science sometimes stood in the way of more homely occupations.

While apprenticed to a merchant in Salem, he formed an intimacy with Thomas Barnard, son of the minister who had taught Governor Hutchinson, and who was then himself a teacher. From this friend he learned ' algebra, geometry, astronomy, and even the higher mathematics,' so that before the age of fifteen he was able to calculate an eclipse.

Having received the best education which circumstances admitted, Benjamin tried various ways of earning his living – mercantile, medical, &c. – till, in 1772, while residing at Concord, a town of New Hampshire, which had once formed part of Massachusetts, the well-to-do widow of Colonel Rolfe, daughter of Timothy Walker, an influential minister, selected him – according to his own account – for her second husband. He was then nineteen and she thirty- three. This marriage introduced him to Governor Went- worth, the popular representative of royalty,1extolled only a few years previously by the Nationalists as a noble contrast to Governor Bernard.2But his popularity was already on the wane, and Wentworth hastened its decline by appointing Benjamin Thompson major in the second New Hampshire company, over the heads of officers with superior claims.

The discovery that the Governor was, at the request of General Gage, secretly providing workmen to assist in the construction of barracks at Boston, finished his reign as the people's hero, and Thompson, his supposed favourite, was involved in this reverse, and even, without any apparent fault of his own, in a persecution which eventually drove him to seek service in the British army.

1 See vol. i. of this Family History, ch. xv.

*See vol. ii. of this Family History, ch. xziv.

VOL. III. T

In 1776 he was sent on a mission to England, and retained by Lord George Germaine, then Secretary of State; in 1780 he held for a short time the appointment of Under-Secretary of State for the Northern Department. In little more than a year after, Lord George retired, and became a peer as Viscount Sackville; meanwhile Thompson had obtained a commission of Lieutenant-Colonel in the British army and returned to America. His conduct was in some respects distinguished, but he has been accused of acts of cruelty while in command at Long Island, from which charges his biographer defends him on the ground that he was not worse than others. Mr. Ellis also suggests that the allegations against him may have owed their origin to the jealousy, evoked by his extraordinary good fortune at various periods of his life, from less successful competitors.

At the peace of 1783, Thompson's regiment was disbanded; he returned to England on half-pay, with the rank of full colonel, and received, it is said, large compensation as a loyalist. In a short time he obtained the King's permission to travel, and crossed the Channel with some idea of serving in the Austrian army as a volunteer against the Turks.

One of his fellow-travellers was Henry Laurens, who had been president of an American Congress, and had just been released from the Tower of London. Another was Gibbon, the historian, who left a comical account of Thompson's stately departure from the British shore.1 How far the three journeyed together I do not know; but Thompson made his way direct to Strasburg, and, appearing at a military parade in his English uniform, mounted on one of the three fine horses he had brought with him from England, he attracted the notice of Maximilian, Duke of Deuxponts or Zweibriicken, then a field marshal in the service of France, and was introduced to officers who had served on the revolutionary side in America. He was next received with distinguished honours at Munich and at Vienna, where COUNT RUMFOED'S CAREER 275

1 In a letter to Lord Sheffield, quoted by Ellis, *Memoir of Sir Benjamin Thompson,* p. 153, also by Dr. Bence Jones, *The Royal Institution,* oh. i.

he remained long enough to hear that the Turkish war had been given up; consequently he went no further, but returned to Munich once more, only to move by slow stages to England.

Charles Theodore, Elector of Bavaria, was uncle to the Duke of Deuxponts, and, like his nephew, succumbed to the unaccountable fascination exercised by the young American on nearly all persons who were brought within the range of his influence. At this time Thompson was already remarkable for his practical scientific knowledge. Gibbon describes him 1 as ' Mr. Secretary, Colonel, Admiral, Philosopher Thompson '; and the Elector appears to have decided that he was the man to superintend the regeneration of his electorate. Thompson therefore visited England only to obtain the permission of his own sovereign, and George III. not only granted his request, but, in February 1774, conferred on him the honour of knighthood. He then entered the service of the Elector of Bavaria, retaining his half-pay as an English officer.

Thenceforth the career of the gifted adventurer reads more like a romance or a fairy tale than ever, as the following passages from his biography2will show:

On the arrival of Sir Benjamin, the Elector appointed him Colonel of a regiment of Cavalry, and general Aide-de-Camp, in order that he might be in immediate contact with himself. A palatial edifice was furnished for his residence in Munich, shared between himself and the Russian Ambassador, with a military staff and a proper corps of servants. Sir Benjamin especially prided himself upon the blood horses which he had brought with him from England. His fine appearance when mounted on parade is frequently noticed. His imposing figure, his manly and handsome countenance, his dignity of bearing, and his courteous manners, not only to the great, but equally to subordinates and inferiors, made him exceedingly popular. This finished courtier and favoured child of fortune – favoured both by native gifts and by opportunities – needed no transformation within or without to adapt himself to circumstances.

1In the letter to Lord Sheffield, quoted by Mr. Ellis and Dr. Bence Jones. *Ellis,*Memoir of Sir Benjamin Thompson,*p. 162.

Sir Benjamin very rapidly acquired a mastery of the German and French languages. Like a true practical philosopher, also, he gave the whole force of his inquisitive and comprehensive mind to the preliminary work of informing himself generally, and in minute particulars, about everything that concerned the dominions of the Elector. The relations of the electorate to other powers, within and outside of the Empire; its population and their employments; its resources and the means of their development; the abuses and evils which admitted of remedies, and the method of applying them – all found in him as curious and intelligent an investigator as could have been chosen among the select few most concerned to examine them.

It may be as well to mention here the titular, military, civil, and academic honours which so rapidly and lavishly were bestowed upon Sir Benjamin while residing in Bavaria. By request of the Elector, the King of Poland, in 1786, conferred on him the Order of Saint Stanislaus, the statutes of Bavaria not then allowing of his receiving any Bavarian orders. In a journey to Prussia in 1787, he was made a member of the Academy of Berlin. He was also admitted to the Academies of Science at Munich and Mannheim. In 1788, the Elector made him Major-General of Cavalry and Privy Councillor of State. He was also put at the head of the War Department, with powers and directions from the Elector to carry into effect the schemes which he had been maturing for the reform of the army and the removal of mendicity. In the interval between the death of the Emperor Joseph and the coronation of Leopold II., the Elector profited by the right going with his functions, as Vicar of the Empire, to raise Sir Benjamin in 1791 to the dignity of a Count of the Holy Roman Empire, with the Order of the White Eagle.

Sir Benjamin chose to be designated Count of Rumford, the name of his home at Concord, during the period when it belonged to Massachusetts. On this subject his biographer remarks:

That he should have selected as his title marking this distinction the former name of the New England village in which he had first enjoyed the favours of fortune, shows that he was not alienated in heart from his native land, and that he gladly associated the memory of it with his own personal advancement.

But he had never seen the wife who had given him theCOUNT RUMFORD'S CABEER 277

first step to fortune since 1775, nor their daughter; while, in Munich, he led a decidedly irregular life.

In 1793, Count Eumford's health failed in consequence of his exertions – one would fain hope that the news of his wife's death in the previous year may have had some effect also; and he was allowed to travel for a twelvemonth. He returned to Munich only partially restored, and, in 1795, obtained leave to visit England, after an absence of eleven years. Mr. Ellis writes:

The principal object of his visit was, as has been said, that he might publish his essays. But he had another leading end in view. He had many warm friends and admirers as well as scientific correspondents in England, with whom he had kept up constant intercourse, communicating his experiments, as we have seen, to the Royal Society, – his membership of which always enlisted his pride and obligation of constant service.1

At what period Benjamin Thompson made the acquaintance of Thomas Bernard I am uncertain. That they ever met in Massachusetts is improbable; and there is nothing to show that during his first sojourn in England he ever saw Sir Francis Bernard. To Governor Hutchinson he was evidently unknown, or he would have been mentioned in the ' Diary.' The date of his first interview with Thomas Bernard may with some plausibility be assigned to 1783, when Thompson was again in England, seeking compensation as a loyalist, while Bernard was engaged in a similar effort on behalf of his brother John.

Thompson was, indeed, accused by his enemies of obtaining for himself most inordinate compensation – no less than 30.000Z.; but Mr. Ellis observes that this is unlikely, since the English Government was by no means profuse in its grants, and in June, 1783, shortly before his arrival, had divided 50,000Z. amongst nearly seven hundred loyalists. Moreover, Thompson had no claim to a large sum, because he had very little of his own when he left his home at Concord, and his wife's property does not appear to have been touchedby the revolutionary government. Nevertheless, it is difficult to understand how he was enabled to travel with three horses and attendants, unless his own slender means had been largely supplemented from some quarter.

1Ellis,*Memoir of Sir Benjamin Thompson,*p. 201.

It may be assumed, however, that Thomas Bernard saw nothing unallowable in the conduct of Thompson, or Rum- ford, as he must henceforward be called – since he was on intimate terms with him in 1795. It would be pleasant to think that he and Mrs. Bernard may have influenced Eumford to send for his daughter Sarah from America, which he did in the course of 1795.1

Count Eumford met with a singular misfortune on his arrival in England. A trunk, containing all his private papers, and his notes and observations on philosophical subjects, was removed from his post-chaise in St. Paul's Churchyard, at six o'clock in the evening; he never recovered the contents, which were probably stolen by some one envious of his luck. This was a heavy blow; but in other respects his visit was prosperous. In Ireland, where he was invited to effect sundry improvements, he was received with honours. It was during this stay in the British Islands that the alterations, already mentioned in Chapter XI., were effected at the Foundling Hospital; and in all likelihood the idea of the Eoyal Institution was at the same time discussed between the Count and Mr. Bernard.

On this subject the Count's biographer2states:

While he was himself one of the most zealous and laborious Fellows of the Eoyal Society, he saw that without trespassing at all upon the range, wide as it was, that was recognized by his associates, there was room for an Institution whose aims should be more practical and popular, coming into direct contact with the agricultural, the mechanical, and the domestic life of the people.

And this theme was expanded by him in a pamphlet,3THE ROYAL INSTITUTION 279

1Ellis,*Memoir of Sir Benjamin Thompson,*p. 204. She left America in January, 1796.

' *Ibid.,*oh. vii., p. 879.

9' Proposals for forming by Subscription, in the Metropolis of the British Empire, a Public Institution for diffusing the Knowledge and facilitating the General Introduction of useful Mechanical Inventions and Improvements, andfor teaching by courses of Philosophical Lectures and Experiments the Application of Science to the Common Purposes of Life.'

the introduction to which contains the following passage:'

1In the beginning of the year 1796, I gave a faint sketch of this plan in my second Essay; but being under the necessity of returning soon to Germany, I had not leisure to pursue it farther at that time; and I was obliged to content myself with having merely thrown out a loose idea, as it were by accident, which I thought might possibly attract attention. After my return to Munich, I opened myself more fully on the subject in my correspondence with my friends in this country [England], and particularly in my letters to Thomas Bernard, Esq., who, as is well known, is one of the founders and most active members of the Society for Bettering the Condition and Increasing the Comforts of the Poor.'

The Count subjoins, in a note, three letters of his to Mr. Bernard, dated at Munich, 28th April 1797, 13th May 1798, and 8th June 1798. The first of these letters returns the writer's grateful acknowledgments for the honour done him by his election as a member of the Society for Bettering the Condition of the Poor. It closes with a characteristic suggestion that visible examples, ' by models,' will advance its objects better than will anything that can be said or written. The third letter emphasises a well-pointed hint that, indolent, selfish, and luxurious persons ' must either be allured or shamed into action,' and that it is very desirable ' to make benevolence fashionable.' The writer also expresses his interest in his correspondent's ' plan with regard to Bridewell. A well arranged House of Industry is much wanted in London.' He closes by asking Mr. Bernard ' to read once more the Proposals published in my second Essay. I really think that a public establishment like that described might easily be formed in London, and that it would produce infinite good. I will come to London to assist you in its execution whenever you will in good earnest undertake it.'

Returning to England in September 1798, the Count says he found Mr. Bernard very solicitous for an attempt for the immediate execution of the plan. ' After several consultations that were held in Mr. Bernard's apartments in the Foundling Hospital, and at the house of the Lord Bishop of Durham, at which several gentlemen assisted who are well known as zealous promoters of useful improvements, it was agreed that Mr. Bernardshould report to the Committee of the Society for Bettering the Condition of the Poor the general result of these consultations, and the unanimous desire of the gentlemen who assisted at them that means might be devised for making an attempt to carry the scheme proposed into execution.

1Ellis,*Memoir of Sir Benjamin Thompson,*p. 388.

For convenience sake the organisation of the Society had been utilised, and a committee of eight members formed to consider the new plan; but it was agreed that so interesting and important a scheme ought not to be made '" an appendix to any other existing establishment," and, therefore, that it ought to stand alone on its own proper basis.'*l*

The Committee consisted of ' the Earl of Winchelsea, Mr. Wilberforce, the Rev. Dr. Glasse, Mr. Sullivan, Mr. Richard Sulivan, Mr. Colquhoun, Mr. Parry, and Mr. Bernard.' It met on January 31, 1799, and thoroughly discussed the elaborate statement prepared by the Count. On the following day it held another meeting – the Bishop of Durham being in the chair – reported what had taken place at the conference, and pronounced a full approval of the scheme. A circular soliciting subscriptions was drawn up, and the recipients were requested to address their replies – ' To Thomas Bernard, Esq., at the Foundling.'*s*

It had been originally proposed ' that subscribers of fifty guineas each should be the perpetual proprietors of the Institution, and be entitled to perpetual transferable tickets for lectures and for admission to the apartments of the Institution.'

As soon as thirty such subscribers were obtained, the question of organisation was to be settled with them. Before, however, any meeting of this description could be called, fifty-eight promises of fifty guinea subscriptions were received from most desirable persons, and it was then resolved to apply at once for a charter. Scrope Bernard, it may be mentioned, was one of these original subscribers.

The objects of the Institution were stated as ' The speedyA EOYAL CHAETEE 281

1Ellis,*Memoir of Sir Benjamin Thompson,*p. 385. See also Dr. Bence Jones,*The Royal Institution, its Founder and its First Professor,*eh. iii.*Life of Sir Thomas Bernard.*

and general diffusion of the knowledge of all new and useful improvements, in whatever quarter of the world they may originate; and teaching the application of scientific discoveries to the improvement of arts and manufactures in this country, and to the increase of domestic comfort and convenience.' It was intended to fill spacious show-rooms with models of mechanical inventions and to fit up a lecture-room with a laboratory and all the requisites for scientific experiments. On March 7, the proprietors – or subscribers of fifty guineas – met in the house of Sir Joseph Banks, President of the Royal Society, who took the chair, and it was decided to apply to the King for a charter, which Count Rumford and Mr. Bernard were requested to draw up.

Mr. Baker speaks of his uncle Thomas Bernard as the sole framer of the charter, and such he must have been in its legal aspect. It passed the royal seals on January 30, 1800. The constitution of the Society is described by Mr. Ellis as follows:

The King appears as Patron; the officers of the Institution were appointed by him at its formation, – the Earl of Winchelsea and Nottingham being President, the Earls of Morton and Egremont and Sir Joseph Banks Vice-Presidents; the Earls of Bessborough, Egremont, and Morton, being respectively the first- named on each of the three classes of Managers, – on the first of which, to serve for three years, is Count Eumford. The Duke of Bridgewater, Viscount Palmerston, and Earl Spencer, lead each of the three classes of Visitors. The whole list proves with what a power of patronage, as well as with what popularity and enthusiasm, the enterprise was initiated. Dr. Thomas Garnett was made Professor of Natural Philosophy and Chemistry, and Thomas Bernard, Esq., Treasurer. A Home and Foreign Secretary, Legal Council, a Solicitor, and a Clerk, complete the list.

The Institution was located in Albemarle Street,1Piccadilly, and some portion of its early history will be told in another chapter.

' ' The Managers have since purchased a large and roomy house, the late Mr. Mellish's, in Albemarle Street.'*Reports of the Society B. C. P.,*by Thomas Bernard, Esq., vol. ii., No. LV., note.

In the meantime, something must be said of another scheme, in which Count Rumford and Thomas Bernard were fellow-workers. It has been stated that the Count expressed in a letter his interest in Mr. Bernard's plan with regard to Bridewell; ' that is, no doubt, to a mode of compelling able-bodied beggars to work.'/It was a subject on which he could bring his own experience to bear; since he had himself conferred a signal benefit on Bavaria by his repression of mendicity, which – owing to the carelessness of former Sovereigns, and the disorganised state of Bavaria during the crisis of the French Revolution – had assumed formidable proportions, and was associated with robbery and violence, to the grave detriment of all peaceable and industrious subjects. Under Count Rumford's management the hordes which infested Bavaria were surrounded and seized by the military in Munich – acting in concert with the civil authorities – and compelled to labour in an establishment called the Military Workhouse, fitted up in a disused manufactory; they were at the same time provided with all reasonable comforts; and every precaution was taken to discriminate between the depraved and the victims of circumstance.

This plan approximated to the mode of procedure adopted in Paris by St. Vincent de Paul, during the previous century. Whether Count Rumford had ever heard of that reform, I cannot say, but the resemblance is striking.2St. Vincent, indeed, wished to act by persuasion, not compulsion, in opposition to the opinion of the ladies who worked with him; but the King decided that under such a system the evil would never disappear, and declared begging prohibited from the day when the General Hospital should be opened. This royal proclamation at once thinned the ranks of the mendicants; and the remaining beggars were in most casesTHE TREATMENT OF MENDICANTS 283

1' Bridewell, in our*customs*denotes a workhouse, partly for the correction of vagrants and disorderly persons, and partly for the employment of the parish poor.'. 'Bridewell near Fleet Street, is a foundation of a mizt and singular nature, partaking of the hospital, the prison, and the workhouse.' *Rees's Cyclopaedia,* 1819.

'Bedford,*Life of St. Vincent de Paul,*ch. xxiii.

willing to avail themselves of the refuge provided for them, in which they were to be trained to industry.

The beggars of London may not have been altogether as mischievous and degraded as those which infested continental towns demoralised by the scourge of war; but their existence was a disgrace to the community, and, except in cases of unavoidable misfortune, to themselves. A paper on this evil was written by Mr. Bernard for the Society's ' Reports,'1 recapitulating some of the evidence collected by Matthew Martin, Esq., Secretary to the Society, and one of a committee appointed to inquire into this matter, with remarks on its tendency.

In order to inform himself on this subject (writes Mr. Bernard), Mr. Martin has from the beginning of the year distributed tickets in London to appoint such of the beggars there as seemed to merit and wish inquiry into their circumstances to come to him for that purpose. Of this as many as 120 have attended in consequence – 21 men and 99 women.

Of the men, the greater part were maimed, or disabled by age or sickness; and only two of them belonged to any place of legal settlement in London.

Of the women there were 48 widows; seven of them the widows of soldiers; only one of them of a seaman. About a third of these consisted of aged women; some were crippled and some distressed for want of work; many of them embarrassed by ignorance of the mode of obtaining parochial assistance, or by the fear of applying for it.

Of the wives in most cases, the difficulty was the want of work, or the incapacity of doing it on account of a child in arms. There were cases of very great distress. Above half of them had two or more children, who were some of them infants, and the greater part of the residue of an helpless age, too young for work.

With regard to the settlements of the women, 24 referred him to parishes in London and Westminster; 33 to parishes in different parts of England; 22 belonged to Scotland and Ireland, and the remaining 20 said they could not give, or at least declined giving him any account of their place of settlement.

By application, in most cases, to their parishes, and in some to their friends, he was enabled to obtain effectual relief for several of them; for others he is now using his endeavours. To all of them, the gift of a little food, and the hearing of their melancholy story, afforded some comfort.

1Extract from ' An Account of an attempt to ascertain the circumstances of the beggars of London, with observations on the best mode of relieving them,' by Thomas Bernard, Esq.*Reports of the Society B. C. P.,*vol. i., No. XXII.

Mr. Bernard added some observations to Mr. Martin's ' Report,' from which it appears that some beggars had become such through the carelessness or neglect of London parish officers, who had not afforded them the assistance to which they were entitled; others had been driven from country parishes, likewise by the parochial authorities, who wished to be quit of their poor, and plied them alternately with menaces and promises till the end was accomplished.

As regarded the remainder, Mr. Baker says,1epitomising his uncle's observations:

Mr. Bernard proposed that a police office should be established solely for the case of the casual mendicant poor in the metropolis, which should enforce the existing laws, and compel parishes to watch over and provide for their own poor; and that inspectors should attend the streets, and bring all common beggars before the Board, whose duty should be to compel labour, or require subsistence, according to the circumstances of the parochial case.

And, in January 1799, shortly after the publication of the Report, the committee waited on the Duke of Portland, Secretary of State, and obtained from him a promise of government assistance. The evil had been long and painfully obvious to the British public, and the prospect of relief was hailed with satisfaction. But the Government took a view of the measures to be adopted which proved fatal to reform.

When, however (continues Mr. Baker), it was agreed to take only*voluntary*examinations of mendicants, without any compulsory process, and without enforcing a penalty on false oaths and declarations, Mr. Bernard despaired of the object being attained, and withdrew from any concern in the measure.

Like others of his benevolent efforts,2indeed, which appeared at the time to fail, the seed then sown bore fruitSTEEET BEGGARS 285

1*Life of Sir Thomas Bernard.*

5Haydn,*Dictionary of Daks*(Tenth Edition), ' Mendicity Society.'

in after years. It would seem, indeed, that the agitation for reform in this matter was continued, and Mr. Martin was the recognised leader of this movement. Some startling disclosures were made before the Committee of the House of Commons1appointed for the purpose of receiving and weighing the evidence – most of which had, however, been known or surmised by the band of philanthropists to which Mr. Martin belonged.

The practice of ' farming ' the poor – that is, the paupers – to persons who made a profit out of their earnings, and in whose power they were virtually placed, was almost universal in London. There was, of course, some variety in these establishments. Overcrowding, underfeeding, insanitary conditions generally, were evils often alleviated by lax discipline, and the inmates, if so inclined, figured as street beggars. As to these street beggars, they included every description of impostor – the blind and the lame, or maimed, the man with fits, women with twins, children brought up to lying and forced to get their living by the same vile means as their parents or employers.

The large earnings and sumptuous living of the cleverest of these people is frequently adverted to, the woeful tales of distress, related both*viva voce*and also in affecting letters; the success of ' the Laudable Institution' for supplying the poor with good meat and vegetables at a low price, whose inventor is supposed to have pocketed at least*500l.*a year – are all related in the evidence, and were probably revelations to a large portion of the public.

But there was much difficulty in getting the authorities to stir in this matter. The majority of magistrates had been accustomed to take it easily, and the Legislature seemed inclined to do the same. It was not until 1819, the year after Thomas Bernard's death, that an Act was passed, commonly known as ' Martin's Act,' which dealt a severe blow at ' Mendicity.' The evil is not, indeed, annihilated, notwithstanding the continuous efforts made to deal with it; but, considering the vast increase in the population, we may perhaps be thankful that it is no worse.

1*The Quarterly Review*(October 1815), Art. VI. ' Minutes of the Evidence taken before the Committee appointed by the House of Commons to inquire into the State of Mendicity and Vagrancy in the Metropolis and its neighbourhood.' (Ordered to be printed July 11, 1815.)*The Edinburgh Review*also had an article on this subject, to much the same effect, but more discursive and general than the one in the*Quarterly.*

FANNY KING 287

CHAPTER XV

PAROCHIAL WORK AND HOLIDAY EXCURSIONS

Fanny King's Interest in the Children of her Parish – The Establishment of Sunday Schools by Robert Raikes – Membership of the S. P. C. K. – Mrs. Trimmer's Work – Mrs. King's Parochial Lending Libraries – Her Love of Nursing – Mr. King a Candidate for the Wardenship of New College – Mrs. King's Letters – A Visit to Alveston – Mrs. King's Acquaintance with Hannah More – Hannah More and the People of Cheddar – Report of Thomas and Margaret Bernard on the Mendip Schools – Attack of Mr. Bere upon Hannah and Martha More – A Charitable Effort in Bath – Thomas Bernard sells his House at Iver.

Thelife of Fanny King, as wife of a country clergyman, did not afford the same opportunities for philanthropy on a large scale as the position of her brother Thomas in London, enjoying the acquaintance, and in some cases the intimacy, of many distinguished persons; but in her narrower sphere she was earnest and diligent in the use of the talents committed to her charge. The writer of a short ' Memoir'1of Mrs. King states, with reference to her work at Steeple Morden and Worthen, that:

In addition to unremitting attention to her children, she was exemplarily useful in those parishes, by administering to the wants of the poor with activity and energy, and particularly by originating the establishment of schools for their children.

The elementary week-day schools of the age, few and far between in country districts, when not the gift of some munificent squire or lady, were generally held in some cottage, and were in most cases the private enterprise of the good woman at their head, often indeed assisted andencouraged by ladies. There girls learned reading and sewing, with the addition of lace-making and other local industries in certain neighbourhoods; and these local industries occupied a large portion of the school hours. Little boys often attended these schools till they went to work. In 1784,1Eobert Eaikes opened a Sunday-school at Gloucester, and thus inaugurated a great popular movement, which became, like many more innovations, or revivals, the subject of much controversy. Something of the kind had been known in France,2and apparently in other European countries, for about two centuries, and even in England he evidently had predecessors; but it was reserved to him to attract the public attention by his labours, and to make England a country where systematic religious instruction was recognised. The new system was a subject of much eulogy on the part of his supporters, and of depreciation by his opponents. For this controversy Eaikes, who appears to have been a single-minded man, was in no way responsible – he was not a hunter after fame.

1' Memoir of the Author,' prefixed to*Female Scripture Characters;*(probably by the Rev. John Collinson).

In connection with the subject of Sunday-schools, there is evidence in the family papers how solemn an affair it then was to be received into membership by the highly orthodox and loyal S. P. C. K.

Mr. King writes,3to Scrope Bernard, from Worthen, apparently in 1786:

I will beg the favour of you to give the enclosed to Smith, who I expect will be in town very soon, and desire him to deliver it to the Society of which I am desirous to become a member, as I have established Sunday Schools in this parish and wish to distribute among the children the useful books that are published by the above Society.

1This is the date in*A Summary of the History of the English Church,*by the Rev. Johnson Gant; and suggested in Rees's*Cycloptedia.*Mr. Eaikes had previously tried the plan of Sunday teaching in his own parish of Painswick. The Sunday-school Society was founded in 1785.

'Sunday Classes for religious instruction appear to have been one of the features of the Religious Revival of the seventeenth century in France; as also of the Ursuline Congregation, founded by St. Angela Merici, in Northern Italy, during the sixteenth century.

' MS. Letter at Nether Winohendon.

MRS. KING'S INTEREST IN SCHOOLS 289

The certificate enclosed, which is a printed form – only the names and descriptions of the three clergymen being filled up by hand – runs as follows:

We, the underwritten do recommend the Rev1*. Richard King

M. A. Rector of Worthen in the county of Salop, to be a Member

of the Society for Promoting Christian Knowledge – and do verily believe that he is well affected to his Majesty King George and his Government, and to the Church of England as by law established, of sober and religious Life and Conversation, and of an humble, peaceable, and charitable Disposition.

Ed. Blakeway,*Minister of St. Mary's Salop.*

ThomasStbdman,*Minister of St. Chad's Salop.*

The fact of Mrs. King's interest in schools, continued from the time when she represented the heroine of ' The Rector's Memorandum Book,'*l*as educating the children of her village, is corroborated by passages in her latest work, ' Female Scripture Characters,' written about thirty years later, in which she displays considerable acquaintance with the efforts of Mrs. Trimmer in that direction, and with the working of the Barrington Training School, as recorded by her brother Thomas. In this book3she exhorts women to follow the example of their Saviour as ' an Instructor of the ignorant and a Teacher of babes,' continuing:

Let us consider ourselves, as we really are, His chosen disciples; and imagine that we hear (as we do in the Gospel) the question put to St. Peter, ' Lovest thou Me?' Should we not, with pious ardour and holy affection, reply with him, ' Yea, Lord; Thou knowest that I love Thee.' Let us then observe the proof required of that love ' Feed My lambs.' – If our hearts answer sincerely to this tender and impressive question, we shall feel ourselves anxious to give the proof by collecting the little lambs of His flock, in order to lead them to the fold of Christ and to train them in His holy laws.

Of Mrs. Trimmer the author states that, while bringing up her twelve children admirably, and discharging all the

1See vol. ii., oh. xxx., p. 323, of this Family History.

' *Female Scripture Characters,*' Dorcas.'

VOL. III. 0

domestic occupations rendered necessary by a limited income,

she managed to create so much time to devote to the benefit of others, that the town and neighbourhood of Brentford, previously a sink of vice and corruption, became, under her instruction, christianized, orderly, moral, and taught in a way ' able to make them wise unto salvation.' *1*

Another writer, Mrs. Papendiek,2who was personally acquainted with Mrs. Trimmer, says:

Horning visits in this exemplary family could not be admitted, for Mrs. Trimmer was occupied in writing her excellent works on education, while the eldest daughter acting as bookkeeper was in the accounting room, and the second daughter, Sarah, was instructing her younger brothers and sisters in the schoolroom.

Mrs. Trimmer, being the daughter of Mr. Kirby, Clerk of the Works at Kew, as well as President of the ' Society of Artists' of Great Britain – from which sprang the Royal Academy – enjoyed the advantage of interesting royalty itself in her schemes:

Mrs. Trimmer's movement in establishing Sunday Schools in many parts of England came to pass during this year (1786 – says Mrs. Papendiek), and her Majesty hearing of it, and being much struck with the excellence and advisability of such a plan, desired that the same might be instituted at Windsor. Her Majesty had several interviews with Mrs. Trimmer, and being much impressed with that lady's clear understanding and sound judgement, requested her to write a work on education, which she did, and it has ever since been considered an authority on the question.

I have not been able to ascertain whether Mrs. King was known to this invaluable woman, but, in ' Female Scripture Characters,' she mentioned Mrs. Trimmer and Miss Hannah More as two women especially worthy of admiration; and Hannah More she certainly knew. The ' Memoir,' entitled ' Some Account of the Life and Writings of Mrs. Trimmer,'PAEOCHIAL LENDING LIBKAEIES 291

1*Some Account of the Life and Writings of Mrs. Trimmer, with Original Letters, Meditations and Prayers.*

*Papendifik (Mrs.),*Court and Private Life in time of Queen Charlotte.*

is too sketchy and fragmentary to throw light upon the subject; but it establishes the fact that the Brentford schools were opened in June 1786. Mr. King's letter to Scrope Bernard about the S. P. C. K. was apparently written a few weeks later; and a little later still – August 27 – Mrs. Trimmer mentions in her Journal a Mrs. K., but not in connection with schools:

I had yesterday great pleasure in receiving from Mrs. Denward a considerable donation for the relief of the sick and aged. After that I attended Mrs. K. to Mary Pearce's and other poor houses. The pleasure I received from these circumstances fatigued my spirits, but I would not but have felt the sensations which so fatigued me for any consideration.

It is obviously not unlikely that Fanny King had taken an opportunity of visiting Brentford to examine the working of the schools, and other charities.

Of Mrs. King's parochial lending libraries a more particular account can be given, because her sister-in-law, Mrs. Bernard, contributed a paper *l* on the subject to the ' Reports' of the Society for Bettering the Condition of the Poor, commencing:

At Steeple Morden, in the county of Cambridge, the poor have been furnished with a circulating library of short tracts of a religious and moral nature. The idea had been originally suggested by a similar plan, useful in its way, but not so peculiarly required, which has been adopted for the benefit of the children at the Foundling. The collection at Steeple Morden consists of the Cheap Eepository Tracts, and some few others of a similar kind, and has already, even at the beginning, proved of considerable benefit to the parish. On Sunday afternoon when the business of the Sunday-school is over, Mrs. King, the lady who has founded the library, reads one of the tracts to the children, and to such of the parents as choose to attend. It is then made the subject of conversation, and a few copies of the tract are lent to the different children, who read it over again in the evening with their parents and neighbours, and by these means spend their Sunday evening well and with useful amusement. Copies of thosame tract are afterwards lent out for the week; aqd generally go round the parish. On the Sunday following they are brought back, when they receive others, which have been first read over to them in the same manner. Fifty-two tracts furnish the year's reading, and ten or twelve copies of each are sufficient for a moderate sized parish. It is very gratifying to contemplate the pleasure, the amusement, and other more material effects which are produced in this parish by a measure perfectly simple and easy in itself, and executed at a trifling expense. It answers in one respect, the end of the Sunday Friendly Societies at Winston and Auckland, and with more general extension to the different ages in the parish.

lExtract of ' An Account of a Parish Library for the Poor,' by Mrs. Bernard.*Report** of the Society for Bettering the Condition of the Poor,*vol. iii., No. LXXXII.

Mrs. Bernard states that this plan has been tried by Mrs. King in two other parishes, and that it has everywhere proved efficacious in keeping the poor from the ale-house. It may be assumed that Worthen was one of these two parishes; the second can only be the subject of conjecture. At one time Mr. King was drawn by circumstances to spend a considerable portion of the year at his brother's house at Alveston, near Bristol; and it is quite likely that having provided his own parishes with curaJtes for a settled period, he may have undertaken the temporary charge of Alveston parish, and thus afforded his wife an opportunity of introducing her favourite scheme. The ' Cheap Eepository Tracts' which she distributed were the composition of Hannah More, and consisted, to a great extent, of narratives and ballads which, in that age, might be considered lively as well as pious.

The failing health from which both her parents had suffered for several years probably impressed the subject of nursing on the mind of Fanny King, and she never forgot her early love for this occupation – first studied, perhaps, at Winchendon under Mrs. Beresford – which the case of her own children must have presented to her in a new aspect. Her remarks on the subject, in' Female Scripture Characters,' show that she had some practical knowledge of its details, and of the disadvantages under which the poor laboured in time of sickness. She writes:/

l*Female Scripture Characters,*'Dorcas.'

NURSING THE SICK 293

Most of us have experienced, in some degree, that greatest of human calamities, loss of health, and those who have, have found it the loss of everything, for with health all calamities may be surmounted, without it no blessing can be enjoyed. If to those who are surrounded by ' all the appliances and means to boot' which affluence furnishes to lessen this evil, it is so heavy a calamity, what must it be to the poor cottager on his pallet of straw, without the common comforts of life? Riches, indeed cannot be enjoyed under the pressure of affliction, but poverty makes a bitter addition to its sufferings. Oh 1 let the happy female, distinguished by the invaluable blessing of health, evince her gratitude to the Great Giver of all good by dispensing aid and comfort to all sufferers under this inevitable evil; let her study nursing the sick as a science, assured that the skill of the nurse is more beneficial than that of the physician. The tenderness, the sympathy, the quietness of her attention, her knowledge in preparing the various little articles of nourishment, and her judgement in producing them at proper times, in small quantities, and in a palatable state, have been found inestimable comforts to those who have languished under the affliction of sickness. She should learn to perform common operations, to administer every kind of remedy, and raise herself above any delicacy of feeling, or nervous weakness, that can impede her usefulness.

These remarks are applicable to the general nursing of the sick in all ranks; but to the sick poor her duties will be still more extensive. Besides administering to their bodily and temporal ease, she should pour into their hearts the comfort of God's Holy Word; she should hold out to them the blessings and comforts that await the patient sufferer, and read and explain to them the many passages in the Scriptures, particularly the Psalms, which mark the value of the poor in the sight of Heaven. She should tell them that our Blessed Lord dignified a state of poverty by His voluntary choice; that the poor were the particular objects of His favour and attention; and that all His doctrines and precepts tended to their comfort and instruction.

Other passages follow in amplification of the same theme, but those already quoted suffice to exemplify Mrs. King's treatment of this topic. One observation here suggests itself: namely, that her plans involved the further task of training some persons of a class or classes above the very poor to aid in their development, whether in the schoolor the sick-room. To a certain extent this would have been the case even had she lived always in one place; but when moving from one parish to another, or quitting them both for a holiday, sometimes of long duration, Mrs. King must have left her work of every sort in abeyance, either in Worthen or Steeple Morden, or both, unless she had assistants to carry on the work on the lines laid down by her. And the following paragraph alludes, it would seem, to some organisation of this kind:

In towns and populous villages much benefit has arisen to the poor from ladies forming themselves into societies, either for the general good of the poor, or for some particular object. Besides the union of the many mites they may collect amongst themselves, here is a union of hearts, heads, talents, time, and exertion; and many agents are enlisted in the cause, who would otherwise for want of activity, thought, or example, have been simply idle and useless.

In Worthen there were probably some women of education and more or less leisure, while even in Steeple Morden there may have been farmers' daughters able and willing to assist Mrs. King and her deputy – who would, of course, be the curate's wife, when he had one – in their labours for the good of the parish.

In 1794 the quiet routine of country life must have been ruffled, though perhaps not seriously, by passing excitement. Mr. King was induced by friends to become a candidate for the headship of his College, somewhat against his better judgment, since he was aware that his long absence from Oxford, and the distance of his actual residence, placed him at a disadvantage, as compared with his rivals, who were certain of strong support on the spot. Mr. Gauntlett was the successful competitor. As Warden of New College Mr. King would undoubtedly have been in a more congenial sphere than as Rector of a country parish, but he philosophically remarks/on his defeat:

I have now the pleasure to reflect that though I have not1MS. Letter at Nether Winchendon.

DEATH OF EMILY BAKEE 295

succeeded in the late object of my wishes, I am not lessened in the esteem of the Society for whom I have ever entertained the highest regard, and – what is better – I am surrounded and in possession of every comfort that any reasonable man can wish for or enjoy.

A greater affliction bad been tbe deatb of Amelia, or Emily, Baker, whicb took place in 1791,1and which evoked her sister's active sympathy for the last born sickly child – William – who was for some time under Fanny King's fostering care;* but she couldnot save his life; he died in 1793.

From a letter, dated ' Alveston, Oct. 3rd,' 3 and which, from its allusion to ' Admiral Nelson's glorious victory,' was probably written in 1798, the year in which the battle of the Nile was fought, it appears that Mr. and Mrs. King were established there for the time; in all likelihood Mr. King had charge of the parish; but he must have lived in a large house – probably his brother's – since his wife then had under her care several young girls besides her own three daughters.4Some of these were daughters of Lady Ingilby, afterwards Lady Ingilby Amcoats, and even her son was for a time in charge of the Kings. Whether the parents were abroad, or the neighbourhood of Bristol offered special advantages for education, I cannot tell.

Another young lady frequently mentioned in the lively letters of the Misses King, dated from Alveston, was Miss Richardson,6afterwards the first wife of Sir Lancelot Shadwell, Vice-Chancellor of England.

In the letter already mentioned Fanny King tells her brother Scrope that:

The book is safely arrived for which I am much obliged to you and a most valuable book it is; I shall study nothing else formonths to come, and I hope to make consider-able use of it in this neighbourhood. I have already done something and shall be very busy this winter.

1By some, the date of the death of Amelia is given as 1795; but I believe that the date I have given is correct.

2MS. Letter at Nether Winchendon. '*Ibid.*

4I was told by a relative that Mrs. King was their guardian; but both the parents were certainly living at this time.

* This information is from MSS. lent by the Collinson family, and from facts stated by its members in conversation.

The paragraph evidently refers to some study she had taken up, and but for the allusion to the winter it might be supposed that the subject was botany, which was her favourite recreation at this period; but as winter was not a good time for that pursuit, it may have been some branch of parochial work – probably schools. Mrs. King continues:

I thank you for your enquiries; my husband and my children are always well, at all times and in every place, and I think I have much less of the rheumatism here than I had at Worthin; it is a very delightful situation, and an excellent house, and I have every comfort about me, more frequent intercourse with our friends and many advantages in the education of my large family of girls, now increased to eight. The old lady, Mr. King's mother, has been with us some weeks, in her 89th year and in perfect health.

I am rejoiced poor old Winchendon is restored to its honours and glories; I still dearly love the place and lamented its desertion.

Mr. King's mother, Priscilla Moon by birth, was a Quakeress of Bristol, related to several leading Quaker families.

The Alveston visit was evidently renewed, perhaps every autumn and winter, for some years; and there seems to have been generally a merry party of young girls in the house.1One of their amusements was writing a magazine of their own composition; it was, however, a laborious business, and not apparently carried on very long.

It is, of course, probable that the Kings had been in the habit of paying visits to Bristol, and perhaps to Alveston, ever since their marriage, though not of such long duration, since Mr. King's nearest relations were domiciled there. Indeed, Mr. King, in an earlier letter to Scrope Bernard,2alludes to a visit which his wife had paid without him to Bristol and Gloucestershire. Her acquaintance with HannahHANNAH MORE 297

1MS. Notes in a book lent by Mrs. Bernard Collinson. * MS. Letter at Nether Winchendon.

More is most likely to have dated from the period of the first long sojourn at Alveston, although it is just possible that they may have met previously in London, or at Monge- well, in Oxfordshire, the private residence of Bishop Barring- ton, where Hannah More was a welcome guest. But even if such was the case, the acquaintance was renewed in the West of England.

The father of Hannah More1was said to come of an impoverished gentleman's family; he had been Master of a Free School, at Fish Ponds, near Bristol; and Hannah was the fourth of five sisters, every one of whom must have been a woman of energy and talent. For many years the three elder sisters kept a ladies' school, in Bristol, which they had started when the eldest was only in her twentieth year, and effectually raised the standard of female education in their neighbourhood. Hannah, who was handsome and brilliant, was early wooed by a man much older than herself, and sold her share in the school. When the engagement was finally broken off, through irresolution on his part, and the determination of her sisters that she should not be trifled with, he insisted on settling an annuity on her. Thus placed in easy circumstances she was soon attracted to London, where she entered much into society, without, however, losing the pious feelings common to the whole family. Ere long she attained celebrity by her writings. Martha, or Patty, who, being fourteen years her junior, was like a daughter to all the elder sisters, frequently accompanied her on her visits to the metropolis, and learned to look up to her with devoted admiration.

As time went on, increased seriousness of thought led Hannah gradually to retire from London gaieties to her old home. The elder sisters had saved enough money to retire, and the five ladies lived together in great harmony, spending the winters in Bath, and the summers chiefly at Hannah's pretty cottage on Cowslip Green in the Vale of Mendip. In 1789, William Wilberforce, who was staying with MissMore in this retreat, drove to Cheddar Cliffs; he was so shocked by the abject misery and lawless savagery of the people, that he exclaimed: ' Miss Hannah More, something must be done for Cheddar.' And presently added: ' If you will be at the trouble, I will be at the expense.' This promise he kept by forwarding a large annual contribution for the purpose. Mr. Henry Thornton also came forward to help, and other friends and well-wishers in their degree. Hannah More wrote to Wilberforce:

1 Thompson,*Life of Mrs. Hannah More;*Roberts (William),*Memoirs of the Life and Correspondence of Mrs. Hannah More.*

I was told we should meet with great opposition if I did not try to propitiate the chief despot of the village, who is very rich, and very brutal; so I ventured into the den of this monster in a country as savage as himself, near Bridgewater. He begged I would not think of bringing any religion into the country; it was the worst thing in the world for the poor, for it made them lazy and useless. In vain did I represent to him that they would be more industrious as they were better principled; and that, for my own part, I had no selfish views in what I was doing. He gave me to understand that he knew the world too well to believe either the one or the other.1

Hannah More was staying at the George Hotel, Cheddar, with her sister Martha, when she wrote this letter; they remained there to pay eleven other visits to fanners. She continues:

Fatty, who is with me, says she has good hope that the hearts of some of these rich poor wretches may be touched; they are as ignorant as the beasts that perish, intoxicated every day before dinner, and plunged in such vices as make me begin to think London a virtuous place.

. I asked the farmers if they had no resident curate. They told me they had a right to insist on one, which right they confessed they had never ventured to exercise, for fear*their tithes shmild be raised.*The glebe house is good for my purpose [that is for a school]. The incumbent is a Mr. R who has something to do, but I cannot find out what, in the University ofDEPRAVED PARI8HES 299

1*Mendip Annals,*or*Narrative of the Charitable Labours of Hannah and Martha More in their Neighbourhood,*being the ' Journal of Martha More,' edited, with additional matter, by Arthur Roberts, M. A., Hector of Woodrising, Norfolk,&o. Memoirs, <tc., of Mrs. Hannah More,*by William Boberts, Esq., vol. ii', chap. v.

Oxford, where he resides. The curate lives at Wells, twelve miles distant. They have only service once a week, and there is scarcely an instance of a poor person being visited or prayed with.1

Mrs. M. reports of the incumbent of a neighbouring parish, that he was intoxicated about six times a week, and was very frequently prevented from preaching by black eyes, caused by fighting. She tells her correspondent in another letter: ' We saw but one Bible in all the parish, and that was used to prop a flowerpot.'

The following year some progress was made:2

We were not long in discovering a sufficient number of wretched ignorant parishes [writes Martha More]. Among the most depraved and wretched were Shipham and Rowberrow, two mining villages, at the top of Mendip; the people savage and depraved, almost even beyond Cheddar, brutal in their natures and ferocious in their manners. They began by suspecting we should make our fortunes by selling their children as slaves. No constable would venture to arrest a Shipham man, lest he should be concealed in one of their pits, and never heard of more; no uncommon case.

In Nailsea, after establishing a school chiefly attended by' inferior farmers" and colliers' children, the sisters visited3' the glass-house people, and entered nineteen houses in a row (little hovels), containing in all near two hundred people,' and Martha describes their condition:

The wages high, the eating and drinking luxurious – the body scarcely covered, but fed with dainties of a shameful description. The high buildings of the glass-houses ranged before the doors of these cottages – the great furnaces roaring – the swearing, eating, and drinking of these half-dressed, black-looking beings, gave it a most infernal and horrible appearance. We had a gentleman with us, who being rather personally fearful, left us to pursue our own devices, which we did by entering and haranguing every separate family. We were in our usual luck respecting personal civility, which we received even from the worst of these creatures, some welcoming us to ' Botany Bay,'4others to ' Little Hell' as they themselves shockingly called it.

1*Mendip Annals,* 'A Journal of the Mendip Schools from the year 1789 to the close of 1791.'2*Ibid.*

* *Mendip Annals,*'Continuation of the School Journal, beginning the year 1792.'

' This was the name of the great settlement for convicts in Australia; thefact is here stated as it is so long since the arrangement was altered that it may be unknown to some English persons born after that time.

No wonder that Hannah expressed her astonishment1 that England should be sending missionaries to the colonies, while its own villages were perishing for lack of instruction. Neither Hannah nor Martha More was a strong woman; both suffered from distressing pains in the head and face, and their previous life had not been good training for evangelising a scattered population of white pagans, in a country almost destitute of roads; yet they kept up the work for many years, only retiring to Bath, of necessity, for the worst of the winter.

Ten years after the beginning of the work, Thomas and Margaret Bernard made some stay in Bath, towards the close of 1799. There it may be assumed that they visited the Misses More, the five sisters being all probably together in the house in Pulteney Street, and obtained from them the materials for the first part of a Report which shows the development of the good work begun in 1789. The account, dated December, 1799, was communicated to the Society for Bettering the Condition of the Poor; it commences:

The Mendip Schools2are situate in the part of Somersetshire between Wells, Bristol, and the channel which divides Wales from England. They extend over twelve parishes, which are dispersed throughout a district of country about twenty-five miles in diameter. They are intended not merely for the education of youth, but for the instruction and reformation of mature life, and for the improvement and consolation of the aged – and, according to the circumstances of each parish, are opened daily, or twice or thrice a week, or on Sundays only. The early part of the Sabbath is devoted to the instruction of the young, who afterwards proceed to church in a body, to attend divine service. Towards the close of the day the room is frequented by others; chiefly by the aged, who come to take the benefit of the evening readings and discourse; and attend with great pleasure and eagerness to derive from religious information and society that solid relief, whichTHE 'MENDIP ANNALS' 301

1To her friend Mrs. Kennicott,*Memoirs of the Life and Correspondence of Mrs. Hannah More,*by William Roberts, Esq., vol. ii., Part III.

2Extracts from ' An Account of the Mendip Schools,' by Thomas Bernard, Esq.*Reports of the Society B. C. P.,*vol. ii., No. LXIV.

alone can give comfort to declining life, and smooth the path to the grave. Their stay in the school is for half an hour, an hour, or more, as their convenience or inclination directs. The number of those who frequent the schools, including children and parents is about three thousand. The anniversary meeting of these societies and schools is, generally, early in July. Of that held on the eighth day of last August, I am able to give a correct account from the relation of my sister Mrs. White, who was one of the ladies then present.

Mrs. White had probably accompanied Mr. and Mrs. King to Bristol and Alveston; her narrative is written throughout in the plural number, implying that she was with friends. It so happens that the ' Mendip Annals,' or ' Journal of Miss Martha More,' which is the fullest account of the sisters' work, does not contain any report of this meeting. Jane White's notice is therefore a contribution to the history of the movement. It is here subjoined: 1

The day begins with a breakfast at Miss H. More's house at Cowslip Green, which is attended by the neighbouring families. From thence they adjourn to Shipham, one of their school-houses, which was decorated by the hands of the children with wreaths and chaplets of natural flowers; every room, and the outside of the cottage, being white-washed, and made a pattern of rural neatness. The company was invited to partake of a collation above stairs, while the better sort of poor were collecting together below, to walk to the Church in a procession which was composed first of the school children of this and the adjoining parish, in number about 120, with their school-mistresses, after them the clergyman who was to preach, the vicar of the parish, and some of the neighbouring clergy, two and two. Then followed Miss Martha More, one of the patronesses, and her sister Mrs. More, of Bath, and the ladies who were members of the society; followed by the poor who were members, and then the ladies and gentlemen, who were introduced by members.

After divine service we had a discourse, exhorting the audience to fulfil all the duties of Christianity, in every rank and condition of society, and to set the example of a virtuous and religious life. The company then returned to the school, where the childrenwere called over; each being noticed in turn, and receiving the present of a plumb-cake, with a particular commendation of every one who had been distinguished for good behaviour. The children were then dismissed; and the poor, and some of the lesser farmers' wives and daughters, sat down to their entertainment of tea and cakes. The ladies assisted to make the tea, and butter the cakes; and in the course of an hour, in three rooms, about a hundred were served with great attention and satisfaction. The yearly account of the Society was then examined by Miss Martha More, with the assistance of the Vicar, and his wife; all the particulars were minutely explained to the members, and the balance in hand, amounting to rather better than $50, was produced, as their fund for sickness or misfortune. It was stated that$50more had, with consent, been lent the preceding year on Government security, which the poor expressed a wish might be continued.

1Continuation of the ' Account of the Mendip Schools.'*Reports of the Society B. C. P.,*vol. ii., lxiv.

After the ladies and gentlemen present had tendered their benefactions to the Society, and some members had been admitted whose character and conduct had previously been inquired into, and others entered, and their names referred for inquiry, the patronesses' wedding-present with some profitable advice was given to a young woman who had been married since the last meeting.

Miss Martha More then addressed herself to her poorer friends with much energy and effect – to mothers on good order in their families, on decency of conduct and the efficacy of example; to young wives, on industry, attention, neatness, gentleness of manners, and good temper; to young women preparing for or going into service, on obedience, simplicity of dress, and mutual kindness and affection to each other. She concluded with an animated detail of the happy effects of a truly Christian spirit; as supplying comfort during life and at the hour of death, and affording the hope of eternal happiness hereafter. The poor then departed to their homes, having expressed their gratitude for the comforts they had derived from the institution during the late severe winter, and having poured forth their earnest wishes and prayers for the health of their absent patroness, Miss Hannah More, who by severe illness was prevented attending this anniversary meeting, which she had originally founded.

Lady Olivia Bernard Sparrow, of Brampton Park,1who was a friend of the sisters, said of the younger lady:

1Introduction to*Mendip Annals,*by the Editor, Mr. Arthur Koberts, M. A., Hector of Woodrising. Lady Olivia Bernard Sparrow has been mentioned invol. i., chap. iv., p. 04, of this Family History. Mr. Roberts dedicated the*Mendip Annals to*her as one who had appreciated the sisters.

A PEEIOD OF SUFFEEING 303

Miss Martha More was a most estimable person, but whose admiration and love for her sister caused her to keep herself, as much as she could, out of observation, so that, in fact, little is known of her.

She certainly threw herself into their mission work at least as thoroughly as Hannah, and her ' Journal' gives a clear account of its progress.

Very soon after the period of this festival just described the sisters were exposed to a virulent attack from Mr. Bere, the curate of Blagdon,1in which parish Cowslip Green was situated. They had not at first undertaken any work there, as it was some distance from the wild district on which Mr. Wilberforce had taken compassion, and Mr. Bere was supposed to be caring for it; the rector was, of course, an absentee. It was at the urgent request of the curate, supported by the churchwardens and overseers, that, at much inconvenience to themselves, they opened a school in Blagdon parish. Early in 1800, when this school had worked much good and was flourishing, Mr. Bere – from what motive, except jealousy, it is hard to see, although the schoolmaster's want of judgment furnished a pretext – accused them, Hannah as the leader especially, of teaching Methodism and Calvinism, and, moreover, principles of infidelity, immorality, and disloyalty, supposed to be derived from France. Of course many partisans of the old state of things in that and other parishes joined in the outcry. The sisters demeaned themselves bravely: Martha perhaps bore the brunt of the battle physically, for Hannah was for some months prostrate with ague. They had, no doubt, many friends, and the Bishop and Rector did them justice; but, as usual, the defence was not as energetic as the attack, and the sisters went through a long period of suffering, without, however, giving up their work.

Either during this or a subsequent visit to Bath, Mr. Bernard probably discovered the existence of some schools at Weston, near Bath, founded recently by a Mrs. Hooker, where children, apparently girls only, were taken from two years old to twelve, received elementary religious instruction, and were taught to sing in church. The very young children were placed singly under the care of an elder child, supervised of course by the Mistress; as they advanced in age they were taught to read, and to work sufficiently well to mend and make for themselves and for their poor neighbours. When arrived at a certain point they were allowed to take orders for paying work.

1Roberts (William),*Memoirs, dc., of Mrs. Hannah More.*(Second Edition), vol. iii., chap. xi. In those days the title Mrs. was given to unmarried as well as to married ladies.

The relatives of these children, and many other persons, were attracted to church by the sight of the whole school, excepting, perhaps, some babes, accompanying its foundress to church, and the consequent introduction of psalmody; indeed the attendance increased so much that the rector was induced to give another service, and a marked change for the better took place in the whole character of the parish.

These schools were only so far connected with the Society for Bettering the Condition of the Poor that an account of them, written by a Miss Masters, appeared in the third volume of the ' Eeports,' which probably means that they were visited by Mr. and Mrs. Bernard. Another charitable effort in Bath was, however, the subject of a paper,1by Margaret Bernard herself, dated '6th Dec., 1799,' beginning:

Towards the end of the year 1796, a Repository was opened at Bath by several ladies, for the reception of works of industry and ingenuity, to be sold for the benefit of the poor. It is supported by subscription, and is conducted by a committee of ladies chosen from among the subscribers; of whom one attends the sale every day from twelve to three, and three or four meet on Saturday, to look over the books, and to pay the poor people. During the two first years articles were sold for the benefit of 200 poor persons, and the receipts amounted to $1133 11s.*id.*The last year's receipt was $700.

1Extract from ' An Account of the Bath Repository for the benefit of the Poor,' by Mrs. Bernard.*Reports of the Society B. CJP.,*vol. ii., No. LXV.

THE BATH EEPOSITOEY 305

There are at present sixty-three poor women, who regularly bring their work, and come every Saturday to be paid for such part as is sold; many of them are widows with large families, and some very infirm, particularly one poor woman who employs herself in making stay-laces, and is paralytic; so much so, as to be unable even to lift her head from the pillow. Her work is remarkably neat and well done, and she not only earns some addition to her means of subsistence, but relieves herself from the weariness of many painful hours.

The children of the School of Industry sent their work thither, and also ladies, who wished to work for the benefit of particular poor persons; the names of the intended recipients were ticketed on the work, and they were required to come in person for the money. Another thoughtful arrangement was that visitors who did not intend to buy were requested to put sixpence into a charity box,' to prevent the inconvenience that might arise from idle visits of curiosity.'

Although Mrs. Bernard states that there was one charity of the same kind in London, it appears that such schemes were by no means common, and were, therefore, worth writing about. She remarks1on the advantage not only to the needy recipients, but also to the rich by giving them an unselfish occupation, 'and making the amusements of the idle and the young contributory to charity and benevolence.'

Especially does Mrs. Bernard dilate on the advantage to the visitors of very tender years:

Amid the pleasures and dissipation of Bath, it must be no small satisfaction to those parents whose health obliges their families to be occasionally resident there, that a place of amusement of this kind should be opened for their children, and that it should be powerfully recommended by fashion; a place, where they may at an early age, be instructed to employ the means, and enjoy the gratification, of being useful to the poor, and of soothing and relieving their distresses. For it must occur to them, before it can be suggested, that habits of this kind, when at anearly and teachable age they are acquired and enjoyed, will remain through life a blessing and an ornament to the possessor.

1' Observations' appended to the ' Account of the Bath Repository,' by Mrs. Bernard.

VOL. III. X

But the most important result of this visit to Bath was the determination formed by Mr. Bernard to publish the good work achieved by the Rev. Mr. Daubeny, in obtaining the funds, superintending the arrangements, and officiating, together with the Eev. Mr. Leigh, in a chapel of the Church of England, to which the poor were admitted free, and invited to attend.

This phenomenon, for such in the usual acceptation of the term it then was, was felt by Thomas to be the first step towards filling a want he had long deplored, and as an example calling for imitation. And the sequel to his resolve that a movement in the same direction should be inaugurated in London will be told in the next chapter.

In the following year, 1800, Thomas Bernard sold his house at Iver to Mr. John Sullivan. It may be conjectured that, as his time and attention became increasingly devoted to philanthropic schemes, he found the country house an encumbrance. From that time he made more excursions to various parts of England – whether for business or pleasure – generally it would seem with a view to some benevolent project; sometimes, perhaps, as aids to health, which had been probably one reason for his visits to Bath.

I have heard an aunt say that Mr. Bernard's wife regretted this change: she was not strong, and thought that the new plan involved more mental and bodily fatigue; but she acquiesced loyally in his wishes, whether they obliged her to make a prolonged stay in London, or a long journey – sometimes to an untried locality.

13

SECTION 13

ME. DAUBENY'S CHAPEL 307
    CHAPTER XVI
    THE FBEE CHAPEL IN ST. GILES'S

    Mr. Danbeny's Chapel at Bath – The First Mention of West Street Chapel, St. Giles's – It becomes John Wesley's West End Mission Station – The Chapel in] Thomas Bernard's hands – The Galleries of the Chapel let to Tradesmen in Order to Defray Expenses – Thomas Bernard's Account of the Progress of the Chapel – The Beligious Destitution of the Day – Neglect by the Church of the Poor – Thomas Bernard's Scheme for the Establishment of Free Chapels for the Poor – Proposed Free Chapel in Douglas, Isle of Man – Offshoots from the West Street Chapel-Public-houses Patronised by Beggars in St. Giles's – The Weakness of English Schemes of Improvement – West Street Chapel passes out of the hands of Thomas Bernard's Trustees – The later History of the Chapel – The Bev. B. W. Dibdin.

    Me. Bebnabdappears to have lost no time in writing an account / of Mr. Daubeny's chapel at Bath for the ' Reports' of his Society; it is dated November 29, 1799, and the subject is introduced as follows:

    The free church, in the parish of Walcot, at Bath, was opened in November, 1798, for the general and indiscriminate accommodation of the poor. The idea was originally suggested by the Eev. Mr. Daubeny, in a sermon delivered at St. Margaret's chapel, at Bath, in April 1792; and afterwards, with the concurrence and approbation of the Eev. Mr. Sibley, the Eector of the parish, published with an address to the inhabitants.

In this discourse, Mr. Daubeny, after enlarging upon the great characteristic of the Christian religion that ' the Poor have the Gospel preached to them,' and upon the expected benefits of the Sunday Schools then established at Bath, proceeded to ask ' where are the children of that place when discharged from the Sunday Schools at a time of life the most dangerous, – where are they to gain that instruction which is calculated to bring to perfection theeducation which they have received? If in conformity to the ideas with which they have been brought up they come to places of worship belonging to the Establishment, they find, alas! the doors for the most part, shut against them.'

1Extract from 'An Account of the Free Church at Bath,1by Thomas Bernard, Esq.*Reports,*vol. ii., No. LXIII.

He then goes on to observe that this is in some degree to exclude them from the Established Church, instead of inviting, and providing places of worship for them; without which (he adds) ' we cannot be surprised that they should no longer continue members of a church, which, in a manner,*excommunicates*them. In which case their infidelity and consequent immorality, will not so much lay at their own doors, as at the doors of those who ought, in charity, to have taken their case into consideration, and to have provided means for their instruction.'

The poor of Walcot had actually been wronged by a measure which should have been beneficial in its effects: namely, the enlargement and alleged improvement of their parish church; this had led to an extension of the system of ' farming ' the pews in order to defray the interest on the expenditure. There were, indeed, four proprietary chapels besides in the parish, but in these the seats were let at very high prices. Mr. Bernard adds: ' I do not mean to suggest that no accommodation is left for the poor. In Laura Chapel, at Bath, I observed one hundred seats reserved for the poor, in the back of the south gallery; and forty for charity children.'1There is sufficient evidence that this state of things was usual throughout England, wherever it was possible to make money by pew rents.

Thomas Bernard did not content himself with giving currency to Mr. Daubeny's appeal, and chronicling its results – which had been most satisfactory; while the paper containing the particulars of the enterprise was passing through the press, he had obtained the lease of a building suitable for his purpose, which was the opening of a free chapel in London, and was able to state the fact in a note to the second volume of the ' Reports,' dated January 29, 1800.*

1Note to the ' Account of the Free Chapel in Bath.'

* Note to the ' Observations ' following the ' Account of the Free Chapel in Bath.' Mr. Bernard received the news of the engagement while the ' Account' or ' Beport' was in the printers' hands.

WORKS OF MERCY 309

While Mr. Bernard was engaged in the negotiation for this building, and in the business of fitting it for the services of the Church of England, he was also helping forward other works of mercy, mentioned elsewhere – the foundation of the Blind

School; the formation of the Cancer Institution; the efforts to obtain a suitable building for a Fever Institution, especially; and was beginning a new crusade on behalf of the unhappy children employed as chimney-sweeps. Indeed, this appears to have been about the busiest period of his philanthropic career. During this winter – 1800-1 – moreover, the scarcity and consequent dearness of provisions reached a point which seriously affected the well-being of the people; and the Society for Bettering the Condition of the Poor was busy with experiments and instruction as to the best means of meeting the emergency. So early as November, 1800,1Thomas Bernard was examined before a Committee of the House of Commons, especially as to the advantages he had found in using rice instead of flour at the Foundling Hospital and elsewhere; and the Committee embodied the details of his evidence in its Report. Bread, in 1800, was Is.*5%d.*the quartern loaf of 4 lbs. 5 ozs., and for some weeks it rose to Is.*W$d.*To remedy the effects of the high price of meat it was proposed to secure for the metropolis a supply of salted or corned fish. The Society elected a committee, which, by the agency of Mr. Patrick Colquhoun, entered into extensive correspondence with Edinburgh on this subject.

On the 29th of November the first cargo arrived containing 390,000 herrings. They wereimmediately announced for sale, which commenced on the 3rd of December, and proceeded with as much rapidity as could have been wished. In the meantime, measures were taken for continuing the supply, at the price then fixed, of 3s.*4d.*per hundred.2

A little later an effort was made to utilise the Cornish fisheries, which had been much neglected, and Mr. HenryBoase, who was a Cornishman, wrote a paper1on the subject for the Society's 'Reports.' Herrings formed the staple of the fish supply; but after a while pilchards, cod, and even several other kinds of fish were sent to London. Fresh sea fish was then impossible at any considerable distance inland, except as an occasional luxury for the rich man's table.

1*Life of Sir Thomas Bernard,*by the Rev. James Baker.

2Extract from ' An Account of the Measures taken during the late Scarcity, for supplying the Poor with corned Herrings and other cheap Fish,' by Thomas Bernard, Esq.*Reports of the Society B. C. P.,*vol. Ui., No. XCV.

The chapel obtained by Mr. Bernard2for the use of the poor was situated in West Street, St. Giles's, one of the streets which converged in a centre called the Seven Dials. West Street Chapel is first mentioned in 1700,3when it was held by a French Protestant congregation, which had moved there from another locality. Soon after that period the neighbourhood appears to have become more thickly populated, and, being much neglected, obtained a bad preeminence in reputation amongst London parishes. This misfortune was no doubt originally due to various changes in the metropolis, such as are still constantly in operation; and it probably owed to this otherwise undesirable distinction the honour of being chosen by John Wesley as one of the scenes of his ministry. He moved into the chapel when it was vacated by the French congregation, and it became his West End mission station.

Wesley still professed to be an attached son of the English Church, and his friend Fletcher, who preached his first sermon in West Street Chapel, lived and died Vicar of Madeley, Salop. Yet the proceedings were altogether irregular, and unsanctioned by ecclesiastical authority; they were, to most intents and purposes, dissenting services, founding their best excuse on the terrible indifference of both Church and State to the spiritual condition of the masses.

The chapel was simply a large room, with galleries on the two sides, entirely devoid of architecture and ornament. ST. GILES'S FREE CHUECH 311

1Extract from ' An Account of the Fisheries in the West of England,1by Henry Boase, Esq.*Reports of the Society B. C. P.,*vol. iii., Appendix xii.

*Life of Sir Thomas Bernard,*by l!ev. James Baker.

*The History of West Street Episcopal Chapel,*by Rev. R. W. Dibdin, M. A. (Nisbet&Co., 1862.)

Adjoining it was a house, apparently built for the officiating minister, and in an upper room of this house were three windows looking into the chapel directly over the communion-table. In Wesley's time many persons, both lay and clerical, some of considerable note, who wished to hear him, occupied this room during the services, though they did not wish – especially if clergymen – to be stigmatised as attendants on his ministry; from this custom these convenient apertures received the name of the ' Nicodemus windows.'

The chapel had no sooner come into Mr. Bernard's hands than he began to realise the semi-starvation to which the poverty-stricken district around had been reduced during the prevailing distress. On April 4, 1800, he wrote:'

Some delay in opening the Free Church in St. Giles's has been unavoidably occasioned by the increased demand of the poor upon the soup-house of that district, adjoining to, and in some degree connected with, that Church. On this account it has been deemed proper to fit up the soup kitchen there, with twice the accommodation originally intended; and until that could be completed, the necessary repairs and preparation of the Chapel could not well be proceeded in. That part of the work is, however, now completed; and the repairs of the chapel are proceeding in; with the hope of its being opened,*not as a solitary free church in the metropolis,*but as one, prior only in time, but inferior in size and accommodation, to many free churches, which the active and persevering benevolence of the inhabitants of the metropolis will establish and open for the benefit of the poor.

These words stamp the Free Chapel in West Street as the first metropolitan place of worship of its kind in connection with the Church of England; but the well-to-do members of that Church did not respond to Mr. Bernard's appeal sufficiently to provide for its maintenance, much less for others of the sort. They apparently looked either with indifference or dislike on the strange idea of preaching the Gospel to the poor, and affording them Christian privilegesin the capital of Christian England, and under the shelter of buildings belonging to the so-called National Church. It was found necessary, as at Bath, to let the galleries to tradesmen in the neighbourhood, by way of paying the expenses of the whole; the body of the chapel was reserved for those who did not pay, and, as the entire number of sittings was over one thousand, they probably obtained about seven hundred.

1In a note to a portion of the Appendix to the second volume of the*Reports of the Society S. C. P.,*No. XIV., entitled ' Notes and Additional Observations,' collected by a Member of the Committee.

Mr. Bernard's biographer writes/concerning this chapel:

It was fitted up by him at the expense of nearly one thousand pounds, the whole of the body being free for the poor, and was opened on the 25th of May, by an excellent and impressive discourse by the late Bishop Porteous, who then presided over the diocese of London. The chapel had been originally intended to be consecrated, but the objection of its being only leasehold for years, together with the Bishop's opinion that consecration was not essential in this more than in many cases of chapels in the metropolis, prevented its taking place. A formal licence was also deemed by the Bishop of London to be unnecessary, he and the Eector of the parish having expressed their approbation by preaching in the chapel; at the same time the appointment of the minister and the attendants was left with Mr. Bernard. In other undertakings of this nature he had received liberal pecuniary assistance from others; to this the contributions were inconsiderable. In addition to the original expense of fitting up, he engaged to pay, during the continuance of the twenty-one years' lease, the further annual sum of fifty guineas, which with the rents of the pews in the galleries defrayed all the expenses.

Thomas Bernard wrote his own account2of the commencement and progress of the chapel in the 'Reports ' of his Society as follows:

On Sunday the 25th of May, 1800, a free chapel was opened in West Street, near the Seven Dials, for the benefit of the Poor. Those who have witnessed the pathos and energy with which the Bishop of London delivers and enforces the divine truths and ordinances of the Gospel, may conceive how powerful and impresST. GILES'S FREE CHUECH 313

1*Life of Sir Thomas Bernard,*by Eev. James Baker.

2Extract from' An Account of the Free Chapel, in West Street, St. Giles's,' by Thomas Bernard, Esq.*Reports of the Society B. C. P.,*vol. iii., No. LXXVHI.

sive his discourse must have been on this occasion; addressed as it was to the feelings, and understandings of his audience, and received by them with silent and unfeigned satisfaction.

The chapel was extremely crowded; not merely by the poor, but by many of the other classes of life. The singing was peculiarly striking and affecting; all the persons who were present, standing up, and uniting earnestly and zealously in this delightful act of devotion. In the afternoon the Eev. Dr. Glasse preached, with much effect upon his audience; if fixed and gratified attention can be admitted as evidence of the impression of the preacher. On the succeeding Sunday the sacrament was administered at the Chapel; and fifty persons, chiefly the aged poor, received the Communion with decency and devotion.

It appears that the Rector of St. Giles's was also Bishop of Chichester. The chapel was placed under the direction of the Bishop of London, the Rector, and eight principal subscribers. The Methodist Society, which was leaving six months before its time, behaved with great friendliness and liberality. For nearly a year, Mr. Vevers was the officiating clergyman, but from Lady-day 1801, Mr. Gurney was engaged, apparently with the idea that he was a very fit person for this difficult post.

It had been conceived (writes Mr. Bernard), that it would be better, and more conducive to the permanency of the institution, that the poor should*gradually*find their way into the chapel; rather than by any special means to press their premature attendance. No hope was entertained that their habits would be suddenly and entirely changed; and that those, who from infancy had passed the Lord's Day in sloth and brutal indulgence, should be *at once* amended; and be prepared regularly to attend with cleanliness and decency, in a place of divine worship. A complete and permanent reform was not to be immediately expected; and a temporary conformity, a mere yielding for the time to pressing instances, compelling them to come in, did not promise any stable improvement.

Everything appears to have been done to make the chapel attractive, according to the ideas of the times, and so far as circumstances permitted; an organ was provided, an organist engaged, and printed copies of the psalms and hymns placed in the free seats; there was also some attention paid to the comfort of the seat-holders in the galleries, on whom the support of the chapel mainly depended, and room was made there for a few additional sittings. Mr. Gurney, who undertook the charge of the district, was evidently considered an eloquent preacher, since many of the inhabitants of St. Giles's had desired to see him appointed to the lectureship of the parish church, and such lecturers were ordinarily chosen on account of their powers of attracting a congregation. He was content to accept the pew rents and the additional *50l.* provided by Mr. Bernard as his stipend. The salary of the organist and other church expenses must have been defrayed by the very moderate contributions of the public.

The ' Observations' appended to Mr. Bernard's paper on the chapel, according to the custom adopted in the Society's ' Reports,' are of unusual length, and contain some curious particulars of the religious destitution of the day:1

Whoever takes a view of the parochial districts of the western end of our metropolis, will find that in the four parishes of Marybone, St. James's, St. Giles's, and St. George's Hanover Square, with a population of some hundred thousand inhabitants, there are only four churches for the reception of those, who are desirous of attending divine worship, according to the rites of the Church of England. Three of these are of a moderate size; but the other, that of Marybone, hardly fit for the chapel of some petty insulated hamlet. In these four parishes, the utmost exertions of the parochial clergy, combined with the greatest talents, must be utterly inadequate to the religious duties of their respective districts.

The writer then recurs to the vexed subject of accommodation; those who did not pay being relegated to ' standing- room in the aisles, and sometimes an occasional neglected bench'; and continues:

It is of very little or no consequence, that in these four parishes, there are many private chapels. These chapels are let at *track*RELIGIOUS DESTITUTION 315

1Extract from ' An Account of the Free Chapel in West Street, St. Giles's,' by Thomas Bernard, Esq. (' Observations' appended to the Account). *Reports of the Society B. C. P.,* vol. iii., No. LXXVIII.

rent, to some speculating undertaker: the pews, and every part of them, being laid out and disposed (as other private property generally is) *so as to produce the greatest possible income with the least outgoings;* and the free admission of the poor being directly opposite to the principle, on which they are built and opened; and perfectly incompatible with the *great object* of making a very large revenue, by the admission of very genteel company.

He notes that

many of the better and more serious of the labouring poor are driven and compelled to take refuge in the different places of worship, which the more accommodating spirit of other sects provides for their religious duties. But this is not all: the greater number of these neglected Christians *preserve their orthodoxy, by never attending any church at all;* and in a country justly boasting of the purity of its religious doctrines, – extremely fortunate in the possession of a learned and pious clergy, – and consecrating very ample funds to the support of a most respectable church establishment – two thirds of the lower order of people in the metropolis, live as utterly ignorant of the doctrines and duties of Christianity, and are as errant and unconverted pagans, as if they had existed in the wildest part of Africa.

Mr. Bernard, though fully admitting the obligation of carrying the Gospel to other lands, remarks how curious an enigma it will appear to future ages that England, while sending missions to distant and unknown countries, should utterly neglect its own metropolis. In the present day we do not look back on the transition years of the eighteenth and nineteenth centuries as particularly distinguished by zeal for foreign missions, but such they apparently were by comparison, since the Church totally ignored the duty of providing for its people at home, where the increase of population demanded an increase of exertion, or where any change of circumstances rendered fresh measures urgent.

In his animadversions on the shortcomings of the National Church, he alludes to ' the awful series of events which is now desolating, and we may hope at the same time reforming, the Christian world' – namely, the great Eevolu- tion in France, and the consequent misfortunes in which other countries had been involved. He continued, in a more animated strain than was usual to him – his feelings having been stirred from their depths by this topic:

It is written in the recent History of Europe, it is inscribed in the summary of the preceding ten years, that there is no protection against the calamities which are now laying waste our quarter of the globe, except that purity of faith and integrity of life, which are to be derived from the vivifying influence of religion, extending, like the solar ray, *to every class* of our fellow subjects, and operating in the moral amendment of the great mass of the people.

And after some further remarks, he adds:

With these sentiments, and with this conviction on my mind, I venture to submit to those, from whom only such a measure can properly originate, the expediency of providing some remedy for this national evil. – What I have to suggest may be considered as a *mission for the instruction and conversion of our neglected fellow creatures, the Pagan Inhabitants in the Centre of London.*

Mr. Bernard's suggestion was the formation of a society for the foundation and establishment of free chapels for the poor in populous towns, ' subject, as all other chapels and churches of the Established Church must be, to episcopal control and government.' The principal subscribers were to be governors of the Society. 'When- ever such a Society shall be formed,' he adds, 'and the directing power placed in unexceptionable hands, I will venture to hope that some addition to its funds may be afforded by government.'

Mr. Baker is silent as to the results of this appeal; it clearly met with little or no response. The West Street chapel struggled on amidst difficulties, and apparently without successors. Some years later, in 1812, Thomas Bernard was engaged in furthering a similar enterprise at Brighton, which, however, had a very troubled career; but, in 1814, his heart was at length rejoiced by the receipt of a letter/from the Isle of Man stating that:

In the principal town of Douglas, which contains about seven thousand inhabitants, there is no accommodation for the poor inGOOD WOEK 317

1 *Life of Sir Thomas Bernard,* by the Bev. James Baker.

the churches belonging to the establishment. It is now in contemplation to erect a Free Chapel on the plan of that in London, West Street, Seven Dials, and his Grace the Duke of Athol, Governor-in-Chief, highly approves of the plan.

It is hardly possible, therefore, that the bishops can have thrown their influence into the movement; most of them probably looked with suspicion on such innovations, while some of the beneficed clergy dreaded the diminution of their rights and incomes. Such were the ideas of the age, indeed, that Mr. Bernard was fortunate in not being opposed in West Street by the Bishop and Rector, whose work he was doing for them. As to the laity, it is not surprising that in such circumstances they, also, should have been generally indifferent, when not hostile to the effort.

The little chapel of the Seven Dials had a subsequent history of some interest. It went through years of bare toleration doing good work in a very unostentatious manner. For some time the majority of the poor inhabitants of the district could scarcely be brought to understand that they were no longer to be repelled from church, but were invited and even expected to attend religious services. The idea was too startling to be quickly realised.

The habitual neglect of Divine Service and of all observance of the Sabbath [writes Mr. Baker'] was so inveterate in the minds of the poor of that neighbourhood, that after the first effects of curiosity were over, the chapel was for some months very thinly attended. Perseverance however, and the assiduity and talent of Mr. Gurney who devoted himself to the duty with extraordinary zeal, produced a numerous and regular congregation of the poor. The Holy Sacrament of the Lord's Supper is folly attended, and a weekly evening Lecture established, and constantly frequented by the neighbourhood.

In a note the same writer adds:

The number of attendants has been from one hundred and eighty to two hundred persons, and the collections among persons so necessitous have amounted to three or four pounds on aSunday. At the first Confirmation the Bishop of London held after the opening of the Chapel, one hundred and fifty young persons went in a body from the Chapel to be confirmed.

1 *Life of Sir Thomas Bernard.*

The soup-kitchen, established in the lower part of the chapel house, may be supposed to have had some influence in attracting persons to the services; but if so, it was within fair bounds; no pious bribery was attempted. The soup was, indeed, as the scarcity increased, supplemented by salt or corned fish, pork, potatoes, bread, and savoury rice. As the scarcity increased and lengthened, these provisions were not given away, but sold at a low price, and to all comers; but the applicants chiefly belonged to St. Giles and the adjoining parish of St. Ann's, Soho. There was also a charity for coals, which were stored under the chapel – this being a customary arrangement in proprietary places of worship – though, perhaps, wine and spirits were the more usual commodities. But it is probable that the provisions were partly discontinued after the times began to mend. Sir Frederick Morton Eden,1who wrote a full account of this institution for the Society's ' Reports,' was against leading the poor to rely on such aid too exclusively.

The success of the chapel [says Mr. Baker *] was followed by the formation of a school, originally containing only about two hundred children. It was however progressively increased to four hundred, consisting of two hundred and fifty boys in the chapel, and about one hundred and fifty girls in the house adjoining.3The parents pay ninepence a month for each child; and the payments are very punctually made, and are adequate to a considerable part of the expense of these schools, which have continued to benefit and improve that part of the metropolis for above fourteen years.

PUBLIC HOUSES IN ST. GILES'S 319

1Extract from ' An Account of the Soup House in West Street, St. Giles's,' by Sir Frederick Morton Eden, Bart.

Life of Sir Thomas Bernard.

'See also, for earlier statistics and other particulars, extract from ' An Account of the Free Chapel Schools in West Street, Seven Dials,' by John Dougan, Esq.,*Reports of the Society B. C. P.,*vol. iv., No. C. The total expense of the day and Sunday-schools, was2831.10s. per annum. Of this 902. was expended in clothing for ninety children nominated by subscribers of one guinea or benefactors of ten guineas each. The parents of the scholars contributed 13s. a year for each child, amounting to1561.,when this account was written.

The chapel produced in 1803 another beneficial establishment – ' A Society of the Poor for the Eelief of their poor Neighbours in Distress,' its objects being to visit, ascertain the circumstances and character, and, as far as may be, relieve the distresses of any poor persons in that neighbourhood, who are suffering in silence and obscurity. In the course of a week from its first proposal by Mr. Gurney from the pulpit, one hundred and eighty-seven of his congregation subscribed to the annual amount of one hundred and twenty-eight pounds; and what makes it singular is that these poor persons subscribe without any preferable claim on the funds, except what may arise from superior character or more urgent distress.1

It is difficult to understand how a population which could undertake a work of this kind could be either very wretched or very depraved. Only from the article in the ' Quarterly Review' on Mendicity,* written some years later, have I been able to glean any particulars throwing light on the darker shades of its social life. It deals with some Minutes of a Committee, printed in 1815, by order of the House of Commons. Some passages relate to two houses in Church Lane, very near West Street.

Joseph Butterworth, Esq., one of the Committee, and an active member of the ' Strangers' Friend Society ' says:

' There are two public-houses in Church Lane St. Giles's whose chief support depends on beggars; one called the Beggar's Opera, which is the Eose and Crown public-house, and the other the Robin Hood. The number that frequent those houses, at various times, are computed to be between two and three hundred. I have been credibly informed that they are divided into companies, and each company is subdivided into what are called walks, and each company has its particular walk: if this walk be considered beneficial, the whole company take it by turns, each person keeping it from half an hour to three or four hours. Their receipts,

1Mr. Baker's notice is chiefly taken from the extract of' An Account of a Society in West Street for the Belief of their Poor Neighbours in Distress,' by Thomas Bernard, Esq.*Reports of the Society B. C. P.,*vol. iv., No. CIV.

2*The Quarterly Review,*October 1815, vol. xiv., Art. vi Minutes of the Evidence taken before the Committee appointed by the House of Commons to inquire into the State of Mendicity and Vagrancy in the Metropolis and its Neighbourhood, ordered to be printed July llth, 1815.

at a moderate calculation, cannot be less than from three to five shillings a day each person. '

Mr. William Dorrell, inspector of the pavement of St. Giles's, has been on an evening, out of curiosity, at the Rose and Crown, kept by a man of the name of Sheen, and the Robin Hood, in Church Lane, by a man whose name is Pearl. ' I have seen them,' he says,' some years back, at a time when the knives and forks, the snuffers, the pokers, tongs, and so on, were chained to the place, take fowls and such things for supper.' He also says that there were two cellars between Plumtree Street and Dyot Street where they used to dress sausages for their supper, and where the things were chained to the table to prevent their being stolen.

Mr. Sampson Stevenson, overseer of the parish of St. Giles's, gives a similar account of another house, called the Fountain, in King Street, Seven Dials, where the beggars assemble, not only at night, but in a morning before they start upon their daily occupations. He has gone into the bar to see their manner of going on: they set out in a morning some with knapsacks on their back; some with none. The former take anything they can collect, old clothes and old shoes, which they bring to a place near Monmouth Street, where ' they*translate*old shoes into new ones; they make sometimes three or four shillings a day by old shoes only '; and ' their mode of exciting charity for shoes is invariably to go barefooted, and scarify their feet and heels with something or another to cause the blood to flow.' He says they are the worst of characters, get violently drunk, quarrel and fight, calling for gin, rum, beer, and whatever they like; ham, beef, and so on; broken victuals none of them will touch.

'There are houses where there are forty or fifty of them, like a gaol; the porter stands at the door and takes the money. For threepence they have clean straw, or something like it; for those who pay fourpence there is something more decent; for sixpence they have a bed. They are all locked in for the night, lest they should take the property. In the morning there is a general muster below.'

It appears that in the parish of St. Giles there are numbers of these houses; the persons who frequent them have no habitations, but live entirely by begging, or something worse.

This evidence was given before a Committee of the House of Commons, whose business was ' to inquire into the State of Mendicity and Vagrancy in the Metropolis,' omitting other forms of vice and crime; the record would

probably be quite as black in each case had other phases been set forth. As the money raised in the parish for the relief of distress was distributed by persons well acquainted with the locality, it may be concluded that it was given to the deserving poor only, for whom these successful vagabonds must have been a sore trial of faith.

The great weakness in every English scheme of improvement is want of continuity. It seems impossible to ensure an organisation for carrying on philanthropic works after the first promoters and benefactors have passed away from the scene. The history of the West Street Chapel has been written, and forms an instructive lesson in the administration of Anglican Church affairs.

It appears from the ' Quarterly Beview' that Mr. Gurney, who gave evidence before the Committee, was then rector of St. Clement Danes, as well as minister of West Street Chapel. Pecuniary reasons may have rendered this arrangement inevitable, but it must have diminished his usefulness in St. Giles's. Within three years from that time Sir Thomas Bernard, as he then was, died – the original lease of the chapel had but another three years to run; but it seems evident that Sir Thomas must have obtained some extension of the term, since Mr. Gurney remained five years longer at his post. The annual sum allowed by Sir Thomas was, therefore, in all likelihood, secured to the officiating clergyman for that period. If the statement of Mr. Samuel Cole, of 98 Great Russell Street, may be received as accurate, the visible results of the chapel teaching had much diminished in the meantime; and Mr. Cole having been converted by Mr. Gurney, was not likely to exaggerate deficiencies which might tell against him.

In the course of his twenty-five years of labour about the Seven Dials Mr. Gurney must have grown sensibly older, and less able to manage large numbers of persons, while the population amongst which he toiled was not of a sort to make allowance for the shortcomings of declining age. Indeed, it may be conjectured that a decided change for the worse had taken place in the character of the inhabitants – Vol. in. Y

that a recent additional influx of lawless and abandoned settlers had proved too much for the clergyman, and had fixed upon St. Giles's,1and especially upon the Seven Dials, the reputation of being the worst quarter of London. This influx of reprobates had, no doubt, led to an exodus of some of the more respectable residents, such as the tradesmen who had occupied the galleries, and the quieter portion of the poor; added to which changes, the death of Sir Thomas Bernard must have been preceded and followed by the loss of some of his contemporaries, who had been friends and fellow-workers, and thus the needful support was withdrawn from the chapel – moral as well as pecuniary. Of the Bishop and Rector at this crisis nothing is said.

Mr. Gurney was succeeded by Mr. Ellaby, who appears to have taken the chapel on his own responsibility, so that it passed out of the hands of Sir Thomas Bernard's trustees. Mr. Cole writes:

At that time there were only ten communicants. A committee was then formed for repairing and altering the chapel; the cooking apparatus for making soup was taken away, and the centre of the chapel fitted up with pews. A benevolent society was formed for visiting the sick and poor.

But the pewing of the chapel must have meant that pew-rents were exacted; so that it became an ordinary ' proprietary chapel,' though not of the most fashionable type. The historical ' Nicodemus windows' were blocked up at this time.

It is not surprising to find that the enterprise ended in disappointment; but it is perhaps remarkable that Mr. Ellaby should have speedily found an opportunity of disposing of the chapel to a new bidder, and, as may be assumed, on satisfactory terms to himself. His widow, who seems to have jotted down some reminiscences as a contribution to the history of the chapel, writes:2

1The stigma which attached to the parish is exemplified in Douglas Jerrold's story – with a purpose – entitled*St. Giles and St. James,*in which, about the middle of the nineteenth century, St. Giles figures as the type of degradation, St. James of exaltation.

2In*The History of West Street Episcopal Chapel,*by Eev. E. W. Dibdin, MA.

A DWINDLING CONGREGATION 323

As far as I can recollect my late dear husband commenced his ministry at West Street in 1826, and closed it in 1830 or 1831, when it was taken by the Irish Society. We lived in the chapel- house for three years. It was not a very desirable locality in which to train up a young family, but we were mercifully kept in health and quietness during our continuance there, with but little occasional annoyance from the turbulent spirits by whom we were surrounded, who knew nothing of the privilege of reverencing the sanctuary or keeping the Sabbath holy.

Daring the years in which the Irish Society held the chapel it was the scene of fierce denunciations of Popery; but even these did not ensure success, apparently, for the Society soon parted with the building, which was taken by the Rev. James Endell Tyler, rector of St. Giles's, in 1836. He probably worked it partly by means of his curates; but he also procured the services of eminent popular preachers. Still the results fell far short of expectation, and when in 1841 or 1842 the Rev. E. W. Dibdin wished for a lease of the chapel under the Hector, the congregation numbered but twenty-five persons, all but one of whom were, however, communicants.

The Rector, who appears to have spoken very frankly to Mr. Dibdin, expressed surprise at his own failure to evangelise the district, after the trouble he had given himself with that view. He stated that he had opened the chapel with twelve judges as worshippers at the service; thereupon Mr. Dibdin observed that judges were the last persons in the world Mr. Tyler should have invited to St. Giles's if he wished the inhabitants to frequent his chapel. The further conversation is instructive:

' You are not risking much money, I hope? ' I told him that I had not much to risk, and that it was not a speculation. He said, ' I am glad that you are not risking money, for you would certainly lose it. I have long looked upon that part of my parish as hopeless. Bring me your chapel book, and I will write in it to authorise you to dispense the sacramental alms as you think fit; but it will not be much, I fear.' He little thought that the communicants would in a few years become nearly ten times as numerous as they were at his parish church.

From this narrative it may be inferred that Mr. Dibdin was a man of great energy and devotion, who was satisfied with the results of his ministry, and had reason to be so; he held strong views on some points – was especially hostile to Popery, and a firm believer in demoniacal possession, in which belief he was probably confirmed by observations made during his residence in St. Giles's. One of his experiences was the loss of his plate, which was stolen; it was, however, replaced by ' friends and well-wishers.'

Mr. Dibdin's account of the chapel is dated 1862; at that period the building had again been put up to auction. Apparently the Rector had previously leased it to St. Clement Danes, since the vestry clerk of that parish was to receive applications. The house and ' extensive cellarage' had been let separately; it may be assumed that the cellarage was now used for the ordinary purposes of such accommodation.

I am indebted to the present ' Missioner,' the Rev. A. C. Holthouse, for a continuation of the narrative, in a letter dated ' December 6, 1892 ':

Mr. Dibdin died about five years ago. He conducted service here and preached right up to the end. On his death the building was put up for auction. Owing to the energy of his sons and of Canon Nisbet, who collected the money, it was bought for the ' Seven Dials Mission' – one of the Diocesan Home Missions.

The Mission before that only had a room-church (rented) in Short's Gardens. Now it is in permanent quarters here, although we keep on the mission-room in Short's Gardens.

After that, ' West Street Episcopal Chapel' had been cleaned and somewhat renovated; we took possession four years ago last Easter.

Some further changes have of course taken place since that time. For two years and a half, ending in April 1903, the Rev. Ernest Schofield replaced the Rev. A. C. Holthouse, who has since taken up the work again. In 1901 an order of the London County Council led to the demolition of the old Mission House. It has been replaced by one of more imposing appearance, and the Short's Gardens Mission has been incorporated in the West Street Mission.

THE 'SEVEN DIALS' 325

Much as the neighbourhood has altered of late years, many of the houses having given place to warehouses, while printing works are carried on in close proximity to the chapel, there is still a sufficient amount of poverty and vice in the district to call forth the strenuous work of the clergy. Even now it includes a region styled ' The Street of the Forty Thieves.' The ' Seven Dials' are gone; they disappeared from the locality early in the last century. ' The old Seven Dials Pillar,' writes Mr. Holthouse, ' is on the Green at Weybridge, where it tells of the virtues of a Duchess of York. The head has been chopped off and lies at a little distance; its new head proudly wears a coronet!'*l*

l Letter to the Author, dated June 8, 1904.

14

SECTION 14

CHAPTER XVII

Chimney-sweepers' Apprentices

The Origin of Climbing Chimneys – The Sale of a Child to a Master Sweep – Appeal in the ' Gentleman's Magazine ' on behalf of Climbing Boys – The Interest taken by Jonas Hanway and Thomas Bernard in Climbing Boys – The Neediness of Master Sweepers – The Act of 1788 – Thomas Bernard's Efforts to abolish the System of Employing Boys – David Porter's Scheme on behalf of Climbing Boys – Thomas Bernard promotes a Movement for the Invention of a Sweeping Machine – Meeting at the Mansion House on behalf of Climbing Boys – Some of the Horrors of Chimney Sweeping – Sydney Smith's Article on the Subject in the ' Edinburgh Review' – Acts of Parliament dealing with the Subject – Final Triumph of the Earl of Shaftes- bury – The Act of 1875.

Thegeneration which in its own childhood remembers the cry of ' Sweep! ' in the streets, and has seen boys commence the ascent of chimneys, and watched them with eager interest emerge partially from the chimney top, nourishing the brush in token that the work had been thoroughly done, is fast passing away, and there remains only a tradition of the boys' miseries. The interest of the last years of that protracted struggle, which ended in the total abolition of the practice, is, moreover, concentrated on Lord Shaftesbury as the hero of the fight, to the oblivion of those previous workers who had to some extent prepared the way.

One who had himself passed through the ordeal of apprenticeship to a master sweep has written: '

Who first discovered the art of climbing internally, or at what period it was introduced, is, I believe, not known. I rather conceive it to be a modern invention, having found no mention of chimneyCLIMBING CHIMNEY SWEEPS 327

1Porter,*Considerations on the Present State of Chimney Sweepers,*London, 1802. The author is evidently the same Mr. Porter who is quoted by Thomas Bernard in the*Reports of the Society B. C. P.*

sweeping or chimney sweepers, before Shakespeare, who, in reflecting on the brevity of human life, and the certainty of death, says:

Golden lads and girls all must

Like chimney sweepers, turn to dnst.

Bat even here though it is fair to conclude there were some who made a business of sweeping chimneys, it is not clear by what method they swept them. Some old men of the trade say that the first climbing chimney sweeper was an intimate of Henry Jenkins, so memorable for longevity. Though climbing chimneys may not be an ancient discovery, it is not so modern that we can trace its original; but, from its nature, it was probably the desperate expedient of a criminal, or the last resource of some poor negro to prolong a miserable life. – I know from experience that no employment is more laborious than climbing chimneys.

Thomas Bernard/believed that the practice of bringing up boys to this occupation dated from about the beginning of the eighteenth century. Before that time, indeed, chimneys were sufficiently wide to admit of easy sweeping; if human beings did ascend them, they were probably men, and the risk and hardship would be much less. The fashion of narrow chimneys was in all likelihood connected with the gradual substitution of coal for wood as fuel.

' The employment of boys,' adds Mr. Bernard, 'is peculiar to England,' and surely this is a subject for humiliation. No doubt there were always benevolent persons who protested against the practice; but the nation generally seems to have adopted it with very few qualms of conscience, even though the chimneys continued to become narrower. That harshness must have been used even by the best disposed masters to drive children of six – or even eight – the age fixed by the Act of 28 George III. – up those steep, dark passages, is obvious. But the majority of the masters were ruffians; the children were forced up the chimneys2' by cruel blows, by pricking the soles of their feet, or by applyingwisps of lighted straw'; their lives were at all times rendered deplorable by privation and suffering; many sank under their cruel tasks; others lived crippled and diseased.

1Extract from ' An Account of a Chimney Sweeper's Boy, with Observations on a Proposal for the Relief of Chimney Sweepers,' by Thomas Bernard, Esq.,*Reports of the Society for Bettering the Condition of the Poor,*vol. i., No. XIX.

*Hodder (Edwin),*The Life and Work of the seventh Earl of Shaftesbury, K. G.,*ch. viii.

A large number of the victims were probably obtained from abandoned or starving parents in the lower ranks.1There is a case given in a pamphlet on this topic of a fine boy of five, the son of a working plumber named Miller – not apparently in want – who was sold by his father to a master sweep, in the absence of his mother from town. On her return the poor woman became almost frantic; with difficulty she traced her child to a vile den, only to discover that the sweep had bought him of his father for three guineas, which she could not replace.

Happily, a humane solicitor took her case in hand; the sweep, Henry Doe of Marylebone, was summoned, and fined by the magistrate sitting at Bow Street 5Z., while the child was restored to its mother. This result, however, would not have been achieved had not the boy been under the age prescribed by the Act just mentioned. Chimney-sweeping was considered a trade like any other, and the masters openly advertised for ' Small boys for narrow flues.'

In the February of the year in which the Act was passed, while the matter was being agitated, there appeared in the ' Gentleman's Magazine 'a notice of a pamphlet called ' An Appeal to the Humane on behalf of the most deplorable Class of Society, the Climbing Boys employed by the Chimney-sweepers,' by J. P. Andrews; the writer was a brother of Sir Joseph Andrews, and the following extract is given:

When we order our chimneys to be swept we little recollect that we often order a fellow-creature to be consigned to death or, what is worse, to a life rendered wretched by deformity, imbecillity, and disease. Surely if the management of our plantations and our chimneys would allow us, it were to be wished that we should have nothing to do with black in either case. We are nowCLIMBING CHIMNEY SWEEPS 329

'*Report of Society for Superseding the Necessity of Climbing Boys.*

''*The Gentleman's Magazine and Historical Chronicle,*vol. Iviii., for the year MDCCLXXXVHI., Part the First, by Sylvanus Urban, Gent.' (February number).

thinking of the poor Africans; let us also think a little of those English men, those English children, who only resemble the Africans in colour; because in point of wretchedness, they are indisputably, a much more poor, and more pitiable race of beings. Many of them, gentle readers, have as yet committed no greater crime than that of being the natural children perhaps, of some relation of yours, or even of*you,*or*you,*or*you.*It is a fact also that they do not often commit crimes; for who remembers a chimney sweeper's coming to be hanged (which calculation would tell us might sometimes happen)? – unless, indeed,*by his own hands,*at the hazard of all that is dear in the next world, in order to avoid all that is dreadful in this.

The story of the boy who, after climbing chimneys in a nobleman's mansion, lay down to rest, and fell asleep on a sumptuous bed, and was not only forgiven, but rescued and educated by the nobleman, because he felt sure that a boy who could venture, in spite of his degradation, to lie on such a bed must have good blood in his veins, is, or was, well known. As it does not appear that the boy was claimed by guardians or kinsfolk, he must have been either a gentleman's illegitimate child or an orphan with hardhearted relations. But if some of the reports current in the eighteenth, and early in the nineteenth, century may be believed, legitimate children were sometimes kidnapped from happy homes to be sold to master sweeps. I had in my childhood a book called ' Timothy Thoughtless,' handed down, I believe, from a previous generation, in which the son of genteel parents having, as far as I remember, played truant, goes through a series of sad adventures, and becomes a climbing boy; he is discovered, long after, by his disconsolate father and mother, who had in vain endeavoured to trace him previously, crying ' Sweep!' in a street, begrimed like his fellows, and laden with his tools and bag of soot.

It has been stated that Mr. Jonas Hanway had taken up the cause of the climbing boys;/he was largely instrumental in obtaining the Act already mentioned, which was passed two years after his death – in 1788. That ThomasBernard may have learned to take an interest in the subject through his acquaintance with Mr. Hanway at the Foundling Hospital is probable. There was a thread of connection between the foundlings and the chimney-sweepers' apprentices, since many of the boys rescued by the Hospital might, but for its intervention, have been in the position of the poor slaves who now swept the chimneys of their comfortable rooms, and Mr. Bernard had evidently collected and stored information as to their condition, which he commenced to utilise so soon as he had formed the Society for Bettering the Condition of the Poor. Some painful facts had recently been brought before Parliament, and he no doubt considered it useless, and even unadvisable, to commence a recapitulation of similar statements. Most of the report he wrote for the Society's first volume was derived from the testimony of David Porter, a master sweep, whom he enlisted as an ally in the crusade, and is of a more encouraging nature, though it begins with the narrative of a breach of the law, induced by hardship:/

1See chapter xi. of this volume.

In December 1791 Charles Eichmond, a little boy, the apprentice of a chimney sweeper in High Street, Marylebone, was convicted at the Old Bailey of a felony in the adjoining house of the Eev. Mr. Buckley.

The circumstances were as follows:

On the preceding Sunday he had run away from his master. He was brought home on Tuesday, and (his master and mistress having occasion to go out) was left locked up by himself. On their return that evening the doors and windows were all fast; but the boy had escaped. On Thursday the master and mistress (on their returning home that day to dinner, and unlocking the door of the house) perceived the boy in the room, with a bundle of woman's clothes, which he said he had found in a cockloft, and had brought home for his mistress. Some circumstances leading to detection, the boy was apprehended, and tried at the Old Bailey; upon his trial it appeared that he had climbed up his master's chimney, and down Mr. Buckley's, where he had stolen the clothes. The boy's account was that' he took the clothes toMASTEE CHIMNEY SWEEPERS 331

1Extract from 'An Account of a Chimney Sweeper's Boy, with Observations and a Proposal for the Eelief of Chimney Sweepers,' by Thomas Bernard, Esq.,*Reports of the Society for Bettering the Condition of the Poor,*vol. i., No. XIX.

prevent his being beat; that when he was unemployed, he was sent to beg in the streets, and that on one Sunday he had begged eight shillings, which his master took from him; another time he brought home a new pair of shoes that some charitable person had given him; they were taken off his feet, and pawned for a few pence.' The boy was convicted; but he was thought more an object of pity than of justice, and on the application of Sheriff Anderson was taken under the protection of the Philanthropic Society.

This was a satisfactory result, so far as the individual boy was concerned, although, from another point of view, it might be called a reward for theft; but it did not alter the system. Mr. Andrews was probably justified in saying that the unfortunate apprentices did not often commit*crimes;*some petty offences, hardly to be called crimes, are no doubt on record, but fewer than might have been expected.

It appears that the masters were in most cases needy men. Mr. Bernard writes:*l*

Of about two hundred master chimney sweepers in London there are not above twenty who can make a decent livelihood by it. in most instances the master is only a lodger, having one room for himself his wife and children, and another, generally a cellar without a fireplace for his soot and his apprentices; without any means of providing for their comfort, health or cleanliness; and without any other bed than the soot bags, which they have been using in the course of their day's work.

It was an aggravation of the unfortunate climbing-boy's lot that as he grew up he became useless.

At the age of sixteen, a period of some additional enjoyment to the generality of mankind, he feels that the increase of stature has unfitted him for the only thing he has been taught; if he then endeavours to become a journeyman chimney-sweeper, (and there are many candidates for one vacancy), his wages, were he to succeed in obtaining a service, are from $3 to $6 a year; and on that miserable pittance, if he should attain the age of twenty-one years without having done anything to incur the penalty of the law, and should*rise*(as it is called) in the world, and become a*master* chimney sweeper, he*then*finds that in London, there are many more persons in the trade than can obtain employment.

1Observations appended to the ' Account of a Chimney Sweeper's Boy,' by Thomas Bernard, Esq.*Reports of the Society for Bettering the Condition of the Poor,*vol. i., No. XIX.

The Act of 1788 (28 Geo. III.) appears to have been mainly procured by the efforts of Mr. Hanway and those he had rallied round him; 1 but it did not represent the wishes of its promoters. The original Bill had passed the House of Commons,' but, unfortunately, the most important and efficient clauses were omitted in the House of Lords '; and the ' Address,' from which I quote, states that ' as it now stands ' it ' is altogether inadequate to the object which it professes to effect.' Its provisoes, moreover, appear to have been disregarded with impunity from the first by a large majority of masters. In order to show what might be done, even under the actual state of the law, and without injury – indeed, with eventual profit to the master – Thomas Bernard gave an account of Porter's treatment of his boys, introducing it with a panegyric as follows:2

I have these facts from a very intelligent and valuable man, Mr. David Porter, a master chimney sweeper in Welbeck Street. An extraordinary energy of mind and body and the protection of Providence, for which he feels a deep and religious gratitude, have preserved him through many hardships and dangers to be the instrument, as I trust, of much good to these unfortunate creatures. Having undergone the sufferings common to a chimney sweeper's boy, he has described them with a warmth and feeling, that do honour to his heart. From the age of eighteen Mr. Porter has lost very few opportunities of improving either his mind or his fortune. He has shown a very favourable specimen of his literary abilities, in what he has written on the subject, and he has brought up and maintained his family, and has improved his fortune, with credit and character. His boys are kindly treated and well kept; and (tho1they make the usual sooty appearance on week days) are cleansed and made neat on Saturday night, or early on Sunday morning; and regularly attend divine service atA GOOD MASTER SWEEPER 383

1In the year before his death Mr. Hanway laid the case before the public in his*Sentimental History of Sweepers in London and Westminster*(1785). (See Hodder's*Life of the seventh Earl of Shaftesbury*,ch. viii.)

2Observations appended to the ' Account of a Chimney Sweeper's Boy,'by Thomas Bernard, Esq.*Reports of the Society for Bettering the Condition of V1e Poor*,vol. i., No. XIX.

church on Sunday. He does not permit his boys to be employed, or sent out on any common work, on the Lord's Day. I lately made him an unexpected visit in order to see them at their Sunday dinner; he had just refused to send two of them to the house of a nobleman, one of his best customers, to do something to the kitchen chimney. I had very great pleasure in seeing his journeymen and boys sitting down to a good meal of boiled mutton and rice pudding, served up with every circumstance of cleanliness and comfort. Their behaviour was decent, orderly, and cheerful. In proof of the good effects of his attention to them, I have to add that in thirty-two years he has lost only two apprentices by death; and as to the dreadful disease called the chimney-sweeper's cancer, a disorder so common and so fatal to the climbing boys (and which appears to be caused by the acrimonious quality of soot, and by an obstructed perspiration in consequence of the children being so seldom washed and cleaned of the soot, and too thinly clad to resist the cold) his apprentices have never had any symptoms of it.

This, however, is an extraordinary and unprecedented history; but it affords valuable information, as it shows what may be done for the benefit of these poor creatures. Of their present condition it is not exaggeration to say, that there is no other species of slavery existing in the world more derogatory to the rights of human nature.

The system of employing boys could not, indeed, be abolished offhand; it has been seen that there was opposition in high quarters even to its alleviation. Mr. Bernard, however, made another attempt in that direction, profiting by the practical experience of the good ' Master Sweeper.' He continues:

What Mr. Porter recommends, is that a Society or Corporation be formed, for the protection of Climbing Boys during the period of their apprenticeship, and for putting them out to other trades at sixteen years of age when that period expires; – that their beds, clothing, and domestic accommodation, shall be put under a regular system of inspection, and from time to time, be reported to the Society; – that the children shall be cleaned, and have a change of dress, so as, on Sunday, regularly to attend Church; and that they shall have, on that day, a comfortable dinner provided for them, at the Society's expense, in a Sunday school; thereby securing to them a periodical return of cleanliness and civilisationevery week; – that no boy shall ever be allowed to cry the streets of London, a practice that has been the cause of the greatest part of the hardships that the Climbing Boys undergo, and which is no more necessary in this, than in any other trade in London; – and lastly, that apprentice fees be given with such of the lads as shall attain the age of sixteen, and prefer a trade, and to those who shall choose to continue as journeymen in the trade, or shall enter into the sea service, a similar fee, at the age of twenty-one, in order to assist them in setting up in business.

Such are the outlines of a plan, which, if the subject is favourably received, may be soon ready to be submitted to the consideration of the public.

This report is dated ' 4th December 1797.' In May 1799 Bishop Barrington contributed another paper on the subject to the ' Reports of the Society for Bettering the Condition of the Poor,' lby which it appears that Porter had published a scheme for the formation of a Friendly Society of Master Chimney Sweepers, whose members should pledge themselves to adopt the suggestions mentioned by Mr. Bernard for the improvement of their apprentices' condition, ' and to apply to the magistrates in those cases where the Act of Parliament remains unexecuted.' Nothing further had as yet been accomplished in London; but the Bishop was able to state that climbing boys had been admitted into the School of Kingston-upon-Thames, and that a benevolent lady had furnished each of these Kingston boys with a suit of clothes, a palliasse, a pair of blankets, and a washing-tub. He also announced that an enlarged account of David Porter's scheme would shortly be published.

This scheme appears to have been cast in its final shape by Mr. Bernard after consultation with the Bishop and other friends. The Duchess of Gloucester became patroness; Mrs. Montague, the accomplished lady who had already signalised herself by feasting all the climbing boys in London every first of May, vice-patroness; the Bishop of DurhamA FAILURE 335

1*Reports of the Society for Bettering the Condition of the Poor.*Extract from ' An Account of a Provision for Chimney Sweepers' Boys at Kingston ' upon-Thames, with Observations,' by the Bishop of Durham, vol. ii., No. L.

President for the ensuing year. A note at the end of the Articles of Agreement/states that:

These articles have been signed by eighteen of the principal masters in the trade, and fifty-six chimney-sweepers' boys have been thereby placed under the care and protection of the Society. The Articles are left for signatures at No 7 Welbeck Street, and little doubt can be entertained, but that they will be speedily signed by every respectable Master Chimney Sweeper, whose conduct will bear inspection and inquiry. The Committee sits every first Wednesday in the month, at three o'clock. 39th May, 1800.

Mr. Bernard's biographer considers that this scheme proved a failure. The re-spectable chimney-sweepers had signed the articles, but they were few in number; those who were not respectable did not sign, but continued to ill- treat their appren-tices, and they formed a large majority. The sole chance of influencing them lay in persuading householders to employ the signing chimney-sweepers in preference to others, and in procuring convictions for flagrant instances of the violation of the Act of Parliament. ' The public mind, however,' as Mr. Baker puts it, ' was not then ready for the consideration of the state of these destitute children,' and so the first suggestion met with little or no response. As to the second, it was so difficult for friendless boys to proceed against their employers, even with the help of the Society, and to establish their grievances, in the adverse condition of public opinion, that all hope of effectual remedy from such proceedings appeared to have been abandoned as fallacious.

Thus Mr. Baker concludes the subject, as if it had ended in despair, which, indeed would not have been surprising. But it was not like Thomas Bernard to abandon a cause into which he had once thrown his energies; and there canbe no reasonable doubt that he was a promoter of the movement, dating from this very time, for the invention of a sweeping machine.

1See ' Copy of an Agreement of the 19th of March, 1800, between several Master Chimney Sweepers within the Liberties of Westminster and the Holborn Division of the County of Middlesex, for forming a Friendly Society for the Protection and Instruction of their Apprentices.' Appendix XL to vol. ii. of the*Reports of the Society B. CJ*.*

In this movement lay the gist of the whole question. It had become clear that little hope could be entertained for the young victims, except by rendering them unnecessary, and that a machine was the most feasible means of thus revolutionising the system. Whose was the original idea, I know not; like other inventions, it had probably occupied many minds before anything was done; but the first mention I have met with is the following:1

In the year 1802 a number of public-spirited and wealthy persons associated for this purpose, and offered considerable premiums to those who might invent and bring into practice a method of cleansing chimneys by mechanical means that should supersede the necessity of Climbing Boys. Feeling themselves, perhaps, inadequate to the task of carrying their laudable intentions into full execution, they applied to the Society for the Encouragement of Arts, Manufactures, &c in the Adelphi, requesting them to engage in it, and to offer premiums on the subject.

Five curious inventions were produced, and the gold medal was gained by Mr. George Smart, ' the patentee of a method of making hollow masts for ships.' His machine was at once brought into use in some houses, and was found to answer everywhere except when a deflection in the flue rendered ascent impossible. In 1803 two patents were taken out, one by Mr. Bell of Hampstead, the other by Mr. Davis of Bloomsbury, for machines to be worked from above. Another method, apparently not modern, was practised at Edinburgh and other Northern places, which consisted in two persons, one below and one above, dragging up and down a cord to which was attached a holly bough.

From a pamphlet published in 18162I gather that theAN INFLUENTIAL MEETING 337

1Bees (Abraham),*The Cyclopadia, or Universal Dictionary,*vol. vii., ' Chimney'; Longman, Hurst, Rees, Orme & Brown, 1819.

' *A. Short Account of the Proceedings of the Society for Superseding the Necessity of Climbing Boys, ttc., $c.*London: Printed by C. Baldwin, New Bridge Street. It was sold for the Society by Baldwin, Cradock,&Jay, – Hatchard, – and Colbum (1816).

association which took up this question called itself the ' Society for Superseding the Necessity of Climbing Boys, by encouraging a new Method of Sweeping Chimneys, and for Improving the Condition of Children and others employed by Chimney

Sweepers.' Its establishment as a society dated from February 4, 1803, and as the Bishop of Durham was president, and William Wilberforce, Henry Thornton, and other persons connected with Thomas Bernard's charitable labours were vice-presidents, his influence may be clearly traced in its formation, although his name does not appear. 1 It would seem, from the article quoted above, that Smart's machine was the favourite; but it required various improvements to adapt it to the varieties of chimneys, and these had been carried out by 1815 to an extent which rendered it suitable for general use. A plan of dropping a weight and brush downwards, borrowed, perhaps, from one or both of the other patented machines, and resembling the simple Scottish arrangement, was substituted in chimneys which could not be swept mechanically from below.

Meanwhile, attempts were made in 1804, 1807, 1808, and 1809 to induce Parliament to grant further protection to the little chimney sweepers. Yet matters remained much as before when an influential meeting was held at the Mansion House on June 12, 1816, on behalf of the cause.

The pamphlet already quoted was published soon after; it notes that several local societies had formed themselves with the view of forwarding the same object; and especially that the inhabitants of Walthamstow and Leyton had passed a resolution at a public meeting against the employment of climbing boys. It might be supposed that the horrors set forth courageously in this pamphlet would have been sufficient to enlist all England on the same side.

Case I. is as follows:

A few years ago, a chimney belonging to the House of Messrs. Coutts & Co., Bankers, Strand, being on fire, a boy was sent up to extinguish it. He climbed up part of the way, but was not able to proceed farther, on account of the fire. This was in a sloping part of the flue, where, having thrust some of the burning soot behind him, he might literally be said to be between two fires; in order to save his life it became necessary to make a hole in the wall from the inside, and he was fortunately taken out alive.

1 It does not appear in the pamphlet of 1816. Whether it may in some other publication of the Society I cannot tell.

VOL. IU. Z

Case II.:

About the beginning of the year 1806 a boy was sent up a chimney in the house of Mr. Creed, Navy Agent, No. 23, Hans Place, Knightsbridge. Being unable to extricate himself, he remained there about half-an-hour, while a person went to fetch assistance. A hole was made through the brickwork, and the boy at length released. It appeared that in consequence of the unusual construction of the flue in one part a vast quantity of soot had accumulated there, into which the boy had plunged, and was not able, probably from partial suffocation, to get back again. So dangerous was the sweeping of this chimney considered, that James Dunn, Chimney Sweeper, No. 46 Hans Town, refused to let his apprentice ascend the flue.

In Case VI.:

A boy employed to sweep a chimney in Marsh Street, Walthamstow, in the house of a carpenter named Jeffery, stuck fast in the flue. Mr. Jeffery heard his cries and sent for help; the chimney-pot and several rows of bricks having been removed, he was brought out alive, but only just alive. His master was sent for, and he arrived soon after the boy had been released. He abused him for the accident, and after striking him, sent him with a bag of soot to sweep another chimney. The child appeared so very weak when taken out that he could scarcely stand, and yet this wretched being, who had been up since three o'clock, had before been sent by his master to Wanstead, which, with his walk to Marsh Street, made about five miles.

I now come to cases which terminated fatally, either on the spot or soon after removal. Whether the child whose misfortune has just been narrated lived long may be doubted.

Cash V.:

In the course of improvements made some years since by the Bank of England in Lothbury, a chimney belonging to a Mr. Mildrum, a baker, was taken down; but before he began to bake, THE HOEEOES OF CHIMNEY SWEEPING 339

in order to see that the rest of the flue was clear, a boy was sent up, and after remaining some time, and not answering to the call of his master, another boy was ordered to descend from the top of the flue and to meet him halfway. But this being found impracticable, they opened the brickwork in the lower part of the flue, and found the first-mentioned boy dead. In the meantime, the boy in the upper part of the flue called out for relief, saying he was completely jammed in the rubbish, and was unable to extricate himself. Upon this a bricklayer was employed with the utmost expedition, but he succeeded only in obtaining a lifeless body. The bodies were sent to St. Margaret's Church, Lothbury, and a coroner's inquest which sat upon them, returned the verdict – ' Accidental death '!

In Case VIII.:

a boy lost his life in Orchard Street through descending into a wrong flue, after he had swept up to the top; faint and giddy, perhaps, even when he had only begun his work, he probably became every moment more exhausted, and attempting to hurry away from his place of torture the first possible moment, was fatally bewildered in the complicated structure; his mistake brought him too near a lighted fire. The verdict' Accidentally suffocated' I In this instance, also, another boy was exposed to danger by being sent up to find the first, but survived.

Case IX. is the story of

a boy of twelve, at Wakefield, in Yorkshire, who was cruelly burned while in the right chimney, because the fire in the neighbouring chimney of John Byron, which communicated by a flue, had not been thoroughly extinguished. He died after four days' suffering. ' N. B. The said Byron and his wife were capitally indicted, and tried at the York Assizes for the alleged murder, but were acquitted.'

Perhaps the most distressing narrative of all is the next Case, X.:

On Monday morning the 29th of March, 1813, a chimney sweeper of the name of Griggs, attended to sweep a small chimney in the brewhouse of Messrs. Calvert & Co. in Upper Thames Street; he was accompanied by one of his boys, a lad of about eight years of age, of the name of Thomas Pitt. The fire had been lighted as early as two o'clock the same morning, and was burning on the arrival of Griggs and his little boy at eight; the fire-place was small, and an iron pipe projected from the grate some little distance into the flue; this the master was acquainted with (having swept the chimneys in the brewhouse for some years,) and therefore had a tile or two taken from the roof, in order that the boy might descend the chimney. He had no sooner extinguished the fire than he suffered the lad to go down, and the consequence as might be expected, was his almost immediate death, in a state no doubt of inexpressible agony. The flue was of the narrowest description, and must have retained heat sufficient to have prevented the child's return to the top, even supposing he had not approached the pipe belonging to the grate, which must have been nearly red hot; this however, was not clearly ascertained on the Inquest, though the appearance of the body would induce an opinion that he had been unavoidably pressed against the pipe. Soon after his descent, the master, who remained on the top, was apprehensive that something had happened, and therefore desired him to come up, the answer of the boy was, ' I cannot come up, Master, I must die here.' An alarm was given in the brewhouse immediately, that he had*stuck*in the chimney; and a bricklayer who was at work near the spot, attended, and after knocking down part of the brickwork of the chimney, first above the fireplace, made a hole sufficiently large to draw him through. A surgeon attended, but all attempts to restore life were ineffectual.

On inspecting the body, various burns appeared; the fleshy part of the legs, and a great part of the feet, more particularly, were injured; those parts too by which Climbing Boys most effectually ascend or descend chimneys, viz., the elbows and knees, seemed burnt to the bone, from which it must be evident that the unhappy sufferer made some attempt to return as soon as the horrors of his situation became apparent.

His death, from this account, cannot have been ' almost immediate,' as stated near the beginning of the report. A jury sat for two days, and returned a most elaborate verdict; but, strange to say, containing no word even of censure on the master. It runs as follows:

That the master was employed to clean a certain chimney at the brewhouse of Messrs. Calvert & Co. situate, &c. and that he set the deceased, an infant of about eight years, to clean the said chimney for him. That deceased accordingly got into and descended the said chimney for the purpose of cleaning the same, THE HORRORS OF CHIMNEY SWEEPING 341

and that by the straitness and narrowness of the chimney, and by the heat thereof, a fire having just been in the grate thereof, the deceased was burned and hurt on divers parts of his body; and also by the foulness and unwholesomeness of the air in the said chimney, the deceased was suffocated; of which said burning, hurts, and suffocation, the deceased then and there died; and so the jurors upon their oath say, that he died in the manner aforesaid, and by misfortune came to his death.

The cause of death was sometimes varied, as in*Case*IV.:

A boy named Sharpless, in the employ of MTM- Whitfield, Little Shire Lane, Temple Bar, fell from the upper part of a chimney in July, or August, 1804, in Devereux Court. The chimney-pot falling, or upper part of the chimney giving way, occasioned this accident. The boy had several bones fractured, and being carried to St. Bartholomew's Hospital, died there in a short time.

It was probably in consequence of the attempts made by a child, about six, to escape ' the horrors of chimney-sweeping,' which enraged his master and mistress, who beat bim to death, that they were tried for murder, though acquitted; the husband, however, ' was detained to take his trial as for a misdemeanour,' and sentenced to two years' imprisonment. In another case, where the guilt was scarcely less, the master escaped scot-free, as will be seen.

On Friday Morning, February 12,1808, a climbing Apprentice to Holland, in East Street, Lambeth, was sent at three in the morning to sweep some chimneys at Norwood. The snow was so deep, and the cold so extreme, that a watchman used the remarkable expression ' That he would not have sent even a dog out.' The boy, having swept two chimneys, was returning home in company with another boy, but at length found the cold so excessive, that he could go no further. After some little time, he was taken to the Half Moon public-house at Dulwich, and died in the course of an hour. It was supposed that by proper care his life might have been preserved. The master-sweep was brought to the Union Hall Southwark, by Mr. Bowes the Magistrate. Upon examining him, his principal fault appeared to be sending the boy out so early, and he was dismissed. A Coroner's Inquest was held upon the body, and a verdict was returned – ' Died from the Inclemency of the Weather.'

The clothing of this boy, as of most of his fellow-slaves, would no doubt be ' a bundle of rags, half stitched together, and half torn to pieces,' his food, if supplied by his master, scanty and unwholesome; but in many cases the boys depended for sustenance entirely on the charity of the persona whose chimneys they swept, and were necessarily driven to begging, and even to thieving, when this resource failed.

Mr. Wright, the doctor who notes these deficiencies in food and clothing, also remarks on ' the stunted growth,' and ' the deformity of the spine, legs, arms, &c., of chimneysweepers '; their ' sore eyes and eyelids,' and further' liability to sores which were generally a long time in healing'; to burns, as a necessary consequence of their employment, to cancer, cough and asthma, which often terminated their miserable lives prematurely.1

From this description it is evident that the survivors must as a rule have recruited the ranks of the pauper and criminal population. Yet it appears that when the Society had promoted ' a Bill in Parliament to supply deficiencies in the existing one,' which passed the Commons, it was rejected by the Lords.

To this Bill Mr. Hodder alludes when he says: * ' The subject was referred in 1817 to a Select Committee, and the printed report is a record of sickening horrors.' Some of these horrors were narrated by the Rev. Sydney Smith in the ' Edinburgh Review.'3The writer was certainly in some matters a fellow-worker with Thomas Bernard – at his first arrival in London he might almost be styled a*prottgi* – and there is every probability that on the failure of the measure on which the friends of the poor little sweeps had foundedTHE HORRORS OF CHIMNEY SWEEPING 343

1These particulars are found in a letter from ' Richard Wright,' dated from ' 389 Rotherhithe, July 16,1816,' and apparently addressed to the ' Society for Superseding the Necessity of Climbing Boys,'in whose ' Short Account' it is included. Mr. Wright is described in this pamphlet as ' a very able medical practitioner.'

*Hodder,*The Life and Work of the seventh Earl of Shaftesbtiry, K. O.*

* *Edinburgh Review,*No. LXIV., October 1819: 'An Account of the Proceedings of the Society for Superseding the Necessity of Climbing Boys.'

their hopes, Sir Thomas, as he then was, urged this young adherent to employ his powerful pen in the cause.

The horrors detailed in the article then written equal or surpass anything that has been previously noted in these pages. It appears that children had sometimes been sent up chimneys at five years of age; that some of the children employed were girls; that some of the master-sweeps, being nightmen, their smallest apprentices were often employed, when chimney work was slack – that is, of course, during the summer – in other loathsome and deleterious work; that they were mercilessly beaten if they showed any fear, and that their sores were not dressed, but rubbed with brine to stop the bleeding. There is a heart-rending account of a boy who was burned to death, slowly, in an Edinburgh chimney, amid the threats and blasphemies of his master. Twice the writer expatiates on the elegances and luxuries of a fashionable dinner-party, and then turns to its dark side:

In the midst of all this who knows that the kitchen-chimney caught fire half an hour before dinner, and that a poor little wretch, of six or seven years old, was sent up in the midst of flames, to put it out?

Yet, after these and other shocking details, the Rev. Sydney Smith concludes:

We should have been very glad to have seconded the views of the Climbing Society, and to have pleaded for the complete abolition of Climbing Boys, if we could conscientiously have done so. But such a measure, we are convinced by the evidence, could not be carried into execution without great injury to property, and great increased risk of fire. The Lords have investigated the matter with the greatest patience, humanity, and good sense, and they do not venture, in their Report, to recommend to the House the abolition of Climbing Boys.

It may be observed that the Bill had been thrown out in 1817; the article did not appear till 1819, and between those two dates Sir Thomas Bernard died – 1818. Had he lived to talk it over exhaustively with the writer, during the process of composition, it would perhaps not have been marred by so lame a conclusion.

A few words are still necessary as to the continuation of the struggle. In 1834, an Act was actually passed containing some important ameliorations; in 1840, when Lord Ashley (afterwards Earl of Shaftesbury)/took up the cause, another Act followed, by which all who should compel or knowingly allow any person under the age of twenty-one years to ascend a chimney or flue were punishable by a fine. The wording of the Act and the feeling of the country against it, led, however, to continual evasion.

Some few years after that time, I can remember the annoyance of my father, who was then a magistrate, at finding that a boy had been sent up his kitchen chimney at Nether Winchendon. This fact he discovered through his habit of early rising; his servants saw no harm at all in the practice. I may state also that even later I was amazed by finding that a very sweet and kind-hearted lady, the daughter of a conscientious clergyman, could not see any objection to making use of boys, and the inconsistency of thus employing them – in a charitable institution for children even – did not strike her.

It is true that in both these cases the chimneys were shorter and wider than most of the chimneys in towns; but the same principle was involved. The argument, however, was in these and other cases that machines were of little or no use – could not, in fact, be got up some chimneys.

And this mention of machines shows the connecting link between the efforts of Thomas Bernard and his coadjutors, and the final triumph of Lord Shaftesbury – member, as he was for many years, first of the House of Commons, then of the House of Peers. A gifted speaker, beginning his contest in the prime of life, and continuing it to old age, he could never have won it at all so far as it is possible to judge, had not one or more of the machines invented in the very beginning of the century been brought to somethingTHE EARL OF SHAFTESBURY 345

1Hodder,*Life of the seventh Earl of Shaftesbury,*chap. viii.

like perfection. So early as 1840l' Every Fire Insurance Company in London, except one, had adopted machines for sweeping chimneys, and recommended their adoption to others,' and they were extensively used in London before other parts of England would reform their ways. Three Bills to amend the previous mistakes failed, and the Commons were as inimical as the Lords. An Act, however, passed in 1864, making the master who made use of climbing boys punishable with imprisonment and hard labour.

Even this somehow failed to annihilate the evil. In 1872 Lord Shaftesbury brought the matter forward once more. Cases were stated of three boys recently killed in flues; and, in 1875, an Act passed, which is supposed to have rolled away this reproach from England – certainly none too soon.

1Hodder,*Life of (ha seventh Earl of Shaftesbury,*chap. viii.

CHAPTER XVIII

CHILDBEN IN COTTON MILLS

Invention of the Fly-shuttle and the ' Spinning Jenny' – The Inventions of Richard Arkwright and Samuel Crompton, and Dr. Cartwright and Robert Millar – The Creation of a Demand for Child Labour – The Use of Parish Apprentices – Edwin Hodder's description of the Employment of Children in Mills – Public Protest against the Employment of Children – Thomas Bernard attacks the System – David Dale's Mills – Thomas Bernard's Strictures upon the System in Force – Regulations suggested by him – Strength of the Mill-owning Interest – Sir Robert Peel introduces a Bill for the Amelioration of the Children's Condition-The Opposition to the Bill – The Second Bill.

I HAVE in this chapter to notice another foul blot on the civilisation and Christianity of England – a blot which stands out in hideous relief all the more prominently in that it defaces the annals of a nation which prides itself particularly on its domestic life. Strange, indeed, is the fact that this country, which glories especially in its religion and virtue, has been so remarkable for utter heartlessness in its treatment of children.

The extraordinary development of manufactures, through the use of machinery in the latter half of the eighteenth century, led to a rapidly increasing demand for hands to work the machinery. How was the difficulty of finding apprentices to be met? According to a French historian, Pitt, the Prime Minister, said: ' Take the children.' I do not know, however, that the onus can be laid in any special manner on the Premier; but the Legislature as a body was certainly guilty, and the whole nation, in its measure and degree, since it condoned and connived at the sacrifice of these innocents to

Mammon, and clung with marvellous tenacity to the system of immolation. As to
theTHE SPINNING-JENNY 347

guilt of those persons who were directly concerned in the traffic it is superfluous to
speak.

Up to the year 1738 the English hand-loom weaver [writes Mr. If odder '] was
in no better case, as regarded his implements, than the ' rude, unlettered Indian';
but in 1738, John Kay, of Bury, substituted the fly-shuttle for the hand-shuttle, by
which the production of the hand-loom was trebled. Other improvements followed;
and in 1767, Mr. James Hargreaves, a hand- loom weaver of Blackburn, patented his
' spinning-jenny.' So great was the saving of labour effected by this machine that
the spinners were up in arms; they broke into his house, and destroyed the machine.
When, however, the advantages became apparent, fresh machines were brought into
use, but these in like manner were destroyed, and Hargreaves quitted Lancashire in
disgust, and settled in Nottingham, where he erected a mill.

Following close upon the inventions of Hargreaves, came those of Eichard Arkwright and Samuel Crompton, by whose genius the production of yarn had increased
three hundred-fold; and to these again succeeded the inventions of Dr. Cartwright,
a clergyman of the Church of England, and of Mr. Eobert Millar, a calico-printer of
Glasgow, so that towards the end of last century the condition of the cotton manufacturing population was completely changed. Instead of working in their homes they
were obliged to work in mills; and instead of being comparatively their own masters,
working when they would, they were under masters who made them work for what
wages they chose to give, and during what hours they chose to dictate.

Eemonstrance was in vain; water could now be employed to do the harder part
of the work formerly done by the men, who, if they were refractory, could be sent
adrift; and machinery was invented which children could manage with almost as much
success as adults.

In this way a demand for child-labour was created, and the supply was not deficient.
But it was effected in a manner which scarcely seems credible to the humanity of to-
day; large bodies of children were drafted from the workhouses of London, Edinburgh,
and other great cities, and placed in the mills as ' apprentices,' where, at the discretion
of sordid overseers, they were worked unmercifully, and treated with such brutality
that the recital is too sickening for narration.

1Eodder (Edwin),*The Life and Work of the seventh Earl of Shaftesbury,*chap. iii.
(Popular Edition),

It appears that the lightness of the labour was put forward at first as an excuse, or
even sufficient reason, for the employment of children. The author of a ' Life of Sir
Bobert Peel,'*l*being naturally anxious to place the system in the best point of view,
observes that:

The real tendency of improvements in machinery is, to substitute the light toil of
feeding the engines, and superintending their work, for mere exertions of physical
strength; hence women and children can be employed in cotton mills without having
their strength overtasked, because the chief requisites of their occupation are regularity,
vigilance, and attention. But a uniformity of work, however light, would, when too

long continued, produce an injurious effect on the physical and mental constitution, particularly in childhood.

After this bland statement, it is instructive to find the details of this trade in children set forth without disguise, as in the following passage:

Under the operation of the Factories' Apprentice System parish apprentices were sent without remorse or inquiry from the workhouses in England, and the public charities of Scotland, to be ' used up' as the ' cheapest raw material in the market.' This inhuman conduct was systematically practised – the mill-owners communicated with the overseer of the poor, and when the demand and supply had been arranged to the satisfaction of both the contracting parties,&day was fixed for the examination of ' the little children' to be inspected by the millowner, or his agent, previous to which the authorities of the workhouse had filled the minds of the wards with the notion that, by entering the mills, they would become ladies and gentlemen. On the day appointed, the children were drawn up to be inspected and selected; those chosen were then conveyed by coach, by waggon, or boat, to their destination, and, as a rule, from that moment were lost to their friends and relatives. It sometimes happened that traffickers contracted with the overseers, removing their juvenile victims to Manchester, or other towns. On their arrival, if not previously assigned, they were deposited sometimes in dark cellars, where the merchant dealing in them brought his customers; the mill-owners, by the light of lanterns, being enabled to examine the children. Their limbs and stature having undergone the necessaryTHE FIRST SIR ROBERT PEEL 349

l*ftife of Bobert Peel*(published anonymously, 1842),

scrutiny, the bargain was struck, and those poor ' innocents' were conveyed to the mills.

The general treatment of those apprentices depended entirely on the will of their masters; in very many instances their labour was limited only by exhaustion, after many modes of torture had been unavailingly applied to force continued action; their food was stinted, coarse, and unwholesome; in ' brisk times' their beds (such as they were) were never cool, the mills were worked night and day, and as soon as one set of children rose for labour the other set retired for rest. Discrimination of sexes was not regarded; vice, disease, and death, luxuriated in those receptacles of human woe. We dare not trust ourselves to write all we know on this subject, much less all we feel, the cases stated hereafter are representative of the system. The moral nature of the traffic between parish authorities and the buyers of pauper children may be judged from the fact that in some cases one idiot was accepted with twenty sane children. A question arises – What was the fate of these idiots? – that secret has not been revealed. (Pp. 16-17).

Space will not allow me to give the detailed accounts of the cases of hardship to which allusion is made in the last extract, and it is the less necessary since students of Lord Shaftesbury's life cannot fail to have a fairly clear idea of this iniquitous system. At this time Lord Shaftesbury was not yet born.1The first Sir Eobert Peel, who, when awakened to the conviction of the means by which his great fortune had been made, did his best to repair the mischief, expressed his remorse for having, night after night, year after year, gone comfortably to sleep while the children in his employ were toiling till daybreak and later.

To return to the pamphlet already quoted. The writer adds:

Little children have been worked for sixteen hours and upwards; with few and trifling intermissions, day and night have been devoted to almost constant labour; a portion of the Sabbath has been for these helpless ones appropriated to toil. In stench, in heated rooms, amid the constant whirling of a thousand wheels have little fingers and little feet been kept in ceaseless action, forced into unnatural activity by blows from the heavy hands andfeet of the merciless overlooker, and the infliction of bodily pain by instruments invented by the sharpened ingenuity of insatiable selfishness. Tens of thousands of' the little children' in those mills have been destroyed because of their owners' lust of gold.

1He was born in 1801, when the system hud been many years in operation.

Mr. Hodder's description is, perhaps, even more forcible; but I have only space for a portion. In process of time he states that:

A horrible traffic had sprung up; child-jobbers scoured the country for the purpose of purchasing children to sell them again into the bondage of factory slaves. The waste of human life in the manufactories to which the children were consigned was simply frightful. Day and night the machinery was kept going; one gang of children working it by day, and another by night, while, in times of pressure, the same children were kept working day and night by remorseless task-masters

Stage by stage they sank into the profoundest depths of wretchedness. In weariness they often fell upon the machinery, and almost every factory child was more or less injured through hunger, neglect, over-fatigue, and poisonous air; they died in terrible numbers, swept off by contagious fevers.

There was no redress of any kind. The isolation of the mills aided the cruelties practised in them. The children could not escape, as rewards were offered for their capture and were eagerly sought; they could not complain when the visiting magistrate came, for they were in abject fear of their task-masters, and, moreover on those days the house was swept and garnished for the anticipated visit, and appearances would have given the lie to complaints; if they perished in the machinery, it was a rare thing for a coroner's inquest to be held, and rarer still for it to issue in anything but a commonplace verdict. And when the time came that their indentures expired, after years of toil, averaging fourteen hours a day, with their bodies scarred with the wounds inflicted by the overlookers – with their minds dwarfed and vacant, with their constitutions in many instances, hopelessly injured; in profound ignorance that there was even the semblance of law for their protection – these unfortunate apprentices, arrived at manhood, found that they had never been taught the trade they should have learned, and that they had no resource but to enter again upon the hateful life from which they were legally freed. Should it happen that they had become crippled or diseased during their apprenticeship, their wages were fixed at the lowest possible sum, and their future was a long lingering death.

A BITTER HERITAGE 351

And thus a bitter heritage was left to succeeding generations – a population, physically, mentally, and morally degraded, and imbued with traditions and memories of their own and their parents' wrongs. Strange that King George, the kind-hearted monarch, whose virtues are popularly supposed to have redeemed the evil deeds of his race, and who was not too constitutional to oppose his ministers and his people vigorously when his own wishes were concerned, had no thought for these infantine victims – nor his ' good Queen Charlotte' either! After reading about the horrors of George III.'s time, it is impossible to wonder at the barbarities of previous ages.

It must not be supposed that the facts were not known. Mr. Hodder says:

As early as 1796 voices were raised in protest against the cruel wrongs inflicted on these poor children, who were continually being sent down to Lancashire by barge-loads by the London workhouses; but in the excitement of the stirring events that were then occurring at home and abroad, those voices were unheeded. Meantime the condition of these unfortunate children was growing from bad to worse, until at last the cruelty of the system under which they were held was hardly paralleled by the abominations of negro-slavery.

It appears, indeed, that voices were raised in protest earlier than 179(5. In a book containing a general review of the duties and responsibilities of the upper classes, of which the third edition was published in 1795, Mr. Thomas Gisborne1 called attention to the abuses in cotton mills. He says:

The ready communication of contagion to numbers crowded together, the accession of virulence from putrid effluvia, and the injury done to young persons, through confinement and too long continued labour are evils which we have lately heard ascribed to cotton mills by persons of the first medical authority assembled to investigate the subject.

1Gisborne (Thomas, M. A.),*An Enquiry into the Duties of Men in the Higher and Middle Classes of Society in Great Britain,*vol. ii., chap. xiii.:' On the Duties of Persons engaged in Trade and Business,' Third Edition, 1795.

It appears that in consequence of an outbreak of putrid fever at the Radcliffe Cotton Mills, the magistrates of the county of Lancaster had requested Dr. Percival and other Manchester physicians to draw up a Report, from which the preceding details were taken by Mr. Gisborne, who continues:

To these must be added an evil, which still brands with disgrace the practice of some cotton-mills, – the custom of obliging a part of the children employed to work all night; a practice which must greatly contribute towards rendering them feeble, diseased, and unfit for other labour, when they are dismissed at a more advanced period of youth from the manufactory.

Important recommendations had been set forth in the Eeport for the better management of mills, but neither magistrates nor physicians appear to have had any hold on the mill-owner. Voices were uplifted elsewhere, and pens set in motion in the cause of humanity, but with little result. Mr. Bernard had resolved to attack this iniquitous system, of which he may have learned some minuter particulars from Mr. Gisborne, who had contributed papers on kindred subjects to the Society's' Eeports.' /But Mr. Bernard began cautiously, as was his wont, avoiding reflections on individuals. In the case of climbing boys, he had brought forward Mr. Porter's regulation of his house as an example of what might be accomplished by a just and benevolent master; and he now set before mill-owners the organisation of Mr. Dale's establishment as a model for imitation.

A letter written by the Rev. Sydney Smith,2apparently to a Mrs. Beach, in 1798, nearly two years before Mr. Bernard took up the subject in the 'Reports,' shows that he had been a visitor to Mr. Dale's mills. Possibly Mr. Bernard may have suggested his paying this call while in the neighbourhood, or it may have been Mr. Smith whoDAVID DALE'S MILLS 353

1I assume his identity with the Bev. Thomas Gisborne, who wrote on Supplying the Poor with Milk '; ' The Duke of Bridgewater's Colliers,' and The Situation of the Mining Poor,' in the Society's*Reports.*

2*Memoirs of the Rev. Sydney Smith,*by his Daughter, Lady Holland, vol. i,, chap. ii.

first mentioned these mills in terms of praise to his friend. On these points I have no information; but I give his account of this visit, as preceding, in order of time, Mr. Bernard's fuller description:

Nothing struck me more than the Courtland Crags, near Lanark. A small river has worked its passage, of ten or twelve feet in breadth, through rocks that tower three hundred feet above it on each side; the passage is hah" a mile long. Consider what a scene this must be! Near Lanark is settled Mr. David Dale; he alone employs in cotton works seventeen hundred souls. He is a very religious and benevolent man, and is remarkably attentive to the morals, as well as to the comfort and happiness of the manufacturing children. They are admirably instructed and brought up, with an attention to cleanliness that is truly delightful. He very often gives them a dance. The evening we were there, after the hours of work, there was a general country dance, of about two hundred couples. We knew nothing of it till the following morning, or of course should not have missed so pleasing a spectacle. I love to see the beauties of nature; but I love better to see the hand of active piety stretch forth to such young orphans as these the innocent pleasures of life, the benefit of instruction and the blessings of religion. It is dreadful to observe in Manchester and Birmingham how manufacturers brutalize mankind, – how small the interval between*a weaver and a beast I* – What does his country not owe to a man who has promoted industry without propagating vice, who has enlarged the boundaries of commerce and strengthened the ties of moral obligation.

Mr. Bernard's paper, dated ' February 24th, 1800,' which appeared in the ' Reports ' of the Society for Bettering the Condition of the Poor, goes more thoroughly into the subject, and is here transcribed in full:*l*

The Cotton Mills at New Lanark in Scotland, are situated in a beautiful and romantic amphitheatre, near the high road between Carlisle and Glasgow. The rapid stream of the Clyde suppliesthat abundance of water which is the powerful operator of the machinery. For the purpose of conveying and directing its power, a subterraneous aqueduct is cut for many hundred yards through the solid rock. The first mill, in length 154 feet, was originally erected in 1785, and, having been burnt down, was rebuilt in 1789. The second is exactly of the same dimensions; the third is 130 feet and the fourth 156 feet in length.

1Extract from' An Account of Mr. Dale's Cotton Mills at New Lanark in Scotland,' by Thomas Bernard, Esq.,*Reports of the Society B. C. P.,*vol. ii., No. LXIX. In vol. iv. of the*Reports,*No. OIL, the subject is followed up by a paper called ' Extract from an Account of the Cotton Mills at Rothsay in the Isle of Bute, by Mr. Carr, of Leeds.' He is able to state that Messrs. Bannatine and Buchanan of Glasgow, who furnished him with particulars, and other mill-

VOL. III. A A

The two first mills contain 12,000 spindles for spinning water- twist; the other two are occupied by jennies for spinning mule yarn. The village of New Lanark owes its existence to the erection of these mills. It consists of neat substantial houses; forming two streets about half a mile in length, and broad, regular, and clean. Near the centre of the village are the mills, and opposite to them a neat mansion, the occasional residence of Mr. Dale, the proprietor, and of his principal manager. The village consisting chiefly of Highlanders from the counties of Argyle, Caithness, and Inverness, contains about 1,500 inhabitants; of whom all who are capable of work are employed in and about the mills.

Of these there are 300 children who are entirely fed, clothed, and educated by Mr. Dale. The others lodge with their parents, in the village, and have a weekly allowance for their work.

The healthy and pleasurable appearance of these children has frequently attracted the attention of the traveller. Peculiar regulations, adopted by Mr. Dale for the preservation of the health and morals of those under his protection, have made this striking difference between his manufactory and many other similar undertakings in this kingdom; so that while some other mills must be regarded as seminaries of vice, and sources of disease, those at Lanark are so peculiarly exempt from these objections, that out of near 3,000 children employed in these mills during a period of 12 years, from 1785 to 1797, only fourteen have died, and not one has been the object of judicial punishment.

In order to supply that first necessary of life, pure and fresh air, the windows of the manufactory are frequently opened; and in summer there are air-holes left under every other window. Cleanliness is another great object of attention. The children wash themselves before they go to work, and also after it beforeDAVID DALE'S MILLS 355

owners, declared themselves satisfied with the Act just passed, ' the abridgement of labour is fully compensated by the continued good health of the children.' (Note to ' Observations.' – Some, I fear many, owners, wished it repealed, on the ground that they could not make profits unless the children worked night and day.) In the Reports Lanark is spelt ' Lanerk.'

they appear in the schools. The floor and the machinery are washed once a week with hot water; and the ceilings and walls twice a year, with unslacked lime. The children who reside in the house, and who have their maintenance in lieu of wages, are lodged in six large airy apartments. The boys and girls are kept distinctly apart, not only in the hours of rest and refreshment, but during the time of occupation. They sleep on cast-iron bedsteads, the bed-tick tilled with straw, which is changed regularly every month. The bedrooms are swept, and the windows thrown open every morning, and kept open all the day. Many of the children have contrived to provide themselves with boxes with locks, in which they keep their books and their little property. Their upper clothing in summer is cotton which is washed once a fortnight. In winter the boys are dressed in woollen; and, as well as the girls, have dress suits for Sundays.

For dinner they have seven ounces each of fresh beef with barley-broth, or alternately five ounces of cheese; and a plentiful allowance of potatoes, or barley bread. This part of the table diet is seldom varied; except in winter by a dinner of fresh herrings as a change. Their breakfast and supper consist of oatmeal porridge, with the addition of milk in summer, and, during the winter, with a sauce made of molasses and beer.

Seven o'clock is the hour for supper; soon after which*(for that pernicious practice, called night-work is entirely excl1tded from these mills)*the schools commence, and continue till nine o'clock. Mr. Dale has engaged three regular masters, who instruct the lesser children during the day. In the evening they are assisted by seven others, one of whom teaches writing. There is likewise a woman to teach the girls sewing, and another person who occasionally gives lessons in church music. The masters preside over the boys' dinner-table. On Sundays they conduct them to the place of divine worship; and, in the evening of Sunday, attend to assist and improve them, by religious and moral information.

In the year 1791, a vessel carrying emigrants to America, from the isle of Skye, was driven by stress of weather into Greenock, and about 200 persons were put on shore in a very destitute situation. Mr. Dale offered them all immediate employment; which the greater part accepted. Soon after he notified to the people of the Highlands and Hebrides the degree of encouragement which he would give to families at the cotton mills, and undertook to provide houses for 200 families. These were finished in 1793; in consequence of which a considerable number ofHighlanders have taken up their residence at New Lanark. Several families also, who were last year driven from Ireland, have found immediate employment here.

I arn uncertain whether Mr. Bernard had himself visited Mr. Dale's cotton mills; he acknowledges having derived the details of his account from ' Mr. Professor Garnett, of the Royal Institution.' But, in any case, by thus placing before the public a sample of a well-organised Children's Department, he drew attention to the right mode of managing such departments, and avoided the necessity of setting forth the shortcomings of other mill-owners so pointedly as to cause irritation. The description also served as a text for his ' Observations ' appended to the Report, in which, without naming any individual, he speaks of the system generally in force with considerable severity:

Observations

Amid the numerous variety of Cotton Mills, that have been erected in this kingdom, I sincerely wish it were in my power to shew many examples, like those of Mr. Dale's mills at Lanark. Some few of these manufactories have been distinguished for attention to health and cleanliness, and many of them for very curious mechanism, and ingenious inventions, by which the operations are produced and facilitated; but I have not had the good fortune to find in any (tho' I doubt not it may exist in some instances) that proper degree of attention, which ought to be paid to the morals and instruction of the children. Where boys and girls are indiscriminately employed at all hours, not only of the day but of the night, and are mingled together without any advantage of education, without benefit of religious instruction or moral principle, and without any friend to advise or protect them, can we be astonished at their plunging at a very early age, and almost during childhood, in every wretched and disgusting species of debauchery? Can we be surprised that our numerous and crowded manufactories should be the nurseries of thieves and prostitutes, sent out at an early age to their own ruin, and to the annoyance of the kingdom, and of every individual of which it is composed?

Such, however, is the present spirit and speculation of this country, that wherever the demon of gain raises his banner, talentsCHILDREN IN COTTON MILLS 357

and exertion are sure to follow it. Cotton Mills are as yet but in their infancy. Whilst great profits and immense fortunes are to be made by them, we know they must rapidly increase; and it is too obvious that, without public attention, they must be destructive of the moral and religious principles of the great mass of the people. The effect of this species of abridgement of labour is so great, that 100 persons in a Cotton Mill will do more spinning, and that of ten times the fineness, and of a superior quality to what can be produced by 3,000 of the very best spinners by hand. In consequence of this, Cotton Mills have almost entirely deprived the cottager's wife and children of these means of domestic industry. The profit of spinning by hand is so reduced, that whole districts of cottagers' families have been obliged to give it up, and apply for relief to the parish.

Our national and individual increase of wealth, from the manufactures of cotton, has been attended with so much injury to the health and morals of the poor, and is so utterly destructive of that which constitutes the essential and fundamental virtue of the female character, that, if I am not permitted to suggest a doubt, whether it would not have been better for us that Cotton Mills had never been erected in this island, I may at least express an anxious wish, that such regulations may be adopted and enforced, as shall diminish, if not entirely remove, the injurious and pernicious effects which must otherwise attend them.

With this view, I will lay before the reader an outline of some regulations, which impelled by zeal, but very little presuming in personal knowledge of the subject, I venture to submit to the consideration of the public; meaning to apply my observations not merely to Cotto Mills, but to all other manufactories under similar circumstances: and particularly to those in which children are engaged as apprentices.

In the first place, I conceive that some general and public attention ought to be paid to the moral and religious improvement of so numerous a class of our fellow-subjects; and that the most essential parts of their education ought not entirely to depend on the caprice, or disposition, of their respective masters; especially as many of them have been apprenticed by lots from distant counties, and have been deserted by those, whose duty it was to have protected them. In addition to this, something should be done for the benefit of these children, to instruct and prepare them to support themselves in life, without thievery or prostitution, when the period of their apprenticeship expires at the age of 16.

It seems to me to be also expedient, that the age and conditions of apprenticeship be regulated; that the hours of work be limited, and night-work (so destructive to health and morals) entirely excluded; that a total separation take place between the boys and the girls; that the works be liable to the periodical inspection of the magistrates, who should have power to order the regular white-washing and cleaning, and the warming and ventilating of the workrooms; and who should receive quarterly or monthly reports from each manufactory, of the number, the health, and the respective ages, of all the apprentices and other persons employed there.

Such are the regulations, which, upon a cursory view of the subject, appear to be proper, and to have a tendency to meliorate the condition, and to preserve the morals, of these unfortunate and neglected children. Other correctives and remedies may probably occur to those who possess more practical knowledge of the subject. At present I have only to add that, as far as my inquiries have extended, I have reason to be satisfied, that almost all the owners of Cotton Mills will concur in thinking that the preceding, or some similar regulations ought to be enforced by the legislature, for the protection of the children employed in those Mills. In order therefore that something practicable and effectual may be done, without injury to the interest of the manufacturers, I would suggest that the outline of any regulations proposed to be adopted, should be first communicated to them, so that they might state any objections, or amendments; and after a proper attention shall have been paid to their observations, I venture boldly to express my confidence, that the measures will have the support of every one, who desires to promote the welfare and happiness of his fellow-creatures, and the essential interests of virtue, morality and religion in this favoured country.1

The question now seems simple enough; but the mill- owning interest was then terribly strong, its social and political influence great, and it found backers in persons of all classes who profited by the iniquitous system in vogue. Fortunately for the cause of the children, Sir Robert Peel, the great mill-owner, and first baronet, came forward to help them. In this case there was no existing Act of Parliament bearing on the subject, and without one nothing could beA GENEROUS DONATION 359

'*Life of Sir Thomas Bernard,*by Rev. James Baker. (See also account of this time in Dr. W. Cooke Taylor's*Life of Sir Robert Peel,*vol. i.)

hoped for; it was Sir Eobert Peel who undertook to introduce a Bill for the amelioration of the children's condition. The framing of this Bill was entrusted to a committee, chiefly consisting of members of the Society for Bettering the Condition of the Poor, and Sir Robert frequently attended their meetings to watch over its progress. An anecdote related by Mr. Baker evidently refers to this period. He writes:

The exclusive and disinterested attention which Mr. Bernard paid to all objects of public charity, was by this time very generally known, and had induced the co-operation of many distinguished individuals in his works of benevolence. One instance which occurred about this time made a considerable impression on his mind. Sir Robert Peel, who had very large concerns in Cotton Mills, called on him one morning, and, after a general conversation on the different philanthropic objects they had in view, said, on leaving the room, that he had to request that he would dispose of something for him in any way he approved. After he had gone, Mr. Bernard opened it, and found to his surprise, a bank note for a thousand pounds. He wrote to Sir Robert, informing him that he could not undertake the disposal of so large a sum, and on his objecting to take it again, proposed that it should be a donation from him to the Society for the Poor. This Sir Robert approved, and it was appropriated as a fund for the melioration of the condition of the Children in Cotton Mills.

The rumour of the forthcoming Bill excited much angry feeling, which eventually led to modifications in its clauses. To preserve a chance of gaining anything, it was necessary to give up something. The following letter from Mr. Wilberforce, 1 addressed ' Thomas Bernard, Esq., Foundling Hospital,' though not fully dated, was evidently written at this period:

Palace Yard, Wednesday morning.

My dear Sir, – I so much respect the judgement of the Committee, and I think so much weight is due to the considerations suggested by Sir Eobert Peel, and even to his feelings, (when our success in the excellent measure in contemplation will be in so great a degree owing to his benevolent and public-spirited exertions) that I will not press any ideas of my own, as to the extension of the plan to any others than apprentices, contrary to what may be the general opinion which the gentlemen of the Committee may form on full consideration. I cannot, however, but earnestly recommend it to them, to consider of some way of securing to the children some religious instruction more effectually than by the plan as it at present stands; and I trust that this subject, on which, it must be confessed, there are difficulties, will be understood to be reserved for further consideration.

1 *Life of William Wilberforce,* by his Sons, vol. iii., p. 44.

It has happened somewhat remarkably, that, whilst we have been engaged on this subject, I have received a letter from a poor but honest and hardworking couple, whose child was barbarously torn from them, and sent down to a distant Cotton Mill. I have since conversed with these people, and seldom have heard a more artless, affecting tale than they related. The letter they wrote me I send, as perhaps the gentlemen present may like to hear it. I am very sorry to be prevented by a House of Commons' Committee from attending you as/had wished this morning. But I am persuaded I shall not be wanted. I beg you however to explain the cause of my non-appearance.

I remain, my dear Sir

Yours very sincerely

W. WILBERFORCE.

On April 7, 1802, Wilberforce notes in his ' Diary ': 'Sir Robert Peel's Bill – motion well received for morals of apprentices &c. in cotton factories.'

The opposition to the Bill [writes Mr. Baker] was composed of a coalition of two classes; those who thought that too little was proposed, and those who thought, or rather felt, that any interference with the excessive profits of the manufacturer was improper. The bill, however, was passed, not with the expectation of its affording a complete remedy, where interest was so actively engaged; but with this degree of satisfaction, that it must, in any event, produce some improvement in the happiness and moral character of the children.

As far as it went the legislation was good [says Mr. Hodder'], it enjoined proper clothing, feeding, and instruction, the limitation of the hours to twelve, exclusive of meals; the abolition of night- work, and the appointment of visitors to inspect the factories.

1 Hodder (Edwin), *The Life and Work of the seventh Earl of Sluiftesbury,* chap. iii.

THE APPRENTICE SYSTEM 361

It was, no doubt, by reason of the onus being thus thrown on the mill-owners that Sir Robert Peel's donation of *1,000l.* was not applied for the benefit of the factory children. This must be the explanation of a sentence in Mr. Baker's book, which does not at first seem very clear:

That object not holding out sufficient demand for it, it has been since applied towards the promotion of education in different parts of the kingdom.

With this sentence Mr. Baker closes his account of the movement on behalf of factory children, as if his uncle's interest in it had suddenly terminated. But I have no loubt that in this instance, as in the case of the climbing boys, he continued to labour for the cause, although it was ostensibly in other hands. It was his friend Sir Robert Peel who moved the next Bill on the subject, thirteen years after the first.

It appears from the letter of Wilberforce, lately quoted, that the promoters of the Bill had, at Sir Robert Peel's desire, confined its provisions to apprentices. This may have been necessary in order to pass the Bill, but it was a serious, almost fatal, defect; for numbers of the children working in factories at that time were not apprentices. After relating the horrors of the original system, Mr. Hodder continues:

Where such abominations were tolerated, the case of the other children and young persons, not apprentices, could not be otherwise than almost as bad, and in point of fact, there grew up as we shall see, consequent upon the rapid increase of trade, a system of iniquity even greater than that we have described, when, instead of churchwardens and overseers of parishes apprenticing the orphans and destitute of their parishes, parents voluntarily placed their children in the factories to do the same kind of work, during the same oppressive hours, and under many of the same heartless conditions. When the mill-owners found that these children were still left entirely at their mercy, the consequences were such as might have been expected.

The effect of the new Act was to do away gradually with the Apprentice System. At first the mills

had been placed where there was plenty of water to drive the machinery; and as this was often in thinly populated districts, the employment of apprentices became a necessity. When however the steam engine was invented, mills could be planted anywhere; and as a matter of fact they were planted in densely populated neighbourhoods, in order that the children of the inhabitants might bs employed instead of the apprentices, and so relieve the masters of the trouble of providing food, clothing, and education.

When Sir Robert Peel brought in his second Bill, in 1815, he stated that:

Although ten times the number of children were employed, compared with the period when the Apprentice Bill had passed, none of them were bound by articles, or anything in the shape of a permanent contract.

The inspectors appointed under the previous Act ' had been very remiss in the performance of their duty. Night work still continued.' Sir Robert Peel said that:

It was his intention, if possible to prevent the recurrence of such a misfortune as had recently taken place; he alluded to the fourteen poor children who were recently burnt in the night in a cotton factory. He knew that the iniquitous practice of working children at a time when their masters were in bed, too often took place. He was ashamed to own that he had himself been concerned where that proceeding had been suffered; but he hoped the House would interfere, and prevent it for the future.

Mr. Peel, the future minister, supported his father in a speech describing: ' The heated atmosphere in which fine spinning was conducted, the large number of children engaged (amounting in Manchester alone to nearly twelve thousand) and the little interest that masters in towns had to protect the health of their operatives, as they could easily supply the place of those who were sickly, or worn out.' When Sir Robert stated, as he did, that ' the loss of life had of late been exceedingly small, not exceeding one per cent, per annum; a loss falling short of the average loss sustainedNIGHT WORK

in every other class of manufacturing industry.' he compared the cotton mills evidently with woollen and silk mills, and establishments of various sorts standing in much need of protection, but for which none had as yet been asked, because the warriors of the cause knew that it would ruin everything to attempt much, and also no doubt because there was no other great owner like Sir Eobert to take the matter up.

KND OF THE THIRD VOLUME

I'll!'. Ml BY

1KD CO. LTD., JtW-6TO!T EQDABl

LONDON

Lightning Source UK Ltd.
Milton Keynes UK
03 June 2010

155035UK00001B/394/P